Successful Coaching

THIRD EDITION

Rainer Martens

American Sport Education Program Founder

HUMAN KINETICS

Library of Congress Cataloging-in-Publication Data

Martens, Rainer, 1942-
  Successful coaching / Rainer Martens.-- 3rd ed.
    p. cm.
  ISBN 0-7360-4012-9 (soft cover)
  1. School sports--Coaching--United States. I. Title.
  GV711.M355 2004
  796'.071'273--dc22

                        2003025833

ISBN-10: 0-7360-4012-9
ISBN-13: 978-0-7360-4012-9

The Facilities Inspection Checklist on pages 476 to 478 was adapted from the *American Coaching Effectiveness Program Level 2 Sport Law Workbook,* Human Kinetics, pp. 40-41, and *Athletic Business,* November, 1985, pp. 36-38.

The Web addresses cited in this text were current as of January 2004 unless otherwise noted.

Acquisitions Editor: Scott Parker; **Developmental Editor:** Christine M. Drews; **Assistant Editor:** Kathleen D. Bernard; **Copyeditor:** Patsy Fortney; **Proofreader:** Sarah Wiseman; **Indexer:** Marie Rizzo; **Permission Manager:** Toni Harte; **Graphic Designer:** Robert Reuther; **Graphic Artist:** Sandra Meier; **Photo Managers:** Kelly Huff, Dan Wendt; **Cover Designer:** Jack W. Davis; **Photographer (cover):** Dan Nierling; **Photographer (interior):** Human Kinetics, unless otherwise noted; **Art Managers:** Kareema McLendon and Kelly Hendren; **Illustrators:** Roberto Sabas (illustrations) and Wendy Beth Jackelow (medical)

Human Kinetics books are available at special discounts for bulk purchase. Special editions or book excerpts can also be created to specification. For details, contact the Special Sales Manager at Human Kinetics.

Printed in Hong Kong   10

Human Kinetics
Web site: www.HumanKinetics.com

United States: Human Kinetics
P.O. Box 5076
Champaign, IL 61825-5076
800-747-4457
e-mail: humank@hkusa.com

Canada: Human Kinetics
475 Devonshire Road, Unit 100
Windsor, ON N8Y 2L5
800-465-7301 (in Canada only)
e-mail: info@hkcanada.com

Europe: Human Kinetics
107 Bradford Road
Stanningley
Leeds LS28 6AT, United Kingdom
+44 (0)113 255 5665
e-mail: hk@hkeurope.com

Australia: Human Kinetics
57A Price Avenue
Lower Mitcham, South Australia 5062
08 8372 0999
e-mail: info@hkaustralia.com

New Zealand: Human Kinetics
Division of Sports Distributors NZ Ltd.
P.O. Box 300 226 Albany
North Shore City, Auckland
0064 9 448 1207
e-mail: info@humankinetics.co.nz

CONTENTS

PREFACE

If you're new to sport coaching, I've written *Successful Coaching* for you. If you're a veteran coach seeking to review, refresh, and expand your coaching knowledge, I've written *Successful Coaching* for you. And if you're a high school or club coach of teenage athletes in any sport, I've written *Successful Coaching* especially for you.

The first edition of this book, titled *Coaching Young Athletes*, sold over 100,000 copies, and the second edition, retitled *Successful Coaching*, sold over 400,000 copies. The book is the text for the American Sport Education Program's (ASEP) Coaching Principles course (see the appendix for more information about this and other ASEP courses) and is widely used as a text in college introductory coaching courses. I revised this third edition to meet and exceed the National Council for Accreditation for Coaching Education guidelines as stated in its publication *Quality Coaches, Quality Sports: National Standards for Athletic Coaches* (Reston, VA: National Association for Sport and Physical Education, 1995).

Successful Coaching will introduce you to many principles of coaching that are applicable across all sports. This book is based on knowledge from the sport sciences integrated with the wisdom of master coaches. It celebrates coaching as an emerging profession that offers you the opportunity to help young people become better athletes and, more important, better human beings. It espouses ASEP's philosophy of Athletes First, Winning Second and explains how you can put that perspective into action.

I've sought to make the book very practical, to give you principles, guidelines, and specific tools that you can use immediately in your coaching. This third edition is almost double the size of previous editions and contains considerably more information. The highlights of the changes in this edition include the following:

▶ New chapters on character education and coaching athletes with diverse characteristics.

▶ A very practical and much expanded chapter on managing athletes' behavior.

▶ In part III, Principles of Teaching, I introduce the games approach to coaching, which is followed by new chapters on teaching technical and tactical skills.

▶ Part IV, Principles of Physical Training, is all new, with much more practical information on energy and muscular fitness.

▶ Part IV also has a new chapter on nutrition that will help you fuel your athletes better, keep them hydrated, and make decisions regarding nutritional supplements.

▶ Part IV concludes with a chapter on drugs in sport, which addresses what you can do to help prevent drug use and what to do if athletes on your team use drugs.

▶ Part V has a much expanded and practical chapter on all the team management functions you will likely have to perform followed by a new chapter on managing relationships with fellow coaches, administrators, officials, and parents.

This book is very special to me. It brings together much of my life as an athlete, a coach, a sport psychologist, and now a sport publisher. My wish is that this book becomes very special to you—that the knowledge in this book created from the labor of many sport scientists and the experience of thousands of master coaches will help you be a successful coach.

ACKNOWLEDGMENTS

Successful Coaching aims to present the foundational knowledge that is essential for coaching any sport. I've had the privilege of authoring this text, but the book is actually the achievement of many people whom I wish to acknowledge.

The content of this book is greatly shaped by my own positive experiences in sport. With few exceptions I've had nurturing coaches who strengthened my intrinsic enjoyment of sport. I've coached many fine athletes and worked with outstanding assistant coaches who, as I think about it, probably taught me more than I taught them. I thank them all for providing me with the experiential knowledge that has shaped this book.

I've harvested the knowledge from the toil of thousands of sport scientists who have applied their intellectual skills to discover better ways of coaching. I'm indebted to them for creating the science of coaching.

Many people have reviewed this book and provided assistance in developing the practical guidelines contained herein. My thanks to Jack Halbert, Alan Launder, Wendy Piltz, Larry Greene, and Jeff Hulsmeyer. I thank Mike Bahrke, Jay Hoffman, Chuck Yesalis, and Roger Earle, who helped with the strength training guidelines. My special thanks to Dan Gould for his thorough review of the previous edition, and to Jean Ashen and Chris Zauner for their input.

I'd like to thank Tim Flannery of the National Federation of State High School Associations for his cooperation and help in developing this book and our entire ASEP curriculum. Thanks to Christine Bolger and the National Council for Accreditation for Coaching Education, who reviewed this text. I've also appreciated the opportunity to work with Jim Page, Peter Davis, and Cathy Sellers of the U.S. Olympic Committee as we've consulted with various national sport organizations about coaching education.

I've had a great team of skilled professionals to work with in producing this book at Human Kinetics. Chris Drews captained the team as my developmental editor. She skillfully guided this book into being from raw manuscript to what you now see, and she made the work enjoyable for all involved. Thanks, Chris. The other members of the team are ASEP's curriculum design director Scott Parker, assistant editor Kathleen Bernard, my capable administrative assistant Kristen Henderson, and photographers Kelly Huff and Dan Wendt. I thank each of you. And I'd like to extend a special thanks to Bob Reuther for his excellent interior design of the book.

She's endured my ramblings as I organized my thoughts about the book during countless walks. She's provided insights as we discussed coaching when driving to numerous softball tournaments. And she nudged me to persist when I needed encouragement. She's my personal coach, my best friend, and my wife, Julie Martens. Thanks, Julie. I'm truly grateful for all your support.

BECOMING A SUCCESSFUL COACH

Welcome to coaching. What a privilege to be a coach—to have the opportunity to guide young people in their sport participation. As a coach think of yourself as being in the "positive persuasion" business!

If you haven't coached before, you have many new experiences awaiting you. Perhaps you've already daydreamed scenes of your athletes carrying you off the field on their shoulders after winning the championship, or your athletes dumping a cooler of sport drink over you in celebration of a victory. Perhaps you see your friends and neighbors congratulating you for masterminding the perfect season. Perhaps your daydreams turn to nightmares—you see yourself making a tactical blunder, and some loudmouth spectator ridicules you. Then you lose your temper and say things you regret. If you have coached before, perhaps these daydreams and nightmares, or similar scenes, are real experiences for you.

Like any profession, coaching has its highs and lows, but if you are prepared, you will experience mostly highs. If you already have the teaching skills of an educator, the training expertise of a physiologist, the administrative leadership of a business executive, and the counseling wisdom of a psychologist, you can throw this book away; it won't help you. If you don't, join me to find out what makes a successful coach.

Is success as a coach the winning of contests? Yes, in part, winning is an aspect of successful coaching. But successful coaching is much more than just winning contests. Successful coaches help athletes master new skills, enjoy competing with others, and develop self-esteem. Successful coaches not only are well versed in the technical and tactical skills of their sports, but they also know how to teach these skills to young people. And successful coaches not only teach athletes sport skills, they also teach and model the skills athletes will need to live successfully in our society.

Coaching indeed is teaching, but it's also more. Coaches not only guide athletes in *learning* technical, tactical, and life skills, they also orchestrate and direct their athletes in the *performance* of these skills. Coaches, unlike teachers, have their teaching skills evaluated by others each time their teams compete. Unfortunately some coaches are guilty of under teaching in practices and over coaching during contests. To help you avoid this tendency, *Successful Coaching* emphasizes teaching in practices so that you'll have less need for coaching during contests.

Coaching also is leading. As a coach you will have enormous power over your athletes. You can do much good with this power—and you can do much harm. Coaching athletes of any age is not a frivolous activity to be granted to anyone willing to volunteer some time. Just as other professionals have great impact on the lives of those they serve, so do coaches. Prepare yourself to use your power to do good.

Coaching is a helping profession. A cardinal principle for all helping professionals is to take care of yourself first so that you can take care of others. Coaching is a demanding helping profession, and the better you care for yourself physically and mentally, the better able you'll be to help your athletes. Throughout this book you'll find advice about taking care of yourself and encouragement to do so.

Being a successful coach is an enormous challenge. Good intentions are not enough to be successful; you need all the knowledge you can get. Most coaches have learned the skills of coaching through years of trial and error. But, oh, how some of those errors hurt! *Successful Coaching* will help you shorten that learning process—and reduce those painful errors—by teaching you the principles of coaching based on the sport sciences and the wisdom of many successful coaches.

This book, and the ASEP Coaching Principles course in which it is used, is only a starting point, a foundation for building your knowledge of coaching. You can also learn much by watching and talking with other coaches. They can teach you both effective and ineffective coaching practices; what you must do is distinguish between the two! By learning the foundational principles in *Successful Coaching,* you will be in a better position to make that distinction.

You will also learn from your own experiences. As you coach, examine your experiences periodically and think about what you are learning. What can you do differently to coach more successfully, and what do you want to do the same because it works well?

Successful coaches are those who can learn new skills, who are flexible enough to change old ways when change is needed, who can accept constructive criticism, and who can critically evaluate themselves. Throughout *Successful Coaching,* I will ask you to do all of these things.

Congratulations on taking this step to become a better coach—a professional coach. I encourage you to continue your learning throughout your coaching career by taking more courses, reading more books, and joining a coaching association in your sport.

CREDITS

Photos © Art Explosion, Platinum Edition, 1997, on page 50 (two bottom).

Photo © Bruce Coleman on page 319.

Photos © Chase Agnello-Dean on pages 17, 80 (right), 437, and 448 (middle of figure 19.4).

Photos © Corbis on pages 387 and 406 (lower right).

Photos © Custom Medical Stock on pages 241 (lower right), 389 (lower right), 390 (upper right), and 392 (upper right).

Photo © David Gonzales on page 13.

Photos © DigitalVisionOnline on pages 70, 71, 72, and 359 (lower right).

Photos © Empics on pages 38 (top), 93, 110 (lower right), 193 (lower left), 229 (upper left), 289, and 293.

Photo © Eyewire on page 379 (upper left).

Photos © Getty Images on pages 46, 53, 56 (lower right), 82 (lower left), 129 (upper right), 359 (third from top), 384, and 396 (lower left).

Photos © Icon Sports Media on pages 6 (upper left), 7, 24 (upper right), 31 (upper left), 32 (upper left), 35 (top), 39 (top), 41 (lower left), 44, 45 (lower left), 62, 88 (lower right), 107 (lower right), and 194 (upper right).

Photos © Jim Whitmer on pages 77, 78, 85 (top), 111, 112, 162, 392 (lower right), 397, 448 (lower left of figure 19.4), and 454 (lower left).

Photo © Joel Rogers on page 141.

Photo © John T. Fowler on page 394.

Photos © Keith Johnston on pages 127, 172 (lower right), and 373.

Photo © Levine B. Roberts on page 391 (upper right).

Photos © MarinMedia.org on pages vi and 115 (lower right).

Photos courtesy of www.20-20photo.com on pages 1, 115 (lower left and second from top), 125, 137 (upper left), 208 (upper left), 272 (lower right), 292 (upper left), 306, and 325.

Photo courtesy of OMRON Healthcare, Inc on page 301.

Photos © Photodisc on pages 264 and 339.

Photos © Photri Inc. on pages 311 (upper right), 389 (upper right), and 406 (upper left).

Photos © Photo Network on pages 69, 95, 235, 236, and 428.

Photos © Raw Talent Photo on pages 41 (second from left), 80 (left), 85 (bottom), 86 (lower right), 108, 132 (upper left and lower right), 134, 217 (upper right), and 396 (upper right).

Photo courtesy of Rhonda Revelle/University of Nebraska Athletic Department on page 3 (upper right).

Photo © Robert Bergstrom on page 271 (middle).

Photo courtesy of Robert Reuther on page 55.

Photos © SportsChrome USA on pages 3, 216 (lower left), 382, and 452 (second from top).

Photos © Sport The Library on pages 86 (upper left), 87, 88 (upper left), 91, 233, 269 (upper left), and 449.

Photo courtesy of Stanford University on page 35 (bottom).

Figure 2.3—Reprinted, from Guidelines for Children's Sports (1979), with permission from the National Association for Sport and Physical Education (NASPE), 1900 Association Drive, Reston, VA 20101-1599.

Figure 13.1—Adapted, by permission, from Harman, 2000, The biomechanics of resistance exercise. In *Essentials of strength training*, edited by T.R. Baechle and R.W. Earle (Champaign, IL: Human Kinetics), 27.

Figure 13.2—Adapted, by permission, from Harman, 2000, The biomechanics of resistance exercise. In *Essentials of strength training*, edited by T.R. Baechle and R.W. Earle (Champaign, IL: Human Kinetics), 29.

Figure 14.2—Reprinted, by permission, from Philip Whitfield, 1995, *The human body explained*, (London, England: Marshall Editions Developments), 93.

Figure 14.4—Reprinted, by permission from Faigenbaum, 2000, Age-and sex-related differences and their implications for resistance exercise. In *Essentials of strength training*, edited by T.R. Baechle and R.W. Earle (Champaign, IL: Human Kinetics), 173.

Figure 16.2—Reprinted, by permission, from L.E. Armstrong, 2000, *Performing in extreme environments* (Champaign, IL: Human Kinetics).

PART I

Principles of Coaching

Your success as a coach will depend more on your coaching philosophy than on any other factor. By *philosophy* I mean the beliefs or principles that guide the actions you take. Your coaching philosophy will determine how wisely you use your knowledge about technical and tactical skills, the sport sciences, and sport management. Part I will help you develop a coaching philosophy, inviting you to think about what you want to accomplish as a coach and how you want to do so with the diverse athletes you're likely to encounter.

Developing Your Coaching Philosophy

You're in the middle of running basketball practice with your high school team when your star guard, Thomas, stops playing and begins to yell at a teammate who missed setting a screen. He then stomps off the court and does not return. One of your team rules is that players must attend all practices if they are to play in games. However, the game you will be playing this weekend is one that could determine whether your team makes the playoffs. Do you suspend Thomas for that game, or let him play?

This is just one of the many tough decisions you may have to make as a coach—sometimes right on the spot. What will help you most in making these decisions is a well-developed philosophy of coaching.

☞ **In this chapter you'll learn**

▸ the value of a coaching philosophy and

▸ the importance of knowing who you are and what kind of coach you want to be.

The word *philosophy* used to turn me off. Nothing seemed more impractical than philosophy, and I see myself as a practical person. I have learned, however, that nothing is as practical as a well-developed philosophy about life and about coaching. My philosophy guides me every day; it helps me interpret the events in my life, and it gives my life direction.

Philosophy to me means the pursuit of wisdom; it helps us answer fundamental questions about what, why, and how. Our philosophies determine the way we view objects and experiences in our lives as well as the way we view people and our relationships with them. Our philosophies also determine the values that we hold about all of these. The philosopher Epictetus said, "The beginning of philosophy is to know the condition of one's own mind."

Do you know the condition of your own mind? Is your philosophy of life well formulated? Is your philosophy of coaching well defined? Or are you uncertain about your beliefs on important issues in life and in coaching? Such uncertainty leads to inconsistency in behavior, which often destroys personal relationships and creates chaotic conditions within a family and a team.

The key to developing a philosophy of coaching—and of life—is getting to know yourself. In this chapter, I'll ask you to consider some facets of yourself and issues pertinent to coaching sports to help you further develop your coaching philosophy.

Why Philosophy?

Coaching is a challenging profession with many difficult decisions and ethical dilemmas. A well-developed philosophy will help you make these difficult decisions and coach more successfully. Without a well-developed philosophy you may find yourself lacking direction and readily succumbing to external pressures, as cleverly illustrated in the following story reported by Ralph Sabock (1985, pp. 49-50):

> " *There was an old man, a boy, and a donkey. They were going to town and it was decided that the boy should ride. As they went along they passed some people who exclaimed that it was a shame for the boy to ride and the old man to walk. The man and boy decided that maybe the critics were right so they changed positions. Later they passed some more people who then exclaimed that it was a real shame for the man to make such a small boy walk. The two decided that maybe they both should walk. Soon they passed some more people who exclaimed that it was stupid to walk when they had a donkey to ride. The man and the boy decided maybe the critics were right so they decided that they both should ride. They soon passed other people who exclaimed that it was a shame to put such a load on a poor little animal. The old man and the boy decided that maybe the critics were right so they decided to carry the donkey. As they crossed a bridge they lost their grip on the animal and the donkey fell into the river and drowned. The moral of the story is that if you try to please everyone you will finally lose your ass.* "

When you are coaching, your philosophy, much more than your knowledge of the sport, will keep you from "losing your ass." Having a philosophy will remove uncertainty about training rules, style of play, discipline, codes of conduct, competitive outlook, short- and long-term objectives, and many other facets of coaching. If you give the same amount of time to the development of your philosophy as you do to the development of your technical knowledge of the sport, you will be a better coach.

Developing Your Philosophy

You already have a philosophy about life and probably a philosophy about coaching. The philosophy may or may not be well developed in your mind. You may be conscious of your perspective of life, or it may reside at a more unconscious level, depending largely on how much you have reflected on it. Even if you do have a well-developed philosophy, remember that philosophies are lifelong in their development.

Many famous coaches are well known for their coaching philosophies. These coaches discovered early in their careers that the art of coaching involved using broad philosophical concepts in a skillful way to enhance the pursuit of their goals, regardless of whether others agreed with their particular coaching philosophies.

Phil Jackson believes that coaches must have compassion in order to help their athletes perform superbly.

Rhonda Revelle, University of Nebraska softball coach, believes in the importance of knowing and caring about her athletes, not just as athletes but as human beings.

A philosophy consists of (1) major objectives (the things you value and want to achieve) and (2) your beliefs or principles that help you achieve your objectives. These principles help you cope with the myriad of life's situations. Often some of your beliefs or principles are formative and shaped by your experiences, as shown in figure 1.1.

Figure 1.1 How life events can affect your coaching philosophy.

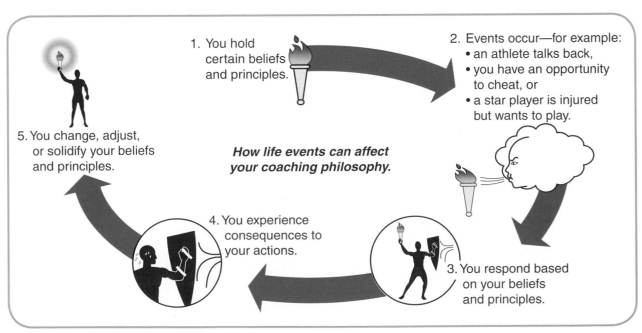

How life events can affect your coaching philosophy.

1. You hold certain beliefs and principles.

2. Events occur—for example:
• an athlete talks back,
• you have an opportunity to cheat, or
• a star player is injured but wants to play.

3. You respond based on your beliefs and principles.

4. You experience consequences to your actions.

5. You change, adjust, or solidify your beliefs and principles.

Your developing principles are tested when you find yourself in situations in which you are uncertain about the best way to respond. Once you have responded, you can then evaluate the consequences of your response against your principles. Favorable evaluations strengthen your principles. Unfavorable evaluations, especially repeated ones, may indicate that you need to search for different principles.

Some coaches, however, give little consideration to this evaluative process. These coaches have philosophies that are insufficiently developed to meet the demands of coaching. Other coaches form philosophies that are inflexible and less productive in achieving their objectives. And still others adopt philosophies that are incongruous with the values of society.

I am especially impressed with John Wooden's philosophy, which emphasizes teaching and performing rather than winning. Wooden's philosophy represents his cumulative wisdom over a lifetime of coaching. He did not begin coaching with the philosophy he espoused at the end of his career. So don't expect to have all the answers immediately. Keep an open mind, examine your beliefs and values from time to time, and benefit from the experience of wise coaches such as John Wooden.

John Wooden, the legendary college basketball coach for UCLA, had a clearly thought-out philosophy of coaching. He communicated his philosophy in the back-to-school letter sent to his players just before the 1972-73 season:

"For maximum team accomplishment each individual must prepare himself to the best of his ability and then put his talents to work for the team. This must be done unselfishly without thought of personal glory. When no one worries about who will receive the credit, far more can be accomplished in any group activity.

You must discipline yourself to do what is expected of you for the welfare of the team. The coach has many decisions to make and you will not agree with all of them, but you must respect and accept them. Without supervision and leadership and a disciplined effort by all, much of our united strength will be dissipated pulling against ourselves. Let us not be victimized by a breakdown from within.

You may feel, at times, that I have double standards, as I certainly will not treat you all the same. However, I will attempt to give each player the treatment that he earns and deserves according to my judgment and in keeping with what I consider to be in the best interest of the team. I know I will not be right in all of my decisions, but I will attempt to be both right and fair."
(Wooden 1988, pp. 237-238)

Wooden also communicated to his players that winning was second to trying their best:

"I tried to convince my players that they could never be truly successful or attain peace of mind unless they had the self-satisfaction of knowing they had done their best. Although I wanted them to work to win, I tried to convince them they had always won when they had done their best." (Wooden 1988, p. 95)

You cannot acquire a philosophy by reading this book or by adopting the philosophy of a famous coach. A philosophy is not acquired from any one source, but rather from all of your experiences. A philosophy is useless unless you own it and nurture it. This chapter and the two that follow are intended to help you develop your own coaching philosophy, but all of the chapters in this book will likely influence it.

Usually your philosophy of life will shape your philosophy of coaching. Sometimes, however, coaches adopt principles in sports that are inconsistent with their larger principles of life. I recall coaching with a math teacher who was one of the kindest people I knew. He clearly followed the principle of the Golden Rule in his interactions with others—until he stepped onto the football field. For some reason, when he coached, he became a tyrant. He abused the players physically and psychologically, only to return to the classroom the next day as a warm, sensitive, highly effective math teacher. I never did learn why he abandoned the Golden Rule when coaching. I suspect that somewhere he had adopted the mistaken notion that a good coach must be highly authoritarian, unkind, and abusive to athletes.

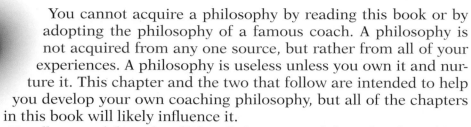

Do to others as you would have them do to you

Approach your athletes in the same way you approach people in other spheres of your life. Of course that does not mean that if you are abusive to others, you should also be abusive to your athletes! My meaning here should be clear.

Developing a useful philosophy involves two major tasks. The first is to develop greater self-awareness, to get to know yourself better. The second is to decide what your objectives are in coaching. Your objectives will shape the way you see your role as a coach, and thus will shape many of your behaviors as a coach. In the next section of this chapter you will learn more about knowing yourself. Then, in chapter 2, I'll ask you to consider your coaching objectives—that is, what you value in coaching. In chapter 3 you'll look at common coaching styles, identify your own style, and learn more about leadership.

Self-Awareness

As a coach, you must know who you are if you hope to help your athletes know who

they are. When you are at peace with yourself, you can help your athletes to be at peace with themselves. If you have direction and commitment, you can impart these to your athletes. When your athletes see you behave with reasonable consistency, they will be more likely to respond with appropriate consistency. If you demonstrate "character" in guiding your athletes through the competitive experience, you will likely build character in those you guide.

Young people seek role models. What they admire in their teachers and coaches they assimilate as their own. As a coach, you must realize that what you teach may well be less important than what you demonstrate through your character and philosophy. Quite literally, the lifetime behavior of your athletes may well depend on the example you set.

Remember this when you assume the tremendous responsibility of being a coach: Your athletes are much more likely to become what you are than what you want them to be. Consequently, you cannot provide consistently positive direction for your athletes unless you know who you are. Once you have clarified your personal values, you will be better able to help your athletes work through conflict and confusion.

Only through self-awareness can you arrive at the conclusion that you want or need to become more competent in some facet of your life. This requires being honest with yourself about who you are—which sometimes is a painful experience. You can increase your self-awareness in two ways:

▶ By reflecting on your own beliefs and assumptions

▶ By requesting feedback from other people on how they see you and how they react to you

A first honest look at yourself may be hard to accept. If you don't like what you see, however, don't run from it or deny it. You have much to learn from it.

Who Am I?

Now is the time for some thought and reflection. Read each of the following questions, reflect for a few moments on your answer, and then note what you think in the space provided. Don't merely read through the list and move on. Take some time to get acquainted with yourself.

▶ Who am I? _____

▶ What do I want in life? _____

▶ Where am I going? _____

▶ Is my behavior appropriate to my life's goals? _____

▶ Am I proud or ashamed of who I am? _____

▶ Am I happy or unhappy? _____

These are tough questions. We should all periodically take a break in our busy lives and answer these questions for ourselves. Now consider the following five questions specific to coaching, and note what you think:

▶ Why do I coach? _____

▶ Am I coaching for the right reasons? _____

▶ What are my goals as a coach? _____

▶ Am I a good coach? _____

▶ What would make me a better coach?_____

Answers to these questions and similar ones form your self-concept—the beliefs you have about yourself. You may have unconsciously assumed many of your beliefs about yourself from how you perceive other people responding to you.

The Three Selves

Your self-concept can be thought of as three selves. The *ideal self* refers to the person you would like to be; it represents your values, your sense of right and wrong. It is what you expect and demand of yourself, and is typically based on moral principles acquired from your family and other important people in your life.

The *public self* is the image you believe others have of you. You want others to believe certain things about you so that they respect you, love you, and help you meet your goals. If others believe the wrong things about you, they may ignore you, reject you, or punish you.

The *real self* is the sum of those subjective thoughts, feelings, and needs that you see as being the authentic you. The real self is continually changing, and healthy people strive to honestly know themselves and to relate their inner selves to the realities of the outside world. Through interactions with others, through the communication process, you come to understand, accept, and experience the real self.

Sometimes conflict arises between the real and the other selves, resulting in anxiety, guilt, and perhaps even self-hatred. When a feeling, thought, or experience conflicts with your beliefs about yourself, you may feel threatened and distort, deny, or ignore the experience. In this way you protect your self-concept, but when you are overly protective, you deny yourself an opportunity to grow from these experiences. To maintain good mental health, you should strive to keep your public and ideal selves compatible with your real self.

Seeing yourself accurately requires insight, or the ability to view yourself objectively. None of us can do so with complete objectivity, but some are able to see themselves more accurately than others can. To help you look at your ideal, public, and real selves, table 1.1 contains a list of some roles and characteristics that are significant to the job of coaching.

Complete the table as follows:

1. For the first role listed, rate yourself first as you would like to be (your ideal self).

2. Then rate yourself as you believe you are seen by others (your public self).

3. Next rate yourself as you perceive yourself really to be (your real self).

4. Then complete the three ratings for the remaining roles and characteristics.

Table 1.1—Knowing Your Three Selves			
RATING SCALE: −3 −2 −1 0 +1 +2 +3			
Negative self Neutral self Positive self			
Item	**Ideal self (as you would like to be)**	**Public self (as you believe you are seen by others)**	**Real self (as you perceive yourself)**
Knowing yourself as . . .			
an athlete			
a coach			
a mother or father			
successful			
honest			
anxious			
empathic			
domineering			
loyal			
humble			
needing recognition			
respected			
stubborn			
powerful			

From *Successful Coaching, Third Edition,* by Rainer Martens, 2004, Champaign, IL: Human Kinetics.

Now look at your ratings. Do you see any substantial discrepancies among your three selves? If so, why do you think they exist? What can you do about the discrepancies? If you are feeling courageous, ask someone who knows you well to review your ratings. Discuss any discrepancies that this person sees. Remember, others really only know your public self.

Self-Esteem

To build a coaching philosophy, you must know yourself. Part of developing self-awareness is understanding your self-esteem, which pertains to an inner conviction about your competency and worth as a human being. Too often coaches and athletes base their self-esteem on their wins and losses in competition. Unfortunately, when they do so, they lose some control of their self-esteem because winning and losing is not fully under their control. The outcome of competition is determined not only by what the competitor does, but also by the opponents, officials, teammates, and of course, luck.

It's not mentally healthy to base your self-esteem on winning and losing. Genuine self-esteem is not something you gain through competition or comparison. Positive self-esteem is viewing yourself as a competent and worthy person, and feeling good about that. Self-esteem is not achieved by defeating others, but by living up to your own realistic standards.

Your success as a coach is strongly related to your self-esteem, to how you value yourself (figure 1.2). If you have confidence, you will help develop confidence in those around you. If you feel worthy as a person, you will recognize worth in others.

How do you judge yourself? Do you believe you are a competent person? Do you believe you are a worthy person? Nathaniel Branden begins his book *Honoring the Self* (1983) by stating: "Of all the judgments that we pass in life, none is as important as the one we pass on ourselves, for that judgment touches the very center of our existence" (p. xi). How we relate to ourselves affects how we relate to others and to the world around us.

Your success as a coach is strongly related to your perception of yourself as a competent person. We make ourselves worthy of living by making ourselves competent to live. Thus self-awareness is the first step toward knowing yourself and your competence, and toward deciding whether to change current ineffective patterns of behavior to effective ones.

Figure 1.2   Your level of self-esteem affects your success as a coach.

- Confidence in yourself
- High self-worth

- You help others develop confidence
- You recognize worth in others

Self-Disclosure

David Johnson expresses the significance of self-disclosure in developing self-awareness in his book *Reaching Out* (1981):

> " By disclosing myself to you, I create the potential for trust, caring, commitment, growth, and self-understanding. How can you care for me if you do not know me? How can you trust me if I do not demonstrate my trust in you by disclosing myself to you? How can you be committed to me if you know little or nothing about me? How can I know and understand myself if I do not disclose myself to friends? " (p. 15)

At the beginning of her stint as the coach of the women's Olympic basketball team in 1996, Tara VanDerveer felt this way about her relationship to her players (VanDerveer 1997):

> " I'm not a coach who gets buddy-buddy with my players . . . A coach needs to keep a certain distance to push her players to be the best they can be. She needs to keep her players on edge just enough to prevent complacency." (p. 52)

Yet, after watching her two assistant coaches work with the team for a while, VanDerveer found herself reconsidering this position:

> " [Yet] I was beginning to understand the power of feelings and of being positive, of tending to your players' souls as well as their minds and bodies. I'd watch Nell and Renee [the assistant coaches] with the players every day and see how well they communicated . . . They loved the players so deeply that the players responded in kind. They would have done anything for one another. As important as X's and O's are, the players don't really care what you know. They just want to know that you care . . . I saw, through Nell and Renee, that being positive and understanding did not necessarily mean you were soft or letting them slack off. " (pp. 186-187)

Some coaches believe it is inappropriate to disclose themselves to their athletes. They believe that they must stay detached to be good taskmasters. I disagree with this view. I believe that detachment serves only one of two purposes: to try to extract more effort from the athletes, or to conceal the coach's doubts about his or her self-concept. John Powell understood this when he wrote: "I am afraid to tell you who I am, because, if I tell you who I am, you may not like who I am, and it's all that I have" (1969, p. 15).

It's true: Our self-worth is our most important possession. I will come back to this theme often in this book.

Jim Bouche, athletic director for Eagan High School in Minnesota and football coach for 20 years, had this to say about his philosophy of coaching:

❝ The success or failure of a coach is not wholly based on his mastery of the X's and O's. He must also be a communicator—let the athletes know what he is all about, where they stand with him, precisely what he expects them to do, and that he will listen to them.

Athletes want to trust their coaches. When they do, they will run through the proverbial wall for them—every day in practice and in every game during the season. Coaching young men, watching them succeed and grow, is tremendously invigorating and rewarding. I approached it with a very simple philosophy:

1. Be honest with the players.
2. Explain decisions on personnel.
3. Keep the players' interests uppermost in mind.

If I did these things, I could win their trust. Every member of my staff was instructed to let each player know his value to the team, whether he was a full-time player or part-time player, or a bench-sitter. The message was simply everyone is part of this team. ❞ (Bouche 1999, p. 26)

How revealing should you be about yourself? *Self-disclosing* does not mean revealing intimate details about your life. It means sharing with your athletes how you feel about what they say and do, or about events that you have shared. Self-disclosure must be relevant to your relationship and appropriate to the situation. For example, if a person is untrustworthy, misinterprets, or overreacts, you would be foolish to be self-disclosing.

Being silent does not mean being strong. Strength is the willingness to take risks in your relationship with your athletes, to disclose yourself with the intent of building a better relationship. Being self-disclosing in this way means being real, honest, and genuine—first to yourself and then to your athletes.

You need to recognize that if you are not appropriately self-disclosing, your athletes will not share their thoughts and feelings with you. Without this intimate knowledge of your athletes, you cannot hope to help them develop character as discussed in chapter 4 or the psychological skills discussed in part II.

You can't disclose your feelings and reactions if you don't know what they are. Self-awareness, therefore, is the first step to self-disclosure. In turn, through self-disclosure you receive feedback from others, and this feedback helps you further your own self-awareness.

Study figure 1.3 for a moment and consider these questions:

▶ How much of the total self that you know is known by others?

▶ How much of you do you purposely choose not to reveal to others?

▶ How much of you is known to others, but not to yourself? You can't answer this question, of course! Do you dare ask others to find out this information? Of course you want to know what others know about you that you don't know . . . or do you?

It's also interesting to wonder how much of you is unknown to yourself and others. What can you do to learn more about this hidden side of you? Provocative questions, are they not?

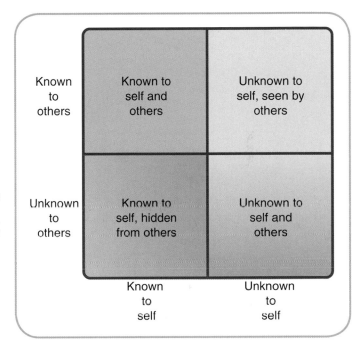

Figure 1.3 Evaluate how much you know about yourself and how much others know about you.

Conclusion

A well-developed philosophy of life and coaching will be among your best friends as you pursue your career in coaching. You develop your philosophy by learning about yourself and thinking through important issues. This will help you establish principles for guiding your actions. Appropriate disclosure of yourself to your athletes helps you to know yourself better, to develop your philosophy further, and to establish a trusting relationship with your athletes. Sharing your philosophy with your athletes by word and deed will help them develop their own philosophies.

Keep these two things in mind:

▶ The most important ingredient of a philosophy is that you own it. Espousing the tenets of someone else's philosophy without acting in a way that is consistent with these tenets is deceiving to yourself and others.

▶ A philosophy is not really expressed by what you say, but by what you do!

Questions for Reflection

▶ Have you formed your own coaching philosophy—the beliefs and principles that will serve as your guides to action? **(p. 5)**

▶ Have you developed greater self-awareness and decided what your coaching objectives are? **(p. 8)**

▶ Are you willing to become more aware of yourself by analyzing your views on many issues and by paying more attention to how others respond to you? **(p. 10)**

▶ What are the characteristics of your ideal, public, and real selves? **(p. 11)**

▶ How do you value yourself? What is your level of self-esteem? Your success as a coach will be strongly related to this. **(p. 12)**

▶ Are you appropriately self-disclosing? It helps others get to know you and, in turn, they can help you to know yourself. It also will help you build a trusting relationship with your athletes and others. **(p. 13)**

References

Bouche, Jim. 1999. Football coaching: A matter of trust. *Coach and Athletic Director* 69 (1): 26.

Branden, Nathaniel. 1983. *Honoring the self: The psychology of confidence and respect.* New York: Bantam.

Johnson, David W. 1981. *Reaching out: Interpersonal effectiveness and self-actualization.* 2nd ed. Englewood Cliffs, NJ: Prentice Hall.

Powell, John. 1969. *Why am I afraid to tell you who I am?* Niles, IL: Argus.

Sabock, Ralph J. 1985. *The coach.* 3rd ed. Champaign, IL: Human Kinetics.

VanDerveer, Tara (with Joan Ryan). 1997. *Shooting from the Outside: How a coach and her Olympic team transformed women's basketball.* New York: Avon Books.

Wooden, John (with Jack Tobin). 1988. *They call me coach.* Chicago: Contemporary Books.

Determining Your Coaching Objectives

The score in the volleyball game is 13 to 14, with your team 1 point down. The opposing team serves, and as the ball arcs down on your team's side, your left-back player digs it. A front line player then sets it perfectly so another player can successfully spike it over the net to tie the game. However, you see that your left-back is limping and in pain; it looks as though she's injured her ankle. You are preparing to pull her off the court, but she's gesturing to indicate that she wants to stay in. Her play has been exemplary all during the game and could be crucial at this point. Do you leave her in, or pull her out?

If a situation similar to that of the volleyball coach hasn't happened to you yet, one day it will. You'll have to make a decision that will affect one of your players and could affect the outcome of a contest. What do you think you'd do?

What you do in difficult situations such as the preceding will be determined in large measure by your coaching objectives, which are an essential part of your coaching philosophy. One of the most important decisions you will make as a coach concerns the objectives you will seek to achieve with your athletes. Have you thought about your objectives as a coach? Is it as simple as saying that you want to be a winning coach, or do you want to achieve other objectives? What do you personally want from coaching?

☞ In this chapter you'll learn

▶ the three major objectives of sport,

▶ society's objectives for sport programs and the compatibility of your objectives with society's,

▶ my perspective on winning as an objective in sport, and

▶ your personal objectives for coaching.

Three Major Objectives of Sport

The goals coaches often list usually fall into the following three broad categories:

▶ To have a winning team

▶ To help young people have fun

▶ To help young people develop . . .

  –*physically,* by learning sport skills, improving physical conditioning, developing good health habits, and avoiding injuries;

  –*psychologically,* by learning to control their emotions and developing feelings of self-worth; and

  –*socially,* by learning cooperation in a competitive context and appropriate standards of behavior

Which of these objectives are important to you? Winning? Having fun? Helping young people develop? Perhaps you believe all three are worthwhile. But are they equally important? What if you must choose among them, which at times you will? Coaches often must decide whether to pursue victory at the possible expense of an athlete's well-being or long-term development. What will your priorities be then?

Assessing Your Objectives

Complete the following questionnaire to help you decide about your objectives for winning; having fun; and helping young athletes develop physically, psychologically, and socially.

1. Read each statement and the three options that follow.

2. Decide which of the three options you believe is most important, and write the number 3 in the white box next to that option.

3. Then decide which option is least important to you, and write 1 in the corresponding white box.

4. Put a 2 in the remaining white box.

5. Add up the scores for each column, and put the totals in the Total Score boxes.

6. Although in some cases you may think all three choices are important, indicate which is the *most* important and which is the *least* important of the three. Try to answer each question as honestly as possible.

Your Coaching Objectives			
The best coaches are those who . . .			
a. give individual help and are interested in their athletes' development.		■	■
b. make practices and games fun.	■		■
c. teach athletes the skills needed to win.	■	■	
If a news story were written about me, I would like to be described as . . .			
a. a coach who contributed to the development of young people.		■	■
b. a coach for whom athletes enjoyed playing.	■		■
c. a winning coach.	■	■	
As a coach I emphasize . . .			
a. teaching skills that young people can use later in life.		■	■
b. having fun.	■		■
c. winning.	■	■	
TOTAL SCORE			
	Development	**Fun**	**Winning**

From *Successful Coaching, Third Edition,* by Rainer Martens, 2004, Champaign, IL: Human Kinetics.

Now let's discuss your responses to the questionnaire. Each total should be between 3 and 9. The higher the total, the more you emphasize that outcome. The first column shows your priority for the development of young athletes, the second your priority for having fun, and the third the importance you give to winning.

Most coaches' scores indicate that they believe winning is least important and helping athletes develop physically, psychologically, and socially is most important. Did you answer the same way? Of course it's the "right thing to say," and it's easy to say in a questionnaire like this. But is it true of how you coach? Do you really believe that winning is the least important of the three objectives?

Nothing is more important in determining how you coach than the significance you give to winning. Some coaches who say winning is least important don't behave that way when they coach. For example, coaches who play only their best athletes, who play injured athletes, or who scream disparagingly at athletes who have erred demonstrate that winning is more important to them than athletes' development.

Be honest. Do you at times overemphasize winning? Do you at times make decisions that reflect more concern about winning the game than the development of your athletes? It is easy to do in a society that places so much value on winning! I'll ask you to think more about this shortly, but first let's consider what society's objectives are for sport programs.

Society's Objectives

As a self-appointed spokesman for "society," I believe that our society offers sports programs primarily to help young people develop physically, psychologically, and socially—and that it expects you as a coach to accept "development" as your number one objective. Moreover, as you strive to achieve this long-term objective, society encourages you to achieve the secondary and short-term objectives of winning and having fun.

Yet, at times society seems to indicate that it values winning more than development because it so clearly rewards winners. That message, however, as powerful as it is, is sent by misguided rascals who do not understand the deeper value of sport in our society. It's a message you must reject.

Recreational Versus Competitive Sport Programs

The sport programs our society offers vary widely in the emphasis placed on winning. As shown in figure 2.1, at one end of the continuum we have recreational sports programs whose primary short-term objectives are to have fun and learn the game, with winning clearly a secondary objective. On the other end of the continuum we have competitive sports programs whose primary short-term objectives are winning and performing well, with fun as a secondary objective.

Both recreational and competitive sport programs are valuable and worthy as long as

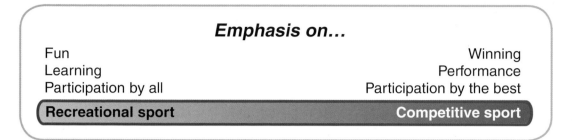

Emphasis on...

Fun	Winning
Learning	Performance
Participation by all	Participation by the best
Recreational sport	**Competitive sport**

Figure 2.1 Recreational and competitive sports programs.

the long-term goal of helping athletes develop remains the first priority. But herein is one of society's significant sport problems: Coaches, administrators, parents, and team supporters may place greater emphasis on the short-term objective of winning than on the long-term objective of development. The second significant problem is the discrepancy that sometimes exists between the short-term objectives of recreational and competitive sports programs and the short-term objectives of coaches.

Look at figure 2.2 for a moment. On the left, the vertical continuum represents the sport program objectives, varying from recreational to competitive, and the horizontal continuum represents the objectives of the coach, also varying from recreational to competitive. Two problems arise when there is an incompatibility between program objectives and coaches' objectives.

▶ Coaches pursue competitive objectives in a recreational sport program (cell D). The players, who likely selected a recreational sport program because their objectives were to learn how to play the sport and have fun, encounter a coach who focuses primarily on winning. Conflict is almost certain because of the incompatibility of objectives.

▶ Coaches pursue recreational objectives in a competitive sport program (cell A). Although this occurs far less frequently, when it does occur, coaches may inadequately prepare their teams to be competitive with opponents and let the less than best players compete, resulting in players, administrators, and parents being dissatisfied with the coach.

To avoid these problems, you must ensure that your short-term coaching objectives are compatible with the short-term objectives of the sport program in which you coach (cells B and C). If your coaching objectives are not compatible with the program's objectives, then you should accept the sport program's objectives and coach accordingly, or you should coach in a sport program that is compatible with your objectives.

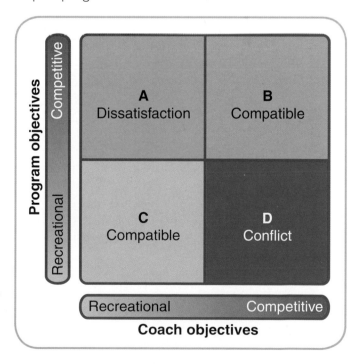

Figure 2.2 Are your coaching objectives compatible with the program objectives?

Problems also arise when administrators', players', and parents' objectives are not compatible with the sport program's objectives, or when the objectives of each party—coach, administrator, player, parents—are incompatible. Here are a few examples:

▶ A player seeks recreational objectives in a competitive sport program. Coaches often are frustrated when confronted with a talented athlete who really isn't committed to pursuing winning and excellence but simply wants to play to have fun.

▶ Parents push their youngster into a competitive sport program when the youngster lacks either the talent or the motivation to seek competitive goals and instead prefers the goals of a recreational sport program.

▶ An administrator gives priority to the long-term development objective, and the coach gives priority to winning.

As you can see, many of the problems in sports are based on differences in objectives—society's priority for the long-term goal of development over winning or having fun, and the differences in short-term objectives seen in recreational and competitive sports programs.

A "Winning" Philosophy

I want you to consider the following objective as the cornerstone for your coaching philosophy. Many national sport organizations, experienced and successful coaches at all levels, professional educators, and physicians endorse this objective. I hope you will endorse it as well, and more important, put it into practice! The objective is this:

Athletes First, Winning Second.

This is the motto of the American Sport Education Program, and it means this: Every decision you make and every behavior you display should be based first on what you judge is best for your athletes, and second on what may improve the athlete's or team's chances of winning.

Athletes First, Winning Second is the philosophical foundation for the Bill of Rights for Young Athletes (figure 2.3). Take a moment to review these rights. Even though they were written for younger children, these rights apply to athletes of all ages. Think about how your coaching might deny an athlete these rights. Then think about how you can coach to help ensure that each athlete enjoys these rights.

Athletes First, Winning Second is simple to state, but not simple to implement. Today some sport organizations are led by administrators who demand that coaches reverse this objective—Winning First, Athletes Second—either because winning is their personal objective or because they are pressured by others. Coaches who skillfully help young people become better humans but fail to win are considered losers, and all too often are fired. This is the regrettable reality in sport today, but through sport education programs, more enlightened sport administrators, and coaches with an Athletes First, Winning Second philosophy, this will change. In the final analysis, what's important is not how many games you win, but how many young people you help to become winners in life.

Striving to Win

Having Athletes First, Winning Second as your objective does not mean that winning is unimportant. The immediate *short-term* objective of any contest is to win. Striving to win within the rules of the game should be the objective of every athlete and coach.

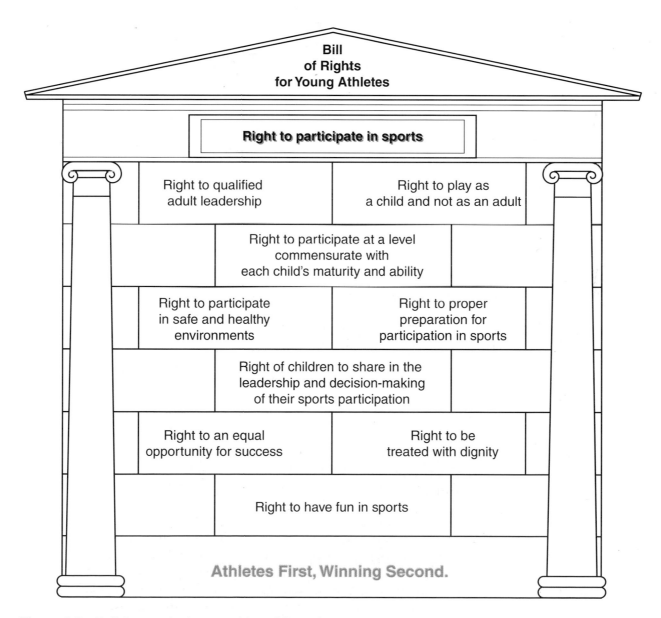

Figure 2.3 Building a winning coaching philosophy.

Reprinted, from *Guidelines for Children's Sports* (1979), with permission from the National Association for Sport and Physical Education (NASPE), 1900 Association Drive, Reston, VA 20101-1599.

To play sports without striving to win is to be a "dishonest competitor," says Michael Novak in *Joy of Sports* (1976, p. 215). Striving to win is essential to enjoyable competition.

"Winning isn't everything; it's the only thing," said Vince Lombardi, or so we are told. Actually Lombardi did not say it quite that way; that was a reporter's mutation. What Lombardi actually said was, "Winning isn't everything, but striving to win is." That statement more accurately reflects his coaching philosophy.

Does it make sense that the emphasis on winning should not be on the winning itself, but on the striving to win? It's the pursuit of the victory, the dream of achieving the goal more than the goal itself that yields the joy of sports. Many outstanding athletes candidly say that their best memories of sport are not the victories themselves, but the months of preparation and anticipation and the self-revelation they received before and during the competition.

Commitment

Competition and the striving to win are significant in another way. Today we hear much about our alienated youth, their lack of commitment to our established institutions, and their lack of desire to achieve excellence. Sadly, many young people are not finding activities in their home, school, or place of worship worthy of their commitment. But youth are often turned on by sport; they find sport a challenge worth pursuing. Why? I believe that they are drawn to the competition—the comparison of abilities and efforts, the striving to win, and the recognition of excellence achieved.

Kaleb Smith was one of these "uncommitted" youth. He was too lazy or uninterested to do his schoolwork; he usually sat around the house watching television and eating, which resulted in his becoming overweight. For some reason Kaleb went out for football, where at last he found a challenge. Before he could join the team, the coach required him to improve his grades and lose 10 pounds. His parents and teachers had tried

to get him to do both for months, but had failed. Now he did them eagerly for the opportunity to play!

In discussing some of our schools' problems, the noted educator James Coleman (1974) observed that humanity's great accomplishments come about when people make an intense commitment to something, when only their total concentrated effort may result in success—but even then success is not guaranteed. Sports attract that type of commitment and often result in great personal accomplishment.

The famous author James Michener wrote in the introduction to *Sports in America* (1976) that sport saved his life by rescuing him from the "streets" and a potential life of crime. It's a story often repeated by famous athletes and not so famous ones, like myself. I deeply believe that my life was greatly influenced for the better because of my participation in sport. One of its lessons—commitment—has certainly helped me to persist in revising this book over the past two years.

Ethical Behavior

The element of competition in sport has value in yet another way. Through sport, young people can develop morally; they can learn a basic code of ethics that is transferable to a moral code for life. Competitive sport—in which winning is a valued prize—provides opportunities for high levels of moral development to occur.

Consider a recreational game of tennis between Sharon and Susan, who hits the winning point on the baseline. Knowing that the shot is good, Sharon so declares it. Susan wins. That's not so hard to do when you're playing tennis only for fun, when there is little at stake. Imagine the same game but now winning means the prestigious state championship. It takes a great deal more character to make the proper call then.

In competitive sport such moral decisions are required often. Young people face opportunities to learn (and have adults to model) appropriate ethical behavior. To make an appropriate moral judgment at the expense of a valued victory is a real test of character, and it is an opportunity to build character (see chapter 4).

Keeping Winning in Perspective

Remember that striving to win the game is an important objective of the contest, but it is not the most important objective of sport participation. It is easy to lose sight of the long-term objectives—helping athletes develop physically, psychologically, and socially—while pursuing the short-term objective of winning the contest because the rewards for winning are immediate and powerful. Winning or striving to win is never more important than athletes' well-being, regardless of the mixed messages our society sends. Ask yourself, Will I be able to keep those long-term goals in sight not only during practice but in the heat of a contest, not only when I am winning but when I'm losing, not only when I have the support of my administrator but when that person is pressuring me to win?

When winning is kept in perspective, sport programs produce young people who enjoy sports, who strive for excellence, who dare to risk error to learn, and who grow with both praise and constructive criticism. When winning is kept in perspective, there is room for fun in the pursuit of victory—or, more accurately, the pursuit of victory is fun. With proper leadership, the leadership you provide, sport programs produce young people who accept responsibilities, who accept others, and most importantly, who accept themselves.

Georgetown University was on the brink of winning the NCAA men's basketball championship. In the championship game, as the final seconds ticked off the clock, GU guard Freddie Brown inexplicably threw the ball into the hands of North Carolina's James Worthy, spelling defeat for the Hoyas. Georgetown coach John Thompson sought out Brown after the buzzer sounded, not to scold him, but to offer words of encouragement as he escorted him off the court, an arm warmly slung around his dejected freshman guard's shoulders. Thompson explained that they would not have gotten to the title game without him.

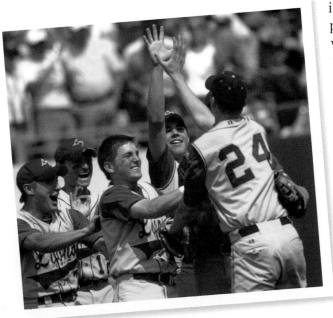

Your Personal Objectives

In developing your coaching philosophy, you need to consider not only your objectives for coaching and those of your sport program, but also what you personally want from coaching. Why do you want to become a coach? Is it because you want to help young people through sport? Or are you coaching to earn a living, to demonstrate your knowledge of the sport, or to gain public recognition, maybe even fame? You may be coaching for the social contact, the love of the sport, to have fun, to travel, or to be in charge. All of these objectives and many others are appropriate personal reasons for coaching. You need to achieve some of your objectives or you are likely to quit coaching.

Coaches sometimes deny their personal objectives. They may believe that the only socially acceptable reasons to give for coaching are altruistic statements about helping athletes. Of course it is desirable for you to have these altruistic motives, but it is entirely appropriate to seek to fulfill your personal objectives in coaching as well—as long as they are not achieved at the expense of your athletes' well-being.

To help you examine your personal objectives, I've listed some personal reasons for coaching in table 2.1.

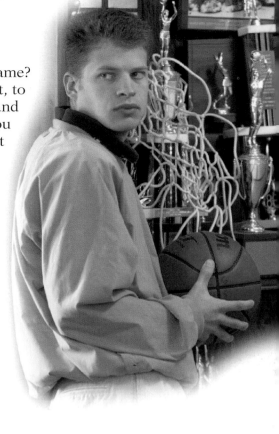

1. Read all of the reasons first before evaluating how important these reasons are to you.

2. Then add any other reasons that you have in the spaces provided.

3. Now, rate how important each reason is to you.

REASON	IMPORTANCE		
	Not at all	Somewhat	Very
1. To be involved in a sport I like			
2. To earn a living			
3. To help secure another job			
4. To have power			
5. To be with people I like			
6. To give something back to the sport			
7. To gain public recognition			
8. To enjoy myself			
9. To demonstrate my knowledge and skill in the sport			
10. To make up for the fact that I was not a good athlete			
11. To travel			
12. To help athletes develop physically, psychologically, and socially			
13.			
14.			
15.			

Table 2.1—Personal Reasons for Coaching

From *Successful Coaching, Third Edition,* by Rainer Martens, 2004, Champaign, IL: Human Kinetics.

Look at the reasons and your rating of each and consider whether a conflict exists between your personal objectives for coaching and the objective of helping athletes develop. If personal recognition or power is among your personal objectives for coaching, for example, you will need to guard against placing this objective above the interest of your athletes. During intense competition you will be especially vulnerable to pursuing your own goals at the expense of your athletes. This risk can be managed, but you must know yourself well and entrench firmly in your mind the philosophy of Athletes First, Winning Second.

they may know that a victory is unlikely, they also know that winning is the purpose of the game and that it should be accomplished within the rules of the sport and without abusing athletes. Successful coaches help athletes develop physically, psychologically, and socially. And successful coaches strive to achieve their personal goals without jeopardizing their athletes' well-being.

Indeed, successful coaches find ways to achieve all three objectives: to have a winning team; to help young people to have fun; and to help them develop physically, psychologically, and socially.

Conclusion

Successful coaches know the differences between their objectives for the contest, their objectives for their athletes' participation, and their personal objectives. Successful coaches strive to win every contest. Although

References

Coleman, James S. 1974. *Youth: Transition to adulthood.* Chicago: University of Chicago Press.

Novak, Michael. 1976. *Joy of sports.* New York: Basic Books.

Michener, James. 1976. *Sports in America.* New York: Random House.

Questions for Reflection

▶ What priority do you give to winning; having fun; and helping athletes develop physically, psychologically, and socially? **(p. 18)**

▶ What are society's objectives for sport programs? Are your objectives compatible with society's? **(p. 20)**

▶ How does the emphasis on winning differ between recreational and competitive sport programs? Are your objectives compatible with the objectives of the sport program in which you coach? **(p. 20)**

▶ Do you embrace the Athletes First, Winning Second philosophy? **(p. 22)**

▶ Do you emphasize striving to win, rather than winning, with your athletes? **(p. 23)**

▶ How does sport impart a sense of commitment and ethical behavior in athletes? **(p. 24)**

▶ What do you consider the long-term objective of sport participation? Although winning is the goal of the contest, do you help your athletes develop physically, psychologically, and socially? **(p. 26)**

▶ What are your personal objectives for coaching? Are you able to achieve them without compromising the well-being of your athletes? **(p. 26)**

3

Selecting Your Coaching Style

You sit down with your soccer team to plan strategy for next Saturday's game.

"OK, as we've talked about before, you all will need to spread out and support the attacker. For example, let's say Chris has the ball and is attacking. What should you do?"

Angie volunteers, "I would try to get up the field to where Chris could pass the ball to me."

"I usually can outrun the player who marks me, so I would try to get on the other side from Angie and be ready for the pass too," adds Tara.

"Great!" you say. "It sounds like you understand what we need to do."

In chapter 2 you considered your coaching objectives. In this chapter we will consider the second important decision you need to make in developing your coaching philosophy—your *coaching style*. That style will determine how you decide what technical and tactical skills to teach, how you organize for practice and competition, what methods you use to discipline players, and most important, what role you give athletes in making decisions.

👉 In this chapter you'll learn

▶ three coaching styles and how those styles affect your athletes,

▶ what leadership is when coaching,

▶ how to develop your team culture,

▶ three other qualities of successful coaches—knowledge of the sport, motivation, and empathy, and

▶ a code of ethics to follow.

Three Coaching Styles

Most coaches lean toward one of three coaching styles: the command style, the submissive style, or the cooperative style.

Command Style (The Dictator)

In the command style of coaching, the coach makes all of the decisions. The role of the athlete is to respond to the coach's commands. The assumption underlying this approach is that because the coach has knowledge and experience, it is the coach's role to tell the athlete what to do. The athlete's role is to listen, to absorb, and to comply.

Submissive Style (The Baby-Sitter)

Coaches who adopt the submissive style make as few decisions as possible. It's a throw-out-the-ball-and-have-a-good-time approach. The coach provides little instruction, provides minimal guidance in organizing activities, and resolves discipline problems only when absolutely necessary. Coaches who adopt this style (1) lack the competence to provide instruction and guidance, (2) are too lazy to meet the demands of their coaching responsibilities, or (3) are very misinformed about what coaching is. The submissive-style coach is merely a baby-sitter and often a poor one at that.

Command Coach

Bobby Knight began his coaching career at West Point, and throughout his career he has characterized playing basketball as war. Recognized as a master teacher and tactician of the sport, he is known for his pugnacity when disciplining his players. He insists that they follow his commands and is sometimes ruthless about leaning on them until they do.

For some college players, Knight provides a wake-up call. By trying to live up to his standards, some players find they can improve their play. Knight's style of play requires that each player execute the offensive and defensive patterns exactly as prescribed by Knight. This highly controlled style is not compatible with the open style of some of his players, which results in some talented players leaving his teams. Others, tired of his incessant demands and in some cases his public humiliation of them, also have left his teams. Although Knight's earlier teams were very successful and close-knit, his teams in later years were marked by dissension.

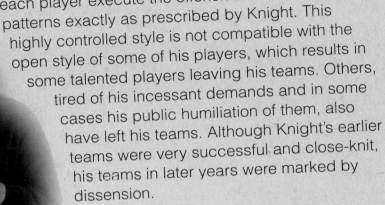

Cooperative Style (The Teacher)

Coaches who select the cooperative style share decision making with their athletes. Although they recognize their responsibility to provide leadership and guide young people toward achieving the objectives set forth, cooperative-style coaches also know that youngsters cannot become responsible adults without learning to make decisions. The challenge of the cooperative style is providing the right balance between directing athletes and letting them direct themselves. That's why I call it the cooperative style—coaches cooperate with their athletes in sharing decision making.

Cooperative Coach

Phil Jackson approaches basketball with the idea that everyone on the team should participate in play, not just one or two stars. As the coach for the Chicago Bulls and the Los Angeles Lakers, he instituted the triangle offense, a difficult system to learn, but one in which all players handle the ball and work together.

As the players become more proficient at the system, Jackson gives them more chances to make their own decisions. He believes strongly that the players who are on the floor often have a better understanding of what's going on in a game than the coaches do. He wants his players to learn how to make decisions on the fly and to rely on each other. To do this, he often lets them solve their own problems during a game rather than calling a time-out and telling them what to do.

Jackson stresses to his players that they should try to work in the flow of the game rather than force plays. He trusts that they can learn to choose the right moves at the right time and doesn't insist that they follow preset patterns. Jackson's cooperative coaching style has made him one of the most successful NBA coaches.

Coaching Styles Evaluated

Let's first dismiss the submissive style. It's not really coaching; it's baby-sitting. As such, it's an abdication of your duties as a coach.

The second coaching style—the command style—has been prevalent in the past and continues among some professional, college, and high school coaches. Sometimes inexperienced coaches adopt the command style because it is the one they have seen modeled by their own coaches or others. Some coaches adopt this style because it helps them conceal their doubts about their capabilities. If they don't permit the athletes to question them, if they can avoid explaining why they coach the way they do, then their inadequacies won't be uncovered—or so they think!

On the surface the command style appears effective. Good athletic teams need organization. They cannot be run effectively as participant democracies; the team cannot vote on every decision that needs to be made. Indeed, the command style can be effective if winning is the coach's primary objective, and if its authoritarian nature does not stifle athletes' motivation. But this risk of stifling motivation is one of the major limitations of the command style. Rather than playing because they are intrinsically motivated, athletes may play for the praise of the coach or to avoid the coach's wrath. Coaches who use the command style also prevent athletes from fully enjoying the sport. The athletes' accomplishments are credited to the coach, not the athletes.

Coaches at all levels of sport are increasingly finding the command style less effective with today's athletes. Coaches are recognizing that the command style alienates all but the highly gifted athlete and that it diminishes their own satisfaction in relating to athletes.

The command style is not compatible with the objective of Athletes First, Winning Second. If your objective is to help young people grow physically, psychologically, and socially through sport; to help athletes learn to make decisions; and to help young people become independent, then the command style is not for you. Even if your foremost objective is to win, the command style is not likely to produce the best performances in your athletes.

Obviously I favor the third coaching style—the cooperative style of coaching. It shares decision making with the athletes and fosters the Athletes First, Winning Second philosophy. Cooperative-style coaches provide the structure and rules that allow athletes to learn to set their own goals and to strive for them.

The Warrensburg-Latham, Illinois, high school volleyball team had a talented group of players. They were coached by Debbie Kiick—a coach who used the cooperative style and was technically very strong, always teaching, always pushing for the best. The team regularly made it to regionals. Becky was an excellent player but too short to play the front line. Instead, she was a back row specialist and came out of the rotation just before she would move to the front. Fans and players alike knew that Becky's short-term dream was to play in the front line, even if just for once.

Before the last home game of the season, on Senior Night, the senior starters initiated a pact with Coach Kiick that if they got up by a certain number of points in the last game, the coach would let Becky play the front line. The girls got up by that number of points, and the captain excitedly reminded Coach Kiick of their agreement. Fans could see Coach Kiick hesitate—she was so used to putting her players in the best positions to win the game, and she didn't want the other team to feel disrespected or that her team was taking the game lightly. But she did the right thing and let Becky play the front line for one rotation. The players and fans were ecstatic. The looks on the players' faces were of pure joy. The girls had worked hard to let their fellow teammate play the front line, the team won the game, and Coach Kiick gained even more respect for understanding what this meant to the team and allowing it to happen.

What would Coach Kiick have communicated to her players had she turned down the pact to begin with? What would she have communicated to her athletes and the parents had she not "cooperated" with her players to let the short senior play the front line this one time?

Some people think that adopting the cooperative style means that you abandon your responsibilities as a coach or let athletes do anything they want. That's not the case at all! Being a cooperative-style coach does not mean avoiding rules and order. Failing to structure team activities is neglecting a major coaching responsibility.

Instead, as a cooperative-style coach, you face the complex task of deciding how much structure will create the optimum climate for athletes' development. It's like handling a wet bar of soap. If you hold it too tightly, it squirts out of your hands (the command style), and if you don't grasp it firmly enough, it slips away (the submissive style). Firm but gentle pressure (the cooperative style) is needed. The cooperative-style coach gives direction and instruction when needed, but also knows when to let athletes make decisions and assume responsibility.

You know there is more to being an athlete than just having motor skills. To perform well, athletes must be able to cope with pressure, adapt to changing situations, keep contests in perspective, exhibit discipline, and maintain concentration. These qualities are nurtured routinely by cooperative-style coaches, but seldom by command-style coaches. The cooperative approach places more trust in athletes, which has a positive effect on their self-image. It promotes openness in the relationship between coaches and athletes, and it improves both communication and motivation. Athletes are motivated not by fear of the coach, but by a desire for personal satisfaction. Thus, the cooperative style is almost always more fun for athletes.

There is a price to pay, however, in choosing the cooperative style of coaching. This style requires more skill on your part because choices are seldom absolutely right or wrong. As a cooperative-style coach you must individualize your coaching much more than command-style coaches do. You may at times have to sacrifice winning in the interest of your athletes' well being. Throughout the remaining chapters of this book you will learn more about how to use the cooperative style.

Leadership in Coaching

If you are like most coaches, you played sports for many years before you began coaching. When you assume the role of coach, you must make the difficult transition of getting things done through others. You can no longer play the game yourself, even though you may yearn to do so. Now you have to help your players play the game. The skills needed to do that are not at all the same skills you needed when you were playing. The skills you need now are leadership skills.

Leadership Defined

Leadership is first knowing how to chart a course, to give others direction by having a vision of what can be. A team without a leader is like a ship without a rudder. Second, leadership is developing the social and psychological environment—what business calls the *corporate culture* and what I'll call *team culture*—to achieve the goals the leader has

charted. This culture is created through selecting, motivating, rewarding, retaining, and unifying members of your team, which includes players, assistants, parents, and others who help your organization.

Excellent coaches—leaders—give the team vision and know how to translate this vision into reality. Coaches, in their leadership roles, seek to develop an environment in which every athlete has the maximum opportunity to achieve success, and in so doing achieve team success. Coaches as leaders are concerned not only with the physical environment, but also with the psychological and social environments.

Cooperative Coach With Vision

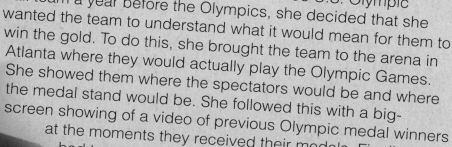

When Tara VanDerveer first went on the road with the 1996 U.S. Olympic women's basketball team a year before the Olympics, she decided that she wanted the team to understand what it would mean for them to win the gold. To do this, she brought the team to the arena in Atlanta where they would actually play the Olympic Games. She showed them where the spectators would be and where the medal stand would be. She followed this with a big-screen showing of a video of previous Olympic medal winners at the moments they received their medals. Finally, she had two actual gold medals that she had borrowed so her players could see and feel them. The players spontaneously tried the medals on to see how wearing them would feel and took pictures of each other. They began to cry and hug each other as they realized the importance of their undertaking.

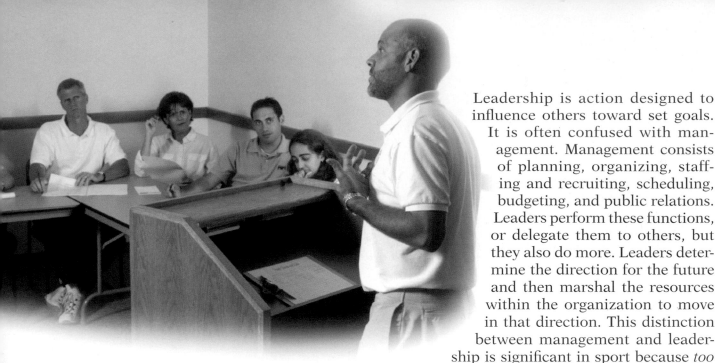

Leadership is action designed to influence others toward set goals. It is often confused with management. Management consists of planning, organizing, staffing and recruiting, scheduling, budgeting, and public relations. Leaders perform these functions, or delegate them to others, but they also do more. Leaders determine the direction for the future and then marshal the resources within the organization to move in that direction. This distinction between management and leadership is significant in sport because *too many teams are overmanaged and underled.*

Leadership emphasizes interpersonal relationships and has a direct impact on motivation, whereas management does not. Tom Peters and Nancy Austin wrote in *A Passion for Excellence* (1985):

> **"** *Coaching is face-to-face leadership that pulls together people with diverse backgrounds, talents, experiences and interests, encourages them to step up to responsibility and continued achievement, and treats them as full-scale partners and contributors. Coaching is not about memorizing techniques or devising the perfect game plan. It is about really paying attention to people—really believing them, really caring about them, really involving them.* **"**
> (p. 326)

Coaching is a people business, and excellent coaches become students of people. To be an excellent leader—an excellent coach—you must develop the interpersonal skills to move people to action. Communication skills are essential—talking, listening, negotiating, encouraging, and consoling. Coaching is as demanding of communication skills as marathoning is of conditioning skills.

I subscribe to the "great person" theory of history—that is, people who exert leadership make a difference. Excellence in teams is a product of superior leadership by people who have acquired specific skills that give them both a vision of a future that can be obtained and the ability to commit others to pursue that vision. Excellence doesn't just happen. It comes from preparing yourself to lead and working hard when leading.

It's been said that people can be divided into three classes: the few who make things happen, the many who watch things happen, and the vast majority who have no idea what happened. There is a ring of truth in that statement. If you want to be a good coach, you must be among the few who make things happen!

Transformative Leadership

In *Leaders: The Strategies for Taking Charge* (1985), Warren Bennis and Burt Nanus described a leader as "one who commits people to action, who converts followers into leaders, and who may convert leaders into agents of change" (p. 3). Leadership viewed from this perspective is congruent with the philosophy espoused in the first two chapters of this book. It's a collective process—you and your players working together to meet each other's individual needs and your common goals.

As shown in figure 3.1, this type of leadership, known as transformative leadership, involves a dynamic relationship in which you influence the team, and the team influences you. It is a psychological contract between you and your athletes. The contract contains a variety of expectations and actions on both sides; your demands on the athletes may be reciprocated by the athletes' demands on you.

Transformative leadership is not unilateral; it is an impressive yet subtle passing of energy back and forth between you and your team. This approach to leadership can move your athletes to become more responsible, more in control of their lives. It can help them acquire the skills that will permit them to lead now and tomorrow.

Power is the basic energy needed to initiate and sustain action; it permits you to translate intentions into reality. Power is essential for you to move your athletes to achieve their objectives. Because it is so often misused, however, power is greatly distrusted. Leadership is the *wise* use of power, and power is gained through effective leadership.

Because you are the appointed coach, you have the authority to direct, but that doesn't make you the leader. As a coach you do not become the team leader until the team members and assistants acknowledge or legitimate your authority. In short, you must earn the respect of the team to have the power needed to achieve excellence. This respect is earned by demonstrating ability through superior skills and knowledge, and by attaining credibility through a clear commitment to the team—Athletes First, Winning Second.

Transformative leaders empower their assistants and players to achieve team goals. Empowered assistants and players

▶ are more likely to believe they are making a difference, a contribution to the team goal;

▶ learn new skills that enhance their physical and psychological performance;

▶ feel more committed to the team, thus increasing their motivation; and

▶ experience more enjoyment from participation, which meets their need for fun.

The team influences the coach

The coach influences the team

Figure 3.1 Transformative leadership.

What Leaders Do

To be a leader, you need to know what leaders do and how they go about doing it. The following six actions set leaders apart from followers; the quality of these actions distinguish the effective leader from the ineffective leader.

▶ Leaders provide direction; they set goals by having a vision of the future. I elaborate on this vital function later.

▶ Leaders build a psychological and social environment that is conducive to achieving the team's goals—what business calls the "corporate culture." I'll discuss this function briefly as well.

▶ Leaders instill values, in part by sharing their philosophy of life. The significance of having values, and of imparting those values to athletes, was addressed in chapter 1.

▶ Leaders motivate members of their group to pursue the goals of the group. You'll learn more about motivation in chapter 7.

▶ Leaders confront members of the organization when problems arise, and they resolve conflicts. You'll learn more about this function in chapter 19.

▶ Leaders communicate. They need this critical skill to engage in the five actions just mentioned. We'll discuss it in more depth in chapter 6.

Providing Direction

You may say that the direction—the goal—in sports is obvious. The goal is to win each game, the league championship, the state title, the national championship, a world record, and so on. This, however, is seldom the goal that excellent coaches pursue when leading their teams. Of course, every team wants to win all that it can; that's the short-term goal. But if winning is your first or only goal, you are far less likely to be a successful coach. Leaders provide direction by focusing not on the outcome of winning or losing, but on the steps that lead to winning, and on the other goals they consider important for the team. Lou Holtz (1998) had this to say about direction:

> *"Leaders are obligated to bring out the best in their people. Most people will not reach their objectives unless you encourage them to take risks. You have to lead them out of their comfort zones. There is nothing more satisfying than knowing you have helped someone do the impossible. If you don't ask much from your team, you'll never scratch their potential."* (p. 157)

Creating the Vision

How do leaders know what the right direction is? Leaders acquire the ability to have vision—to set realistic goals that beckon the group to action. Hickman and Silva (1984) wrote, "Vision is a mental journey from the known to the unknown, creating the future from a montage of current facts, hopes, dreams, dangers, and opportunities" (p. 151).

Once coaches have direction, have charted a course, they focus not only their own attention, but the attention of the team, on this course. First they must communicate the direction successfully, striving to obtain commitment to it. Such commitment cannot be achieved by edict or coercion, although many coaches have sought to establish direction in this way. True commitment comes through persuasion; it comes from creating enthusiasm by helping the team to see that it is possible to achieve a certain goal. Effective coaches appeal to the emotions and to the spirit of the team members, addressing their values and aspirations. Excellent coaches do not state their goal just once, but repeat it again and again and arrange the physical and psychological environment to reinforce that goal.

Vision comes mostly through preparation. Leaders acquire vision by seeking information from any appropriate source—from history, books, reports, observation, and especially from other people. Because leaders rely so heavily on other people for their information, they must possess good listening skills and must be able to ask good questions. Once they have obtained the available information, they sift through it, analyze it, and interpret it. The quality of this interpretation determines whether they are able to gain true insight.

Vision also comes from intelligence, and intelligence comes from preparation—from educating yourself to be able to out-think, out-plan, and out-teach others. Those who can select the right strategy for the right situation, under the pressure that sport often imposes, earn the right to be called leaders. Superior strategy does not come from raw intelligence, although that helps; it comes mostly from educated intelligence—and that involves becoming a student of the game. To provide direction, to have a vision, to implement strategy—all require that you know your sport, your athletes, and your competitors well. As Thomas Edison said, "Genius is 1 percent inspiration and 99 percent perspiration."

Nurturing Team Culture

Having direction—a vision—for your team is the first vital act of leadership. But it's your ability to put this vision into action—to make it become reality—that makes you a leader. Putting a vision into action requires that you develop and maintain an effective team culture. Developing physical skills and conditioning and planning tactics for the next game is important, but of equal importance is nurturing the culture of your team.

Team Culture Defined

Team culture is the way things are done on a team—it's the social architecture that nurtures the team psyche. A healthy team culture creates a climate for success. When coaches talk about developing a winning attitude, instilling commitment, inculcating pride, and building team spirit, they are talking about team culture.

Team culture is concerned with how rewards are given, who communicates with whom about what, practice procedures, game protocols, acceptable reactions toward winning and losing, dress codes, and so on. The style of leadership you use, which determines how power is distributed and how decisions are made, is part of the team culture.

Team culture, then, comprises the formal organizational systems that you establish for moving your team toward its goal, and the many informal factors that operate in any dynamic team. These formal and informal processes have great influence on the soul and spirit of your team—what is called the *team psyche.*

If your team culture is not adequately developed, or is incompatible with the team direction, then your team will function substantially below its performance capabilities, and widespread dissatisfaction is likely. Poor team culture results when athletes are constantly subjected to criticism, when conflicts develop between athletes and coaches or among athletes themselves, when athletes feel alienated, when coaches exert too much control, and when feelings of futility and frustration reach a threshold.

Far more coaches fail to achieve their objectives because they lack an awareness of, or the ability to develop, team culture than because they lack good direction or knowledge of the game. John Wooden's last national championship team was considered by many to be weaker in talent and ability than other prominent teams in the country that year. By all accounts, UCLA won the national title more because of a very powerful and effective team culture than because of superb talent.

Building team culture does not mean that every member of the team must conform rigidly to the dictates of the coach. It is a team process and thus must involve the team. Dictating every standard of appropriate behavior is not leading the development of your team culture; it is imposing your power on the team and is highly likely to have an adverse effect on the team. A positive culture must have room for individualism and the sharing of responsibility.

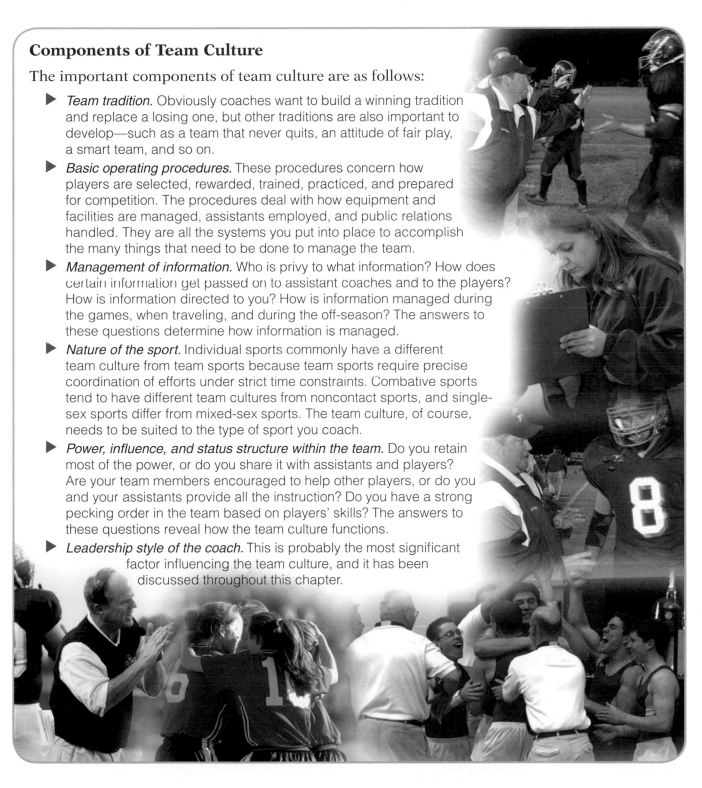

Components of Team Culture

The important components of team culture are as follows:

▶ *Team tradition.* Obviously coaches want to build a winning tradition and replace a losing one, but other traditions are also important to develop—such as a team that never quits, an attitude of fair play, a smart team, and so on.

▶ *Basic operating procedures.* These procedures concern how players are selected, rewarded, trained, practiced, and prepared for competition. The procedures deal with how equipment and facilities are managed, assistants employed, and public relations handled. They are all the systems you put into place to accomplish the many things that need to be done to manage the team.

▶ *Management of information.* Who is privy to what information? How does certain information get passed on to assistant coaches and to the players? How is information directed to you? How is information managed during the games, when traveling, and during the off-season? The answers to these questions determine how information is managed.

▶ *Nature of the sport.* Individual sports commonly have a different team culture from team sports because team sports require precise coordination of efforts under strict time constraints. Combative sports tend to have different team cultures from noncontact sports, and single-sex sports differ from mixed-sex sports. The team culture, of course, needs to be suited to the type of sport you coach.

▶ *Power, influence, and status structure within the team.* Do you retain most of the power, or do you share it with assistants and players? Are your team members encouraged to help other players, or do you and your assistants provide all the instruction? Do you have a strong pecking order in the team based on players' skills? The answers to these questions reveal how the team culture functions.

▶ *Leadership style of the coach.* This is probably the most significant factor influencing the team culture, and it has been discussed throughout this chapter.

Developing Team Culture

A group of Harvard professors in the late 1920s and early 1930s conducted a series of studies at the Western Electric Company in Hawthorne, Illinois, that have taught us much about team culture. These studies initially tested the hypothesis that workers would be more efficient if their lighting were increased. The results were positive. Then the lighting was decreased. Again the workers increased their productivity, much to the astonishment of the professors. This led to a series of other studies in which researchers lengthened workers' rest periods, shortened them, offered refreshments and took them away, shortened the work week, and changed the method by which workers were paid. In every case production increased, which initially baffled the professors. After much analysis, however, they realized that the significant factor in the studies was not the change in the work environment, but the attention being paid to the workers because they were part of a special group. This attention fostered a sense of group cohesiveness and motivation. The researchers also observed that the boss in the experimental group behaved differently from the boss in the control group. He

▶ showed interest in each employee's achievement,

▶ demonstrated pride in the accomplishments of the group,

▶ helped the group work together,

▶ regularly posted feedback about performance, and

▶ consulted the workers before changes were made.

The workers in the experimental group, as compared to the control groups, exhibited other changes. They

▶ took pride in their own achievement,

▶ felt satisfaction from the interest shown by outsiders in their work,

▶ did not feel they were being pressured to change, and

▶ developed a sense of confidence and candor.

The conditions discovered over 70 years ago in the now classic Hawthorne studies still have much to teach us about developing team culture. If you show interest in each athlete's achievement, show pride in the team's accomplishment, help the team play together, and provide clear feedback about performance, you'll most likely see the same results among your players as the researchers found among the Hawthorne workers. Your players will show pride in their achievements,

have feelings of satisfaction and enjoyment from being part of the team, believe that they are part of the decision-making process, and develop a sense of confidence.

Developing team culture is not something successful coaches delegate to anyone else. They recognize that it is the most difficult task facing coaches. When coaches talk about "turning a team around," they are recognizing the need to change the team culture. Just how do you recognize the need to change the team culture?

You should always be working on the team culture. Every time you meet with an athlete, every practice, every contest, and every action you take has some influence on the team culture. Nevertheless, some definite signs indicate when your team culture is in trouble:

▶ The team is not playing as well as it used to, or it appears to be playing below its capability.

▶ Your assistant coaches are complaining.

▶ There are conflicts among members of your team.

▶ You feel uncomfortable communicating with assistants and players, and they with you.

▶ There is confusion about assignments, messages are missed, and relationships are unclear.

▶ Signs of apathy and disinterest are evident.

▶ There is little response at team meetings.

Changing the team culture is not accomplished overnight or in a few weeks; it is a gradual process. When teams are constructed quickly, such as all-star teams that represent a region or national teams that represent a country, there is little time to develop team culture. This is probably one reason that these teams with enormous individual talent do not play as well as might be expected. Sport administrators increasingly are recognizing this problem and are now having national teams play together longer before engaging in international competition.

Some coaches also err by not fully grasping the scope of team culture and its complexity. If your team is experiencing internal friction, simply announcing, "We'll have no more bickering on the team" will not bring about any type of permanent solution to the problem. Nor is giving a pep talk about how everyone needs to be more committed likely to result in any lasting change. When the team culture is in trouble, you must look hard to discover what is interfering with maximum effort. Then you must devise a strategy to remove the obstacle or to build the right system. Tinkering with the team culture thoughtlessly can cause devastating problems. Thus it is vital that you involve the other members of the team in determining what the obstacles are. Remember—they are part of the culture.

You can build commitment to a dynamic team culture by

▶ involving players in defining team goals and recognizing that team goals must be compatible with individual goals;

▶ giving players responsibilities that they can accommodate;

▶ demonstrating superior skill and knowledge of the sport;

▶ treating each player with respect;

▶ rewarding competency by taking time to notice it and rewarding it promptly;

▶ rewarding excellent performance and effort, not outcomes that are beyond the control of the athletes; and

▶ teaching the players to reward each other.

You can maintain consistency by

▶ developing a sound coaching philosophy;

▶ adopting a long-term rather than a short-term perspective; and

▶ sticking with a well-thought-out plan when adversity occurs.

When you chart out a meaningful course for the team and build an effective team culture, you become an excellent leader.

Three Other Qualities of Successful Coaches

In this chapter I have recommended that to be successful, you should adopt a coaching style compatible with the Athletes First, Winning Second objective—that is, the cooperative style. I've also explained what leaders do and how they especially focus on developing the team culture. Now let's briefly consider three other attributes of successful coaches:

▶ Knowledge of the sport
▶ Motivation
▶ Empathy

Knowledge of the Sport

There is no substitute for knowing well the rules and technical and tactical skills of the sport you coach. This is just as true for teaching beginning athletes as advanced ones. In fact, to teach the fundamentals well to beginners you must have as much knowledge as you would need to coach professional athletes. (Actually they require different types of knowledge.)

Not knowing how to teach technical skills puts you in the position of risking injury to your athletes and frustration from their repeated failure. The more you know about the basic technical skills of your sport and about teaching these basics in the proper sequence, the more success and fun you and your athletes will have.

Moreover, your ability to teach both technical and tactical skills will earn you great respect from your athletes. This respect gives you credibility that you can use in teaching athletes life skills such as ethical behavior, emotional control, and respect for others and oneself.

The most common way coaches acquire knowledge about rules and technical and tactical skills is by playing the sport themselves, but that most likely will not give you all the knowledge you need. On the other hand, not having played a sport does not mean that you can't acquire the knowledge needed to coach it. Most coaches enjoy being a "student" of the sport, and I encourage you to learn all you can about every facet of it.

Pat Head Summitt, women's basketball coach at the University of Tennessee, is known for her technical knowledge of the sport.

▶ Consider learning about coaching as a lifelong journey. For example, complete the courses in the Professional Education Program of the American Sport Education Program described in the appendix.

▶ Join a coaching association. Many sports have state and national coaching associations, and every sport has a national governing body. National coaching associations and national governing bodies usually offer publications, courses, and conferences that provide rich opportunities for learning more about your sport.

▶ Many books and videos are available for most sports; read them, view them, learn from them. See the appendix for resources available from the American Sport Education Program and visit the Human Kinetics Publishers Web site at www.HumanKinetics.com for an excellent selection of books and videos.

▶ Attend clinics that are frequently offered in larger cities. Check with your school athletic director or fellow coaches for information about availability.

▶ Watch and talk with other coaches. When watching other coaches, don't just casually observe; study them carefully. Look for opportunities to talk with coaches about how they practice their profession. Just remember that as you observe and talk with colleagues, you need to determine for yourself what methods are consistent with your personal coaching objectives and coaching style.

Motivation

You can have all the skills and knowledge in the world, but without the motivation to use them, you will not be a successful coach. You need only come across a player who has the ability but not the motivation to develop into an excellent

Pat Riley, coach of the Miami HEAT, has a long-standing reputation for motivating his players to perform their very best.

LeRoy Walker, former track and field coach at North Carolina Central University, has long been recognized as being understanding of his players.

athlete to see full well the importance of motivation.

Sometimes coaches have the motivation to be successful but not the time. Or rather they don't have sufficient motivation to make the time for doing what is necessary to be a successful coach. I encourage you to have the motivation; young people need your time.

Empathy

Empathy is the ability to understand the thoughts, feelings, and emotions of your athletes and to convey your sensitivity to them. Successful coaches possess empathy. They understand athletes' joy, frustration, anxiety, and anger. Coaches who have empathy are able to listen to their athletes and express their understanding of what was said. They don't belittle, chastise, or diminish the self-worth of their athletes because they know how it feels to experience the loss of self-worth. Coaches with empathy more readily communicate respect for their athletes, and in turn they receive more respect. Empathy—it's essential to be a successful coach!

Coaching Code of Ethics

In these first three chapters you've been formulating your coaching philosophy. I have advocated that you build your philosophy on the cornerstone of Athletes First, Winning Second. In the next chapter I'll ask you to become not only a coach of the technical and tactical skills of your sport, but also a coach of character, helping your athletes develop moral values and good sporting behavior. To be a coach of character, you must be of good character—which may be a work in progress as it is for most of us.

As coaching continues its journey toward being a respected profession, some organizations have developed codes of ethics for coaches. These are guidelines arrived at by coaches and sport administrators prescribing what is acceptable and unacceptable behaviors by coaches. I'd like you to carefully consider the National Federation of State High School Coaches Association code of conduct, which follows.

Code
of
Conduct

NFHS
Coaches Code
of Ethics

The coach shall be aware that he or she has a tremendous influence, for either good or ill, on the education of the student-athlete and, thus, shall never place the value of winning above the value of instilling the highest ideals of character.

The coach shall uphold the honor and dignity of the profession. In all personal contact with student-athletes, officials, athletic directors, school administrators, the state high school athletic association, the media, and the public, the coach shall strive to set an example of the highest ethical and moral conduct.

The coach shall take an active role in the prevention of drug, alcohol and tobacco abuse.

The coach shall avoid the use of alcohol and tobacco products when in contact with players.

The coach shall promote the entire interscholastic program of the school and direct his or her program in harmony with the total school program.

The coach shall master the contest rules and shall teach them to his or her team members. The coach shall not seek an advantage by circumvention of the spirit or letter of the rules.

The coach shall exert his or her influence to enhance sportsmanship by spectators, both directly and by working closely with cheerleaders, pep club sponsors, booster clubs, and administrators.

The coach shall respect and support contest officials. The coach shall not indulge in conduct which would incite players or spectators against the officials. Public criticism of officials or players is unethical.

The coach should meet and exchange cordial greetings with the opposing coach to set the correct tone for the event before and after the contest.

The coach shall not exert pressure on faculty members to give student-athletes special consideration.

The coach shall not scout opponents by any means other than those adopted by the league and/or state high school athletic association.

Reprinted with permission of the National Federation of State High School Associations (NFHS).

Questions for Reflection

▶ What are the three coaching styles most coaches adopt? **(p. 30)**

▶ What is your coaching style? Can you see how the cooperative style fits with the Athletes First, Winning Second philosophy? **(p. 32)**

▶ How do you define leadership? What is the difference between leadership and management? **(p. 34)**

▶ Are you a leader who addresses not only the physical but the psychological and social environments of your athletes? **(p. 35)**

▶ Are you a transformative leader, influencing your team but also being influenced by it? **(p. 37)**

▶ Is your authority as a coach legitimated by your athletes and assistants? Do you use that authority, or power, wisely to help your athletes achieve their objectives? **(p. 37)**

▶ How do you provide direction for your athletes? Do you focus on the steps that lead to winning as well as other goals? **(p. 38)**

▶ Do you seek information from outside sources to inform your visioning process? How do you interpret that information? **(p. 39)**

▶ What are the components of team culture? Do you foster a positive team culture, including your athletes in its creation? **(p. 40)**

▶ Are you knowledgeable about the sport you coach? Are you motivated to be the best coach you can be? Do you have empathy for your players? These three qualities are important to the success of any coach. **(p. 44)**

▶ Do you agree with the coaching code of ethics of the National Federation of High School Coaches Association? **(p. 47)**

References

Bennis, Warren, and Burt Nanus. 1985. *Leaders: The strategies for taking charge.* New York: Harper Collins.

Berger, Phil. 2000. *Knight fall: Bobby Knight, the truth behind America's most controversial coach.* New York: Kensington Publishing, Pinnacle Books.

Hickman, Craig, and Michael Silva. 1984. *Creating excellence: Managing corporate culture, strategy, and change in the New Age.* New York: New American Library.

Holtz, Lou. 1998. *Winning every day: The game plan for success.* New York: HarperCollins Publishers, HarperBusiness.

Jackson, Phil, and Hugh Delehanty. 1995. *Sacred hoops: Spiritual lessons of a hardwood warrior.* New York: Hyperion.

Peters, Tom, and Austin, Nancy. 1985. *A passion for excellence: The leadership difference.* New York: Random House.

4

Coaching for Character

It's the end of a very close game, and your men's soccer team is ecstatic about their win. Some of the players are dancing in the field; one has taken off his jersey and is waving it over his head; and others are pointing their fingers at the opposing team's players, taunting them for the loss. They're boasting about their own prowess and calling the other players names. What should you do? What could you have done earlier to prevent this behavior?

The coach I admire and respect the most taught me not just the game of baseball, but the game of life. He taught me how to pitch, hit, and field; but far more significant, he showed me how to be respectful, responsible, and caring. I don't remember how many games we won that year, but I remember how we played—with good character—because he would not let us play any other way.

I was fortunate to have a coach who believed that building character counted more than building a winning team. Coach effectively and you'll win your fair share of contests, but in the end your win–loss record is not what really counts. What really counts is the influence you have or had on your players' character. Coaching for character is putting the philosophy of Athletes First, Winning Second into action. It's about helping your players to become better human beings—to be moral, to display sportsmanship—both inside and outside of sport.

☞ **In this chapter you'll learn**

▶ why character education is an essential duty of coaches,

▶ the definitions of character and sportsmanship, and

▶ how to coach to help your players develop good character.

As you study this chapter, think about whether you have the "character" to become a coach of character. Writing this chapter certainly caused me to think about who I am and what I want to be.

Why Character Education

In the past, character development was a primary function of the family, the school, and religious institutions. Today the breakdown of the family has made it difficult for many families to provide moral

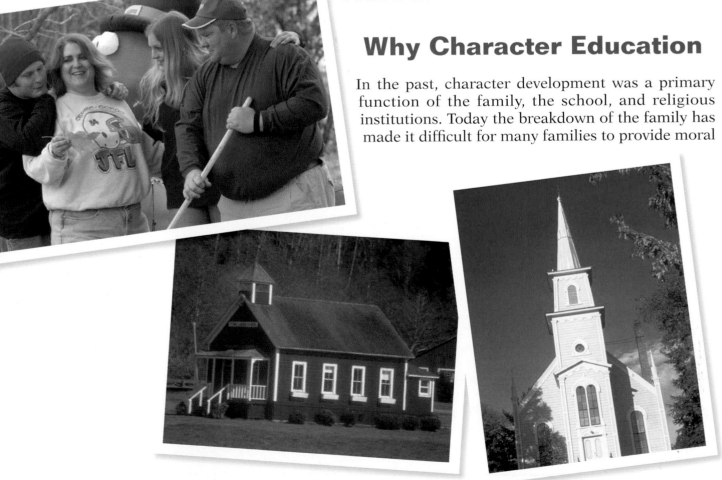

guidance, schools abandoned moral education in the last half century, and only now as our society is confronted with a moral crisis are they returning to character education. In addition, a smaller percentage of youths today are being exposed to the moral values of any religion.

The neglect of character education for our youth is seen in these distressing statistics:

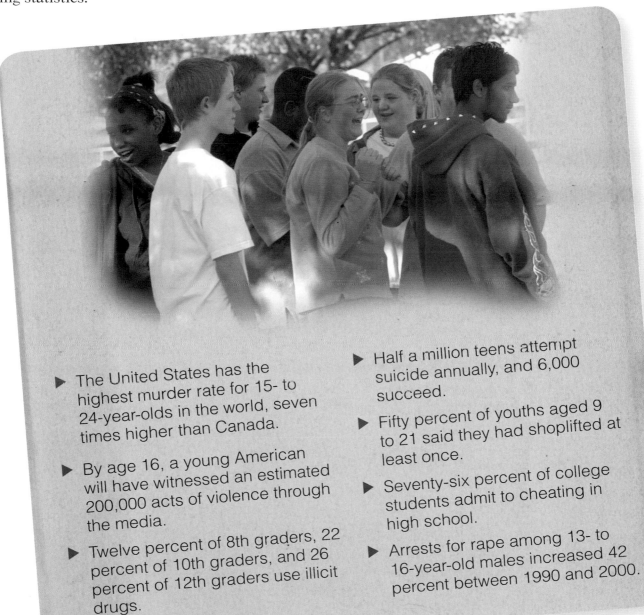

▶ The United States has the highest murder rate for 15- to 24-year-olds in the world, seven times higher than Canada.

▶ By age 16, a young American will have witnessed an estimated 200,000 acts of violence through the media.

▶ Twelve percent of 8th graders, 22 percent of 10th graders, and 26 percent of 12th graders use illicit drugs.

▶ Half a million teens attempt suicide annually, and 6,000 succeed.

▶ Fifty percent of youths aged 9 to 21 said they had shoplifted at least once.

▶ Seventy-six percent of college students admit to cheating in high school.

▶ Arrests for rape among 13- to 16-year-old males increased 42 percent between 1990 and 2000.

Sexual precocity, sexual abuse, foul language, disrespect for authority, and peer cruelty by teens are frequent news stories. Although self-centered behavior is typical for teenagers, some believe teens are showing a declining civic responsibility. Educators and government officials alike report a lack of basic moral knowledge among our youth.

Because sport is a mirror of our society, we see erosion in moral behavior in sports as exemplified by such incidents as these:

▶ Players on a Chicago girls' soccer team are arrested for a violent "hazing" incident that sends several girls to the hospital.

▶ New York father of a 14-year-old alters the boy's birth certificate so that he can play as a 12-year-old in the Little League World Series.

▶ Eleven percent of high school football players are taking anabolic steroids to gain an advantage over their opponents.

▶ High school basketball players in Los Angeles are charged with gang rape of the opposing team's cheerleaders.

▶ Coaches resign in increasing numbers, citing player disrespect as the primary cause.

▶ A soccer official in Atlanta is hospitalized after players on the losing team attacked him over a disputed call.

That's the bad news. The good news is that we know what to do about these problems. We need to reinstitute character education through the major institutions of our society—family, schools, religious organizations—and sports. According to a Gallup survey in April 2001, preparing young people for the future is the public's highest priority. As a coach, you can help.

What Is Character Education?

Intuitively we each have a good idea of what character education is. It's been defined as "teaching young people the knowledge, attitudes, beliefs, skills, and behaviors to be a good, fair, kind—in a word, moral—people" (Kirschenbaum 1995, pp. 26-27). It's also been called "gradual soul turning" (Ryan and Bohlin 1999, p. 140). Our character determines how we respond to the events in life—whether we contribute to or take from society.

Character education is not just a 10-minute discussion of sportsmanship after a display of poor behavior. It's not just a series of slogans posted on the wall. It's a total commitment to educating your athletes about moral behavior so that these behaviors are continually practiced, corrected when flawed, and celebrated when demonstrated.

It's Your Responsibility

Can coaches really build character? Think back about your own coaches and the influence they had on you—positive and negative. Your coaches may have reminded you that you could work harder, encouraged your talents, demanded that you behave responsibly, and treated you with respect while insisting that you be respectful. You bet coaches can build character! Coaches are far more than skill instructors, conditioning experts, and game tacticians. They are mentors, counselors, and unrecognized heroes who "turn souls."

Chapter 2 addressed the significance of helping athletes develop physically, psychologically, and socially. Well, nothing is more important than helping athletes develop good character. I urge you to grasp this responsibility with enthusiasm, to make it your highest priority in coaching.

Eddie Robinson, the head football coach at Grambling State University from 1941 to 1997, can lay claim to 408 wins; he is the most winning coach in the history of college football. Robinson, an African American, began coaching at a time when racial prejudice worked against him, yet he always maintained a positive attitude. Here's a glimpse of his philosophy of coaching (Robinson 1999):

▶ "When you are coaching these guys, they are somebody's baby, somebody loves them—I don't care how big he is, how small he is, somebody at home loves him. You can't coach him unless you love him. You coach him as though he were the boy you want to marry your daughter. You want him to be the greatest" (p. 254).

▶ "We not only try to motivate our guys to be better players but also to be better people. We talked a lot with the players. We asked them to watch what other people were doing and what they were experiencing. We used everyday happenings on the campus as examples. If a student got into trouble, we talked about that. If a student got an award, we talked about that" (p. 255).

▶ "We had to put the whistle down every so often to get after them and tell them what they were supposed to do. I wanted each of my student-athletes to be good family men and good citizens. I was rarely disappointed" (p. 261).

Perhaps you're thinking, I'm an ethical person, a good sport, a good role model. Isn't that enough in teaching my players to be good sports? Yes, that's important, but it isn't enough. You need to plan for it as surely as you plan your game strategy. You must actively teach character development.

You may be thinking, This is not my responsibility. It's enough of a challenge just to coach players to play the game. Character education is the responsibility of parents, the school, and religions. Although you can rightfully say that character education is the responsibility of these institutions, society needs your help too.

Coaching is becoming a profession, and professions demand certain behaviors or practices from their members. As a member of the coaching profession, your leaders are asking you to be a coach of character, to turn souls. See the Arizona Sports Summit Accord summary opposite.

Get the picture? As a coach, character education is your professional duty. It's not your job alone of course. It's the job of parents, teachers, and the clergy; and in sport, it's also the job of sport administrators, officials, and assistants. With you as a vital part of the team, we can reverse the decline in moral behavior among young people.

Character and Sportsmanship

OK, you agree that it is your duty to be a coach of character. Better yet, you enthusiastically embrace this challenge. Now let's learn more about character development and sportsmanship.

What Is Character?

Fundamentally, character is about who we are and what we stand for. Thomas Lickona (1991) wrote:

> **"**Good character consists of knowing the good, desiring the good, and doing the good—habits of the mind, habits of the heart, and habits of action. . . . When we think about the kind of character we want for our children, it's clear that we want them to be able to judge what is right, care deeply about what is right, and then do what they believe to be right—even in the face of pressure from without and temptation from within.**"** (p. 51)

In short,
Coaching for Character is helping your players know the right thing to do, and then helping them do it right.

In a giant step forward for coaching, on May 25, 1999, the Arizona Sports Summit Accord was released and endorsed by most sport organizations in the United States. The accord encourages character development through sport as stated in its preamble. Portions of the intercollegiate version of the accord related specifically to coaching are presented here.

Arizona Sports Summit Accord

At its best, athletic competition can hold intrinsic value for our society. It is a symbol of a great ideal: pursuing victory with honor. The love of sports is deeply embedded in our national consciousness. The values of millions of participants and spectators are directly and dramatically influenced by the values conveyed by organized sports. Thus, sports are a major social force that shapes the quality and character of the American culture. In the belief that the impact of sports can and should enhance the character and uplift the ethics of the nation, we seek to establish a framework of principles and a common language of values that can be adopted and practiced widely.

It is therefore agreed:

► The essential elements of character-building and ethics in sports are embodied in the concept of sportsmanship and six core principles: trustworthiness, respect, responsibility, fairness, caring, and good citizenship. The highest potential of sports is achieved when competition reflects these "six pillars of character."

► It is the duty of sports leadership—including coaches, athletic administrators, program directors and game officials—to promote sportsmanship and foster good character by teaching, enforcing, advocating and modeling these ethical principles.

► To promote sportsmanship and foster the development of good character, sports programs must be conducted in a manner that enhances the mental, social and moral development of athletes and teaches them positive life skills that will help them become personally successful and socially responsible.

► Sports programs should establish standards for participation by adopting codes of conduct for coaches, athletes, parents, spectators and other groups that impact the quality of athletic programs.

► Everyone involved in athletic competition has a duty to treat the traditions of the sport and other participants with respect. Coaches have a special responsibility to model respectful behavior and the duty to demand that their athletes refrain from disrespectful conduct including verbal abuse of opponents and officials, profane or belligerent trash-talking, taunting and unseemly celebrations.

► The leadership of sports programs at all levels must ensure that coaches, whether paid or voluntary, are competent to coach. Minimal competence may be attained by training or experience. It includes basic knowledge of (1) the character-building aspects of sports, including techniques and methods of teaching and reinforcing the core values comprising sportsmanship and good character; (2) first-aid principles and the physical capacities and limitations of the age group coached; and (3) coaching principles and the rules and strategies of the sport.

► To safeguard the health of athletes and the integrity of the sport, athletic programs must discourage the use of alcohol and tobacco and demand compliance with all laws and regulations, including those relating to gambling and the use of drugs.

► The profession of coaching is a profession of teaching. In addition to teaching the mental and physical dimensions of their sport, coaches, through words and example, must also strive to build the character of their athletes by teaching them to be trustworthy, respectful, responsible, fair, caring and good citizens.

Russell Gough (1998) wrote, "character is what you are in the dark" (p. 23). He asked,

If I could do whatever I wanted, without any consequence of being seen by others, would I tend to be

Kind	or	Unkind?
Honest	or	Dishonest?
Trustworthy	or	Untrustworthy?
Respectful	or	Disrespectful?
Faithful	or	Unfaithful?
Self-controlled	or	Not self-controlled?
Responsible	or	Irresponsible?

As humans, we are what we repeatedly do, and thus our character is the sum of our habits, our unique assortment of virtues and vices. Aristotle said, "No one who desires to become good will become good unless he does good things." Developing good character habits is like developing good sport skills; they must be repeatedly practiced until they become habits. A good example of such practice is the trend in many high schools of encouraging or requiring students to participate in community service projects.

Almost every day you are faced with opportunities to practice good character and to help your athletes to do so. For instance, if you repeatedly hold back from yelling at officials, you are practicing a good habit that will eventually become part of your character. If one of your athletes routinely swears, directing that athlete to keep the language in check will help the athlete develop a good habit, a habit that with practice will become part of the athlete's character.

Coaches of character help young people know what's right, instill the desire to do what's right, and guide them in the process of doing right.

What Is Sportsmanship?

Perhaps you find oft-quoted cliches trite, but the two that follow are often quoted because they ring so true, stating so well the essence of sportsmanship. Sportsmanship is simply good character when participating in sports. Sportsmanship is about respect for opponents, officials, teammates, coaches—and especially for the game itself.

Grantland Rice.

Why Is Sportsmanship Important?

Craig Clifford and Randy Feezell answer the question well in their fine book *Coaching for Character* (1997):

"*Because the nature of sport requires it. Sport understood as rule-governed competitive athletic play requires—and therefore can teach—certain character traits. Without sportsmanship, sport is no longer sport, the game is no longer a game. If the game is valuable—if we play the game for its joy, for its educational value, for its intrinsic beauty, for the truth about ourselves that it opens up—then sportsmanship is indispensable. Why sportsmanship? Because it matters what sort of human beings we are—and what sort of human beings our children become. Because it is better for human beings to be courageous, disciplined, fair, honest, responsible, humble, and wise than not to be.... Why sportsmanship? Because good character is good for its own sake, whether we are "rewarded" for it or not.*" (p. 24)

"*When the one Great Scorer comes
to write against your name,
he marks—not that you have won or lost,
but how you played the game.*"

Grantland Rice, sportswriter

"*The most important thing in the Olympic Games
is not to win but to take part
just as the most important thing in life
is not the triumph but the struggle.
The essential thing is not to have conquered
but to have fought well.*"

**Baron de Coubertin, founder of the
modern era of the Olympic Games**

How to Teach Character and Sportsmanship

Ultimately we each are responsible for the development of our own character. But just as the development of athletic talent can benefit from coaching, so can the development of character. Becoming a person of character involves a similar learning process to becoming a good athlete—it takes knowledge, desire, effort, and practice. It seldom is done alone; it takes support from others.

As shown in figure 4.1, coaching for character involves three steps that are similar to the steps in coaching sport skills. We'll consider each of these three steps more closely in the remainder of this chapter.

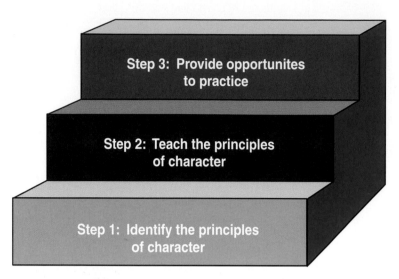

Figure 4.1 Coaching for character.

STEP 1: Identify the Principles of Character

The principles of character are the moral values that tell us what we ought to do. We are to abide by them even when we'd rather not do so. These principles of behavior that prohibit injustice to others are considered to be natural or universal laws. They are not the teachings of any one religion, although most religions incorporate these moral values.

Thomas Lickona (1991) believes there are two great moral values: *respect* and *responsibility*. They are worthwhile because they promote the good of the individual and the good of the whole community.

> " *Respect means showing regard for the worth of someone or something. It takes three major forms: respect for oneself, respect for other people, and respect for all forms of life and the environment that sustains them.* " (p. 43)

> " *Responsibility is an extension of respect. If we respect other people, we value them. If we value them, we feel a measure of responsibility for their welfare. . . . Responsibility emphasizes our positive obligations to care for each other.* " (p. 44)

The YMCA of the U.S.A., long an advocate of character development, espouses Lickona's *respect* and *responsibility* and adds *caring* and *honesty* as essential moral values. I'd like to add two more: *fairness* and *citizenship*. The "fair play" movement is the most visible

Coach Johnson lived and coached in one of the wealthiest suburbs in the nation. The players on Coach Johnson's basketball team had grown up with pretty much everything they needed. In an odd sort of way, his athletes had not learned some simple values of compassion and helping others because they hadn't needed much compassion or help in their own lives. Coach Johnson decided to fill this gap, and throughout the year he looked for opportunities to encourage his players to help others in need.

One night when the team was riding home from a game, they passed a softball field where Special Olympians were practicing for an upcoming competition. Coach Johnson heard a few snickers from his athletes. He let the comments go at the time, but the next day at the weekly team meeting, Coach Johnson brought up the incident. He asked his players what they thought the Special Olympians needed. After some awkward moments, one of the athletes offered that they probably needed a friend. Another one wondered aloud if they could play basketball. Before Coach knew it, the athletes had decided to put on a half-day basketball camp at their high school for the Special Olympians. They would teach some basic dribbling and shooting skills and set up a few informal games. Coach Johnson had taken a disappointing situation, where his athletes had made fun of the Special Olympians, and created a valuable character lesson in showing compassion and helping people in need.

proponent of fairness in sports and all aspects of life. Good citizenship is fundamental to an orderly society and is espoused by the National Federation of State High School Associations through its Citizenship Through Sports course.

These six moral values are widely advocated by character educators and are embodied in the Athletes Character Code shown next. I encourage you to embrace these six virtues and nurture them in your athletes as you fulfill your responsibility as a coach of character.

Athletes Character Code

Moral Values	Actions in Life	Actions in Sport
▶ Be Respectful	Be respectful of other people Be respectful of others' property Be respectful of the environment Be respectful of yourself	Be respectful of the game and to its rules and traditions Be respectful of your opponents Be respectful of the officials Be respectful in victory and defeat
▶ Be Responsible	Fulfill your obligations Be dependable Be in control of yourself Be persistent	Prepare yourself to do your best Be punctual for practices and games Be self-disciplined Be cooperative with your teammates
▶ Be Caring	Be compassionate and have empathy Be forgiving Be generous and kind Avoid being selfish or mean	Help your teammates play better Support teammates in trouble Be generous with praise; stingy with criticism Play for the team, not yourself
▶ Be Honest	Be truthful and forthright Act with integrity Be trustworthy Be courageous to do the right thing	Play by the spirit of the rules Be loyal to the team Play drug free Admit to your own mistakes
▶ Be Fair	Follow the Golden Rule Be tolerant of others Be willing to share Avoid taking advantage of others	Treat other players as you wish to be treated Be fair to all players, including those who are different Give other players an opportunity Play to win within the rules
▶ Be a Good Citizen	Obey the laws and rules Be educated and stay informed Contribute to the community Protect others	Be a good role model Strive for excellence Give back to the sport Encourage teammates to be good citizens

STEP 2: Teach the Principles of Character

Now you know the content, but how do you teach these six principles of character? I can't give you a "play book" or set of recipes to be a coach of character. It doesn't work that way. What I can give you are six strategies to help you meet this most challenging responsibility of being a coach.

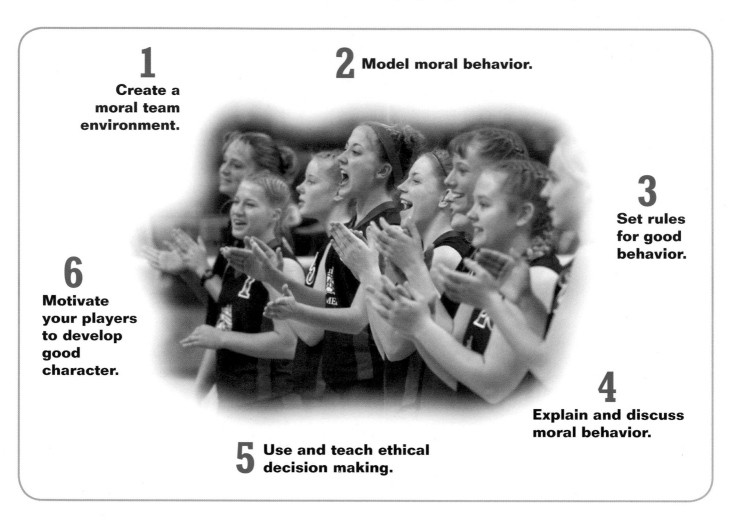

1 Create a moral team environment.

2 Model moral behavior.

3 Set rules for good behavior.

4 Explain and discuss moral behavior.

5 Use and teach ethical decision making.

6 Motivate your players to develop good character.

Create a Moral Team Environment

Character education begins with a fundamental duty of a coach—building a team culture as discussed in chapter 3. This involves developing shared values, including moral values, and motivating players to achieve a common goal. These values and goals unite a team, and successful coaches have long known that you build a team first and then win games. Coaches often must teach players how to be good team members, learning when to cooperate and when to compete, when to lead and when to follow, and when to put the team ahead of themselves.

How you run the team greatly influences the team culture, which has an enormous influence on the character development of your players. Table 4.1 lists characteristics of team culture that affect character development either negatively or positively.

Table 4.1—How Team Culture Influences Character Development

Negative influence	Positive influence
Overemphasis on winning	Athletes First, Winning Second emphasis
Ignoring or even rewarding unsportsmanlike behavior	Recognizing and rewarding sportsmanship
Demanding a period of "mourning" after losing	Helping athletes put winning and losing into proper perspective
Dictating all team actions and discouraging questions and input from team members	Encouraging questions and sharing the decision making with the team
Being distant from players, their parents, and others involved with the team	Being appropriately warm, involved, and caring with all who are involved with the team
Showing favoritism toward the better players and picking on the weaker ones	Respecting all players and helping each to become a better player and person
Encouraging cutthroat competition within the team	Encouraging cooperation among teammates and respect for opponents within the competitive environment
Failing to develop traditions and rituals that encourage team spirit	Creating valued and enjoyable traditions and rituals in cooperation with team members

Adopting the cooperative style of coaching—sharing the decision making in appropriate ways—is essential to a team climate that nurtures good character development. Remember: To build a moral team, you must give your players a stake in its construction.

Model Moral Behavior

You know that actions speak louder than words. What you do will have far greater impact than what you say about moral behavior. As a coach, you are always on "exhibit," especially with your players. They watch your every move because you're so important to them. They know your behaviors well. In fact, in a study I did years ago, we found that high school players knew the pregame anxiety level of their coaches better than the coaches themselves did.

If you want your athletes to develop character, you need to demonstrate good character yourself. How you manage your responsibilities as their coach, how you show respect for them, and how you respond to winning and losing influence their character. They watch to see if you are consistent in what you say and do, and in what you do today and then tomorrow. They make note if you put on a good face in public and then act differently in private

> "*One man practicing good sportsmanship is far better than fifty others preaching it.*"
>
> **Knute Rockne, the legendary Notre Dame football coach**

with your team. If you act inconsistently, if you're hypocritical, they conclude that you're not trustworthy, which damages your credibility to teach character development.

Coaching for character does not mean, however, that you must be a paragon of virtue. (I heard that sigh of relief!) As with your players, as with us all, you can be a "work in progress," striving to improve your own character and acknowledging your mistakes. You need to be a good role model, but not a perfect one!

Another way to model moral behavior is to introduce your players to heroes and heroines in sport and life through stories and news reports. William Bennett, the former U.S. secretary of education, wrote the best-selling *Book of Virtues* (1993) for this very purpose, and we've learned that Bennett's gambling shows that he also is not a perfect role model. From literature, newspaper accounts, and stories of past players on your team, your players can learn about both moral and immoral behavior.

For example, take NBA star Grant Hill as a positive role model. Even before he signed with the Detroit Pistons, he used part of his money from endorsements to fund a summer basketball and academic program for 1,800 boys and girls in the inner city. This program gave these teens the opportunity to learn more about basketball and to sharpen their intellectual skills, as well as the chance to compete with other teams in the suburbs.

Young people need your guidance in selecting the right role models, the right heroes. They need your guidance in interpreting events in sports that reflect moral and immoral behaviors. Find opportunities with your team, such as when you're traveling, to discuss news reports of athletes committing acts of violence, using performance-enhancing drugs, and making great sacrifices to achieve difficult goals. Encourage your players to reflect on these stories.

Set Rules for Good Behavior

I encourage you to establish team rules to help inculcate the values of our society, and recommend that you adopt the Athletes Character Code as a basis for your team rules. Team rules create boundaries for acceptable and unacceptable behavior to help develop character and help you manage your players so that you can be a successful team. We'll spend a lot more time on creating and enforcing team rules in chapter 8, pages 149 to 154.

Explain and Discuss Moral Behavior

Before they are teens, children learn moral values more through imitation and practice than through instruction. As they become teens and their reasoning abilities develop, although they still learn from modeling and practicing, they now also want to know why they should behave in certain ways. At this stage you can help them by providing explanations that justify your request for them to behave ethically.

Posting rules is not enough. For example, you may have a rule that the team will shake hands with the other team after each game. One of your players may ask why you have this rule. You could see the question as a challenge to your authority and respond with "Because I said so," or you could explain that it demonstrates sportsmanship and reflects well on the team and school. The first response would have missed a valuable opportunity to discuss why this postgame tradition is meaningful, and would likely close the door to future discussions about such issues. The second response provides a reason for your action that is understandable and justifiable.

Because character traits cannot be directly observed but are inferred from behavior, it is important that you help players see the connection between their behavior and the trait or value it represents. You can do this by labeling the behaviors. Some examples are as follows:

▶ **Respect.** When a player argues with an official, you can point out that it shows disrespect.

▶ **Self-discipline.** When a player walks away from a provocation, you can reinforce his self-discipline by saying, "I'm proud of you for walking away from the fight. That took real courage."

▶ **Responsibility.** When a player skips practice for no good reason, you can let her know that she has not acted responsibly.

▶ **Self-control.** When you lose your cool over an injustice, you can explain to your players that you have a right to do so because you're the coach. No, just checking to see if you're reading carefully. You should explain that you failed to show self-control and will work at doing better the next time.

Once you help your players understand the connection between the behavior and the trait it reflects, be it positive or negative, then you must express your expectation about that behavior in the future. For example, after discussing an athlete's tardiness, you might say, "Show me you're responsible by coming to practice on time tomorrow." Encourage and reward moral actions, and discourage and punish immoral actions. You'll actively build good character by consistently doing so.

I'm not advocating that you become a zealot—a moral missionary—preaching about good and evil at every turn. But share your beliefs and reasons for the Athletes Character Code with your players, and share your experiences related to them as well. Don't preach; find ways to discuss these issues. Spend more time listening than talking. When you do all the talking, teenagers see it as just another adult lecturing them. You'll be more effective if you don't try to "hammer" the message home. Instead nudge, suggest, and encourage, steadfastly guiding your players to better behavior.

Hazing—A Growing Problem

Hazing in sport is any action or situation created intentionally to produce mental or physical discomfort, embarrassment, harassment, or ridicule among new members of a team. An NCAA survey found that 8 percent of college athletes reported having been hazed, and ESPN reports a substantial increase in hazing incidents in high school sports. Consider the following:

▶ **Connecticut**—High school seniors sodomize a new wrestling teammate, who had a learning disability, with a plastic knife handle. The coach apparently did nothing to stop the incident.

▶ **Illinois**—High school football players pinned younger players on the locker room floor and poked them in the buttocks with sawed-off broom handles. The players were suspended.

▶ **California**—The senior girls of a high school soccer team forced four freshman girls to drink alcohol until the girls vomited or collapsed.

▶ **Illinois**—Three high school baseball players overpowered a sophomore player and cut his hair. They were suspended and charged with battery.

▶ **New Jersey**—Freshman soccer players were abused physically and thrown in the mud as part of an annual hazing event. The head coach and two assistants were dismissed because they allowed it to happen.

After decades of darkness, hazing of athletes by athletes is being recognized as serious misbehavior. In the past coaches often saw hazing as part of a ritual to build team cohesiveness, and condoned or even encouraged such practices. But hazing is contrary to the moral values of the Athletes Character Code we've considered in this chapter. As a coach you should recognize subtle and outrageous hazing practices for what they are—the mistreatment of fellow human beings. Be proactive and have a strong antihazing policy as part of your team rules, and counsel your athletes to recognize that hazing is not acceptable behavior.

Use and Teach Ethical Decision Making

You've taught your athletes to "know the good" and "desire to do good." Now you need to give them chances to "do good" by making appropriate ethical decisions. Ethical decision making is the process of evaluating alternative courses of action and choosing the action consistent with one's moral values.

There are two kinds of ethical decisions—choosing right from wrong and choosing the best right alternative. When faced with an ethical decision, we should ask ourselves these questions: (a) Is this action illegal? (b) Is this action dishonest? and (c) Is this action immoral? If the answer is yes to any of these three questions, then the course of action is unethical. With right-versus-wrong decisions, the right course of action is often clear, but what makes it a dilemma is that the wrong course of action may greatly increase our chances of obtaining a desirable outcome, such as winning the game or obtaining money or sexual gratification.

In the second type of ethical decision making—choosing the best right alternative—there is no obvious wrong decision. Instead we are faced with deciding the better course of action among two or more alternatives. For example, you are likely to be faced with decisions about whether to play your best athletes today or those that may be your best athletes tomorrow (to be good tomorrow, you know they will benefit by playing today). Or you may be faced with a "problem athlete," someone who gives you headaches repeatedly. You would be justified in cutting the player from your team and being rid of your problem today, but you could also invest more time in this athlete in the hope of "turning a soul." In these types of decisions there is no illegal, dishonest, or immoral action. You must learn to apply reasoning and problem-solving skills that include evaluating the relevant facts, identifying alternative courses of action, and foreseeing the potential consequences of each course of action.

Motivate Your Players to Develop Good Character

The public thinks of coaches as teachers of sport skills who motivate their players to play their best. But coaches are also teachers of character who motivate their players to behave their best.

Creating a moral team environment, demonstrating good character, and explaining and discussing moral actions all help develop good character, but motivation or inspiration provides the fuel to "turn souls." It's been said,

*A mediocre coach **tells,***

*A good coach **explains,***

*A superior coach **demonstrates,***

*But the great coach **inspires.***

Inspire your charges to be the best they can be both on and off the sport field.

Now that you know the principles of character you want to teach and the ways you want to teach them, let's look at how you can help your athletes practice good character skills.

STEP 3: Provide Opportunities to Practice

Sport provides players with many opportunities to learn and practice moral actions and resolve ethical dilemmas. Thus, you don't need to arrange contrived situations in which to practice moral decision making—they occur frequently in sport, an activity that has great significance to many young people. Teachable moments will arise, but you need to be prepared to respond to them in the appropriate way. You can do so by making character development a priority and taking the steps described in the previous section. You can also help your athletes practice moral behavior by establishing routines.

Establish Routines

Rituals and traditions, what we call routines in sports, are important ways that societies pass on their culture—including their values—to the next generation. They are a valuable way to help your players practice moral behavior. Here are some examples:

▶ Have your players practice respect by asking them to shake hands with the opposing team.

▶ Develop good citizenship habits in your players through fund-raising activities and school and community service projects.

▶ Develop habits of caring in your players by adopting a mentoring program in which your players help younger players learn the sport.

▶ Encourage responsibility by developing routines of putting away equipment and cleaning up the locker room after practice.

Be creative in thinking up team rituals and routines that are fun and encourage practicing the moral values of the Athletes Character Code.

Reward Good Character

Remember that the development of good character is not unlike the development of sport skills. Few players get them right the first time. You'll need to be tolerant of mistakes, provide immediate and accurate feedback, demonstrate the appropriate action, and give your athletes repeated chances to practice. Reward progress even if the behavior is not totally what you want. There are many ways to reward your players for demonstrating good character—season-end awards for sportsmanship, special privileges such as being named honorary captain for a game, stickers to place on lockers or equipment, certificates, or a simple recognition at a team meeting or practice-ending huddle.

Also remember that your athletes are likely to come to you with a wide range of moral skills. Some will be superstars of good character, and others you may see as villains of vice. Your challenge is to mold them all into a team of good character.

Questions for Reflection

▶ What is character education, and why is it important? Do you believe it is your responsibility as a coach? **(p. 52)**

▶ What is sportsmanship? **(p. 57)**

▶ List the three steps to teaching character and sportsmanship. **(p. 58)**

▶ What is the Athletes Character Code? **(p. 59)**

▶ What are six strategies you can use to help build character in the athletes you coach? **(p. 60)**

▶ What can you do to model good character and moral behavior for your athletes? **(p. 61)**

▶ Do you discuss moral behavior with your athletes? Stories of sport figures can be a good way to help athletes reflect on issues of morality and ethics. **(p. 62)**

▶ How can you give your athletes opportunities to practice moral behavior and make ethical decisions? **(p. 65)**

▶ Do you provide rituals and routines and reward good character to encourage your players to be people of good character? **(p. 66)**

References

Bennett, William. *Book of virtues.* 1993. New York: Simon & Schuster.

Clifford, Craig, and Randolph M. Feezell. 1997. *Coaching for character.* Champaign, IL: Human Kinetics.

Gough, Russell W. 1998. *Character is destiny.* Rocklin, CA: Forum.

Kirschenbaum, Howard. 1995. *100 ways to enhance values and morality in schools and youth settings.* Needham Heights, MA: Allyn and Bacon.

Lickona, Thomas. 1991. *Educating for character.* New York: Bantam Books.

Robinson, Eddie (with Richard Lapchick). 1999. *Never before, never again: The stirring autobiography of Eddie Robinson, the winningest coach in the history of college football.* New York: St. Martin's Press, Thomas Dunne Books.

Ryan, Kevin, and Karen E. Bohlin. 1999. *Building character in schools.* San Francisco: Jossey-Bass.

5

Coaching Diverse Athletes

Meet your new players for this season:

- ➤ Miguel is a 15-year-old Latino whose devout Catholic parents immigrated into a tough inner-city neighborhood two years ago.

- ➤ Vanessa is a very mature 17-year-old African American lesbian.

- ➤ John, a prepubescent 14-year-old Caucasian, is obese and struggles with attention-deficit/ hyperactivity disorder (AD/HD).

- ➤ Sixteen-year-old Marcia is a Native American who spent most of her life living in poverty on a reservation.

- ➤ Li, an Asian American who is 17 years old, lost a leg to cancer. ☞

As in the movie *Mission Impossible,* your job, should you choose to accept it, is to integrate these newcomers with your returning players and make them a team. How do you do it?

Although you're unlikely to see as much diversity as just described, to be an effective coach you need to understand the uniqueness, the individual differences, of each of your players, and that is no easy task.

I've heard coaches proudly say, "I treat every kid the same regardless of who they are." While that message is usually meant to say they treat each player fairly; it's not good coaching to "treat every kid the same."

☞ **In this chapter you'll learn why, as I introduce you to a variety of young people who differ in**

▶ maturation,

▶ culture,

▶ gender, and

▶ physical and mental abilities.

In the past, players with special needs often were cut from sport teams or didn't dare try to participate, but that day is gone. You need to be prepared to coach players who differ widely and have special needs, be they physical, mental, medical, social, or cultural. I won't be able to tell you all that you'll need to know about these individual differences in this one chapter, but I'll help you recognize them, provide you with some recommendations for coaching different kind of players, and guide you to additional sources of information. We begin by looking at the "typical" teenager!

Understanding Teenagers

Coaching teens or adolescents is an adventure because this is one of the most dynamic periods of human development. The adolescent years, ages 11 to 21, are witness to the remarkable transformation from childhood to adulthood, a metamorphosis more fascinating than a butterfly escaping its cocoon. In this section we'll briefly look at the developmental characteristics of early adolescents (ages 11 to 14), middle adolescents (ages 15 to 17), and late adolescents (ages 18 to 21).

Early Adolescence (11 to 14 years)

▶ The average age for the start of the growth spurt is 9.5 years in females and 11.5 years in males. Girls experience the fastest growth in height at an average age of 11.5 years, and boys at an average age of 13.5 years.

▶ Many believe that when adolescents go through the growth spurt they experience awkwardness (lack of agility, balance, and coordination) until they have a chance to accommodate these changes. Scientific evidence, however, does not support this view.

▶ Strength, which increases in both males and females during this period and throughout adolescence, can be further increased through well-designed strength training programs. However, boys have a small advantage over girls in strength prior to puberty, and a substantially greater advantage after puberty.

▶ For activities such as jumping, throwing, and running, boys and girls steadily improve their performance throughout adolescence, but girls tend to level off at ages 12 and 13 and boys continue their steady improvement until the later teen years.

▶ Because they grow so rapidly and are so active, teens in this age range need good nutrition and extra sleep.

▶ The tallest, strongest boys, especially those with athletic talent, command the greatest stature among their peers. That's one reason sport is so important in the lives of this age group.

▶ This is the age period when both boys and girls go through puberty, experiencing considerable sexual changes about which they are often very self-conscious. Girls' breasts develop, and they begin menstruating. Boys' voices lower and penile erections are more frequent, often at embarrassing moments. Early adolescents become sexually curious and begin wanting privacy as modesty becomes an issue.

▶ Their physical appearance is exceptionally important, especially in comparison with their peers.

▶ There is an increasing dependence on peers, mostly of the same sex, and thus a desire to conform to the popular culture of this age group.

▶ They want to be more independent and may express this by being more argumentative with adults who supervise them.

▶ They are searching to discover who they are and where they belong in the world, and they often are insecure about the physical and emotional changes they're experiencing. Consequently teens this age can be irritable and moody. One day they can be on top of the world and the next be overwhelmed by it.

▶ They tend to think more concretely or literally but are beginning to think abstractly and consider the possibilities of what could happen in a situation based on their actions.

▶ As their intellect matures, teens are working on developing their personal values, and they are especially influenced by their peers and by adults they admire.

▶ During this period teens are working hard at learning to accept others and themselves.

Middle Adolescence (15 to 17 years)

▶ Most physical growth is completed by girls at about 14.5 years and by boys at 16.5 years. Males gain muscle, and females gain fat.

▶ Teens at this age are less concerned about their changing bodies and much more concerned about their sexual appeal. They are searching to deal with what it means to be masculine or feminine in their culture.

▶ These teens will assert their independence by demanding the right to make their own decisions, but often they show poor judgment and impulsiveness. This combined with their feeling of invulnerability and willingness to take exceptional risks results in these teens having a disproportionately high accident rate as seen in auto fatality statistics. Parents, teachers, and coaches must protect these youth from dangerous risks by setting and enforcing clear limits.

▶ The peer group profoundly influences their thinking and life choices. Their dress and hairstyle, their recreational and cultural activities, and their decisions about tattoos and body piercing are substantially influenced by their peers.

▶ They take pride in being given responsibility and fulfilling it, and they increasingly show respect for others.

▶ These teens are increasingly able to think abstractly, developing a better understanding of how present actions affect future consequences.

▶ Although they are generally self-centered, with guidance teens become more empathic and recognize the value in helping others as they shift their focus from themselves to the larger world.

Late Adolescence (18 to 21 years)

▶ These maturing young people are more secure and understand who they are. They know what they are good at and not so good at, and yet many are seeking to figure out what they want to do with their lives. Fortunately, because they are more capable of abstract thinking at this age, they are better able to make long-term plans.

▶ They are able to function independently, and because they now are more secure about themselves, they're willing to seek advice from family and trusted adults.

▶ They set goals based on feelings of personal needs and priorities, and they are more likely to reject goals set by others.

▶ Peers are important in influencing decisions, but these teens evaluate their decisions more critically and make more rational judgments.

▶ Intimate relationships become very important.

These general characteristics of adolescents describe no one person, but they provide insight into these turbulent but exciting years in a young person's life (in case you've forgotten). Keep these characteristics in mind as you coach teen players.

Now let's look at the many diverse players you'll be coaching, beginning with diversity in maturation.

Maturational Differences

Each of us has many ages—and herein is the problem. Chronological age is not always closely related to players' physical, intellectual, emotional, or social maturity, and thus often is not the best way to group teens for competition because it is unsafe and unfair. In this section we'll look at maturational differences and consider how they can affect your coaching.

Understanding Maturation Differences

The range of individual differences in physical structure is greater between the ages of 10 and 16 than it is at any other time in the human life span.

▶ Boy A and B are the same chronological age, 13 years, but differ greatly in their anatomical age (usually measured by X rays of the wrist bones that reveal the biological age of the skeleton).

▶ Boy A has an anatomical age typical for boys of a chronological age of 10 years.

▶ Boy B has an anatomical age of a chronologically aged 15-year-old.

▶ Boy A is 54 inches (137 centimeters) tall and weighs 105 pounds (48 kilograms), and boy B is 69 inches (175 centimeters) tall and weighs 195 pounds (88 kilograms), a difference of 15 inches (38 centimeters) in height and 90 pounds (40 kilograms) in weight.

▶ In contact and collision sports boy A is at considerable risk of injury playing against boy B, and in sports in which speed, strength, and power are likely to determine the outcome, boy A has a decided disadvantage. Herein lies the problem in competitive sports for adolescents.

Maturation Matching

Young people are usually grouped for competition according to chronological age and sex, along with weight in sports such as wrestling, because it's objective, easy to do, and traditional.

Boy A   **Boy B**

But early-maturing athletes have a decided advantage. In two studies, of the players who made it to the Little League World Series, nearly 50 percent were one year advanced in anatomical age. The starting pitchers, first basemen, and left fielders were nearly two years advanced. In another study, those who made their interscholastic teams were 11 to 13 months advanced in anatomical maturity. In several other studies, the best predictor of success in football and track was not a measure of motor skill or physical size, as might be expected, but anatomical age.

Failing to consider maturational differences not only risks injury to the later-maturing athlete, but it also makes for inequitable competition. In the ideal world we would measure players' anatomical age and match them for competition based on physical maturity, not chronological age. But that won't happen until we can easily assess anatomical age—and it's not easy or affordable now. However, there are two things you should do. First, if your sport involves speed, power, and strength, match players more by their physical size and apparent physical maturity. Second, if you see that an athlete is going to be greatly mismatched in competition and in your best judgment is at risk of injury, do not let the athlete compete. Letting the athlete play

would be irresponsible and a potential basis for legal action even though the athlete may be the same chronological age as the other competitors. You'll learn more about your legal duty to provide for the safety of your athletes in chapter 20.

When the Early Maturer Loses the Biological Advantage

During the middle teen years the players who matured early in grade school or middle school and became star athletes sometimes lose their biological advantage to the average- and late-maturing players. In a famous study done years ago, only 25 percent of the youngsters who were stars in elementary school continued as stars in high school. This is encouraging news for later-maturing youngsters because it tells them their day is coming. For the early-maturing player the loss of stardom may be a difficult psychological adjustment. Sometimes coaches mistakenly attribute a player's fall from stardom not to the improvement of the other players, but to the erroneous belief that the early-maturing player is no longer putting forth the needed effort. Because both the coach and the player fail to understand the biological basis for the player's initial advantage in sports and the subsequent loss of it, the player may become frustrated and quit.

Other Maturational Differences

You need to consider not only physical differences, but also intellectual, emotional, and social differences in the players you coach. Your players will vary in intellectual ability, affecting the rate at which they can learn the cognitive aspects of the sport. Some may be slower in their intellectual maturation, and some may just be slow. Some young people take longer to mature emotionally and socially than others, and others never seem to mature in these ways. These differences will influence the rate at which you teach your players and how you guide them in their sporting experience.

Letter to My Football Coach

DEAR COACH:

You won't remember me. It was just a few years back. I was one of those kids that turn out every year for freshman football without the slightest idea of how to play the game. Think hard. I was the tall, skinny kid, a little slower than the others.

Still don't remember? Well, I remember you. I remember how scared I was of you when you'd slap your hands together and yell "Hit!" I remember how you used to laugh at me and guys like me when we'd miss a tackle or get beat one-on-one in practice.

You see, you never let me play in a game. Once in a while, when you'd be giving a chalk talk to the first string, I'd get to play a couple of downs of scrimmage.

I really admired you. We all did. But now that I'm a little older and a little wiser, I just wanted to let you know that you blew it. I didn't play football after my freshman year. You convinced me that I didn't have what it took, that I wasn't tough enough.

I remember the first day of practice, when you asked for all the linebackers. I wanted to be a linebacker. The first time I tried to tackle someone, I got my helmet ripped off. All I had done was lower my head and hit. No technique. No tackle.

You laughed. You told me I ought to be a quarterback, that I tackled like one. All the guys laughed. You were really funny.

Another time, after I became a guard. I missed a block—in practice. Of course. The guy sidestepped and I wound up with my face mask in the mud.

"C'mon! You hit like a girl," you said. I wanted to hit. I wanted to tell you how much I wanted to hit. But if I had, you'd have flattened me because you were tough and didn't take any backtalk.

We ran the play again, and I hit the same guy a pretty good shot this time. When I looked at you, you were talking to another coach.

I'm the first to admit that I was pretty bad. Even if I had been coached on technique, I still would have been a lousy football player. I was one of those kids who was a couple of years behind my peers in physical maturity and strength.

That's where you messed up. I grew up. By the time I was a senior, I stood 6′5″ and weighed 220. I couldn't fly, but I could run pretty well. That nonathletic freshman could now throw a baseball harder than anyone in the state. I was drafted and signed by a major league baseball team.

Looking back I really regret not playing football. It would have been a lot of fun. Maybe I could even have helped the team. But thanks to you, I turned against the game before I ever really got into it. A little coaching, a little encouragement, and who knows? I guess I'll never find out.

How sad. You're in a position to do a lot of boys a lot of good. But I doubt that you will. You'll never give up a chance to look tough and sound tough. You think that's what football's all about.

I know better.

LARRY D. BROOKS

Reprinted from National Federation Press Service, V36 (9), April 1976.

Coaching Recommendations

Here are my suggestions for coaching young people who differ widely in physical, intellectual, emotional, and social maturity:

1. In your practices, match your players based on physical maturity to reduce the risk of injury to the less mature players.

2. Help your physically immature athletes understand that their biological clock is just a little slower than others and that their time is coming. Seek to match them in practices with players of similar ability, but also occasionally give them the opportunity to learn from the better players. Encourage their progress rather than focus on the outcome of winning and losing.

3. Help physically early-maturing players who no longer are the stars to understand and accept that it is no failure in them, but that others have simply caught up and in some cases surpassed them. Encourage them to sustain their effort, and help them find a role on the team that they can fill well.

4. Recognize that you may have gifted athletes who physically matured early, but are not equally mature emotionally or socially. You may need to provide them with more assistance in dealing with their sport success and in some situations protect them more from the media and others who may want to exploit their talent.

5. Your players will differ widely in intellectual capability. For slower learners you may need to repeat instructions more often, break down the technical and tactical skills even further, and have them practice with more repetitions. You may need to simplify the language you use to communicate with these players and provide more guidance than you do with intellectually more mature players.

6. Of course you should never make fun of a player's physical, intellectual, emotional, or social immaturity, and you should not permit anyone on your team to do so. Help your players learn respect by respecting these maturational differences.

Cultural Differences

Who we are and how we respond to our world is greatly influenced by the environment in which we're raised and live. *Culture* is the term we use to describe those social forces that shape our thoughts, ideas, and ways of interacting with our world. Heredity is the other significant factor that determines our behavior. In sport, we often speculate about a player's talent, wondering how much of it is inherited and how much is acquired through the player's social environment (culture).

In this section we'll consider how our cultural heritage creates individual differences, differences that you'll want to consider when coaching.

Understanding Cultural Differences

Culture refers to the human-made part of our environment as opposed to the aspects occurring naturally. It includes such tangible things as the way we dress and eat, the decorative and ritual objects we create, and even the sports we play. It also includes intangible things such as attitudes, values, norms of behavior, learning styles, and social roles. We teach culture to our young through our social institutions including the family, school, peer groups, media, religious groups—and sports. As you'll recall from chapter 4, we strive to teach moral values through sports not just so young people demonstrate good sportsmanship when they play, but also so they will demonstrate good character in all aspects of their lives.

Cultural Heritage

Culture operates at many different levels as shown in figure 5.1. The society of a nation has a culture as does your local community, your school or sport club, and as we discussed in chapter 4, your team. There are many factors that identify cultural differences, with race, ethnicity, gender, sexual orientation, and social class being primary factors. Other factors include age, health, religion, language, and ability. Collectively, all of these factors influence each of us to shape our cultural heritage, making us similar in some ways and uniquely different in other ways.

Our society clearly is becoming culturally more diverse. Recent estimates show that among high school students in the United States, 69 percent are white, 13 percent are black, 12 percent are Hispanic, 5 percent are Asian, and 1 percent are American Indian.

As more and more immigrants settle predominantly in larger cities, our cultural diversity increases. Although this cultural diversity is widely recognized to be a strength of our society, it also is a source of racism, ethnic discrimination, religious intolerance, sexism and homophobia, and social class prejudice, and these problems do not escape sport. An advanced course in sociology of sport would be needed to examine these issues in depth. In this section we'll consider only how cultural differences among your players may influence your coaching.

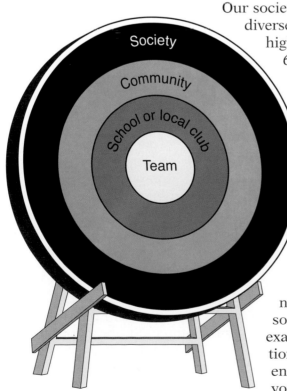

Figure 5.1 The levels of culture.

Stereotypes and Prejudice

We tend to categorize things in our world because it helps simplify the complex. We tend to develop stereotypes about people because it helps us understand complex human behavior. Here are a few oversimplified examples:

▶ Red-headed people have tempers.
▶ Jews are wealthy but frugal.
▶ Football players are dumb.
▶ Germans are stubborn.
▶ Short people have an inferiority complex.
▶ Female athletes are lesbians.
    ▶ Latinos are great lovers.
    ▶ Blacks have rhythm.
    ▶ White men can't jump.

Sometimes these stereotypes have some basis in fact, but they are usually gross overgeneralizations. Stereotypes become prejudices when they are negative opinions about a group of people that result in bigotry toward them. As a coach, you must guard against unfounded stereotypes and prejudices that may result in treating your players unfairly. It's a real challenge to put aside prejudices when selecting the members of your team or the starting lineup, or assigning players to positions. It's a challenge because you come to coaching with your cultural heritage, and how you coach is inevitably affected by your culture.

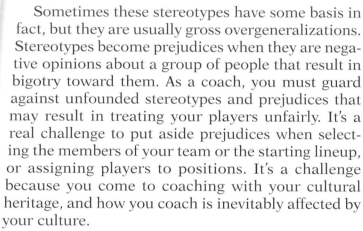

For example, you may have a cultural heritage that emphasizes hard work, dedication, and seriousness—what some call the Protestant work ethic. Your players also come to your team with their personal cultural backgrounds that influence their perception of you, their teammates, and the sport itself. Sometimes the culture of the coach and those of some players clash over communication style, how players respond to mistakes and criticism, aggressiveness or assertiveness, and dedication to the sport.

A common cultural difference among racial and ethnic groups is how serious they seem to be when playing sports. A coach with a Protestant work ethic will have difficulty understanding a fun-loving Latino who may be just as committed to achievement in the sport, but does not express the seriousness considered so important by the coach. Some coaches mis-

takenly think that players are defying them when they don't respond according to the expectations of the coaches—expectations based on their cultural heritage—instead of recognizing that players may have different views based on their own cultural heritages. The best way to avoid these cultural clashes is to learn more about the culture of your players so you can better understand their attitudes and beliefs.

Expectations

Another more insidious form of prejudice can occur in the form of holding negative expectations of certain players based on their cultural heritages. Most of us know that minorities and low-income youths have performed less well in schools than others, but many don't know that a major reason is that teachers expect less from them. Instead, many people believe they perform poorly because they don't try, their parents don't care, or their culture does not value education. As you'll learn in chapter 7, the expectations teachers—and coaches—hold of the young people they guide are subtly but clearly communicated to them, and those with low self-esteem often decide to perform as they are expected to perform.

You need to be vigilant in guarding against communicating low expectations to your players based on cultural differences. It's a very subtle, but powerful and destructive form of discrimination.

Culturally Responsive Coaching

You may be thinking that as a coach you shouldn't have to address issues such as cultural heritage, that players should forget about their differences and learn to adopt the prevailing culture of the team. To some extent, this is true, but what about your commitment to recognizing the uniqueness of each player and working with them as individuals? How can you recognize players' individual differences if you don't recognize cultural heritage, which is so much a part of who they are?

Culturally responsive coaches recognize the importance of cultural heritage, learn about their players' cultural heritage, and then coach them in light of these differences. They find the right balance between expecting players to adapt to the team culture and respecting each player's cultural heritage.

Coaching Recommendations

You can do many things to be a culturally responsive coach. Consider these ideas as you work with youths from diverse cultures:

1. Be sensitive to the cultural heritage of different categories of people, recognizing that they may hold values and beliefs different from yours. Take time to learn more about these differences and show respect for them in your coaching.

2. Teach your players to respect their own cultural heritage and those of other groups. Find opportunities for your players to share their cultural heritage with team members to foster an appreciation for cultural diversity.

3. Have a clear sense of your own ethnic and cultural heritage and how it may influence your coaching. Examine the rituals and routines you establish for your team to see if they are inclusive. Be ever mindful of imposing your cultural heritage on players who have differing perspectives.

4. Check yourself for discrimination against players of racial, ethnic, and social backgrounds different from your own. Watch for subtle differences such as providing less instruction, less opportunity to play, and less opportunity to communicate with you. Avoid preferential treatment of players who have the same cultural background as you, recognizing the tendency we all have to prefer to be with people who are like us.

5. Guard against subtly communicating low expectations of players because of their race, ethnic background, or social class. Hold high but realistic expectations of each player.

6. Use stories from diverse cultural groups when discussing character development as mentioned in chapter 4.

7. Discipline all players fairly, watching that you don't treat a player of a certain cultural heritage more harshly.

8. Seek to achieve the difficult balance of forging a unified team from culturally diverse players by teaching the culture of your team and also respecting the cultural distinctiveness of your players.

9. Do not allow your players to engage in racist, sexist, antigay, or homophobic language or actions. Instead help your players identify and dispel false stereotypes and prejudicial attitudes. Developing a strong team culture will be impossible if you permit prejudice and discriminatory behavior by some players against others.

10. Encourage active participation of parents and guardians, especially those from minority cultures, in team activities. In this way, players will get to know each other better.

Gender Differences

In this section we'll look at gender differences and what implications these differences have for your coaching. We'll also briefly consider gender equity.

Understanding Gender Differences

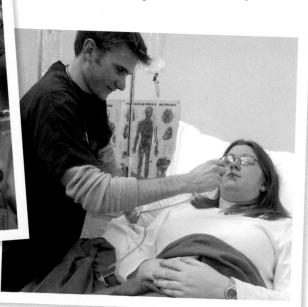

The term *gender differences* refers to socially determined factors that define masculinity and femininity; sex differences, on the other hand, are biologically determined. For example, the fact that women are on average shorter and lighter than men and have a higher percentage of body fat is biologically determined (a sex difference), but the fact that men rarely wear skirts and many women do is socially based (a gender difference).

We learn through our culture to associate certain characteristics with one sex or the other. Do you think of men as more competitive and women

Gender Equity

In the past the biggest gender issue in sport has been the inequality of opportunities for girls and women to play sports and therefore acquire the benefits of sport participation. The problem is being corrected, but it certainly is not completely solved.

On the positive side consider the huge increase in women's participation in sport at the high school and collegiate levels shown in figure 5.2.

Most people have positive attitudes toward girls' and women's participation in sport. Myths that women aren't physically capable of playing sports, and that sport participation will harm their reproductive organs and make them masculine have been debunked. Title IX legislation, which became law in 1972 and is supported by 79 percent of the public, has done much to give girls and women greater opportunities to participate in sports.

And yet girls and women are still striving for equal opportunity in sport in terms of facilities, budgets, media exposure, and the number of women coaches

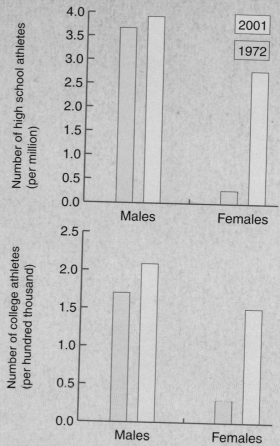

Figure 5.2 Change in male and female participation in high school and college sports from 1972 to 2001.

and sport administrators. Although achieving equity is a societal task, I believe every coach has a responsibility to address this problem in the following ways:

► Whether you're coaching boys or girls, as an important role model, encourage girls to participate in sport.

► If you're a male coach it is especially helpful if you encourage your organization to provide girls and women more sport opportunities.

► Encourage girls and women athletes to pursue careers in coaching.

► When speaking to students, parents, and the public, deliver the message that sport should be "an equal opportunity employer."

► Encourage your sport organization to give males and females the same recognition for participation in sport.

as more compassionate, or men as aggressive and women as cheerful? Then you may need to rethink whether you stereotype people on the basis of sex. From 30 years of gender research, we've learned that males and females are more similar than different. The principles of coaching advocated in the first four chapters of this book and most of the chapters to follow apply equally well when coaching athletes of both sexes.

Coaching Recommendations

Consider these recommendations for treating male and female athletes equally:

1. Be sensitive to stereotyping that may lead you to make invalid assumptions that boys and girls should be coached differently because of their gender.

2. Regardless of gender, get to know your athletes as unique individuals and coach them accordingly.

Sexual Issues

Now let's tackle some tough issues typically not discussed in the coaching profession—sexual harassment, coach–player sexual relationships, and homosexuality in sport.

Sexual Harassment

Sexual harassment is any unwelcome sexual advance, request for sexual favors, and unwelcome verbal or physical conduct of a sexual nature. It is a concern not only in the workplace but also in education and across all sectors of society, including sport.

When coaches make sexual advances toward their athletes or assistant coaches, or when players make sexual advances toward other players, it may be sexual harassment. Courts consider sexual harassment to have occurred if submitting to or rejecting these advances can (1) affect decisions about the person, (2) interfere with the person's performance, or (3) create a detrimental environment. Here are some behaviors that may constitute sexual harassment:

▶ Unwelcome remarks, jokes, comments, and innuendo about a person's body, appearance, sex, or sexual orientation

▶ Inquiries or comments about a person's sex life

▶ Obscene or suggestive gestures

▶ Use of inappropriate or derogatory sexual language

▶ Inappropriate physical contact including sexualized touching, kissing, patting, and pinching

▶ Promises or threats contingent on the performance of sexual favors

Sexual harassment by coaches is illegal, and more important, unethical. Coaches need to understand the power they have over players and assistants, how vulnerable players and assistants are, and how much they are affected by such harassment. Sexual harassment not only harms the athlete or assistant being harassed, but often hurts the entire team, risks imprisonment for the coach, and undermines the coaching profession.

Coaching Recommendations

Follow these recommendations to avoid sexual harassment on your team.

1. Not only must you not sexually harass your players or assistants, but you must also guard against any action that has the slightest appearance of harassment.

2. In addition to not engaging in sexual harassment, you have a duty as a coach not to let your players or assistants engage in this action. Watch for this especially with mixed-sex teams. In the past, sexual harassment has been dismissed as "harmless teasing," but ignoring it sends a message that sexually abusing a player is acceptable behavior or at least not a serious matter.

3. Review the preceding list of what is considered harassment, and review your behaviors as a coach to identify any actions that could possibly be interpreted as sexual harassment.

4. To avoid unintentional sexual harassment claims, discuss this at the preseason meeting with athletes and parents (described in detail in chapter 18), and ask them to notify you immediately if they experience or perceive any action on your part as harassment. And of course ask them to also notify you if they experience or perceive sexual harassment by another player or anyone associated with the team.

5. False accusation of sexual harassment has become an occupational hazard of employers and professionals, including coaches. Here are some things you can do to minimize the risk of being falsely accused:

a. Try to always have others present when interacting with players. If that is not possible, leave the door open so it does not appear that you're trying to talk secretly.

b. Be extra careful about any physical contact. Although psychologists call for more human contact (we all need more hugs), our litigious society makes touching risky. Sometimes you may need to touch players to guide their movements to learn a skill or treat an injury. Do so only with others present. Otherwise touch your players only in socially responsible ways. A pat on the fanny by a male coach to a male player is common, but it is not appropriate with a female player. A "high five" or pat on the back would be a wiser choice.

c. If you accidentally touch an inappropriate body part during your coaching, don't just ignore it. Apologize and make it clear that the action was unintentional.

d. If you are accused of sexual harassment, listen carefully to the complaint and don't try to make light of the accusation. Instead, respect the other person's viewpoint, identify the offending behavior, and stop it.

e. Work with your sport administrator to develop a sexual harassment policy (see the Women's Sports Foundation policy in the sidebar).

Women's Sports Foundation Policy on Sexual Harassment and Sexual Relationships Between Coaches and Athletes

1. Sexual harassment and sexual relationships between coaches and athletes subvert the mission of sports organizations and educational institutions to provide leadership and resources for the purpose of improving the physical, mental, and emotional well-being of all [athletes] through sport and fitness participation.

2. Sexual harassment has debilitating consequences both for its victims and for the society as a whole. In the context of athletic programs it lowers the self-esteems and limits the ability of [athletes] to develop their full potential in sports and fitness activities. It impairs the future capacity of its victims to experience full athletic participation and to pursue employment and leadership roles in athletics.

3. Romantic and/or sexual relationships between coaches and athletes undermine the professionalism of coaches, taint the atmosphere of mutual trust and respect between coach and athlete, and hinder the fulfillment of the overall educational mission of athletics. The WSF views it as unethical if coaches engage in romantic and/or sexual relations with athletes under their supervision, even when both parties have apparently consented to the relationship.

4. In order to effectively deal with cases of sexual harassment in athletics, as well as to prevent future abuse of [athletes] by coaches, the WSF encourages officers of sports governance bodies, athletic directors, and school administrators to formulate policy guidelines and procedures that include training, distribution of the policy, and subsequent evaluation of its effectiveness.

Adapted, by permission, from Women's Sports Foundation Position on Sexual Harassment and Sexual Relationships Between Coaches and Athletes.

Sexual Relations

When coaching, you develop close relationships with your players and experience many powerful emotions with them. These relationships give you the opportunity to be a powerful positive role model, but they can also lead to sexual intimacy. This is a line in the coach and player relationship, though, that you must not cross. Close is good, but sexually intimate is not.

It is illegal to have sex with your players if you coach for an *educational organization,* regardless of the age of the player or whether the player consents to having sex. It is illegal for adults to have sex with minors, and for good reason. It is an abuse of power, unethical, and grossly irresponsible. Everybody involved loses from such behavior—it's harmful emotionally to the player; it can destroy a coach's career; it can lead to legal action against the coach and sport organization; and it usually devastates a team's cohesiveness.

It is legal of course for a player of legal age to have a sexual relationship with a coach of legal age when it is consensual by both, but not within an educational organization unless they are married. However, whether it's love or merely a sexual relationship, such a relationship between coach and player creates potential problems on a team. If known by the other players (and it usually is), it places added pressure on the player because of the likely perception that the player receives special treatment, and it changes the relationship between the coach and all other players too.

Coaching Recommendations

Occasionally remind yourself of these guidelines, to avoid inappropriate sexual relations with your athletes.

1. You know that it is unethical, and perhaps illegal, for you to have sexual relationships with any players on your team. You must be prepared to resist any such temptation.

2. If the player is a consenting adult and you decide to have a sexual relationship with the player, either you or the player should resign from the team in the best interest of the other players.

Homosexuality and Sexual Orientation

Even though more and more homosexual players have been coming out of the closet in recent years, coaching gay, lesbian, and bisexual players is rarely discussed. The number of homosexuals participating in sports is not known, but we might suspect that gays and lesbians are represented in sport to the same extent as in the general population, which is estimated to be between 5 and 10 percent.

As a coach, ask yourself whether you are biased or prejudiced against homosexuals. Can you coach someone effectively who has a different sexual orientation than your own? Can you fulfill your professional duty to your players even if you have a strong personal opinion about your differences? As a coach, you have the responsibility to set aside your personal prejudices to provide an environment that supports all of your players. Part of coaching with character is treating all athletes with respect regardless of your personal views on their lifestyles.

An irrational fear or intolerance of gay men, lesbians, and bisexual people is called *homophobia*. It's prominent and destructive in sport. It rears its ugly head in the form of subtle, demeaning comments and jokes about a person's sexual orientation, and labeling of individuals as fags and queers. It can even be more overt in the form of verbal aggression and physical violence. Regardless of how it appears, homophobia is a form of sexual harassment.

In school and club sports heterosexual males sometimes tease women athletes about being lesbians. Such teasing creates fear in heterosexual women about participation in sport, and it closets lesbian women.

Homophobia can also dissuade gay men from participating in sports perceived to be more masculine, encouraging them instead to engage in sports that are perceived as being more tolerant of all sexual orientations. Homophobia can cause great distress and depression in players, harm their performance, and destroy relationships. It's not a matter to be taken lightly.

In the past, most coaches turned a blind eye to homosexuality, either denying its existence or sending a message that any discussion of the subject was forbidden. As homosexuality has become more visible in society and in sport, such an attitude is no longer acceptable.

Coaching Recommendations

Follow these recommendations to give athletes who are homosexual fair treatment and equal opportunities.

1. You have a responsibility to provide a safe and fair environment for players of all sexual orientations.

2. Come to terms with your own prejudices by learning more about homosexuality.

3. Establish and enforce policies that stop your players from engaging in antigay or homophobic behavior, explaining why it is harmful.

4. Consistently portray lesbians and gay people in neutral, matter-of-fact language.

5. Encourage your sport organization to include sexual orientation in its nondiscrimination policy prohibiting bias, stereotyping, and harassment of lesbians and gay people.

Being a Woman Coach

In an ideal world, being a woman in the coaching profession should be no different from being a man, but of course it is. The time demands of coaching are not very accommodating to the family and child-rearing responsibilities commonly assumed by women. Consequently some women avoid coaching as a career or leave it when they begin raising a family.

Women are also discouraged from entering the profession because of the sexual harassment they have seen or experienced in the male-dominated world of sport. Some women also perceive that they are judged by more demanding standards than male coaches and are rewarded less for equal work. This inequity leaves them less than enamored with the coaching profession.

But the world of sport is changing for the better, and coaching is becoming a more acceptable profession for women. If you're a woman considering a coaching career or have just begun coaching, I encourage you to continue with your plans to coach and to join with fellow coaches of both sexes to remove the barriers for women coaches. Help sport become an equitable experience for both sexes.

Physical and Mental Differences

It's remarkable to see an athlete with one leg and a prosthesis run a 100-meter dash in the Paralympics in less than 12 seconds. It's thrilling to watch the skilled movement of athletes in a college wheelchair basketball game. And it's inspiring to witness the joy of participation in athletes who are mentally retarded in the Special Olympics. Sport today is no longer the domain of the gifted few; sport is for everyone—those with loads of ability and those without; people of every race, ethnic origin, and sex; and those of all ages, young and old alike.

Although you may coach the best of the best, the able-bodied people who are physically gifted, you may also have the opportunity to coach athletes who have physical and mental disabilities. In this section you'll learn more about coaching these athletes, whether they are playing with other able-bodied athletes or with athletes of similar disabilities.

Understanding Physical and Mental Differences Among Players

There is a preferred language when discussing players with disabilities, and I've just used it in this sentence. Refer first to the person, not the disability. Thus, it is preferable to say *an athlete with mental retardation* or *a runner who is blind* or *a skier who is paraplegic* than to say *a mentally retarded athlete, a blind runner,* or *a paraplegic skier*. Also, when an impairment adversely affects a person's performance, it is preferable to refer to the impairment as a disability, not a handicap.

Types of Disabilities

Athletes with disabilities are people who are unable to participate in most sports without some accommodation in the form of special equipment or training or rule modifications. The range of impairments or disabilities that challenge athletes in sport participation are described here along with a brief definition or explanation.

Common Disability Groupings for Disabled Sports

Sensory Impairments

Deafness. This refers to a hearing loss that makes it impossible to understand speech through hearing alone. For national and international competition, the hearing loss must be at least 55 decibels in the better ear.

Blindness. This includes the entire range of vision impairments. For national and international competition, there are three classes of competition ranging from total blindness to a visual acuity greater than 20/600 up to 20/200 and a field limitation from 5 to 20 degrees.

Physical Disabilities

Amputation. This refers to people who have an elbow, wrist, knee, or ankle joint missing or no functional movement in one of these joints. There are nine categories for amputee competition in sports.

Cerebral palsy. This is a disorder of movement and posture due to brain damage. The degree of impairment can vary widely, and thus competition among athletes with this disability is organized into eight classes based on the extent of impairment.

Spinal cord injuries. This refers to people with cervical lesions who have complete or incomplete quadriplegia or paraplegia. Athletes with spinal cord injuries constitute the major group of athletes who play wheelchair sports, but other wheelchair participants include people with spina bifida and polio, double leg amputees, and nonambulatory les autres athletes. There are seven classes of competition in wheelchair sports based on the functionality of the athlete.

Les autres. This term means "the others" in French and refers to athletes with conditions that limit movement who do not fit into the other established disability groups. There are six classes of competition for athletes in this category.

Mental Disabilities

Mental retardation. People with intelligence quotients of less than 70 are considered to have mental retardation. Special Olympics International does not have a formal classification system for matching competitors, but uses an informal approach of matching by considering age, sex, and ability in the sport.

Learning disabilities. This is a broad category for developmental speech and language disorders, academic skill disorders such as dyslexia, and several motor coordination disorders. No special categories or special sport programs exist for people with these disorders.

Attention disorders. These are technically not learning disorders, but they often result in learning problems. Attention-deficit/hyperactivity disorder (AD/HD) is the better known problem in this category.

Together or Separate

On a moral ground, persons with disabilities have the same right to play sports as able-bodied people. On a legal ground, the Americans With Disabilities Act requires that organizations that offer sport programs, regardless of whether they are federally funded, provide comparable opportunities to people with disabilities. No sport program may discriminate against players or coaches with disabilities; they must make reasonable accommodations to ensure that athletes with disabilities have equal access to sports. All people have the right to play on recreational sport teams and to try out for elite, competitive teams, but the law recognizes that not everyone has the right to play on elite sport teams.

As a coach of an able-bodied team, you may have an athlete with a disability who wants to play on your team. Obviously for some disabilities this would be impossible, but for other disabilities it may be possible. The decision to permit a person with a disability to try out for a nondisability sport should be made jointly by the athlete, the athlete's parents, medical consultants, the sport organization, and the coach. These decision makers should consider any special accommodations for the athlete and of course the safety of the athlete with a disability as well as the safety of all athletes.

When athletes with disabilities are unable to play with able-bodied athletes, they can seek opportunities to play with people who have similar disabilities. Fortunately, more and more opportunities exist for athletes with disabilities to participate in a wide variety of sports. Of course athletes with disabilities benefit from good coaching just as much as any athletes, and they deserve the best coaching possible.

Coaching Recommendations

Follow these recommendations so that athletes with disabilities have equal athletic opportunities.

1. If you're coaching an able-bodied team, you should make reasonable accommodations to help people with disabilities to play on the team. It is unreasonable, however, if the accommodation puts the able-bodied members of the team at risk or a disadvantage, it represents substantial risk to the well-being of the athlete with disabilities, or the cost or assistance required is more than what is reasonable. After you have made reasonable accommodations, athletes with disabilities should be expected to play at the same level as all members of the team to earn a position on the team.

2. When coaching athletes with disabilities, your first obligation is to understand the disability of your athletes. See the list of references at the end of this chapter for additional information.

3. Know your sport well, including how to modify it to accommodate your athletes with disabilities.

4. Know your athletes with disabilities well; treat them as special, not for their disabilities, but just as you would treat each of your athletes as special. As you work with athletes with disabilities, focus on what they can do, not on what they cannot do.

Here is a list of additional recommendations for you to consider developed by Karen DePauw and Susan Gavron in their excellent book *Disability and Sport* (1995, p. 171):

▶ Ask athletes for information about what they can do and how to adapt activities.

▶ Develop reasonable skill progressions based on the disability.

▶ Assist athletes when requested, but do not become overbearing and smother them.

▶ Allow athletes to experience risk, success, and failure. Do not overprotect them.

▶ Do not underestimate what athletes with disabilities can do.

▶ Have a smaller coach-to-player ratio when coaching athletes with disabilities.

▶ Find ways to match athletes with comparable abilities.

Questions for Reflection

▶ What are some key characteristics of early adolescents (11-14), middle adolescents (15-17), and late adolescents (18-21) that you should understand as a coach? **(p. 71)**

▶ How do you best match athletes for safe practices and competition? **(p. 76)**

▶ What is culturally responsive coaching? **(p. 79)**

▶ What can you do to promote gender equity in sports? **(p. 81)**

▶ Should the sex of your athletes affect the way you coach them? **(p. 82)**

▶ What constitutes sexual harassment? How can you protect yourself from accusations of sexual harassment? **(p. 82)**

▶ Are there any situations in which sexual relations would be appropriate between a coach and a player? **(p. 85)**

▶ What can you do to be sure that all of your athletes feel safe from harassment and can fully participate, excel, and be judged based on their athletic performance and not on their sexual orientation? **(p. 86)**

▶ How can you accommodate athletes with disabilities in your sport program? **(p. 91)**

References

DePauw, Karen, and Susan Gavron. 1995. *Disability and sport*. Champaign, IL: Human Kinetics.

To Learn More

Australian Sports Commission. 1992. *Coaching athletes with vision impairments*. Canberra, Australia: Australian Sports Commission.

Australian Sports Commission. 1994. *Coaching amputee and les autres athletes*. Canberra, Australia: Australian Sports Commission.

Australian Sports Commission. 1995. *Coaching athletes with disabilities: General principles*. Canberra, Australia: Australian Sports Commission.

Australian Sports Commission. 1996. *Coaching wheelchair athletes*. Canberra, Australia: Australian Sports Commission.

Australian Sports Commission. 1997a. *Coaching athletes with an intellectual disability*. Canberra, Australia: Australian Sports Commission.

Australian Sports Commission. 1997b. *Coaching deaf athletes*. Canberra, Australia: Australian Sports Commission.

Australian Sports Commission. 1998. *Coaching athletes with cerebral palsy*. Canberra, Australia: Australian Sports Commission.

Cushner, K., A. McClelland, and P. Safford. 1996. *Human diversity in education: An integrative approach*. New York: McGraw-Hill.

Gains, C., and R. George. 1999. *Gender, 'race' and class in schooling: A new introduction*. London: Falmer Press.

Griffin, P. 1998. *Strong women, deep closets: Lesbians and homophobia in sport*. Champaign, IL: Human Kinetics.

Malina, R.M., C. Bouchard, and O. Bar-Or. 2004. *Growth, maturation, and physical activity*. 2nd ed. Champaign, IL: Human Kinetics.

"It takes a team! Making sports safe for lesbian, gay, bisexual, and transgender athletes and coaches." 2003. The education kit for athletic directors, coaches, teachers, parents/guardians, and athletes includes a 15-minute video. To obtain a kit, contact the Women's Sports Foundation at 800-227-3988 or visit the Web site at www.homophobiainsport.com.

Winnick, Joseph P. 2000. *Adapted physical education and sport*. 3rd ed. Champaign, IL: Human Kinetics.

PART II

Principles of Behavior

Successful coaches are good sport psychologists. They are skillful communicators, motivators, and behavioral managers. In part II you'll learn valuable psychological principles to help you be a better coach. Remember, however, that human behavior has few absolutes. These chapters offer recommendations, not laws. They must be understood and used not as a replacement for, but in conjunction with, good common sense.

6

Communicating With Your Athletes

The Newton Railroaders were behind by a touchdown but had the ball and were driving toward the Hutchinson Salt Hawks goal line. It was third down and long with only a minute remaining in the game. In an obvious passing situation, Salt Hawks coach Mike Giovanini yelled to his defensive backs, "Loosen up, loosen up." Angel Delgado, the left safety, looked at his coach and starting doing jumping jacks! ☞

Coach Giovanini's intended message was for the defense to back away from the line of scrimmage more than usual so that the pass receivers would not get behind the defense, but in that stressful moment Angel misunderstood "loosen up" to mean to relax his body more. Even in that tense moment it brought a smile to Coach Giovanini's face and a big laugh in the locker room later.

Coaching is all about communication. Successful coaches are masterful communicators, and unsuccessful coaches often fail not because they lack knowledge of the sport but because of poor communication skills. As a coach you must be able to communicate effectively in countless situations, including speaking with an irate parent about why her daughter is not starting, explaining to athletes how to perform a complex skill, introducing your team to the school pep assembly, and speaking to an official who just made a call you're sure was incorrect. Effective communication is essential to successful coaching just as it is to successful marriages, parenting, and careers.

☞ In this chapter you'll learn

▶ the basics of the communication process,

▶ eight major communication problems common to the coaching profession, and

▶ how to improve your communication skills for six of these problems (the other two problems will be discussed in later chapters).

Although coaches must be able to communicate equally well with athletes, fellow coaches, parents, administrators, and the public, in this chapter we'll focus on the communication between coach and athlete. All of the principles put forth, however, are applicable to any communication situation.

Three Dimensions of Communication

Let's begin with some basics about the communication process. First, communication includes not only *sending* messages, but also *receiving* them. Generally coaches are known much more for their oratorical skills than for their listening skills. But as I'm sure you know, coaches must be skillful not only at sending clear, understandable messages, but also at listening to understand what their athletes are communicating in return.

Second, communication consists of *verbal* and *nonverbal* messages. Gestures of hostility, facial expressions of joy, movements of intimidation, and acts of kindness are all forms of nonverbal communication. It is estimated that over 70 percent of communication is nonverbal, which reinforces the previous observation that what you say is not nearly as important as what you do.

Most of us tend to demonstrate greater control over our verbal messages than we do over our nonverbal ones. Because coaches are often intently observed by players, administrators, and the public, they must be especially attuned to how their gestures, body positions, and facial expressions communicate.

Third, communication has two parts: *content* and *emotion*. Content is the substance of the message, and emotion is how you feel about it. Content is usually expressed verbally, emotion nonverbally. Pressure-packed competitive sports challenge coaches to be in control of both the content and the emotions they communicate.

Coaches are typically more skilled in sending messages than receiving them, in expressing themselves verbally rather than nonverbally, and in controlling the content of their message compared with the emotion of it. Is that true of you? If so, through practice and effort you can develop your listening, nonverbal, and emotional communication skills. Let's learn how.

Six Steps in Communicating

The goal of communication is mutual understanding between the person sending the message and the person receiving the message. The process of delivering a message to your athletes involves six steps as shown in figure 6.1.

Figure 6.1

Six Steps in Communicating

Step 1

You have thoughts (ideas, feelings, intentions) that you wish to convey.

Katie needs to improve her position.

Step 2

You translate these thoughts into a message appropriate for transmission.

I'll tell her she needs to keep her hips level.

Step 3

You transmit your message through some channel (verbal or nonverbal).

Katie, work on keeping your hips level next time you try that.

Step 4

The athlete receives your message (if he or she is paying attention).

Step 5

The athlete interprets the message's meaning. The interpretation depends upon the athlete's comprehension of the message's content and your intentions.

I'm still making this same mistake. Coach has told me this before.

Step 6

The athlete responds internally to his or her interpretation of the message.

...I'm going to keep working on this until I get it right...

Sometimes this sequence of events flows smoothly, with you and the athlete clearly understanding each other's messages. But sometimes problems develop in one or more of the six steps. Let's look at two examples.

Example 1

COACH (shouting): *"How many times do I have to tell you to use a crossover step?"*

JOHN (meekly): *"Sorry. I forgot."*

COACH'S INTENTION: *To give John feedback about a technique error and to encourage him to remember the right technique in the future.*

JOHN'S INTERPRETATION: *"He thinks I'm lousy. I want to do it right, but there are so many things to remember. The harder I try, the more nervous I get and the more mistakes I make. I wish he'd get off my back."*

What went wrong in this communication? The coach's intention was good: to give constructive feedback. But the method he chose to transmit the message was flawed in both content and emotion. John received the message negatively, and instead of helping him to correct his error, the message added to the pressure he felt.

The same message expressed to another athlete, however, might be interpreted to mean, "Darn, I did it wrong again. Coach is upset. I don't blame him. I ought to be getting it right, and he's just trying to help." Even though the coach was not skillful in delivering his message, the second athlete understood the coach's intent and interpreted the message positively.

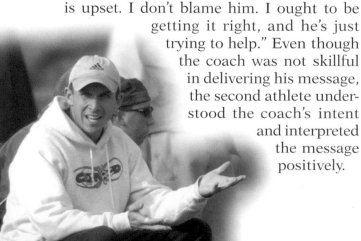

Example 2

COACH: *"I thought you really played well today, Denise."*

DENISE (with a tone of disbelief): *"Uh, huh. Thanks."*

COACH'S INTENTION: *To praise Denise for a good performance in the hope that she will repeat it.*

DENISE'S INTERPRETATION: *"Coach is only saying that because we won. When we lose, even if I play well, she yells at me and the team."*

The coach's thoughts were good, and she accurately transmitted the message she intended to send. Unfortunately, Denise's perception of the message's intent, not the content, was skewed. This may have been the result of previous messages that led her to believe that winning is more important to the coach than the players are. Because the coach had lost credibility with Denise, a well-intended message was received negatively.

Why Communication Is Sometimes Ineffective

The reasons for ineffective communication between coach and athlete are shown in figure 6.2.

Communication problems tend to occur more when people are under stress or duress, when they are passionate about the subject, or when the outcome is very important to them. Stress, passion, and importance reign supreme in the world of competitive sports, which is why communication is such a challenge for coaches.

Ineffective communication is not always the fault of the coach; the problem may lie with the athlete, or with both coach and athlete. But you can do much to avoid problems of miscommunication by developing your own communication skills. We will discuss these skills after you evaluate yours.

Evaluating Your Communication Skills

From interviewing and observing hundreds of coaches I have identified eight communication skills that coaches need most. I'll introduce you to eight coaches who will acquaint you with these skills by demonstrating their lack of them. Read the description of each mythical coach and then rate yourself on the skill discussed. Circle the number that best describes you. If you have not coached before, answer according to how you communicate in a leadership position. After you've rated yourself, we'll look at how to develop each of these communication skills.

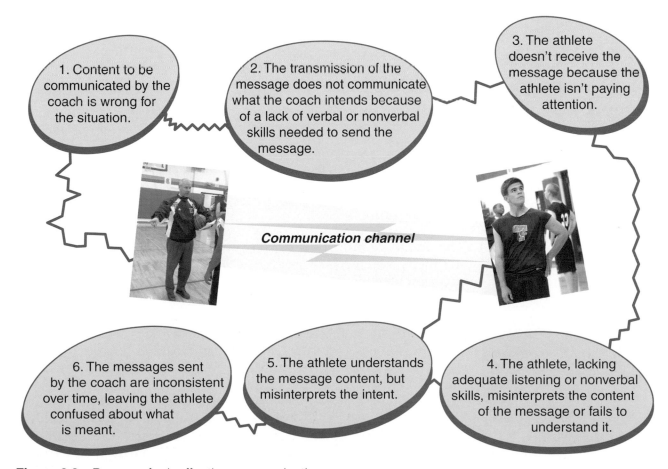

Figure 6.2 Reasons for ineffective communication.

Coach Incredible

Coach Incredible

Never admitting to an error, Coach Incredible finds he doesn't get the respect he demands because he doesn't show any for his athletes. He often doesn't follow through on what he says he will do, he thinks he's far more knowledgeable about the sport than he is, and he's very self-centered. When he speaks, he preaches rather than coaches so his athletes tune out because what he says never amounts to much. Coach Incredible has not yet learned that he cannot demand respect; instead it must be earned. Hence he has no credibility with his athletes.

Think about how you communicate with your athletes and others. Does it add or detract from your credibility? Rate yourself on how credible your athletes perceive your communication.

Very low credibility			Very high credibility	
1	2	3	4	5

Coach Naysayer

Coach Naysayer

Most of the words and actions of Coach Naysayer are negative, sometimes almost hostile. She frequently criticizes her athletes, increasing their self-doubts and destroying their self-confidence. Coach Naysayer is slow to praise, as though she believes it is not "coachlike" to say a kind word, and when she utters an infrequent kindness, she usually overshadows it with other negative comments.

Think back to your recent communications with your athletes. Are you primarily positive in the messages you deliver, or are you like Coach Naysayer? Rate the degree to which your messages are positive or negative.

Negative messages			Positive messages	
1	2	3	4	5

The Judge

The Judge

The Judge continually evaluates his athletes instead of instructing them. When a player errs, the Judge places blame rather than providing feedback or information about how to correct the error ("Who screwed up here?" "Why can't you get this right?" "You cost us the game with that dumb move."). When the players do well, the Judge cheers them on but doesn't know how to instruct them to achieve advanced skill levels. The continuous judgments, even when they are occasionally positive, cause athletes to feel uncertain and uncomfortable around the Judge.

Reflect a moment on the type of messages you send to your athletes. Do you give ample feedback and instructions, or are you like the Judge? Rate the extent to which the content of your communication is high in information or high in judgment.

High in judgment			High in information	
1	2	3	4	5

Coach Fickle

You are never sure what Coach Fickle will say next. Today it's one thing, tomorrow another. Last week she punished Janeen for fighting but not Sara, her star goalie. She tells players not to argue with the officials, but she does so regularly.

It's not easy to detect our own inconsistencies, but ponder for a moment how consistent you think you are in the messages you send and between what you say and what you do. Is your message consistent, or are you more like Coach Fickle? Rate the consistency of your communication.

Coach Fickle

Inconsistent messages			Consistent messages	
1	2	3	4	5

Coach Glib

Coach Glib is the most talkative person you ever met. He gives instructions constantly during practice, and when he's not yelling advice to his players during the contest, he's muttering to himself on the sidelines. He's so busy talking that he never has time to listen to his athletes. It has never occurred to him that his players might like to tell him something rather than always being told.

Are you a good listener, or are you like Coach Glib? Rate how good a listener you are.

Coach Glib

Not good listener			Very good listener	
1	2	3	4	5

Coach Stone

Coach Stone never shows emotion. She doesn't smile, wink, or give her athletes pats on the back. Nor does she scowl, kick at the dirt, or express disgust with them. You just don't know how she feels, which leaves her players feeling insecure most of the time.

Do you communicate your emotions effectively both verbally and nonverbally, or are you like Coach Stone? Rate how effective you are in expressing your emotions constructively.

Coach Stone

Weak in expression			Strong in expression	
1	2	3	4	5

The Professor

The Professor

The Professor is unable to explain anything at a level understandable to his players. He talks either above their heads or in such a roundabout way that they are repeatedly left confused. In addition, the Professor, who is used to dealing with abstractions, is unable to demonstrate the skills of the sport in a logical sequence so that the athletes can grasp the fundamentals.

Are you able to provide clear instructions and demonstrations, or are you like the Professor? Rate your ability to communicate instructions.

Weak in instructing			Strong in instructing	
1	2	3	4	5

Coach Skinner

Coach Skinner

Coach Skinner just doesn't seem to understand how the principles of reinforcement work. Although he gives frequent rewards to his athletes, he reinforces the wrong behavior at the wrong time. When faced with misbehavior, he either lets the infraction pass or comes down too hard.

Do you understand the principles of reinforcement, or are you like Coach Skinner? Rate your skill in rewarding and punishing athletes.

Not good in reinforcement			Very good in reinforcement	
1	2	3	4	5

Coaching Style and Communication

Well, how are you as a communicator—outstanding, good, weak in some areas? If you're like most of us, you can always improve your communication skills. I'll show you how in a moment, but first let's examine how command-style, submissive-style, and cooperative-style coaches typically communicate. Which of these styles characterizes your communication?

Command-Style Communication

As you would expect, the command-style coach communicates in an aggressive way by ordering athletes to do whatever, often accompanied by intimidating body language. Command-style coaches do most of the talking and little listening, and when things go wrong, they accuse and blame.

Command-style coaches often approach communication as competition—to outdo the other person, to have the last word, to "talk down" the other person. They win, not by listening, but by interrupting, shouting, and attacking the other person rather than speaking to the issue at hand. It's a communication style that prevailed in sport years gone by, and when seen today is embarrassingly out of place. This approach can be successful in sports for the short term because the coach has so much power. Over the long term, however, it drives athletes and others away, destroys relationships, and injures and scars those who are victims of the coach's tongue lashings.

Submissive-Style Communication

The submissive style, which allows others to dominate the conversation, is far less prevalent among coaches, although it does exist. Submissive-tyle coaches seldom express their own viewpoints and will tend to express agreement, even when they don't agree. They are uncertain, speak in a soft voice, and qualify what they say with *perhaps, maybe, hopefully,* and other such tentative terms. They beat around the bush and express nonverbally their lack of confidence. They avoid direct eye contact and stay at a distance from those with whom they are speaking.

Particularly troublesome about submissive-style coaches is their avoidance of difficult issues. They disdain confrontations and conflict, and by avoiding them often let small hot spots within their team turn into roaring fires.

Cooperative-Style Communication

I am an advocate of the cooperative style of communication because this style is based on mutual respect between the coach and athlete (and others with whom the coach communicates). Cooperative-style coaches communicate in a straightforward, positive, and confident way and allow and encourage others to do the same. These coaches don't play games in their communication, but take the initiative to make things happen. They speak up and are direct and constructive, focusing on moving the team forward in a positive way. Cooperative-style coaches are good listeners, seeking to understand what the other person is striving to communicate, and thus encourage two-way communication.

Stop for a moment to reflect on your communication style. Are you more a command-, submissive-, or cooperative-style communicator? Do you use the command style when coaching, but the submissive style at work? What style do you use with your significant other and family? Do you think the style you use is effective in each of these contexts, or would you like to become a better communicator? If you would like to make improvements (and most of us would), the next section will help you be a more successful cooperative-style communicator.

Developing Your Communication Skills

In the remainder of this chapter I'll share with you the advice of communication specialists regarding the first six of the eight communication skills discussed previously.

- ▶ Developing credibility when you communicate
- ▶ Communicating with a positive approach
- ▶ Sending messages high in information
  - ▶ Communicating with consistency
    - ▶ Learning how to listen
      - ▶ Improving your nonverbal communication

The seventh skill, instructional communication, is examined in chapters 10 and 11, and the eighth skill, applying the principles of reinforcement, is discussed in chapter 8.

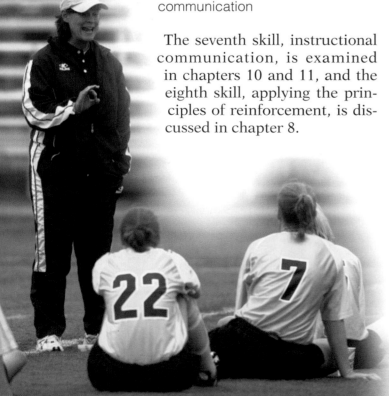

Developing Credibility When You Communicate

Can you think of someone who has very little credibility with you—a fellow worker, a neighbor, or a politician perhaps? Do you know coaches like Coach Incredible? You don't put much stock in almost anything these people say, probably for one of the following reasons:

- ▶ You don't believe they are knowledgeable about what they say.
- ▶ Usually what they say makes little sense or is of no importance to you.
- ▶ They often distort things or simply lie, so you have little trust in them.
- ▶ They constantly speak negatively.
- ▶ They speak to you as though you were stupid or less important than they are.

Your credibility is probably the single most important element in communicating effectively with your athletes. Your communication credibility is reflected in the degree to which your athletes trust what you say. At the outset, athletes will give you credibility simply because you occupy the prestigious role of the coach. From then on, however, you maintain and build this credibility or diminish it based on your own actions and communication.

Coach Lee was having a bad day. At breakfast she told her daughter to put on a less revealing blouse, which led to an argument. At work her boss reprimanded her for failing to complete an assignment on time, and when she arrived at the soccer field for the game, the officials were late. Then in the first period when an official failed to call a tripping foul, Coach Lee let the day's frustrations loose by charging onto the field complaining bitterly until the official ejected her from the game. Later in the locker room, after reflecting on the incident, Coach Lee apologized to the team for her actions. She explained her difficult day and that she had lost control and demonstrated poor sportsmanship. She asked that her players not follow her example but instead learn from her mistake. That went a long way in enhancing the credibility of Coach Lee with her players.

 Coaching Recommendations

There are many ways to build and maintain your credibility as a coach. Some of the more important ones are listed here.

- ▶ By being a cooperative-style coach
- ▶ By being knowledgeable about the sport or at least honest about whatever knowledge you possess
- ▶ By being reliable, fair, and consistent
- ▶ By following through on what you say you'll do
- ▶ By expressing warmth, friendliness, acceptance, and empathy
- ▶ By being dynamic, spontaneous, and open
- ▶ By remaining calm under pressure
- ▶ By using the positive approach—the next communication skill I'll discuss

Communicating With a Positive Approach

When I was growing up, I remember saying to kids who taunted me, "Sticks and stones can break my bones, but words can never hurt me." I was wrong. The words you say to others can hurt a lot.

One of the most important skills you can learn, for coaching or any other aspect of life, is to communicate with a positive approach. The positive approach emphasizes praise and reward to strengthen desirable behaviors, whereas the negative approach uses punishment and criticism to eliminate undesirable behaviors. The positive approach helps athletes value themselves as individuals, and in turn it gives you credibility. The negative approach increases athletes' fear of failure, lowers their self-esteem, and destroys your credibility.

Using the positive approach does not mean that every message should be full of praise and gushy compliments. Too much praise leaves youngsters doubting the sincerity of your messages and reduces the value of your rewards. Being positive also does not mean that you turn your back on athletes' misbehaviors. At times athletes should be punished, but even punishment can be given in positive ways (see chapter 8).

The positive approach is an attitude that you communicate in both verbal and nonverbal messages. It is an attitude that communicates a desire to understand, an acceptance of others, and an expectation of mutual respect. It is the attitude of a cooperative-style coach.

Encouragement is a vital part of the positive approach as eloquently expressed by Jim Grassi: "I'm convinced that encouragement has to be the most important trait of all. You can lack a little in talent, you can play in a small unknown school, but you will most likely never develop the commitment and dedication you need without someone in the balcony of your heart rooting you on and guiding you to the next opportunity" (2002, p. 194). As a coach, you have the opportunity to be that cheerleader.

Bad Habits

Why do so many coaches behave like Coach Naysayer? One reason is that they have simply fallen into the habit of telling athletes only what they do wrong rather than what they do right. Is this true of you? Think not only about the content of your messages—the words you say—but the way you say them. For example, when you give athletes feedback, is your tone upbeat or harsh and on edge?

Breaking habits is difficult, especially ingrained habits such as the negative approach. If you are uncertain about whether you use the positive or negative approach, or about the degree to which you use them, ask a fellow coach or friend to observe you for a constructive evaluation. Warning: This takes courage and a very good friend.

If you know you are in the habit of using the negative approach, three things will help you change to the positive approach:

▶ You must want to change.

▶ You must practice the positive approach not only when coaching but in all of your communications. The positive approach is often most difficult to use with those to whom you are closest, so practice with a friend or significant other. (Who knows, learning to be a successful coach may help your career or relationship.)

▶ You need to monitor yourself or get help from someone whom you will permit to tell you when your bad habit rears its ugly head.

Unrealistic Expectations

Another reason coaches use the negative approach is that they have unrealistic expectations about acceptable and unacceptable behaviors. Sometimes coaches forget that 14-year-olds are not 28-year-olds, or that one 16-year-old is not as skilled as another. When coaches have unrealistically high expectations, they seldom view their athletes as successful. If coaches communicate their judgment of failure to athletes—as they often do—athletes will feel frustrated and unaccepted.

It is important to have realistic goals not only about your athletes' performance abilities, but about their emotional and social behavior as well. Remember, it's natural for kids to "horse around" and have fun.

Being realistic in your expectations and remembering that people aren't perfect will help you shake the habit of communicating negatively. Just remember: If athletes behaved perfectly, they wouldn't need you as a coach!

Short-Term Success

The third reason coaches use the negative approach is that they honestly believe it gets the best results, possibly because some successful college and professional coaches use it. The negative approach does work! It can help athletes learn the skills you want them to learn and motivate them to achieve. But when criticism is frequent or continuous, the strong negative emotion it creates in athletes often also interferes with learning and motivation. Athletes start playing it safe, taking as few risks as possible to avoid their coach's wrath. The negative approach has a short life. After a while athletes "turn off," and the coach loses credibility.

A perennial winning high school soccer coach makes a practice of calling one or two parents of her players after each game to praise the athlete's play, effort, and commitment to the team. Sometimes those calls go to parents of athletes who didn't get to play in the game. In those cases the coach comments on their athlete's contribution to the team and provides a brief critique summary of the progress the athlete is making.

 ## Coaching Recommendations

Most of us would rather be ruined by praise than saved by criticism. You can adopt the positive approach by following these guidelines:

- ▶ Provide honest, direct, and constructive messages.
- ▶ Embrace an attitude in which you look to catch your athletes doing good or right, and then tell them they've done so (we'll discuss "catching them doing good" more in chapter 8).
- ▶ Avoid sarcasm and put-downs, but at the same time don't sugarcoat athletes' behaviors by falsely putting a positive spin on them.
- ▶ Emphasize what can be done, not what cannot be done, and avoid language that dwells on problems, but instead use language that focuses on solutions.
- ▶ Seek to build character rather than destroy it.

Sending Messages High in Information

Some coaches seem to think that a whistle, a cap, and the title "Coach" qualify them to be the Judge. They constantly give verdicts to their players, telling them what they did right or wrong—usually wrong. Athletes need more than to be told that they did something wrong; they need specific information about how to do it right. Successful coaches are not judges; they are skilled teachers.

Why Coaches Judge

Some coaches communicate like the Judge for the same reasons they adopt the negative approach—sheer habit and imitation of other coaches who engage in this practice. Other coaches become judges because they lack the technical knowledge of the sport necessary to give athletes the information they need. When this occurs, coaches may become judges to cover up for their own deficiencies. Command-style coaches are especially likely to communicate like the Judge.

Being a judge is dangerous, however, because you assume you always know what is good and bad, right and wrong. Too often judgmental coaches label something as bad or wrong, only to learn later that *they* were wrong.

Let's consider an example: Doug is late to practice, so Coach Stanley makes him run 15 laps as punishment without letting him explain. Later, Coach Stanley learns that the boy's mother was late getting home from work and that he was responsible for baby-sitting his little sister. Under these circumstances, the athlete behaved responsibly.

Consider another example: Jody strikes out by swinging at a ball a foot over her head. Coach DuPuy yells, "For Pete's sake! What's wrong with you? Don't you know a ball from a strike?" Although Jody made a poor judgment in swinging, the coach's message is highly destructive and provides no useful information. Instead of judging, an instructive coach would first determine if Jody knew that the pitch was not a good one to swing at and then indicate that they would continue working in practice to learn to swing only at strikes.

Remember, sport tends to evaluate participants enough through competition. Usually athletes know when they have made a mistake or played poorly. You hardly need to be told you made an error when the ball goes between your legs and the game winning run scores. Athletes need some room to make mistakes—that's part of learning.

Providing Feedback High in Information

As a coach, you should provide evaluative comments only when athletes clearly don't know what is correct or incorrect. If a behavior is good, praise them for it and tell them what is good about it. If it's wrong, give them specific instructions on how they can improve.

The last season the legendary John Wooden coached UCLA basketball, two psychologists recorded all of his verbal communication with the team during practice. Nearly 75 percent of Wooden's messages gave specific instructions to the athletes. His remaining messages were 12 percent requests to hustle, 7 percent praise, and 6 percent scolds.

Another study found that Little League baseball coaches who provided specific instructions were evaluated more positively by their players than were coaches who gave general encouragement. This was especially true for players who were low in self-esteem. Athletes so dearly want to learn sport skills that not only will they respect you for helping them learn, but they will also respect themselves for their learning.

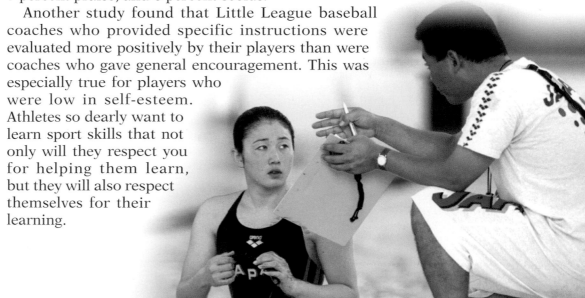

Habitually communicating in judgmental language tends to make people around you feel uneasy. They become cautious, even defensive, always wondering how you are evaluating them at the moment.

Although there is a time to communicate your evaluations, they should not dominate your interactions with athletes. Save evaluations for instructional sessions when you can put them into a constructive framework.

One final caution: Do not evaluate the athletes' selves. Instead, evaluate their behavior. Rather than saying to a youngster who has made a tactical error, "What's wrong with you, Joe?" say, "That was the wrong decision, Joe," commenting only on the behavior.

 ## Coaching Recommendations

Follow these guidelines to be a better communicator and less judgmental:

- ▶ Provide athletes with specific information that helps them correct mistakes rather than general information that judges their performance.
- ▶ Be certain you understand the reason for your athletes' actions before you judge their behavior.
- ▶ Avoid making evaluative comments when athletes know they've made a mistake.
- ▶ Focus your comments on the athletes' behaviors, not on them as people, to avoid damaging their self-worth.

Communicating With Consistency

Communicating with consistency is a real challenge, in coaching or any endeavor because each of us has a little Coach Fickle in us. It is so easy to preach one thing and do another, or to do one thing one day and the opposite the next. Your brain may tell you to say one thing verbally, but your emotions may express something else nonverbally. When youngsters receive these mixed messages, they become confused or question your credibility.

Look at it from the perspective of the athletes. A coach asks them to show emotional control when playing, but then the coach throws a temper tantrum at an official. A coach asks players to respect their teammates, but treats them without respect. A coach teaches that physical fitness is important, but does nothing to stay fit. A coach tells athletes to be self-confident, then turns around and destroys their feelings of self-worth by yelling at them for their errors. A coach penalizes a bench-sitter for being late to practice, then ignores the same behavior by a starting player. When coaches behave in this way, it is no wonder that athletes think of them as hypocrites!

The Value of Consistency

Keeping your word is a form of consistency that will enhance your credibility. For example, if you promise your athletes a reward for a good practice, you'll want to deliver; if you say you'll help a player with a problem, be sure to follow up. When you're true to your word, athletes learn to trust you, which enhances your credibility and thus your

Coaching Recommendations

Strive hard to be consistent in your verbal messages and to ensure that your nonverbal actions are consistent with your verbal messages.

▶ When you promise to do something, be sure to follow through.

▶ Avoid gossiping, and discourage your athletes from gossiping.

▶ Develop a sense of trust with your athletes by being consistent and positive. Through trust you become a coach of character.

Learning How to Listen

Are you a good listener? How much of what is said do you actually hear? Researchers estimate that untrained listeners probably hear less than 20 percent of what is communicated. Think of that for a moment—you miss 80 percent of what people are trying to communicate to you!

Although listening may seem deceptively easy, it's quite difficult. Coaches are sometimes accused of being poor listeners because (1) they are so busy "commanding" that they never give others a chance to speak, and (2) they assume that they know it all and that "athletes should be seen and not heard." I think these are stereotypes from the past and that coaches today recognize the importance of listening. Dr. Leroy Walker, Olympic track coach and former president of the U.S. Olympic Committee, said, "The essence of coaching is understanding your athletes. You have to listen to them and find out what they felt, how they interpreted their race. Then you can tell them how you interpreted it or saw it through your eyes as the coach" (Dale and Janssen 2002, p. 179).

Poor listening skills cause breakdowns in the communication process. For example, after repeatedly failing to get you to listen, athletes will simply stop speaking to you, and are less likely in turn to listen to you. When athletes stop talking to you, you can't get to know them, to understand them; when they stop listening to you, you can't influ-

influence. If you don't provide a promised reward, you lose the power to use rewards in the future, and you may be forced to resort to punishment as a means of control.

Athletes, however, are not out looking for inconsistencies in their coaches. Because of the great respect they have for the position of coach and those who hold it, most athletes begin with the attitude that the coach can do no wrong, and are therefore slow to see inconsistencies. Because of this initial deep sense of trust, it can be a shattering experience when athletes recognize a coach as untrustworthy, or worse yet, a hypocrite or liar.

I was fortunate to have Charlie Lyons as my high school wrestling coach; he was honest and consistent in his communication with me. I trusted him fully. I never heard him speak derogatorily of other athletes. If he had, I would have wondered if he spoke that way of me when I was not present. Moreover, Coach Lyons didn't permit his athletes to speak ill of others. Instead he would gently turn negative comments by others into positives. Because I trusted Coach Lyons, he was an important character coach for me.

Of course, we do not intend to be inconsistent or hypocritical; usually we are just careless. It is easy to forget the influence we have on the athletes under our charge.

ence them. Coaches who are poor listeners also often have more discipline problems. Athletes may misbehave just to get attention—a drastic way to get you to listen.

Improving Your Listening Skills

You can do a number of things to improve your listening skills as shown in the following list.

▶ Most important, of course, is to *recognize the need to listen.*

▶ *Concentrate on listening.* This means that you must give your undivided attention to what is being said. Has someone ever accused you of not listening? Although you may have heard the words and could repeat them, you were not really listening. What the accuser sensed was that you were not "with" her or him psychologically. When you listen, search for the meaning of the message rather than focusing on the details. Especially in disagreements, we are inclined to listen for and respond to details that we can attack or refute, failing to listen to the major point of the message.

▶ *Avoid interrupting your athletes.* We sometimes interrupt others because we anticipate what they will say and complete their thoughts for them. Then we respond to what we thought they were going to say, but perhaps later discover that the intended message was quite different. It's especially tempting to interrupt those who speak slowly because we are too impatient to wait for them to complete their messages. Remember that you can listen considerably faster than a person can speak.

▶ *Respect the rights of your athletes to share their views with you.* It is important to listen to not only your athletes' fears and problems, but also their joys and accomplishments. Your response to athletes' views is important in shaping their attitudes. Repress the tendency to respond emotionally to what your athletes say, but don't be like Coach Stone, who never shows any emotion. Think about why an athlete said what he or she did and how you can respond constructively. (I know this is easier said than done, but isn't that true of most complex skills?)

Active Listening

Educators distinguish between two types of listening—passive and active. Passive listening is what we typically think of as listening—being silent while another person speaks. Although passive listening is sometimes desirable, it has limitations in that the speaker is not sure whether you are paying attention or really understand. Although passive listening communicates some degree of acceptance, athletes may think you are evaluating them. Silence does not communicate empathy and warmth.

Active listening involves interacting with athletes by providing them with proof that you understand. Here are some examples of how it works:

One of your players is worried about meeting your expectations for an important game.

PLAYER: *"Do you think we can beat this team?"*

COACH: *"They are a pretty good team, but we have a good team too."*

PLAYER: *"But what if we don't play well?"*

Now you must interpret these questions. Is she really worried about the team winning, or is she worried that she may not be able to play well enough herself? In active listening, you don't just guess at your player's meaning; you work to find it out. You do this by feeding back to the player what you think she means:

COACH: *"Are you worried about how you might play?"*

PLAYER: *"Well, a little."*

COACH: *"As long as you try to do the best you can, I'll always be proud of you."*

The coach's reassurance lets the player know that her acceptance on the team is not contingent on her performing well, but only on her trying. Here is another example:

GYMNAST: *"What's the worst injury you've seen on the high bar?"*

COACH: *"I saw a fellow fly off and break his neck."*

The coach may have answered the question without thinking about what was really being asked. The player may have been expressing concern about the possibility of his own injury. Active listening by the coach might change the conversation this way:

GYMNAST: *"What's the worst injury you've seen on the high bar?"*

COACH: *"I haven't seen too many injuries. Are you worried about getting hurt?"*

GYMNAST: *"Sometimes I think about it."*

COACH: *"With today's better equipment, the use of a spotter, and the coaching you've received, the chances of serious injury are really small."*

Active listening is a tremendous skill that brings together many of the ideas we have discussed in this chapter. Active listening, however, works only when you convey that you accept your athletes' feelings and that you want to understand and help. Otherwise, you will come across as insincere, patronizing, or manipulative. Because active listening lets athletes know that you understand and respect their ideas and feelings, they will be more willing to listen to you in return.

 ## Coaching Recommendations

It's been said that "it shows a fine command of language to say nothing." Here are some keys to improving your listening skills:

▶ Show the person speaking to you that you're interested in listening and trying to understand.

▶ Once someone has spoken to you, check that you understand what was said by paraphrasing the message, not only the content but the emotion behind it.

▶ Express empathy, not sympathy, by showing that you care and respect what the person speaking to you has to say.

Improving Your Nonverbal Communication

If you have ever needed to communicate with someone who does not speak your language, you know both how important and how effective nonverbal communication can be. It is estimated that 70 percent of our total communication is nonverbal. In the world of sport, especially team sports, numerous situations arise in which effective nonverbal communication is essential to good performance—a nod of the head, a glance of the eyes, or a hand signal can communicate vital information to teammates. It is equally important in your role as a coach.

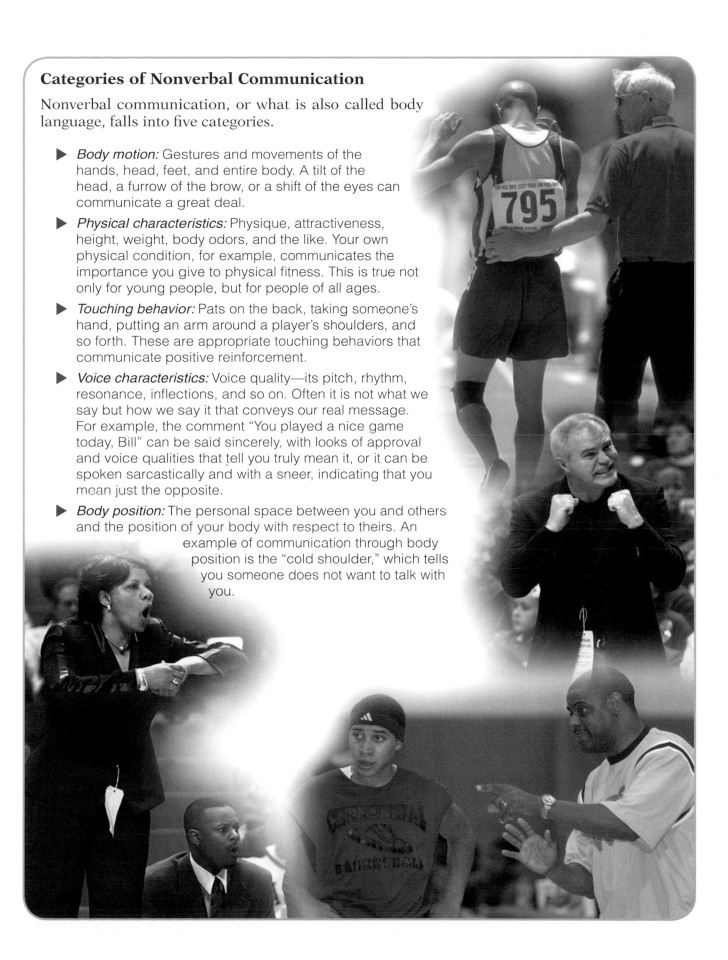

Categories of Nonverbal Communication

Nonverbal communication, or what is also called body language, falls into five categories.

▶ *Body motion:* Gestures and movements of the hands, head, feet, and entire body. A tilt of the head, a furrow of the brow, or a shift of the eyes can communicate a great deal.

▶ *Physical characteristics:* Physique, attractiveness, height, weight, body odors, and the like. Your own physical condition, for example, communicates the importance you give to physical fitness. This is true not only for young people, but for people of all ages.

▶ *Touching behavior:* Pats on the back, taking someone's hand, putting an arm around a player's shoulders, and so forth. These are appropriate touching behaviors that communicate positive reinforcement.

▶ *Voice characteristics:* Voice quality—its pitch, rhythm, resonance, inflections, and so on. Often it is not what we say but how we say it that conveys our real message. For example, the comment "You played a nice game today, Bill" can be said sincerely, with looks of approval and voice qualities that tell you truly mean it, or it can be spoken sarcastically and with a sneer, indicating that you mean just the opposite.

▶ *Body position:* The personal space between you and others and the position of your body with respect to theirs. An example of communication through body position is the "cold shoulder," which tells you someone does not want to talk with you.

Are you aware of each of these dimensions of nonverbal communication, and are you effective at both sending and receiving nonverbal messages through each type? Whatever skills you have in nonverbal communication were probably derived in on-the-job training—that is, the job of daily living. Teaching nonverbal communication skills by written or spoken words alone, or learning nonverbal skills without practicing them, is not easy.

Your first step, then, is to recognize the importance of nonverbal messages in the total communication process. One way to develop nonverbal skills is to observe the feedback others give you as you both send and receive nonverbal messages. The value of that feedback depends on your sensitivity and receptivity to it. The more sensitive you become to nonverbal cues, the more likely you are to be able to express your feelings and attitudes nonverbally and to understand athletes' feelings and attitudes. This is an important aspect of developing empathy, which was mentioned in chapter 3.

You As a Model

Once again, keep in mind that your every action in and out of the playing arena is a form of nonverbal communication, not just the good ones. Perhaps one of the most important things you communicate by your

The "house rules" developed by the YMCA of the USA in the YBA Director's Manual say it well:

Speak for yourself
Not for anybody else.
Listen to others
Then they'll listen to you.
Avoid put-downs
Who needs 'em?
Take charge of yourself
You are responsible for you.
Show respect
Every person is important.

actions is respect, or lack of it, for people and the sport. How you walk, how you approach others, your gestures, and both what you say and how you say it all convey your attitudes about sportsmanship and other people. Impressionable athletes who hold you in high esteem are influenced by everything you do.

Your actions can teach athletes much more than just the skills and rules of your sport. Lead the way in congratulating opposing teams after both victories and losses. Show athletes how you want them to behave after having played well and not so well, after having won or lost. Model how they should react when you think the team has been treated unfairly.

Young people, you'll find, are more influenced by what you do than by what you say. You know the axiom: Actions speak louder than words. If you want your athletes to display good sportsmanship, it is not enough to just tell them; you must show them!

Coaching Recommendations

Follow these tips to improve your nonverbal communication skills.

▶ Recognize how much of what you communicate is in the form of nonverbal messages.

▶ Learn how to both send and receive messages by effectively using and reading body position, body motion, voice characteristics, and touching behaviors.

▶ Remember that it's not so much what you say but what you do that influences your athletes.

References

Dale, Greg, and Jeff Janssen. 2001. *The seven secrets of successful coaches.* Phoenix: Winning the Mental Game.

Grassi, James E. 2002. *Crunch time: What football can teach you about the game of life.* Minneapolis: Bethany House.

"Introduction: The YBA Philosophy," *YBA Director's Manual* by J. Ferrell (Ed.), 1977. Copyright 1977 by the YMCA of the U.S.

Questions for Reflection

▶ What are the three dimensions of communication? What can you do to develop your listening, nonverbal, and emotional communication skills? **(p. 96)**

▶ What are the six steps in communicating? What are some common ways communication breaks down? **(p. 97)**

▶ What eight communication skills do coaches need most? **(p. 101)**

▶ What coaching communication style do you tend to adopt most often? Are you a command-style, submissive-style, or cooperative-style coach? **(p. 104)**

▶ How can you develop credibility with your players? **(p. 106)**

▶ Do you use a positive approach when coaching? What can you do to make your interactions with athletes more positive? **(p. 107)**

▶ When you coach, do you usually send messages high in information or high in judgment? **(p. 109)**

▶ In what way does consistency enhance your relationship with your athletes? **(p. 111)**

▶ Are you a good listener as well as communicator? What are some ways you can incorporate active listening into your coaching? **(p. 112)**

▶ What are the five categories of nonverbal communication? How effective are you at using them when you coach? **(p. 115)**

7

Motivating Your Athletes

Baseball was my passion growing up, and I could hardly wait for spring to arrive so I could play. When I was 12, all my school friends tried out for a new team, so I joined them. Coach Archer, the father of the pitcher, told me to go to right field. At the end of the first practice he told me I wasn't good enough to be a starter and that I wouldn't get to play much that year, but if I wanted to stay on the team maybe I'd get to play the next year. I quit.

I could hardly see to bike home because of the tears. Rejected from the game I loved and the friends with whom I had always played, the despair was almost more than I could bear. Ashamed to go home and tell my parents that I didn't make the team, I biked around aimlessly when I happened to pass a school playground where another team of my age group was practicing. I stopped and watched.

After a while the coach, Mr. Hickey, probably noticing my dejected look, came over and asked if I wanted to play. With some reluctance, perhaps fearing another rejection, I mumbled that I did but that I didn't know anyone. Mr. Hickey put his arm around me and introduced me to the team. He asked what position I played, and I told him I liked to pitch. He said, "Great, we need a pitcher."

I threw hard but wild that day. Coach Hickey offered words of encouragement, something I desperately needed at that moment. In the next few practices he taught me a lot about pitching, and my control improved quickly.

Two weeks later we played a five-inning game against Coach Archer and all my friends. We won the game 1 to 0, and I struck out 14 of the 15 batters. After the game Coach Archer said, "I didn't know you could pitch like that. Why don't you come back and play for us." You know what I would have liked to have told him . . . but I think I said something about the fact that he never asked if I could pitch, and that I was happy with my new team because the coach encouraged me.

Most coaches I meet recognize that even the most skillful athletes will not be successful unless they are sufficiently motivated. Many coaches have experienced the frustration of coaching a talented athlete whom they could not motivate. So coaches typically want answers to two questions:

▶ Why are some athletes so motivated and others so unmotivated?
▶ How do we motivate our athletes to be the best they can be?

I often answer by asking a question of my own: How do I motivate you to be the best coach you can be? I don't ask this question to beg the issue. Instead, I want coaches to examine their own motives in the hope of discovering a basic principle of motivation:

> **People are motivated to fulfill their needs.**

If you understand what your athletes' needs are, and you are able to help them fulfill those needs, you possess the key to their motivation. Coach Hickey knew my needs—encouragement and instruction—which motivated me then and I believe greatly affected my motivation to achieve in the future.

To meet the needs of your athletes, you need to get to know them really well, something I encourage you to do throughout this book. You should know why each athlete wants to play the sport and what the athlete wants from the sport. The more you understand why your athletes are playing the sport, the easier it will be to understand their behavior throughout the season—and to help motivate them or at least avoid stifling their intrinsic motivation.

Sport psychologists have learned that the two most important needs of athletes are

▶ to have *fun*, which includes the need for stimulation and excitement, and

▶ to *feel worthy*, which includes the need to feel competent and successful.

☞ **In this chapter you'll learn**

▶ how you can help your athletes fulfill their needs to have fun and to feel worthy,

▶ how optimal arousal and flow are related to fun,

▶ how sports can threaten self-worth and what you can do to remove the threat,

▶ how you can motivate athletes by helping them focus not on winning but on achieving their own performance goals, and

▶ how to reduce anxiety and stress in your athletes and yourself.

Extrinsic and Intrinsic Rewards

If you remember nothing else from this chapter, remember this: Athletes are motivated to fulfill their needs, and their primary needs when participating in sports are to have fun and to feel worthy by experiencing success. With that knowledge, consider what actions you can take that will positively motivate your athletes and what actions may demotivate them. We've already discussed many actions by coaches that make sport fun or not, and that enhance or decrease self-worth. With this key principle in mind, let's look more closely at what is rewarding to athletes.

It's important that you understand the difference between extrinsic and intrinsic rewards, and which are more meaningful to your athletes. Trophies, medals, money, praise, and trips to a tournament are examples of *extrinsic rewards*—that is, they are provided to players by others, or externally. *Intrinsic rewards* are those things that are internally satisfying when players participate in sport. Having fun and feeling competent and successful are intrinsic rewards.

Extrinsic rewards such as recognition from others and trophies can be powerful motivators, but over time these rewards may become less valued as intrinsic rewards become more valued. The nifty thing about intrinsic rewards, unlike extrinsic rewards, is that they are self-fueling; that is, you as the coach do not need to provide them. In fact you can't provide them. What you can do is create the conditions in practices and games that provide your players opportunities to attain their own intrinsic rewards—those rewards being fun and success. Again, think about your coaching actions. Do you create the conditions that help your athletes experience these intrinsic rewards?

Coaches who are great motivators understand this key to motivating their athletes. They know that they do not motivate players. Instead they create the conditions or the climate in which players motivate

themselves. And they skillfully use extrinsic rewards to help build intrinsic motivation. When players fail to achieve the intrinsic rewards of having fun and feeling worthy, they will lose motivation to play and are likely to quit. I'll discuss the specific use of rewards in more detail in chapter 8, but for now remember that intrinsic rewards are the best motivators for the long term. Now let's take a closer look at the two most important intrinsic rewards: having fun and feeling worthy.

Need to Have Fun

Why do people play—not only sports, but other games as well? This question has intrigued philosophers and scientists alike for centuries. Only recently have we begun to know why. Each of us is born with the need for a certain amount of stimulation and excitement—what is often called the need for arousal, and what most of us simply call fun.

Optimal Arousal

When our arousal level is too low, we become bored and seek stimulation. We call this play-

ing when the primary purpose of the stimulation we seek is to have fun. Sometimes, however, we find ourselves in situations that are more arousing than we would like, and we become fearful or anxious. Then we try to decrease our arousal however we can.

In other words, people have a need for an optimal amount of arousal or stimulation—not too little and not too much as shown in figure 7.1. This optimal level of arousal differs from person to person. We all know people who seem to thrive on a great deal of stimulation and others who are quite content with only a little.

The Flow Experience

What makes optimal arousal so desirable? Why do we seek it? The answer lies in how we feel when experiencing optimal arousal, what Mihaly Csikszentmihalyi (Jackson and Csikszentmihalyi 1999) calls the "flow experience." Flow occurs when we are totally immersed in an activity; we lose our sense of time, feeling everything is going just right because we are neither bored nor anxious.

When experiencing flow, our attention is so intensely centered on the activity that concentration is automatic. When in flow, we are not self-critical because our thoughts are totally focused on the activity. Because we are neither bored nor threatened, we feel in control of ourselves and our environment. One athlete explained it this way: "You are so involved in what you are doing you aren't thinking of yourself as separate from the game."

The flow experience is so pleasing that it is intrinsically rewarding. We will engage in activities for no other reason than to experience flow, because it is fun. Sports, of course, are popular with

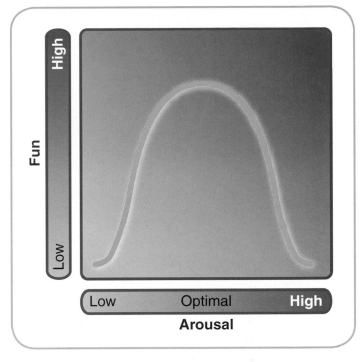

Figure 7.1 Relationship between fun and arousal.

young people because they increase arousal often to an optimal level, and therefore are fun. But not always. For some young people, sports aren't fun—they don't increase arousal enough or they create too much. As a coach you can work to ensure that your athletes are neither bored (not enough arousal) nor threatened to the point of anxiety (too much arousal).

Here are some ways you can help your athletes experience optimal arousal and thus flow:

▶ Fit the difficulty of the skills to be learned or performed to the ability of the athletes. You want the task to be difficult enough to be challenging, but not so difficult that they see no chance of success. This very important point is illustrated in figure 7.2. If athletes' abilities are high but the challenge is low, they will be bored. If athletes' abilities are low and the challenge is high, they will experience anxiety. But if their abilities are reasonably close to the challenge at hand, athletes are more likely to experience flow and have fun.

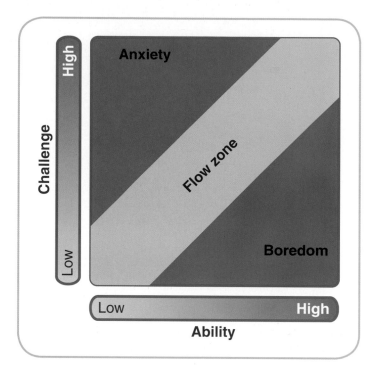

Figure 7.2 Increase the probability of experiencing flow by matching the challenge of the task to the ability of the athletes.

▶ Keep practice stimulating by using a wide variety of drills and activities to work on skills. Moreover, let your athletes help design some of the activities that will help them learn new skills.

▶ Keep everyone active rather than standing around for long periods waiting their turns. By following the suggestions presented later in this chapter and in chapter 8, you can make practices nearly as much fun as games.

▶ Avoid constant instruction during practices and games. Give athletes time when they don't have to pay attention to you and can get absorbed in the activity. Your yelling instructions constantly from the sidelines during contests does not permit athletes to experience flow.

▶ Do not constantly evaluate your athletes (as we discussed in chapter 6). The flow experience cannot occur when young athletes are being continuously evaluated or made to evaluate themselves— whether the evaluation is positive or negative. There is a time for evaluation, but it is not when the contest is in progress.

Other Sources of Fun

Besides the experience of optimal arousal and flow, athletes find fun in being with other young people who share their interest in sport. By recognizing this reason for participation in sports, you can create a team environment that gives athletes the opportunity to enjoy social interaction with their teammates. Try not to overregiment practices and contests, which greatly reduces opportunities for players to socialize and to engage in spontaneous and frivolous activities, both of which are enjoyable aspects of sport participation. Also, try to create an environment that is not so competitive that players feel they are playing *against* each other rather than *with* each other.

The results of several studies examining the reasons athletes quit sports reveal how important fun is to athletes. The most frequent reasons given for quitting are these:

▶ I found other activities more enjoyable.
▶ I lost interest.
▶ I didn't play enough.
▶ It was all work and no fun.
▶ I didn't like the coach.

Take the fun out of participating in sport, and you'll take the athletes out of the sport. And if they don't quit, their motivation will be seriously impaired.

How do you motivate athletes? One key way is to help them meet their need for fun by making the sport experience challenging and exciting, not boring or threatening. Another is to help athletes meet their need to feel worthy, which we consider next.

Need to Feel Worthy

We all share basic needs to feel competent, to experience some success, to believe we are worthy persons. In our society we quickly learn that our worth depends largely on our ability to achieve. Children as young as 5 years old understand this, and with respect to sports, they translate it to mean

Winning = Success
Losing = Failure

Consequently, participation in sports is potentially threatening to athletes because they equate their achievement with their self-worth. To win is to be successful, to be competent, to be a worthy person; to lose is to be a failure, to be incompetent, to be unworthy.

A reasonable amount of success reinforces athletes' sense of competency, which in turn reinforces their further pursuit of excellence. But if athletes fail to experience success, they may blame themselves for failure and attribute it to a lack of ability. With repeated failure, athletes may decide that if they cannot be certain of success, they can at least protect their dignity by avoiding failure. Emerging then from early success and failure experiences are two very different types of athletes: one who is *motivated to achieve success* and another who is *motivated to avoid failure*.

How Winners Think

Success-oriented athletes engage in drastically different reasoning about winning and losing than do failure-oriented athletes. Wendy Winner, a model success-oriented athlete, sees winning as a consequence of her ability, which gives her confidence in her ability to succeed again. When Wendy encounters an occasional failure, she is likely to blame it on insufficient effort; this robs failure of its threat to her self-worth because it doesn't reflect on her ability. To succeed, Wendy believes, she simply needs to try harder. Thus, failure increases her motivation rather than reduces it.

State of Mind

If you think you are beaten you are;
If you think you dare not, you don't;
If you want to win but think you can't;
It's almost a cinch you won't.

If you think you'll lose you're lost;
For out of the world we find
Success begins with a person's will;
It's all in a state of mind.

Life's battles don't always go
To the stronger and faster man,
But sooner or later the man who wins
Is the man who thinks he can.

—Author unknown

125

For Wendy, an occasional failure is inevitable when playing sports and is not a fault within herself. Thus she is willing to take reasonable risks of failure—risks that are necessary to achieve success. Wendy and athletes like her direct their energies to the challenges of the sport rather than to worry and self-doubt. They take credit for their success and accept responsibility for their failure. This is a healthy attitude, one you want to foster in your athletes. In my work as a sport psychologist over the years, I found that "Wendy Winner" resides in all great athletes.

How Losers Think

In contrast, meet Larry Loser, a failure-oriented athlete who is filled with self-doubts and anxiety. Larry tends to attribute his failures to a lack of ability and his infrequent successes to luck or to weak or incompetent opponents. Such thinking produces disaster; Larry blames himself for failure, yet takes little or no credit for his successes.

Athletes like Larry Loser believe they are powerless to change their plight because their early sport experiences have convinced them that no matter how hard they try, the outcome is always the same: failure. They conclude, "Well, trying didn't help, so my problem must be low ability. So why try?"

Because sport so clearly identifies winners and losers, failure-oriented athletes like Larry Loser have little choice in protecting their self-worth but to not participate or to maneuver to avoid failure. Although many such young people choose not to play sports, parental, coach, and peer pressure may keep Larry playing. When he does play, he has learned to protect his threatened self-worth in a variety of ways.

How Larry Loser Protects His Self Worth

The Token Effort Game

Rather than putting forth maximum effort, Larry almost unknowingly gives only token effort so that if he fails he can say he just didn't try hard enough. Why does he do this? Because if he gave maximum effort and failed, others would know he didn't have ability. Not to put forth maximum effort is less threatening, in Larry's thinking, than to have others discover that he lacks ability, which he equates with being unworthy. The tragedy of choosing not to put forth full effort, however, is that it increases the likelihood of failure in his desperate attempt to avoid it.

But the tragedy becomes even greater. Coaches usually reward effort because it seems fair—not everyone is skilled, but everyone can try. Yet for Larry Loser and failure-oriented athletes like him, to put forth full effort risks discovery that he lacks ability, so he doesn't. His failure to put forth full effort after encouragement from the coach leaves the coach puzzled or angry. The coach attributes it to a lack of motivation, but in reality Larry is far from unmotivated. Instead, he is highly motivated—but motivated to avoid the threat to his self-worth. It becomes a vicious circle.

Excuses, Excuses

Another common ploy of Larry Loser is to stay well armed with excuses. "I was robbed by the ump." "My leg hurts." "I don't have the right shoes." "Something got in my eye." "I don't feel good." And on and on.

Rejecting Success

Coaches with Larry Losers on the team often try to solve the problem by arranging some successful experiences for them. But once athletes begin thinking like Larry, they tend to reject success, which mystifies and frustrates coaches even more. Although failure-oriented athletes want to accept success to enhance their self-worth, they reject it because they fear they will be expected to succeed again. They may so fear impending success that they purposely perform so as to avoid winning. Not until failure-oriented athletes can learn to accept their own successes is there hope of enhancing their confidence in their ability and thus their self-worth.

You will find both Wendy Winners and Larry Losers on your team, as well as players with varying degrees of both athletes' characteristics. It's especially important that you recognize Larry Loser and those athletes who tend to be like him so that you do not misdiagnose their motivational problems. Although the problems of Larry Loser may seem unsolvable, they are not. You have to change the way they perceive winning and losing. I'll describe how to do that shortly.

Self-Fulfilling Prophecy

Just as athletes assign reasons to their successes and failures, so do you as a coach. These reasons—called attributions—in turn lead you to have certain expectancies of your athletes, which if conveyed to them may affect their motivation to perform. Kandace's case illustrates how this can occur.

Kandace ran track satisfactorily last season under Coach Woods, who encouraged her frequently in practices. This season, playing for a new coach, Ms. Clarkson, Kandace just can't get "on track." Never too confident, Kandace begins attributing her poor playing more and more to a lack of ability. She senses that Coach Clarkson doesn't think very much of her ability because she spends little time helping her and encourages her far less than Coach Woods did. As Kandace's self-doubts increase, she runs even worse, and slowly begins giving up. After a while, she shrugs off even an occasional good performance and encouragement from Coach Clarkson as flukes.

When Kandace fails to respond to her encouragement, Coach Clarkson becomes discouraged with Kandace's lack of effort, attributing it to laziness. Finally, in the hope of instilling the missing enthusiasm, Coach Clarkson takes Kandace off the first team and

has her run with the B team. Now convinced more than ever that she is worthless, Kandace quits the team.

Coach Clarkson clearly communicated to Kandace that she had lowered her expectations by sending Kandace to the B team. But coaches often communicate expectations in more indirect ways. For example, they more often reward players for whom they have higher expectations and spend less time with those for whom they have low expectations (privately thinking, Why waste my time with this kid?). Coaches may have closer relationships with their better players, permitting them to have more input about what the team is doing. Although these messages may be indirect, athletes easily pick them up.

When these expectations are conveyed to athletes, they may become self-fulfilling prophecies; that is, athletes may act in ways to fulfill what coaches have prophesied for them. These expectations-turned-prophecies may, of course, be either positive or negative. The steps in creating a self-fulfilling prophecy when coaching are summarized in figure 7.3.

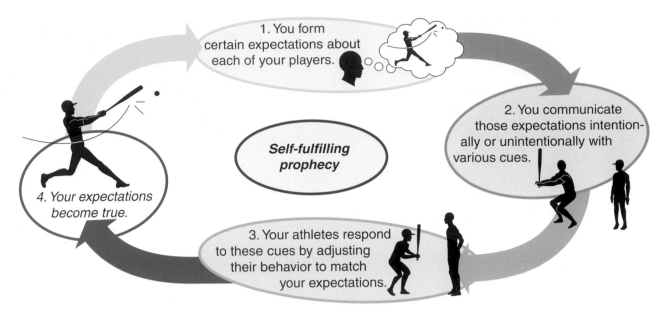

Figure 7.3 Steps in creating a self-fulfilling prophecy.

As we would expect, failure-oriented athletes are most vulnerable to negative expectations. When such athletes, already full of self-doubt, perceive that the coach has low expectations of them, what they suspected is confirmed: Coach thinks I'm no good, so why should I try? When positive expectations are communicated to failure-oriented athletes, they reject them for the same reasons they reject occasional success.

On the other hand, success-oriented athletes—whose self-confidence is strong—most often reject negative expectancies conveyed by coaches or others. Instead of fulfilling what has been prophesied for them, they work even harder to show that others are wrong. Positive expectations, of course, strengthen success-oriented athletes' beliefs in their own abilities.

By now you may be wondering what you can do to influence the motivation of your athletes. The success-oriented athlete apparently doesn't need to be motivated by you, and it seems you can do little to help the failure-oriented youngster. But don't despair—read on!

How Athletes Learn to Fear Failure

Organized sports are very different from the backyard sports most children first learn to play. Some differences are obvious: uniforms and regulation playing surfaces, rules and officials to enforce them, spectators and scorekeepers, and you: their coach. But you should be aware of other subtler differences, which are the root causes for athletes learning to fear failure. Understanding these causes will help you appreciate what I prescribe for overcoming motivation problems.

Emphasis on Performance, Not Learning

When young people are left to themselves to learn sport skills—without coaches, peer pressure, or spectators—they have an ingenious way of avoiding failure. Each time they do not obtain their goals, they simply lower them slightly, learn from their mistakes, and try again. A few practices and adjustments like these and success is virtually guaranteed. But they'll never achieve any difficult goals that way, you say? Wrong! When young people do succeed, they naturally raise their goals a little to keep the activity challenging. The result is that athletes tend to keep their goals near the upper limits of their current abilities. Through this self-regulated learning process, athletes see mistakes not as failures, but as a natural part of the learning process.

When young people begin playing organized sports, however, evaluation becomes public and official. The emphasis may shift from learning to performing. The mistakes and errors that are a natural part of the learning process may now be misinterpreted as failure to perform.

Unrealistic Goals

Something else happens when young people begin playing organized sports. They quickly observe that coaches prefer superior performance and tend to give greater recognition to the athletes who excel. Envious of their superior skills and desirous of similar recognition, less-skilled players attempt to be like the more-skilled ones. In doing so, these young athletes may set their goals too high for their present levels of skill.

If athletes themselves don't set unrealistically high goals, coaches or parents sometimes do. Coaches, for example, may set a performance goal for the entire team that is only within the grasp of the few best athletes. Parents who aspire to be stars vicariously through their children may also make the mistake of convincing their children to pursue goals that are beyond their reach.

Regardless of who is at fault, the result is the same—unrealistically high goals almost guarantee failure. They cause athletes to play in order to attain the goals set for them by others, not to meet their own. For example, if a parent pushes the goal of obtaining a college athletic scholarship, the odds are about 1 in 100; the odds of going on to play professionally in basketball, football, or baseball are less than 1 in 10,000. Tragically, athletes do not realize that such goals are unrealistic; they believe their performance is out of kilter and mistakenly accuse themselves of not having ability and thus being unworthy.

Extrinsic Rewards and Intrinsic Motivation

A third reason athletes learn to fear failure once they start playing organized sports is that the skills they have been trying to master for the sheer satisfaction of doing so (intrinsic reward) become subject to an elaborate system of extrinsic rewards. Trophies, medallions, ribbons, plaques, all-star team recognition, and so on, may cause a change in why young people play sports—a change that is not desirable. Rather than playing sports for self-satisfaction, athletes may begin to play primarily to earn these extrinsic rewards. The extrinsic rewards are given not for achieving personal goals, but for achieving goals set by others. Once again, athletes can find themselves pursuing unrealistic goals, thus dooming themselves to failure.

Overemphasis on extrinsic rewards has another negative consequence; it may result in an addiction. Hooked on the glitter of trophies and medals, such addicted athletes continually want more and bigger rewards to feed their growing habits. When the gold is no longer offered or within their capability to achieve, they see no value in continuing to participate.

How many athletic "junkies" are there? How often do trophies and medals (extrinsic rewards) undermine athletes' intrinsic motivation to play sports? We don't really know, but it need never happen if you help your athletes understand the meaning of these rewards.

The fact that extrinsic rewards can undermine intrinsic motivation does not mean that you should never give extrinsic rewards. As you'll learn in chapter 8, extrinsic rewards, when properly used, are excellent incentives for motivating athletes who are struggling to learn sport skills. And of course we all like to be recognized for our achievements and to have mementos of past accomplishments.

Our concern is not with the extrinsic rewards as such, but the meaning athletes attach to them. You should continually let your athletes know by word and deed that extrinsic rewards are only tokens of recognition for achieving the larger goal of acquiring and performing sport skills. These tokens do not make one person better than another, they do not guarantee future success, and they are not the primary reason for playing sports. You should help your athletes remember instead that the most important reason for participating in sport is the participation itself. When athletes understand this message, extrinsic rewards are unlikely to undermine their intrinsic motivation to play the game.

Now you know three ways that participation in organized sports may cause athletes to fear failure.

▶ The mistakes and errors that are a natural part of the learning process are misinterpreted as failures.

▶ As a result of competitive pressures, athletes set unrealistically high goals that, when not attained, lead them to conclude that they are failures.

▶ Athletes begin to play for extrinsic rewards rather than to attain personal goals.

Do you know any athletes who think this way? Do you coach in ways that help athletes develop these destructive perceptions? It's easy to do if winning is your sole focus. Keep reading to find out how to help your athletes overcome these misperceptions.

Enhancing Athletes' Motivation

Nearly everything I have suggested in previous chapters and will discuss in chapters to come will be directly or indirectly helpful in enhancing the motivation of your athletes. Your decision to put the well-being of athletes first and winning second, along with adopting a cooperative rather than a command style of coaching, are essential prerequisites. The communication skills discussed in chapter 6 and the positive discipline methods described in chapter 8 also are integral to successfully motivating athletes. In this chapter I have specified some ways that you can help athletes fulfill their need to have fun. What remains is to find a way to help each young athlete feel worthy. The goal is a difficult one; *you must find a way for every athlete to experience success in an environment in which winners are few and losers are many.*

The simplest solution is to eliminate losing; in that way, the vicious cycle that produces failure-oriented athletes can never begin. Of course that's not possible in sports; besides, learning to lose has positive aspects. But as a coach once said, "Every time I lose, I learn something, but I don't want to get too smart!" The solution lies in changing the way athletes (and coaches) interpret their losing experiences.

Success Is Not Winning

The basic problem about this issue of worthiness is that athletes learn from parents, coaches, teammates, and the media to gauge their self-worth largely by whether they win or lose. The devastating result is that athletes can maintain their sense of self-worth only by making others feel unworthy. The most

important thing you can do as a coach to enhance the motivation of your athletes is to change this yardstick of success.

Winning is important, but it must become secondary to striving to achieve personal goals. This is the cardinal principle for understanding motivation in sport:

> **Athletes must see success in terms of achieving their own goals rather than surpassing the performances of others.**

It is a principle easy to state, but oh so difficult to achieve. If you can help athletes understand and implement this principle, you will do more to help them become excellent athletes—and successful adults—than through any other coaching action.

Team goals should not be confused with personal goals. In fact, team goals are hardly needed if one of the personal goals of each team member is to make the best contribution possible, given his or her current skill level. Team goals such as winning so many games or this or that championship are not useful, and they actually undermine the type of personal goals just described. Team goals more appropriately deal with learning to play together as a unit, respecting each other, having fun, and playing with good sportsmanship. Accomplishing these team goals and each athlete's personal goals is more important than winning. Besides, when athletes achieve both individual and team goals, winning usually takes care of itself.

Personal goals are specific performance or behavioral milestones rather than goals concerning the outcome of winning or losing. The following are examples of personal goals that focus on performance and other behavioral objectives:

▶ My goal is to jump 1 inch farther than I did last week.

▶ I want to improve my backhand so that I can hit it deep into the corner 75 percent of the time.

▶ I want to learn to relax more and enjoy playing.

Consequence of Setting Personal Goals

When winning the game becomes secondary to achieving personal goals, athletes are much more motivated to practice. Practices provide athletes opportunities to work toward their personal goals with assistance from the coach. Contests are viewed not as the end-all, but as periodic tests along the way toward achieving personal goals. Athletes do not judge themselves as having succeeded or failed on the basis of whether

Setting Realistic Personal Goals

By placing greater emphasis on achieving personal goals, athletes can gain control over an important part of their sport participation—their own success. The important thing here is to set realistic goals; by doing so, athletes ensure themselves a reasonable degree of success. In the face of all of the competitive pressures and parental and teammate influences, you must help each athlete keep a realistic perspective in setting goals suitable for him or her alone.

they win or lose, but in terms of achieving the specific performance and behavioral goals they have set.

Evidence from many sources indicates that not only outstanding athletes but also less successful ones who have most enjoyed and benefited from sport focus on personal goals, not the defeat of others. The consequence of this perspective is incredibly positive. When athletes are allowed to set their own goals, guided by the coach when necessary to make sure they are realistic, they become responsible for their own progress. They feel in control and take credit for their successes and responsibility for their failures. As stated earlier, this is the first step in motivating athletes.

To help athletes set realistic goals, you must be able to assess each athlete's skill level. This brings up another crucial point, one you perhaps have thought about while reading this chapter.

Recognizing Athletes' Limitations

Athletes do not always perform poorly because they lack motivation. Poor performance may be a signal that personal limits have been reached, that athletes are performing up to their ability. Neither increased effort nor all the confidence in the world will improve their ability to perform. One

of your more difficult tasks as a coach is to determine whether an athlete is performing at her or his limits.

Many athletes need help in learning to face their limitations without devaluing themselves. Rather than conveying the nonsense that every athlete can become a superstar or a professional, you should encourage your athletes to learn their limits for themselves. Only in this way can they learn to maintain realistic goals. But if coaches make athletes believe that they have no limits, that to accept limits is loathsome, then athletes may push themselves to seek unrealistic goals, leading to eventual failure, and perhaps even to personal injury.

Realistic Personal Goals

When coaches help athletes set realistic goals, athletes inevitably experience more success and feel more competent. By becoming more competent, they gain confidence and can tackle skills of moderate difficulty without fearing failure. They discover that their efforts do result in more favorable outcomes and that falling short is most likely caused by insufficient effort. Realistic goals rob failure of its threat. Rather than indicating that athletes are not worthy, failure indicates that they should try harder.

De-emphasize winning and reemphasize attaining personal goals. This principle is

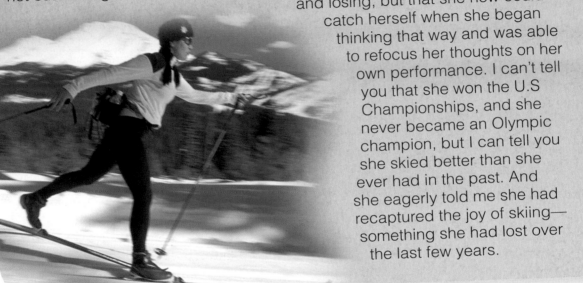

Performance Goals

After months of working with a talented cross-country skier who was a member of the U.S. Olympic Ski Team, I got a call from her after the U.S. National Championships. "I got it. I got it," she blurted out. "I finally got it!" For years she had been shackled with focusing on winning when racing, which often meant focusing on "not losing." We had spent many hours practicing to refocus her goals on realistic times for a 5K race, and evaluating her success or failure on how well she achieved those goals.

She enthusiastically told me how learning to focus on performance goals, not outcome goals, did not come easy after years of thinking about winning and losing, but that she now could catch herself when she began thinking that way and was able to refocus her thoughts on her own performance. I can't tell you that she won the U.S Championships, and she never became an Olympic champion, but I can tell you she skied better than she ever had in the past. And she eagerly told me she had recaptured the joy of skiing— something she had lost over the last few years.

the key to meeting athletes' needs to feel worthy—not only to maintain their self-worth but also to develop it further. This principle is essential to enhancing the motivation of your athletes.

From Motivation to Anxiety

To this point we've been concerned exclusively with maintaining and increasing motivation because we know that being motivated is essential to performing well and enjoying participation. Be wary of the belief that more motivation is always better, however; athletes can be too motivated or aroused. Let me explain.

Arousal–Performance Relationship

Just as there is an optimal level of arousal for having fun, there is an optimal level of arousal for performing well as shown in figure 7.4. When athletes are aroused too little or too much, they do not perform as well as they might; but if they are aroused just the right amount, their performance will be better.

Optimal arousal level varies for different sport skills. As shown in figure 7.5, high-precision sport skills requiring fine motor control, such as putting in golf or any skill in the shooting sports or bowling, are best performed with lower levels of arousal; sports such as basketball, baseball, and volleyball are played better at slightly higher levels of arousal; and skills requiring large muscle movements, such as weightlifting or tackling and blocking in football, are best done with even higher levels of arousal. Optimal arousal levels also differ from athlete to athlete. One athlete may perform a sport skill better with considerably less arousal than another athlete may need.

If some motivation is good, why isn't more better? When athletes are too motivated or aroused, they become anxious and worried about whether they will be able to succeed—especially failure-oriented athletes. Anxiety causes muscles to tense so athletes' movements are not as smooth and easy as when their muscles are more relaxed. Players think about how they are doing rather than concentrating on just doing. Consequently, their attention is not well centered on the contest, and they may feel out of control.

As you probably recall, these conditions are precisely the opposite of those necessary for experiencing flow. Athletes perform their best (have their peak performances) when they are in the flow state, which by definition means that they are optimally aroused.

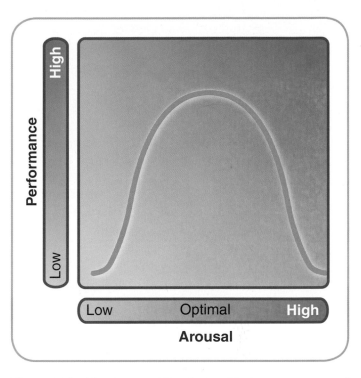

Figure 7.4 The inverted **U** relationship between arousal and performance.

Just as you must help your athletes increase their motivation to an optimal level, you must also help them decrease it when they are too anxious. To do so, you need to understand why they become anxious.

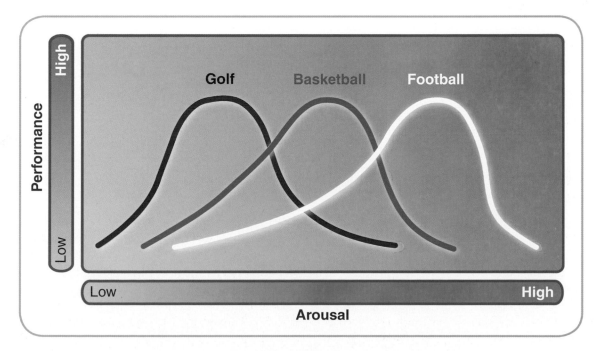

Figure 7.5 Optimal arousal levels for peak performance in different sports.

Causes of Anxiety

The fundamental cause of anxiety in sport is athletes' uncertainty about whether they can meet the demands of coaches, parents, peers, or themselves when meeting these demands is important to them. The more uncertainty athletes have and the more important an outcome is to them, the greater their anxiety.

Keeping athletes uncertain about whether they will make the team or the starting lineup, or get to play at all, can increase their levels of anxiety. Other causes of anxiety are being reminded about the uncertainty of winning, or being made to feel insecure about their social status or importance to the team.

The Pep Talk

Some coaches seem particularly insensitive to the emotional states of athletes and thus do not recognize the need to reduce the anxiety of some athletes by decreasing the uncertainty and importance of the game. Instead, they give a traditional pregame pep talk that reminds athletes of the importance of the game and the uncertainties associated with competition. For insufficiently motivated athletes, a pep talk may increase arousal toward the optimal level. For athletes who are already optimally aroused, this additional hype may push them beyond their optimal arousal level, creating anxiety. And for already anxious athletes, it is petrifying!

Most coaches probably give pep talks out of tradition and to help alleviate their own anxiety. Unfortunately, pep talks may do as much harm as good. Words of encouragement by the coach prior to the game of course are appropriate, but seeking to instill motivation in athletes through an oratorical firestorm fails because it does not address the needs of individual athletes. Although one athlete may need a coach's verbal "kick in the behind," another may need quiet reassurance.

Many factors make sport important to athletes. As we have already seen, winning itself has a great deal of importance because athletes link winning with their self-worth. In addition, publicizing the outcome of the game, adding pageantry to the game, and of course offering all types of extrinsic rewards increase the game's importance.

You can help alleviate the anxiety of overly anxious athletes by finding ways to reduce both the uncertainty about how their performance will be evaluated and the importance they attach to the game. We already have discovered one powerful way to do this. Helping athletes change the criterion for evaluating themselves from winning to achieving their realistic personal goals goes a long way toward removing the threat that causes anxiety. With an emphasis on personal goals, athletes are not attempting to defeat an opponent of uncertain ability, but only to achieve their own performance goals. When athletes do not link their self-worth to winning and losing, sports are defused of their threat and athletes do not fear failure.

Help your athletes focus on achieving personal goals, not winning, and they'll be less anxious and have less fear of failure.

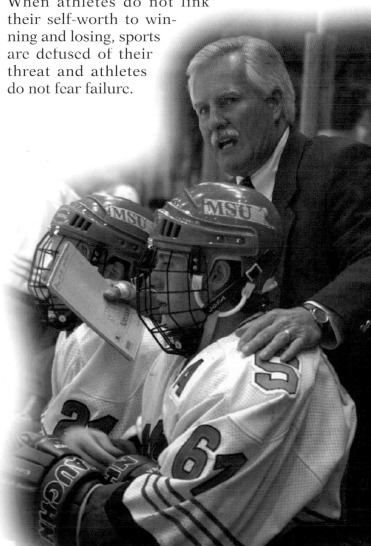

Coaching Yourself:
Managing Your Stress

Coaching can be immensely stressful, and when stress is experienced over an extended period without relief, it leads to "burnout," one of the major occupational hazards of coaching. Coaches experience stress when they are uncertain about the outcome of their situation and the outcome is important to them. Uncertainty occurs (1) when you perceive that more is being demanded of you, either by others or by yourself, than what you perceive you may be capable of delivering, or (2) when the outcome will be determined by factors out of your control. For example, you may worry about your relationships with players (the leading cause of stress among coaches) and about winning, both factors that are not entirely under your control, but for which you are commonly held accountable.

The first step to managing your stress is understanding that stress is caused by a combination of environmental, or situational, factors and your perceptions of those factors. Without a doubt the coaching environment is loaded with potential sources of stress, including

▶ sport administrators and supporters demanding that your team win;

▶ complex and demanding relationships with players;

▶ time pressures to complete many tasks, some of which seem to have little to do with coaching;

▶ invasions of privacy; and

▶ time-pressured decision making before and during contests.

Although these demanding situations are the stimuli that trigger stress, they are not the *cause* of stress. The cause of stress is your perceptions of these situations. You can see the situation as demanding an overwhelming amount from you or as a challenge and opportunity to demonstrate your capability. You can worry endlessly about the things you cannot control, or you can focus on being certain you have done everything in your control to achieve a favorable outcome. You can perceive the situation as absolutely the most important thing in your life (and if a favorable outcome is not obtained, life won't be worth living), or you can place the outcome in a more reasonable perspective.

Here are four general steps to help you address the stress you may encounter as a coach:

1. Identify what you believe are the sources of stress in your environment and determine which ones you may be able to change so that they are less stressful and which ones are out of your control. For example, you can't change the uncertainty about winning or how your players will play on any certain day (although good coaching can reduce that uncertainty), but you may be able to organize your time better so you can manage all those tasks that distract you from planning your practices better. You can't change the pressure parents may place on you, but you can use your improved communication and relationship skills to educate them about your coaching philosophy and team goals, and to develop better relationships with them.

2. Of course you won't be able to remove all of the potential sources of stress in your environment, but you can change your *perceptions* about these factors. After failing to convince your sport administrator to stop pressuring you to engage in unethical activities, you can change your perception of the situation by ignoring such requests, finding comfort in coaching ethically,

and discounting the importance of this coaching position should you be terminated. Changing your perceptions about your environment is not easy to do, but it is entirely under your control and thus is an effective way to manage your stress.

3. Find strength in a moral coaching philosophy that embraces the principles discussed in part I. When you give your best in an effort to do "right" by all those you influence as a coach, you can always be at peace with yourself.

4. If you're unable to work through these first three steps by yourself, seek professional assistance. Psychologists have a rich set of tools to help you find ways to manage stress effectively and enjoy your coaching more.

For additional information on stress management I recommend reading Martha Davis, Elizabeth Robbins Eshelman, and Matthew McKay's book, *The Relaxation and Stress Reduction Workbook, Fifth Edition*. Oakland, CA: New Harbinger Publications, 2000.

Questions for Reflection

▶ What motivates you to coach? Do you believe that people are motivated to fulfill their needs? **(p. 120)**

▶ What are the two most important needs of athletes? **(p. 121)**

▶ Why is intrinsic motivation superior to extrinsic motivation for athletes? **(p. 122)**

▶ What can you do to help your athletes experience optimal arousal, or flow? **(p. 123)**

▶ How do success-oriented athletes view winning and losing? **(p. 125)**

▶ How do failure-oriented athletes view winning and losing? What are some strategies they adopt to protect their sense of self-worth? **(p. 126)**

▶ In what way do coaches' expectations for athletes become self-fulfilling prophesies? **(p. 127)**

▶ Why are failure-oriented athletes especially vulnerable to self-fulfilling prophesies? **(p. 128)**

▶ What are three causes of athletes learning to fear failure? **(p. 130)**

▶ Do you focus on your athletes' personal goals rather than on winning? Doing so can enhance athletes' motivation. **(p. 131)**

▶ How can you help your athletes set realistic personal goals and recognize their limitations? **(p. 132)**

▶ What are some appropriate team goals? **(p. 132)**

▶ What are some causes of athlete anxiety? How can you help your athletes manage their anxiety levels? **(p. 136)**

▶ How can you manage your own stress as a coach? **(p. 138)**

Reference

Jackson, Susan, and Csikszentmihalyi, Mihaly. 1999. *Flow in sports*. Champaign, IL: Human Kinetics.

8

Managing Your Athletes' Behavior

"I decided to try rowing with a crew, and from the very beginning, I was happy with my choice. I enjoyed the sport and the camaraderie, and I especially liked my coach. Ken's thoughtfulness and good-natured personality earned him the admiration of the wide-eyed freshman that I was at the time. Unlike so many of the male coaches I'd had, he was not macho at all, but very soft-spoken, rarely raising his voice ☞

in disapproval or for emphasis. He was sweet-tempered, patient, intelligent, charismatic, and inspirational. He could motivate me as no one ever had before, or will again.

On the rare occasions when Ken did get angry, it commanded our attention. The only such moment I can remember was early in the fall semester, when our crew members were still learning about team commitment and the importance of timeliness. One morning, one crew member showed up at practice about ten minutes late. . . . It is critical that all the members of the team arrive on time, since practice consists of rowing in boats made for a set number of athletes. When there's a no-show, the boat is impossible to row properly.

Ken waited until all the other teams had launched their boats. Then he called our novice team together in the boathouse bay. After everyone had gathered, he slammed the door and stood quietly for a few moments in the eerie solitude of the deserted boathouse. He proceeded to explain how tardiness was not merely a matter of slowing down practice. It was effectively 'cursing out' every other member of the team. It was saying that you didn't care about the goals that the team had set. Ken's point came through loud and clear. For the rest of the year, practices began on time." (Glennon and Leavitt 2000, 116-117).

Reprinted, by permission, from Glennon and Leavitt 2000.

You've learned the basics of communication and motivation as it applies to coaching sports. Now let's apply this knowledge and other information to helping you manage or guide your athletes' behavior, which is an essential part of being a successful coach. It will determine how administrators, fellow coaches, parents, your players, and the public perceive you as a coach. It will influence the quality of your practices and the team's cohesiveness when facing challenging competitive situations. And it will be a major factor in determining your enjoyment of coaching and thus how long you're likely to coach.

Most people begin their coaching careers with little or no training in managing player behavior. Instead it's strictly on-the-job learning, but the mistakes that go with such learning can be ever so costly to you and your players. So in this chapter I'll show you how to manage your players' behavior using positive discipline, not only to correct misbehavior but also to help players learn essential life skills. Through positive discipline your players will play better because they'll have more productive practices, be more motivated, and enjoy playing under your leadership. You'll find far greater job satisfaction, and thus hopefully continue coaching for many years.

What Is Positive Discipline?

Discipline is a negative term to most of us, but the root word of *discipline* is *disciple,* which conjures up more positive images. A disciple is a person who follows the teachings of a mentor. As a coach you are a mentor, and your players are disciples. The positive discipline* approach views discipline as training that develops self-control in your disciples.

Discipline begins with *instruction,* not only to develop sports skills, but also to develop life skills. Instruction is followed by *training,* which provides your players with opportunities to practice these skills. As they practice, you help them by *correcting* their mistakes (figure 8.1).

Sometimes coaches assume that their athletes know certain sport skills, know how to manage their emotions, know right from wrong, and possess self-discipline. Thus when players err or misbehave, coaches immediately correct the behavior. However, the player may not know how to perform the skill or behave appropriately, or may not have mastered self-control. In such cases the coach needs to first instruct, then provide opportunities to practice, and finally to correct mistakes. Positive discipline is about understanding that discipline is more than just correcting behavior; it's about teaching behavior too.

When using the positive discipline approach, you must distinguish between two types of mistakes or misbehaviors. The first is when players try to perform the skill or behavior but cannot because they do not know how to or have not yet mastered it. The second is when the player willfully misbehaves. When players have been instructed and they possess the skill or behavior to respond appropriately but willfully choose not to, then you need to take prompt action

*Jane Nelson first coined the term *positive discipline* in her book by the same name. I have adapted the term for coaching in this chapter.

| Instruction | Training | Correction |

Figure 8.1 The discipline process.

to correct the behavior. The key here is knowing when your players need instruction and when they need correction.

Positive discipline is an attitude toward coaching players that is constructive, not destructive. It helps you provide enough guidance to direct and teach without directing so much that you stifle players' growth and motivation. It's knowing how to hold that bar of soap—not squeezing so hard that the bar squirts from your hands, but applying just enough pressure to keep it in your hand. As the coach, you are responsible for providing direction and setting limits on players' behaviors, but you do so seeking to teach self-discipline and to enhance every player's self-worth.

Why Positive Discipline Is Better

I believe that most coaches begin their coaching career thinking they'll be positive, encouraging their players to master skills and compete effectively. But then they're confronted with players who challenge their authority by skirting the rules, seeking attention by disrupting practices, provoking other players by taunting, and displaying poor sportsmanship when competing. Without training, many coaches resort to the command style

(see chapter 3) for managing misbehavior, which I'll call negative discipline and at its extreme can only be described as "mean and nasty." Others try to ignore the misbehavior or address the problems so ineptly that the behavior problems escalate to the point at which the coach loses control of the team.

Command-style coaches who use negative discipline manage behavior using blame, shame, and pain. They make all of the decisions and rarely permit players to have any input about the team's activities. In fact, thinking and problem solving by the players are discouraged. Players are blamed for defeats by publicly identifying their mistakes. Discipline is maintained through humiliation, making players feel insecure about their status on the team, and fear of punishment.

Sport has a long history of coaches using negative discipline, probably because it works in the short term, but the cost is monstrous. It creates hostility among players, which creates a viperous team environment harming performance and destroying enjoyment for both players and coaches. When playing out of fear rather than enthusiasm to succeed, players are more anxious and cautious and perform less well. More important, the negative approach denies athletes the opportunity to gain all of the benefits of sports—learning life skills, developing values, and enhancing self-worth. Some players will quit teams with coaches who use negative discipline; others love playing the sport so much that they will endure coaches who use this approach.

Cooperative-style coaches, as described in chapter 3, exemplify the positive discipline approach. These coaches create a team environment that nurtures players' self-esteem and is based on mutual respect between coach and player. Players are made to feel that they are an important part of the team, and thus are encouraged to practice sport and life skills without blame, shame, or pain. Mistakes are seen as part of the learning process, and because players feel "psychologically safe," they learn and perform much better. Coaches who use positive discipline inspire excitement, enthusiasm, and positive motivation. They use a wide variety of activities with well-planned lessons that keep players maximally engaged and motivated. Positive discipline coaches strive to teach players self-discipline so that they don't need to discipline.

If an Athlete Is Coached With . . .

If an athlete is coached with criticism, she learns to condemn;
If an athlete is coached with hostility, he learns to fight;
If an athlete is coached with ridicule, she learns to hate;
If an athlete is coached with shame, he learns to feel guilty;
If an athlete is coached with tolerance, she learns to be patient;
If an athlete is coached with encouragement, he learns to be confident;
If an athlete is coached with praise, she learns to appreciate;
If an athlete is coached with fairness, he learns justice;
If an athlete is coached with consistency, she learns to trust;
If an athlete is coached with respect, he learns to respect himself.

Author unknown.

The positive discipline approach may not come easy to you. Perhaps you've used negative discipline to varying degrees for years, maybe in raising your children. There's a good likelihood it's how you were coached and how coaches you greatly admire coach. But if you believe that participation in sport can do more for young people than teach them how to win games, that it can teach them how to be better human beings, then positive discipline is well worth mastering.

Positive discipline involves preventive discipline and corrective discipline. You'll drastically reduce misbehavior when you implement the six preventive discipline steps described in the next section. In the last section you'll learn the guidelines for corrective discipline, to use when infrequent misbehaviors do occur.

Preventive Discipline

The cliche "The best defense is a good offense" expresses what preventive discipline is about. There are six offensive steps you can take to defend against the disciplinary problems that drive some coaches out of the profession. These six steps—a pyramid to preventive discipline success—are shown in figure 8.2, and each is discussed in detail in the sections that follow.

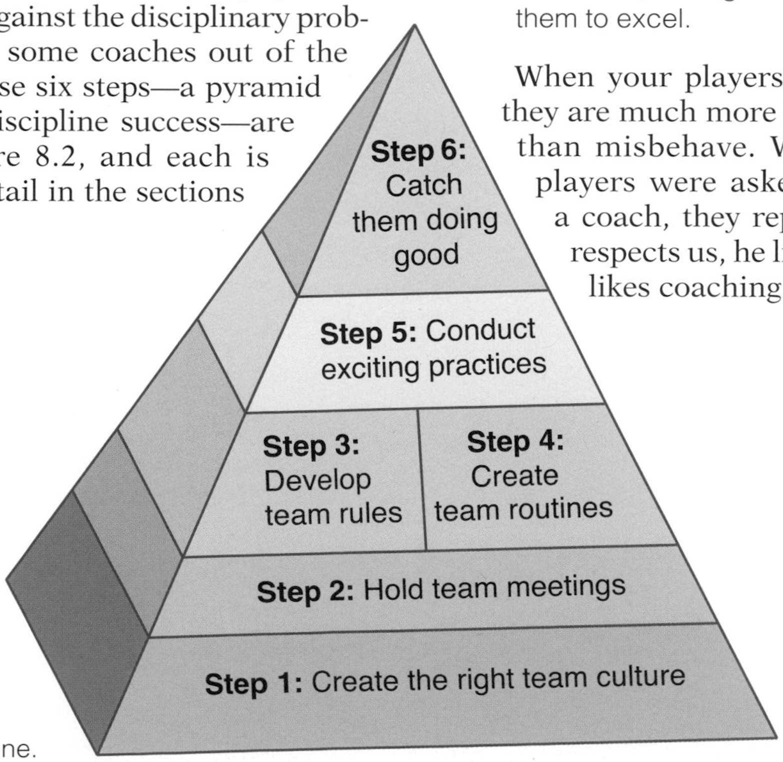

STEP 1: Create the Right Team Culture

We considered team culture in chapter 3, and you may have a sense of what constitutes the right team culture from the previous discussion of positive discipline. With regard to managing your players' behavior, nothing is more important in creating the right team culture than caring about your players, caring based on kindness but also firmness. Players quickly discern that you care when you

▶ take the time to learn who they are on and off the field;

▶ listen to them and take their viewpoints seriously;

▶ believe in them and let them know they are an important part of the team;

▶ encourage them to see mistakes as opportunities to learn;

▶ respect them enough to involve them in team decision making; and

▶ skillfully and respectfully guide their behaviors, setting limits and challenging them to excel.

When your players feel cared about, they are much more likely to cooperate than misbehave. When high school players were asked why they liked a coach, they replied, "Because he respects us, he listens to us, and he likes coaching."

Figure 8.2
The six steps of preventive discipline.

Step 6: Catch them doing good

Step 5: Conduct exciting practices

Step 3: Develop team rules

Step 4: Create team routines

Step 2: Hold team meetings

Step 1: Create the right team culture

and needed on the team. It's one in which coaches build players' self-esteem rather than humiliate them. In a psychologically safe environment players feel they can risk making mistakes to progress to a higher level without condemnation or embarrassment.

Have you noticed that when you're treated with respect and dignity, you feel much more inclined to reciprocate that respect and dignity? So create a team environment in which your players feel obligated to treat you and their teammates with respect and dignity.

STEP 2: Hold Team Meetings

If there is anything that the world has too much of, it's meetings. Nevertheless, I'm a strong advocate for purposeful team meetings that are effectively organized and conducted.

Reasons to Meet

Team meetings have traditionally been used to introduce offensive and defensive tactics and to review video of previous performances; these are valuable uses of team meetings. However, one caution when having team meetings to review previous performances. It is so easy to focus on errors and do so in a way that embarrasses and humiliates players who have made mistakes. The likely consequence of doing this to a player is not a better performance, but greater anxiety and caution in future play. Here are five good reasons for team meetings.

1. Team meetings can provide your players with information that will help them be better athletes. Here's a sample list of topics:

   —Nutrition for athletes, including pregame meals
   —Playing in the heat
   —Psychological preparation for competition
   —Strength and power training
   —Maintaining flexibility
   —Anabolic steroid use
   —Alcohol and tobacco use
   —The facts on various food supplements
   —Off-season training

When you like what you're doing, it shows—and it rubs off on those around you. Coaches who are positive and encouraging create a team culture that nurtures winning attitudes among their players. Be happy when you coach; it's a privilege you should enjoy!

If it's part of your personality, use humor to decrease tension or frustration and to simply add levity to the hard work of conditioning and mastering skills. But use humor correctly. Don't make players the brunt of your jokes by diminishing their self-worth. Laugh with, not at, your players.

The right team culture is also a safe environment both physically and psychologically. A physically safe environment includes good facilities and equipment, good instructions and appropriate progressions to master complex skills, and constant supervision of the players. A psychologically safe environment is one in which players feel they are wanted

2. As mentioned in chapter 4, team meetings are valuable opportunities to discuss important character education issues. The team meeting is a good place to discuss incidents in practice and games of good and poor sportsmanship. Present the situation and then invite your players to comment on what they think is appropriate and inappropriate behavior. Don't make this a lecture; skillfully guide the discussion.

3. The team meeting is the appropriate place to develop the consequences for violations of team rules. When a serious violation of a team rule occurs, you may want to have the team determine the appropriate consequence for the athlete.

4. Team meetings are also valuable for problem solving. If team practices are uninspired, see if you can root out the reason through a constructive conversation with your players. If the team is struggling with one aspect of their performance in games, see if the team can identify the cause and recommend solutions. If the team needs to decide a course of action, such as going to one tournament versus another, you can share making this decision with them in a meeting.

5. Team meetings are wonderful opportunities to exchange compliments and appreciations— that is, to give players "warm fuzzies." Although players and coaches initially are often uncomfortable telling other players something positive in a public forum, some guidance from you in encouraging such action will produce positive results. I recommend that at every team meeting you call on three to five players to stand up and give a compliment to a teammate. It's a great way to end a meeting.

Team meetings take time, both to prepare for and to conduct. Some coaches see this meeting time as time that could be spent conditioning or practicing the techniques and tactics of the sport. I believe that well-planned team meetings are a valuable way to help your athletes become better players and better people.

Conducting Team Meetings

How frequently should you hold team meetings? That depends on your situation, but for many sports two 30-minute meetings per week during the preseason and one 30-minute meeting per week during the season provides sufficient opportunity to address the many issues that merit team discussion. Here are a few guidelines for conducting the team meeting:

▶ Decide on the appropriate time and location for the meeting. Should the meeting be held as part of your practice, or before or after your practice session? Or should you have the team meeting separate from regular practice? Will the meeting work best on the court or playing field, in the bleachers, or in the classroom? Consider where you will maximize the players' attention and opportunity to learn in selecting the location.

▶ Arrange the seating to be appropriate for the purpose of the meeting. If you will be

providing information or using visual aids, then classroom-style seating is best. When you discuss team issues or exchange warm fuzzies, a team circle is better so that everyone can see one another.

▶ At the first meeting agree on rules for conducting the meeting. See the YMCA rules on page 116 as a starting point.

▶ Invite players to submit topics to you for the agenda.

▶ Keep the meeting informative and positive.

▶ Don't let a planned 30-minute meeting become an hour-long lecture by you. Your players will quickly dread such meetings.

▶ End the meeting with a quick round of "warm fuzzies" expressed by the players to one another.

STEP 3: Develop Team Rules

An essential part of preventive discipline is providing players with guidance on appropriate and inappropriate behavior and their responsibilities as members of the team. You provide this guidance partly through a formal set of team rules, and partly by establishing team routines (routines are discussed in the next section). In this section, you'll have an opportunity to thoughtfully establish a set of rules that will form your team policy. First, we'll look at guidelines for creating team rules, and then we'll look at examples of rules that you may want to consider for your team policy (i.e., your collection of rules). When players break rules, there must be consequences. So we'll provide some examples of, and guidelines for creating, consequences.

Rules About Making Rules

▶ Rules are best when they describe specific behaviors that can be observed and enforced. Unenforceable rules will not be taken seriously by athletes.

▶ Develop a list of rules that are needed to govern team behavior, but keep the list as brief as possible.

▶ State rules in positive terms, defining what players ought to do, not just what to avoid. Rules such as "No shirt, no shoes, no service" are a turnoff to many people.

▶ Rules should reflect mutual respect and responsibility between you and your players.

▶ Rules should be specific and clear. Imagine a road sign that said: Drive at a prudent speed. Vague rules leave room for misinterpretation. On the other hand, don't make rules overly restrictive so that they violate dignity or common sense.

▶ Rules and responsibilities should serve your players, not vice versa. Players are less likely to follow rules that they see as stupid or punitive. Rules should be created for a good reason, not just because you said so.

▶ Establish logical consequences for rule violations. We'll discuss these further later.

▶ Provide the players with the rules and their consequences—what becomes your team policies—as part of their player handbook (see chapter 18 about guidelines for a player handbook). Some coaches like to post the team rules on the walls of the locker room, but I think this is unnecessary if you've discussed the rules in a team meeting and you provide players with a team handbook containing the rules.

▶ Remind the players of your team policies periodically.

Guidelines for Creating Rules

You'll first need to decide whether you want to set the rules yourself or involve your players. Some coaching educators believe that players should help set the team rules because they will own them more, and the process of developing them through a team meeting teaches responsibility. If that can be achieved, it is highly desirable. However, what commonly happens in such a meeting is that coaches find they need to direct their players to such a great extent to develop acceptable rules that the coaches in fact have set the rules—and the players see this for what it is.

Consequences for Rule Violations

Rules obviously are ineffective if no consequences exist for violations. Players should know that if they break a rule, they can expect an appropriate consequence. For example, you may have a team rule that players will not use profanity. If players use profanity, you can have the following schedule of consequences:

▶ *First incident:* The player is warned.

▶ *Second incident:* The player must spend one hour picking up trash or cleaning the facility.

▶ *Third and repeated incidents:* The player misses one game per incident.

Although I recommend that coaches establish the team rules, I think it is very helpful to ask your players to help develop the consequences for violating team rules and then agree to them. Players who have been involved in setting the consequences are more likely to make better choices about their actions.

Coaches often want to know when it is appropriate to cut a player from the team as a consequence for misbehavior. There is no easy answer to this difficult question. You will have to weigh how much the player's misbehavior is hurting the team versus how much the team may help the problem player. Sometimes coaches cut players because they don't want to hassle with irritating and disrupting misbehaviors, and they are more inclined to do so with players who are less likely to help the team win. If you embrace the challenge of helping young people become not only better athletes but also better human beings, then you should only cut a player when you conclude that the cost to the team of the player's misdeeds is greater than the potential help you can give the player.

Guidelines for Developing Consequences for Rule Violations

▶ Consequences need to be seen by the majority of the team as being fair, appropriate to the misbehavior, equitable, and sufficient in response to the offense. Your goal in setting consequences is to control misbehavior and provide justice for victims, and at the same time to encourage and maintain appropriate behaviors while discouraging inappropriate behaviors.

▶ It is helpful to have three to five consequences that are listed in sequential order for each rule. Consequences may include a five-minute time-out, not being allowed to practice, calling the athlete's parents, or suspension from a contest. Each consequence should be more severe than the previous one. Multiple consequences let you provide more severe consequences for more severe violations or for repeated offenses that were not discontinued when a less severe consequence was invoked.

▶ Consequences should be logical, not just punitive. Consider the example of a player who shows up late to practice and is made to run 2 miles after practice. First, the consequence uses physical activity as a punishment, something you definitely want to avoid if you hope to encourage your players to be active for a lifetime. Second, being late has nothing to do with the player's conditioning, the logical reason for making the player run (unless the entire team had run 2 miles to warm up and the player avoided that exercise by being late). A logical consequence would be to require the tardy athlete to come to practice 30 minutes earlier than the other players and help the coach or assistants prepare the facility for the practice.

▶ Don't develop consequences that you cannot live with.

▶ Plan consequences in advance for common misbehaviors, and don't respond in haste when you're uncertain what an appropriate consequence should be. It's OK to take some time to think about an appropriate consequence and let the athlete know that.

▶ Consequences should be delivered respectfully, and definitely not with anger.

Developing Your Team Policies

▶ Your team policies must be in compliance with the policies of any governing body that has authority over your team. You must know these policies and incorporate them into your team policies.

▶ Revisit your coaching philosophy by reviewing part I to reaffirm or modify your coaching objectives and coaching style. Your team policies should be an expression of your coaching philosophy.

▶ Obtain copies of other team policies from coaches you know or by searching the Internet. Evaluate these policies, adopting those compatible with your coaching philosophy and modifying others to make them consistent with your viewpoint.

▶ Use chapters 4, 5, 8, and 17 of this book to help prepare your team policies.

▶ Create a team policy committee consisting of your assistant coaches, team captains or other veteran players, sport administrator, and a parent or two to review and revise your team policies.

▶ Present the team policies to your team by incorporating them into a player handbook. After the players have had a chance to review the team policies, at a team meeting invite them to ask for any further justifications or explanations of any of the rules.

Outline for Developing Team Policies

To further help you develop your team policies I've developed an outline of rules that you will likely want to address. They are based on the moral values presented in the Athletes Character Code on page 59.

Rules About Being Honest
- Stealing
- Cheating
- Lying

Rules About Being Respectful
- Profanity
- Fighting
- Hazing
- Interacting with coaches, teammates, officials, and opposing players
- Destroying property
- Insubordination (following instructions; doing what you're supposed to do)
- Sexual harassment
- Substance abuse
- Drug use

Rules About Being Responsible
- Attendance and promptness
- Dress when practicing, competing, and traveling
- Self-discipline
- Academic performance
- Curfews
- Travel policies

Rules About Being Fair
- Complying with sports rules
- Blaming others
- Taking advantage of others
- Criteria for awards

Rules About Caring
- Showing kindness and compassion
- Helping your teammates
- Following safety guidelines

Rules About Being a Good Citizen
- Being cooperative
- Obeying laws and rules
- Respecting authority

You should also have a rule that if a player does not accept the consequences for breaking a team rule, the player will not be allowed to remain on the team until the consequence is accepted.

Player Code of Conduct

I recommend that you ask your players to sign a team code of conduct pledge at the beginning of the season, which is something many teams now do. This code of conduct is based on your team policies.

Athlete Code of Conduct

I, [name of athlete], hereby pledge to honor and support [name of team] by adhering to the team's Athlete Code of Conduct as stated below.

I will be respectful by using appropriate language in appropriate tones when interacting with other athletes, coaches, officials, parents, and spectators. I will not taunt, use obscene gestures, or engage in boastful celebrations that demean fellow athletes.

I will treat everyone fairly regardless of gender, ethnic origin, race, religion, or sexual orientation.

I will treat all athletes, coaches, officials, parents, and spectators with dignity and respect.

I will not provide, use, or condone the use of tobacco products or alcoholic beverages.

I will not provide, use, or condone the use of performance-enhancing or mind-altering recreational drugs.

I will arrive on time for all practices, meetings, and contests, with only emergencies and illnesses being acceptable reasons for tardiness or absence.

I will seek to become the best athlete I can be by practicing appropriately and eating right.

I will play by the rules of the sport, demonstrating and encouraging good sportsmanship both in victory and defeat.

I will be honest. I will not lie, cheat, or steal.

I will be respectful by not fighting or damaging the property of others.

I will do my best to play safely so as not to injure myself or any other athlete.

I will cooperate with medical personnel in their efforts to care for my well-being.

I will respect the dignity of others by not sexually harassing or molesting them.

I will reject and report any individuals who request sexual favors or who threaten reprisal for rejecting such advances.

I will protect the integrity of the game by not gambling on the sport or having any involvement with those who do.

I will encourage and assist my teammates in becoming better athletes and human beings.

I have read and understand the above statements and agree to conduct myself in a manner consistent with each.

Signature of athlete _____ Date _____

Signature of parent/guardian _____ Date _____

(Optional)

From *Successful Coaching, Third Edition,* by Rainer Martens, 2004, Champaign, IL: Human Kinetics.

Enforcing Rules Consistently

Once you have established your team rules and schedule of consequences, you must apply the rules consistently and fairly. For example, if you have a no practice, no play rule and you ignore the rule when your team's best player violates it, you'll quickly destroy your credibility. Enforcing rules inconsistently is worse than not having rules at all. Also remember that one of the best ways to enforce the rules is for you to follow them as well: Practice what you preach, and your athletes will too.

It's not a pleasant task to enforce team rules, but it shows you care about your team and developing good character. If you're reluctant to enforce team rules, think about what Ogden Nash (1938) wrote in the poem "Yes and No."

Sometimes with secret pride I sigh

To think how tolerant am I;

Then wonder which is really mine:

Tolerance or a rubber spine.

STEP 4: Create Team Routines

I've mentioned several times the value of creating routines; they let players know what to do in certain situations and can help build team spirit. Routines also reduce the time you must spend instructing and supervising your players. Players are more likely to misbehave when they don't know what to do. Both rules and routines provide them with direction.

Identifying areas in which routines would be beneficial can be fairly easy. Look for situations in which players seem not to know how to proceed or ask for a lot of instructions, or situations in which misbehaviors occur. Here is a list of some routines that may be helpful for your team:

▶ *Prepractice locker room routines.* These may involve checking personal equipment, checking injuries with athletic trainers, receiving therapy, preventive taping, receiving clean clothing, weighing in, checking assignments on the bulletin board, and of course dressing appropriately.

▶ *Prepractice practice.* First, do you permit players to use the practice facility before formal practice begins? If so, what do you want players to do when they arrive early at the practice facility? A routine that involves a proper warm-up and practice of certain skills may be useful. If your situation requires the players to bring out equipment or prepare the facility for practice, then a routine for this task is useful.

▶ *Starting practice.* Most coaches have some type of routine to start practice, which may be as simple as blowing the whistle, expecting everyone to drop whatever they're doing immediately, and make haste to gather around the coach to hear the plans for the day.

▶ *Transitioning from one activity to another.* You will make better use of practice time if you have a routine that directs your players to move from one activity to another. You may call for an instructional session in which everyone takes an appropriate position so they can see a demonstration. An established routine for an instructional session will expedite the transition. Or you may want players to move from one drill or practice game to another, or from one conditioning activity to another. All of this can be done more efficiently with an established routine.

▶ *After-practice locker room routines.* After practice can be a time when players are likely to engage in mischief. Routines for this time period can be very useful.

▶ *Precontest routines.* These routines may start the day before a contest and carry over to the day of the contest. You may have routines for the locker room just prior to the contest, warming up for the contest, and team behavior during the contest.

▶ *Postcontest routines.* How do you want your players to acknowledge the other team and coach? How do they celebrate a victory and respond to a loss? When is it permissible for players to be interviewed by the media, and how are they to conduct themselves in such interviews?

▶ *Travel routines.* What are the routines with regard to dress, luggage allowance, responsibility for equipment, and behavior in hotels and restaurants?

Be careful not to create so many routines that are so specific in what you expect of the players that they are offensive to them and deny them the opportunity to be responsible for themselves. Use good judgment in thinking about what routines are beneficial to you and the players and when to permit your players to direct themselves. For some routines, such as precontest warm-up, I suggest letting your players recommend the routine. Also, if a routine seems to be getting old and you see signs of players' lack of motivation to comply, consider changing the routine by asking your players for suggestions. Sometimes just occasional changes of routine are enough to keep players from becoming bored.

STEP 5: Conduct Exciting Practices

Players who are bored will make their own entertainment. If your players are enjoying practice, they are far less inclined to misbehave. Traditional coaching lore contends that to become a good player one must endure endless hours of boring practice. Hogwash! I contend that practices can be exciting, interesting, and fun—and at the same time much more productive. Here's how.

An overemphasis on drilling—especially when drills are irrelevant to the actual skills needed to play the game—can result in demotivated athletes. Try replacing drills with gamelike activities that are more enjoyable and more relevant to learning to play the game well. The games approach, described in detail in chapter 9, is a great way to master the technical and tactical skills of the sport using modified games.

Another way to keep practices interesting is to come with a well-thought-out practice plan. I'll show you how to create these plans in chapter 12. One of the criteria you should use in designing practices is to make it fun for the players by varying methods and having a sense of how long to work on one activity before switching to another.

Also design practices so everyone stays busy; practices in which players are standing in long lines waiting their turns not only invite misbehavior but also steal valuable practice time from the players. If you find that your players are standing around in practice, you need to design better practices!

Players who fail repeatedly become discouraged, and as their motivation wanes, they may begin to misbehave. By teaching skills using progressions that are appropriate for each player, your players will experience more success and enjoy learning. If you fail to appropriately adjust the progression to learn a skill, players may fear for their safety, and in some cases rightfully so. For example, you obviously wouldn't ask a gymnast to do a complex routine without having first learned one of the components of the routine.

Successful coaches have a way of knowing when to back off from intense practices and let players recover. Coaches may not only reduce the intensity of practice but actually let the players play another sport just for fun and light conditioning.

The bottom line is this: If you take the fun out of sport for your athletes, you can expect some athletes to misbehave—or worse yet, to take themselves out of sport. You may think that is the athlete's loss, but it's your loss too because you no longer have an opportunity to help a young person through sport. Moreover (permit me to be blunt), you lost them because you were unable to design exciting practices.

STEP 6:
Catch Them Doing Good

I've saved the most potent preventive discipline method for last—catching your players doing good. It's easy to get in the mind-set of ignoring good performances and positive behaviors and focusing only on correcting mistakes and misbehaviors. But by recognizing and rewarding appropriate behavior, you reinforce these behaviors, and reinforced behaviors are more likely to occur. So look less for mistakes and look a lot harder for good performance and appropriate behavior, and let your players know that you appreciate these actions.

For example, you might respond to a difficult but successful pass with "Nice pass, John. Way to read the defense." When you catch a typically negative player offer encouragement to a teammate, you might say, "Good attitude, Jessica. Keep it up!"

Catching them doing good serves a couple of functions. First, it reinforces players' appropriate behavior. Second, it creates a positive rapport between you and your players. If you want them to listen to your message, they have to like and respect the messenger.

Encouragement is an important ingredient in catching them doing good. You communicate your belief in your athletes' ability to improve and achieve. For example, you might say, "I know you can master this skill. You'll get it, Marcus, just keep practicing." Catching your players doing good and encouraging their efforts motivates them to persist in mastering difficult skills, and they feel it is safe to make mistakes in the process of learning.

I played on an adult team once with a coach who used criticism and sarcasm as his predominant style of communication. As you can imagine, morale was low and a couple of players quit, primarily because of the coach's comments. I mentioned to the coach how his communication made me feel and how I thought it affected the other players. He explained that this was his form of communication, and that he saw it as a form of humor; he didn't realize the impact it was having on our team. He discontinued that style of communication, and our team enjoyed playing much more, and we even won a national championship.

Types of Rewards

Different rewards are reinforcing to different athletes. Athletes will reveal what rewards they like if you observe them or ask them. Study the list of rewards in table 8.1 and find out which of these (or others) are reinforcing to each of your athletes.

You'll recall that we discussed extrinsic and intrinsic rewards in chapter 7. Extrinsic rewards come from you or another external source. Most athletes respond positively to extrinsic rewards such as praise and recognition for their accomplishments. These rewards are powerful reinforcers that you can skillfully use to shape and motivate behaviors.

Table 8.1—Types of Rewards for Athletes

Tangible rewards	People rewards	Activity rewards
Trophies	Praise	Playing a game rather than doing drills
Medals	Smiles	Being able to continue to play
Ribbons	Expressions of approval	Taking a trip to play another team
Decals	Pats on the back	Getting to take a rest
Athletic letters	Publicity	Changing positions with other players
T-shirts	Expressions of interest	Playing another sport for a day

What to Reward

Let's learn about how to use praise and rewards effectively as you catch your players doing good.

▶ *Reward the performance, not the outcome.* When a player hits a line drive to the shortstop, who makes a great diving catch, the performance is good (line drive), but the outcome is not (an out). When another batter hits an easy fly ball to the left fielder, who loses the ball in the sun, and the batter ends up with a double, the performance is not good (easy fly ball), but the outcome is (a double). Rewarding the double reinforces luck, not skill, and not rewarding the line drive may cause the player to change his hitting method in search of a more favorable outcome. Although you may know that you should reinforce performance and not outcome, in the midst of competition it's easy to forget this principle. You may find yourself thinking about winning and losing (the outcome) more than about how your athletes are playing (the performance).

▶ *Reward athletes more for their effort than for their actual success.* When athletes know that you recognize they are trying to hit the ball, make the shot, or run as fast as possible, they do not fear trying. If they know you will reward them only when they succeed, then they may begin to fear the consequences of failing. This causes anxiety in some players. For example, your swimmer gives a 100 percent effort, but because she needs a lot of work on her technical skills, she places last. Praise the effort and let her know that you'll work together in practice to develop her technique.

▶ *Reward little things on the way toward reaching larger goals.* If you wait to reward only the achievement of major goals, you may never reward a player; reward the little steps on the way to bigger successes (see the section on shaping on page 176 in chapter 9).

▶ *Reward the learning and performance of life skills as well as sport skills.* Reward your athletes for showing self-control, good judgment, and the ability to handle responsibility (but remember to give them responsibility first). Reward them too for displaying sportsmanship, teamwork, and cooperation. One school gives out "Caught in the Act" awards to students who do good things without being asked.

▶ *Reward frequently when players are first learning new skills.* Generally, the more frequently you reward players, the faster they learn. One caution, though: Rewards given insincerely or too freely lose their value.

▶ *Once skills are well learned, reinforce them only occasionally.* Be careful, though, not to make the mistake of taking your athletes' positive behaviors for granted, forgetting to reinforce them for their accomplishments. Athletes have been known to perform poorly intentionally to get recognition from the coach.

▶ *When athletes are first learning, reward them as soon as possible after correct behaviors or their approximations occur.* Shouting "good" as a player executes a skill correctly is reinforcing; a postpractice debriefing an hour later is less so. However, once skills have been learned and as athletes mature mentally, it is less important to give rewards immediately after appropriate behaviors occur—with one exception. Athletes low in self-confidence always need to be reinforced soon after making appropriate responses.

▶ *Reward athletes only when they have earned it.* When players have made repeated errors, cost the team a victory, or had an all-around miserable day, praising them for some insignificant behavior makes them feel misunderstood and subtly manipulated. When players have poor performances, communicate empathy (understanding) but not sympathy (feeling sorry for them). All athletes have bad days, and they will appreciate that you understand that.

Intrinsic rewards, though not directly available for you to use, also have powerful effects on athletes. These rewards come from within the athlete. They include such things as feeling successful, having a sense of pride in accomplishment, and feeling competent. Although you cannot directly offer these rewards to your athletes, by belittling them or not recognizing their accomplishments, you may deny them the opportunity to experience intrinsic rewards.

Successful coaches use extrinsic rewards to motivate their athletes while encouraging them to recognize the intrinsic rewards of sport participation. The neat thing about intrinsic rewards is that they are self-fueling; that is, self-satisfaction and pride lead to a greater desire to succeed without any extrinsic rewards. Coaches who emphasize extrinsic rewards may find that athletes want ever increasing amounts, until the demand exceeds the supply. The trophies can be only so big; the social recognition can be only so great.

Athletes who play only for extrinsic rewards seldom maintain the long-term motivation needed to succeed in sport. Athletes such as Michael Jordon obviously expect to be paid for playing, but they excel because of intrinsic rewards—the test of self, sense of achievement, and pride in accomplishment.

Coaches can help athletes be more intrinsically motivated in two ways. They can help athletes experience the intrinsic rewards of enjoyment, satisfaction, and feeling competent by administering extrinsic rewards effectively through the principles of reinforcement. They can also help athletes understand that although extrinsic rewards are nice to earn, the intrinsic rewards associated with participation are of greater value.

Corrective Discipline

You've implemented the six steps to preventive discipline, yet your athletes still occasionally misbehave. In this section you will learn how to correct misbehavior using the

positive discipline approach—an approach that minimizes the negatives of punishment and motivates athletes to perform better and behave as responsible team members. Your goal is to help misbehaving athletes develop self-discipline—an important life skill.

Discipline Versus Punishment

Remember that positive discipline involves instruction, training, and correction for the purpose of helping your athletes develop sport and life skills. Negative discipline uses punishment, which is perceived by your athletes as penalizing them for an offense so that you can get even or retaliate. When a player seriously misbehaves, you may feel disrespected or thwarted, and thus administer punishment with anger. After being punished, the player may harbor hostility toward you, which is not a desirable emotion for building a positive relationship with that player in the future.

Besides damaging the coach–athlete relationship, punishment hurts players' self-esteem, leading them to believe they can do nothing right. Punishing misbehavior doesn't "teach them a lesson" because punishment alone doesn't teach your players what to do correctly and doesn't encourage them to change their behavior. Controlling athletes through punishment causes them to resent you, rebel against you, seek revenge, or retreat.

So why do so many coaches rely on punishment to discipline? Because it works—at least in the short term. It stops disruptive, destructive, and violent behavior and therefore is necessary in extreme cases in which the misbehavior puts you or your team at risk. You may be tempted, however, to use punishment for minor misbehaviors, and even for a person's inability to perform a skill that is not yet mastered, which is certainly not a misbehavior. The long-term consequence of using punishment in this way makes it all but impossible to help athletes develop life skills and motivate them to optimal performance. Jane Nelsen and colleagues sum it up in their text *Positive Discipline* by stating: "Where did we ever get the crazy idea that to make people do better, we first have to make them feel worse? People do better when they feel better" (Nelsen 1996, p. 120).

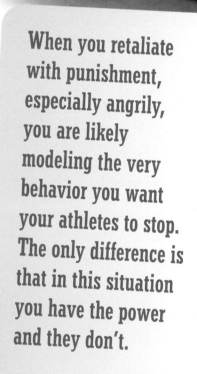

When you retaliate with punishment, especially angrily, you are likely modeling the very behavior you want your athletes to stop. The only difference is that in this situation you have the power and they don't.

Why Athletes Misbehave

If you understand why your athletes misbehave, especially those who repeatedly misbehave, you'll be much better able to help them through instruction, training, and correction. Athletes usually misbehave for one of two reasons:

▶ Misbehaving athletes are likely to be discouraged athletes. You need to find out why they are discouraged. Could it be conditions at home, in school, or with friends? Is it the way their teammates treat them? Is it the way you're coaching them?

▶ Misbehaving athletes may believe they do not belong and are not significant to the team. Why do athletes feel insecure or unimportant on your team?

If athletes can't get attention for their positive behaviors, they may decide to get attention by misbehaving. They may decide to make your life miserable by arguing, contradicting, lying, resisting directions, and distracting the team. If they feel unfairly treated, they may try to get revenge by treating teammates or you cruelly. Conversely, some athletes who are discouraged or feel insignificant will display feelings of inadequacy and despair. They think trying is useless because they always fail. These players may resort to becoming the team clown, refusing to give much effort, or simply quitting. (We discussed this type of player in chapter 7.)

The point here is for you to look beyond the immediate misbehaviors and search for the cause of the action. If you talk with the misbehaving athletes, sometimes they will tell you why they are misbehaving, but other times they will not. You need to secure as much information as you can about the player to help you determine the underlying cause for misbehavior.

Strategies for Correcting Behavior

When misbehaviors occur, take the following steps:

1. Determine whether the misbehavior is a violation of the law or your team rules. If legal or police action is warranted, your first decision is whether to turn the matter over to the appropriate authorities.

2. If it is a minor offense occurring during practices or contests, request a change in behavior—either that the athlete stop doing something or begin doing something. Be respectful, yet firm. For offenses that occur outside of your supervision, you will not have a chance to request a change in behavior.

3. If the player has broken a team rule, you need to invoke an appropriate consequence. With your team rules and schedule of consequences to guide you, you'll be much better prepared to respond to the misbehavior. Remember to address misbehaviors quickly, consistently, and respectfully.

Guidelines for Administering Consequences for Misbehaviors

▶ Be highly predictable in your dealing with misbehavior. Athletes respect coaches who are firm and decisive while also being caring, understanding, and encouraging.

▶ Be specific about what you want the player to do or stop doing. Avoid generalities such as "Act responsibly." Remember, the player may not know what you think responsible behavior is. "Bill, stop horsing around with Jerome and help him practice his stroke," is more effective.

▶ Be succinct. Avoid lecturing, nagging, interrogating, and moralizing. This is not the time to give a sermon.

▶ Be confident when you speak, but if you're not quite certain about the appropriate consequence, tell the player you need to give it some thought and will talk later. If you think consulting with your team about the consequence is appropriate, do so at your next team meeting.

▶ Even if you feel angry, remain calm and in control. If you react in anger, the situation can become explosive, and you may be demonstrating the very behavior you're trying to stop.

▶ Once you gain compliance, don't keep the player in the "doghouse." Forgive and forget.

More Discipline Tips

1. Use nonverbal communications to promote self-control among your players. A tilt of the head, a slight frown, a wink, a stare, and moving close to the player, maybe even putting a hand on the player's shoulder without saying anything can be effective actions to stop inattentiveness and horseplay.

2. Sometimes just reminding players of appropriate behavior is sufficient. Try to do so privately without embarrassing them. When in public, do so with comments such as, "Hey, Liz, you were just about to practice that backward somersault. Right?" "Michael, you were just about to start your stretching routine, weren't you?"

3. If players are seeking attention by misbehaving, ignoring it usually results in their escalating the behavior until you pay attention. Try to redirect the behavior by giving them attention when they are not demanding it. Related to this, sometimes it is effective to ask players to answer a question or demonstrate a skill to refocus their attention.

4. When a player misbehaves, address the behavior, not the character of the player.

5. Consequences should never be harmful physically or psychologically.

6. Make players understand that they have chosen the consequences because they misbehaved. This helps to teach them responsibility for their actions.

7. Avoid public confrontations if possible. Remove the player and address the misbehavior privately. This eliminates an opportunity for the player to show off and possibly show you up.

8. An effective consequence is the loss of privileges. The most important is the opportunity to play in games, to practice, to travel with the team, and as a last resort to be on the team. Removing a player from the team should be a last resort because it eliminates your opportunity to help the player.

9. Reward other players for the type of behavior you want a misbehaving player to demonstrate, and do so when the offending player is clearly observing. Then, when the offending player demonstrates the appropriate behavior, reward it immediately.

Coaching Yourself:
Being Perfect

Sport is about the pursuit of excellence, but some coaches push over the top and strive unrelentingly for perfection. Perfectionism can be very debilitating to coaches, athletes, and the coach–athlete relationship. When coaches are perfectionist about themselves, they are never satisfied, and thus they get little enjoyment from coaching. When they direct that perfectionism at others, their constant demand for players and assistants to perform perfectly destroys relationships and damages self-esteem.

High standards and the pursuit of excellence are positive coaching qualities, but excessive demand to achieve perfection is corrosive. Perfectionist coaches tend to think as follows:

▶ There is only one correct way to do things.

▶ My standards are very high, and I will not lower them.

▶ Don't muddle the issue: It's either right or wrong, black or white.

▶ Why is everything screwed up? Why can't people do it right?

▶ I know what they're thinking about me. I'll show them they're wrong.

Perfectionists often have trouble seeing the big picture because they pay too much attention to the details. They also tend to believe that they have more control over events than they do.

Perfectionist coaches tend to be overorganized, incessantly checking to see that everything is in order. They overpractice and are unable to judge when to quit. They overcorrect their players, which comes off as being overly critical. Because they have a high need to control, they have difficulty trusting others to complete tasks and thus are poor at delegating to their assistant coaches and entrusting their athletes with responsibilities.

The first step toward developing a healthy striving for excellence is to *recognize that perfectionism is destructive.* Here are some other steps that may help you eliminate the "excess" associated with perfectionism:

1. *Identify perfectionist triggers.* Determine if you are overly perfectionist with certain people and in specific situations. Is your perfectionism directed mostly at yourself or others, or both? Try to catch yourself engaging in perfectionist behaviors when you are in the situations you've identified.

2. *Take a reality check.* Evaluate your standards to determine whether they help you and your athletes achieve your goals or get in the way of achieving them?

3. *Cost–benefit analysis.* Assess what it costs you in striving for perfection and what the benefits would be of lessening your standards. For the perfectionist, this is often a difficult analysis; you may need someone who can be objective to help you weigh the costs and benefits.

4. *Gain perspective.* Step back to look at the big picture of your coaching. What are your coaching objectives? Are you achieving these objectives by the actions you're taking?

5. *Seek assistance.* If your perfectionism dominates your life and perhaps is now compulsive, you may benefit from seeking professional help.

6. *Educate yourself.* Learn more about perfectionism by reading on this subject. I recommend Martin M. Antony and Richard P. Swinson's book *When Perfect Isn't Good Enough*, Oakland, CA: New Harbinger, 1998.

Questions for Reflection

▶ What is positive discipline? Do you practice positive discipline, instructing your athletes in sport and life skills, training them by providing opportunities to practice these skills, and correcting their mistakes? **(p. 143)**

▶ How can you distinguish between a mistake or misbehavior that stems from a lack of instruction, and one that is purely willful? How should you respond to each? **(p. 143)**

▶ What constitutes negative discipline? Why is this style of coaching less effective in the long run than positive discipline? **(p. 144)**

▶ What are the six preventive discipline steps? **(p. 146)**

▶ How can you create a physically and psychologically safe environment for your players? **(p. 147)**

▶ What are some appropriate uses for team meetings? **(p. 147)**

▶ What consequences have you (or you and your players) established for rule violations? Are they fair, appropriate, and sufficient in response? Are you able to deliver them respectfully and without anger? **(p. 151)**

▶ Have you established team rules that are specific, observable, enforceable, and logical? How good are you at enforcing them consistently? **(p. 152)**

▶ What are some situations in which routines can be helpful in guiding athletes and keeping them out of trouble? Do you have routines for before and after practice, transitions during practice, before and after contests, and travel? **(p. 154)**

▶ How can you make your practices more exciting and fun? Do you teach skills through the games approach? Do you come to practice with well-designed practice plans? **(p. 155)**

▶ What are some things you can do to catch your players doing good? **(p. 156)**

▶ What are the key principles of rewarding effectively? **(p. 158)**

▶ What are two primary reasons that athletes misbehave? **(p. 161)**

▶ What are some key points for administering consequences of misbehavior? **(p. 162)**

▶ Are you a perfectionist coach? What can you do to lessen your need for perfection and control? **(p. 163)**

References

Glennon, Lorraine, and Roy Leavitt. 2000. *Those who can . . . COACH!* Berkeley: Wildcat Canyon Press/Council Oak Books.

Nash, Ogden. 1938. *I'm a stranger here myself.* Boston: Little, Brown and Company.

Nelsen, Jane, and H. Stephen Glenn. 1996. *Positive discipline.* New York: Ballantine Books.

PART III

Principles of Teaching

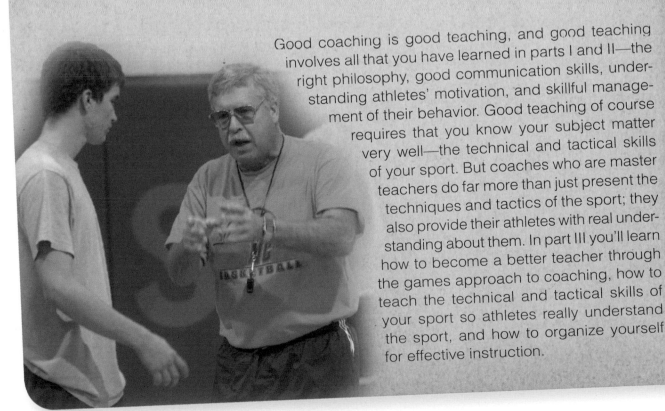

Good coaching is good teaching, and good teaching involves all that you have learned in parts I and II—the right philosophy, good communication skills, understanding athletes' motivation, and skillful management of their behavior. Good teaching of course requires that you know your subject matter very well—the technical and tactical skills of your sport. But coaches who are master teachers do far more than just present the techniques and tactics of the sport; they also provide their athletes with real understanding about them. In part III you'll learn how to become a better teacher through the games approach to coaching, how to teach the technical and tactical skills of your sport so athletes really understand the sport, and how to organize yourself for effective instruction.

9

Coaching the Games Approach Way

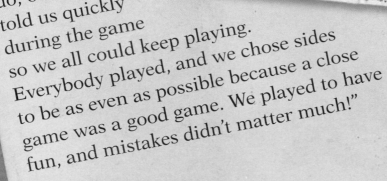

"I recall the good old days when we learned sports through 'pickup' games," said Steve Ruhlig. "We didn't have coaches or umpires—or screaming parents! We didn't practice first; there was no time for that. We began playing immediately. If we didn't know the basic things to do, our friends told us quickly during the game so we all could keep playing. Everybody played, and we chose sides to be as even as possible because a close game was a good game. We played to have fun, and mistakes didn't matter much!"

Many of us wax nostalgic about the good old "sandlot" days and mourn their departure. Critics of today's youth sport programs often contrast the joy and spontaneity of sandlot sports with the reported violence, cheating, and stressful world of adult-organized youth sport programs. But the sandlot days were not so perfect either. Youngsters' talents went undeveloped because they received no instruction. Play was often unsafe, less-talented players were occasionally abused or neglected, and cheating and fighting unfortunately were no strangers to sandlots.

One of the reasons adult-organized youth sport programs have become so popular is that they address some of the problems of sandlot play. They give more young people an opportunity to play safely, to receive helpful instruction, and to learn life skills from coaches like you. But with those advantages has come a new risk. We adults may be in danger of overinstructing our athletes on the technical skills and underinstructing them on how to play the game (the tactics). In doing so, we take the fun out of sports.

Can you recall how you were taught by adults to play a sport? The coach or teacher probably taught you the basic technical skills using a series of drills that you likely found boring. As you began to learn the basic technical skills, the coach eventually taught you some of the tactical skills, and then finally you were able to play the game. If you were like me, you became impatient during what seemed to be endless instruction and drills and very little playing of the game.

On the surface, what I call the traditional approach (playing the game only after practicing the basic technical and tactical skills) makes sense, but we've discovered that this approach has serious shortcomings. Today we know more about the way young people learn, and this knowledge has led to the development of a better way to coach. It's called the games approach. It teaches athletes how to play the game better and retains the joy of participation more commonly seen in sandlot play. I'll introduce you to the games approach to coaching in this chapter and encourage you to embrace this approach because it is so well aligned with the principles advocated in parts I and II of this book.

 **In this chapter you'll learn**

▶ what technical and tactical skills are,

▶ the limitations of the traditional approach,

▶ what the games approach is all about,

▶ how to teach through the games approach, and

▶ how to make the games approach work for you.

Technical and Tactical Skills

To understand the games approach, you need to know what I mean when using the terms *technique* or *technical skills* and *tactics* or *tactical skills*.

Technical Skills

We'll use the terms *technique* or *technical skills* here to mean *the specific procedures to move one's body to perform the task that needs to be accomplished.* That procedure may be to move quickly to a particular space and then to gain control of and direct an object such as a ball, puck, or shuttle by trapping, kicking, catching, throwing, or hitting it. Or it may be to control one's body to execute a prescribed movement such as in diving or a gymnastics routine. Or it may be to repeat a certain movement as efficiently as possible such as in running or rowing. Some sports require that athletes learn many technical skills, and others require that they learn only a few. The degree of difficulty of the technical skills can vary considerably between sports and within sports.

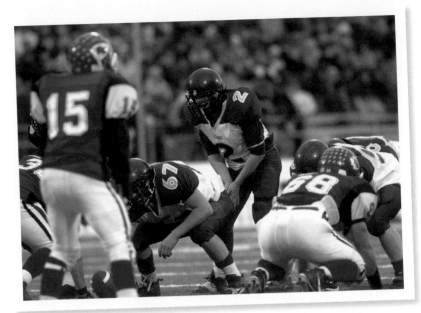

Tactical Skills

Tactical skills are *the decisions and actions of players in the contest to gain an advantage over the opposing team or players.* A tactic can be as simple as hitting the ball to a player's weak side, placing the ball in the space away from the player, the give-and-go in basketball, or starting out fast in a race in the hope of tiring the opponent early. A player who demonstrates good tactics knows where to go and how to use space and time intelligently, both alone and with teammates.

The rules of the sport define what tactics are permitted, and through experience and careful study of how the sport is played, athletes can learn the range of possible tactics used in the sport. Yet it's one thing to understand the tactical options in a sport, and another to execute the appropriate tactic when playing the sport. Many sports require athletes to take in extraordinary amounts of information and then process it in nanoseconds to reach a decision. I'll use the term *game sense* to refer to the ability to make tactical decisions within a game.

In sports we often use the terms *strategy* and *tactic* synonymously, but as we go forward in part III, I'll use the term *strategy* to refer to *a plan of action for your team for a season or series of contests.* If you have a small but quick group of basketball players, you may decide that your strategy will be to run and shoot. If you have a big and powerful offensive line in football and not a good passing quarterback, you may decide to run the ball much more than pass. Your strategy is a plan of action based on the talent of your team and what you expect will be the attributes of your competition to give you the best chance of success. In short, *strategy is the big plan, and tactics are the plans within the game to gain an advantage.*

Defining Skill

Skill has two meanings. It may mean a task. For example, I could say, "The skill of rifle shooting is underappreciated in the sport world." You could easily substitute the word *task* for *skill* in this sentence. Skill also may mean the quality of a person's performance at some task. When I say, "She demonstrates excellent shooting skill," I use *skill* to mean the *quality* of the shooter's performance.

Technique and *skill* are two terms often used synonymously, but they shouldn't be. *Skill in sport is being able to execute the techniques required at the right time and place.* The overall use of skill is different from the more narrow use of technical and tactical skills. Remember that technical skills, or techniques, refer to the specific motor skills used to perform a task; and tactical skills, or tactics, refer to the mental skills to know when and where to execute the technical skills. Skill in general is the proficient use of techniques and tactics to play the sport (see the sidebar for an example).

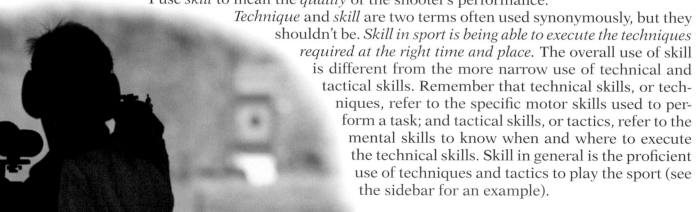

Technical and Tactical Skills

I took up the sport of handball in graduate school, and after a couple of years I was able to defeat the small group of players at our local gym. I decided to enter my first interstate tournament to see how I might fare. When I arrived for my first match, my opponent was warming up in the court. He looked very fit, wore a very nice warm-up outfit, and repeatedly threw the ball against the back wall and hit nothing but kill shots against the front wall (that's good). His technique looked flawless to me.

As the game started, my heart was racing, and I had cottonmouth so thick I thought I would choke; I was surely going to be humiliated. But it wasn't 5 points into the game that I realized that my opponent, while having excellent technical skills, lacked tactical skills. He didn't know how to position himself in the court, select the right shot for the situation, or adjust to the various tactics I employed. Consequently I won the match easily.

Now who was the more "skillful" player? My opponent may have had superior technical skills, but I had better tactical skills.

We've all seen players who had superb technique but in contests didn't know how to use that technique at the appropriate time or place. When I first began coaching using the traditional approach, I was unable to recognize when an athlete lacked tactical skills. Instead I became frustrated with such athletes, thinking that they either were "choking" in competition or needed more practice on technical skills. Now I realize I had failed to teach them the tactical, or decision-making, skills they needed to know when and where to use their technical skills.

As we go forward, keep in mind the difference between technique and skill and between strategy and tactic as we compare the traditional approach of coaching with the games approach.

Traditional Approach

In the traditional approach to coaching a typical practice session begins with a warm-up, followed by the teaching of a basic or advanced technical skill, and then the repeated practice of this technical skill through one or more drills. This may be repeated for a variety of technical skills, and perhaps some instruction on tactical skills, which are also practiced through a series of drills. Next the players play a practice game, or what is often called a scrimmage, during which the coach hopes that they apply the technical and tactical skills practiced in the drills. The session concludes with some physical training if the practice session did not involve sufficient physical conditioning.

Instructional methods using the traditional approach tend to be dominated by command-style teaching of technical and tactical skills. Typically, the coach teaches new skills during the early parts of the practice, then provides feedback to the players as they practice them through a series of drills. The coach does very little actual teaching during the scrimmages or practice games. This

approach has several shortcomings, as discussed in the following sections.

Overemphasis on Technical Skills

In the traditional approach coaches overemphasize the teaching and practicing of technical skills at the expense of teaching and practicing the decision-making skills needed to develop tactical skills. Drills to learn technical skills dominate practice time, and often are structured to de-emphasize any thinking or decision making by the athletes. Although properly structured drills can provide valuable learning in some aspects of skilled play, gamelike experiences are often more beneficial in developing both technical and tactical skills.

Overemphasis on Direct Instruction

Direct instruction—the coach telling the athlete how to perform the skill—is the dominant method used for teaching in the traditional approach. Although direct instruction is a useful way to teach some of what athletes need to learn, it is less suitable for the development of thinking skills required for problem solving and decision making in sport. In contrast, the games approach relies more on

indirect methods such as problem solving or guided discovery. These methods are better for developing thinking athletes because they involve athletes much more in the learning process and therefore enable them to take greater responsibility for their learning.

Mindless Drills

The traditional approach often teaches the technical and tactical skills of the sport out of the context of the game. Athletes learn the basic skills through drills, but find it difficult to apply these technical skills within the game because they don't practice them enough in gamelike situations. Experience has shown that athletes often do not automatically see the relevance of a drill and are unable to apply the learning from drills in the game setting.

The well-established principle of specificity says: *Practice like you play, and you're more likely to play like you practiced.* In football, for example, players practice hitting two- and seven-person sleds. They run through tires and ropes and tackle large stuffed dummies. Do you think what is learned in these drills transfers to playing football? Is blocking a sled or a dummy anything like blocking an agile linebacker? Hardly. Could the time be better spent practicing what players actually do in the game? Absolutely!

In baseball, players often swing weighted bats prior to hitting. The principle of specificity indicates that this is not a good idea. Another common practice in baseball is to have players hit 25 to 50 balls at a time during practice. This may be useful when the coach is trying to help the player master the hitting skill, but when preparing for a game, wouldn't it be better to take maybe three swings, step out to let someone else hit three, and then step back in? The practice would be aligned more with game conditions.

Basketball coaches often use drills to teach offensive patterns. Players learn stereotyped responses, often without any defensive resistance, whereas in real games the pressure of the defense and the action of the game call for much more flexible responses. It's one thing to learn a technical or tactical skill in a repetitive drill in which the decisions are minimized, and quite another thing to perform it in a game.

Boredom

Another problem with the traditional approach's overreliance on nongame-like drills is that they are boring, sometimes because athletes spend much of their time standing in lines and sometimes because the drills are just tediously repetitious. Drills also often eliminate or reduce the opportunities for players to problem solve as they would in a real game. Part of the joy of sport is the intellectual challenge of making the right decisions to maximize the chances of winning—that is, to demonstrate good tactical skills.

Many coaches believe that highly repetitive, monotonous drills are the only way to master technical skills, but that's not true. The games approach can make practice of technical skills much more enjoyable and relevant by making drills more gamelike and eliminating athletes standing in lines to take their turns.

How frequently have you heard athletes say that they loved playing the games, but hated practice? The traditional approach to practicing takes much of the fun out of playing the sport. Overly structured practices using drills that have little direct relevance to playing the game destroy the playful element of participation and stifle players' intrinsic motivation to play. Many athletes love the sport so much that they endure these practices in order to have the opportunity to play in real games. Others simply quit.

Essence of the Games Approach

There's a quiet revolution going on in coaching—a sport coup d'etat of sorts. The traditional approach is being ousted by the new games approach, in which the emphasis is on learning the game through gamelike practice activities that create realistic and enjoyable learning situations. As athletes play, they learn what to do; this is called tactical awareness.

When your athletes understand the tactics they must use in the game, they are then eager to develop the technical skills that let them execute those tactics. Because your athletes are motivated to learn or refine their technical skills, they'll be more receptive to your instruction because you are teaching them what they want to learn.

Holistic Approach

The games approach is a more holistic approach to learning the sport, focusing first on helping athletes understand what the game is all about, and then helping them learn how to play the game. Through this approach players discover what to do in the game, not by you telling them, but by them experiencing it. What you do as an effective coach is help them understand what they've experienced.

With your guidance, for example, your athletes may discover that they need to master certain techniques to execute a particular tactic or that they need to be able to "read the play" to select the appropriate tactic. In contrast to the highly structured and coach-centered traditional approach, the games approach is an athlete-centered, guided discovery method of teaching. It empowers your athletes to solve the problems that arise in the game, and that's a big part of the fun of playing a sport.

How the Games Approach Works

The games approach is based on practice being as closely aligned as possible with what actually occurs in games, but it is not simply a throw-out-the-ball-and-let-them-play approach. It's an approach that requires skillful analysis of the game by you to structure gamelike situations so that players learn what they need to know to play well.

Coaches do this using three methods.

▶ Shaping play

▶ Focusing play

▶ Enhancing play

I'll describe these coaching tools using team sports as examples, but these tools can be applied to individual sports as well. ASEP's Bronze Level sport-specific technical and tactical skills courses, which are based on the games approach, apply these methods in both team and individual sports.

Shaping Play

Shaping the play of your athletes is about *teaching through the game.* Here are four aspects of the game that you can change to create a variety of learning situations:

1. The rules define what players can and cannot do in a game. You can change the rules in practice to create the learning environment you want.

2. You can alter the number of players to increase player participation and active learning time. Examples are games such as two-on-two basketball or three-on-three soccer. The advantage of using these games is that they increase the opportunity to learn technical and tactical skills in a microcosm of the full game. You can also create imbalances between the number of offensive and defensive players to simulate certain game situations. The fast-break drill in basketball in which two offensive players attempt to score against one defensive player is a common example.

3. You can alter the size of the playing area or change the size of the goal to help your athletes focus on learning a particular aspect of the game. For example, in soccer you could have three attackers against one defender practicing in a 15-by-15-meter grid, which would allow the attackers time to develop their passing skills. Gradually you could reduce the space, making it more difficult for the attackers because the defender can cover the space more easily.

4. You can shape play by modifying the goal and the scoring.

Other ways of shaping play include modifying the playing equipment, controlling the actions of the better players who may tend to dominate the game, and manipulating playing time. *The key in shaping play is to redesign the game so that your athletes have the opportunity to practice what is relevant in the real game.*

Focusing Play

Of course you don't just "shape" the game by modifying the variables described earlier and hope the athletes will teach themselves the techniques, tactics, and decision-making skills they need to learn. Nor will athletes always fully understand the similarities and differences between the practice game and the real game. So as they play, you need to "focus" your players' attention on the key elements of

the game that you want them to learn. When you watch master coaches at work, they excel at focusing their players on the critical elements of the game as they practice. This vital process determines the quality of practice and helps athletes transfer what they are learning in practice games to real games.

Focusing can be done by explaining the purpose of the practice game and labeling the key elements to be learned, and then during play reminding players of these actions. You can also stop the play and correct the incorrect action or positively reinforce the correct action.

Questioning is a primary tool that games approach coaches use to help players recognize what they need to learn. Part of the art of coaching is knowing when to use questions and when to provide answers. Generally, when athletes are learning something new and don't have the knowledge, you need to provide the answers. When they are likely to know, but are not focused on what they should be, then questions are a good way to direct their attention.

A more elaborate focusing technique is called the freeze replay. The coach gives an agreed-on signal to "freeze" the players, who must immediately stop. Play is then rewound back to the critical point and then, through questioning, the coach helps the players "replay" the situation to draw out the key elements of good play. The freeze replay, skillfully used, is a great tool for capturing those teachable moments and provides opportunities for players to think about their actions.

Enhancing Play

You can enhance your athletes' play by presenting challenges during practices, using handicapping techniques to make close contests, and of course encouraging them and recognizing them for the progress they make. Your personality and knowledge of the game, and the respect players have for you, are also important factors that help enhance play.

The games approach to coaching gives you a huge advantage in motivating your athletes because practices are much more game-like and thus much more enjoyable. Moreover, your players will quickly recognize that in the games approach the practice is focused on helping them, whereas in the traditional approach it often seems that practice is focused on obeying the commands of the coach. In other words, practices using the games approach are athlete-centered rather than coach-centered.

A Games Approach to a Basketball Practice

Here's an example of how to use a games approach in basketball using the processes of shaping, focusing, and enhancing play. The coach identifies the purpose of the practice as follows:

▶ To improve passing and develop midrange set shot execution on offense

▶ To develop the defensive principles of putting pressure on the ball, providing defensive support by sagging, and recovering one's position

The coach calls the game Slick Shot. (It is useful to name your games to help your players remember them for future practices.) The aim of the game is for the offensive players to pass the ball and locate an unguarded team member who can put up a set shot within the designated area. The two defensive players work as a team to cover the passes and deny the shot. Each team gets five attempts to score on offense.

How the Coach Shapes Play

Playing area: The area is inside the 3-point line of the court and bounded by the baseline.

Numbers: Teams of three players. The game involves three offensive and two defensive players. The extra defender observes the others and then rotates into the defense. You can have as many of these games going on as your facility allows, with you and your assistant coaches moving from game to game.

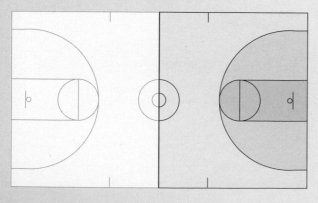

Scoring: The offensive players score 1 point for shooting when unguarded (the defender must be a meter or more away) as well as for shooting from anywhere in the area outside the key and within the 3-point line. An additional 2 points are scored for sinking the basket. A maximum of 3 points can be scored with each attempt to score. The defending team scores points for intercepting the ball or for forcing the offensive team to make more than three passes before shooting. Each team keeps a record of the points it scores.

Rules of the game: The offensive players may not dribble, and they may only receive the ball in the designated area (outside the key and within the 3-point line). If the offensive players break this rule, they cannot score any points on that attempt. Defensive players may only intercept the pass; they cannot take the ball from the offensive players' hands. If they do, the offensive team gets to repeat the attempt to score.

How the Coach Focuses Play

The coach focuses the offensive team's attention on the following:

▶ Scanning the court to identify the open player (by reminding players to look up)

▶ Moving into position to provide passing and shooting options

▶ Recognizing when a player is open for a shot, then receiving the pass and squaring up for a well-balanced shot

The coach focuses the defensive team's attention on the following:

▶ Applying pressure to the ball and then recovering

▶ Providing defensive support by sagging, and then moving "out" to pressure the ball

(The additional player in defense can be directed to observe these elements as the others are playing and then provide information to improve this aspect of play.)

The coach can use a variety of methods for focusing the play, including the following:

▶ Providing direct instruction and then giving feedback as play is observed

▶ "Freezing" play and asking questions of the players

▶ Giving the team time-outs so that players can reflect on and discuss their performances

How the Coach Enhances Play

Following some initial practice of the game, the coach announces that teams will now have a mini-competition titled the Slick Shot State Tournament. The coach determines the number of divisions or levels of competition, and then the teams decide on their team names and in which division of competition they will play (e.g., Division 1 or 2). Results are recorded and awards and recognition given. During the competition, the coach focuses on catching players doing good.

The games approach is consistent with the coaching philosophy advocated in part I. Once you fully understand the games approach, you'll quickly see its advantages. Not only will your athletes learn and play the game better, but also they (and you) will enjoy the sport much more, and as a result you'll have far fewer discipline problems. To understand the games approach better, read *Play Practice* (2001) written by Alan Launder, a pioneer in the games approach.

Skills to Teach Through the Games Approach

The skills needed for success in sports are not limited to technical and tactical skills, although of course those skills are essential. They also include physical training skills, mental skills, and communication skills. I believe every coach should also add character development skills to this list.

To help you identify the range of sport skills that your athletes need to become "stars," I have created the Celestial Map of Sport Skills shown in figure 9.1. The skills are organized into six constellations. As you review

Traditional Approach Compared With the Games Approach

Traditional Approach	Games Approach
Uses drills primarily to practice technical skills.	Uses drills that are closely aligned with the game to teach technical and tactical skills.
Teaches the specific elements of the game and then combines them into the whole.	Teaches the whole game and then refines the parts.
Coach-centered. (The coach uses direct instructional methods that may or may not consider the players' needs.)	Player-centered. (The coach creates a learning environment that focuses on the players' needs using a variety of teaching methods.)
Practices are often boring and therefore unmotivating to the players.	Practices are fun, relevant, and challenging, and therefore increases intrinsic motivation.
Players become highly dependent on the coach.	Players develop increasing independence from the coach by being actively involved in the learning process.
Through extensive drilling coaches strive to develop automatic responses that promote mindlessness when playing.	Practices are designed to develop the thinking, understanding, and decision-making skills that are required to play well.
Players provide little or no input to the coach, who makes most or all of the decisions.	Players have considerable input to the coach and help the coach make decisions.
Players are not encouraged to help each other master the skills of the sport.	Players are encouraged to help each other master the skills of the sport.
Preferred approach of command-style coaches.	Preferred approach of cooperative-style coaches.

them, be thinking about creating your own map by applying the general skills described in each constellation to your sport. Obviously the importance of each category of skills varies from sport to sport and from situation to situation within a sport.

Next I'll briefly comment on the teaching of these six categories of skills. In chapter 10 we'll look at technical skills in depth and do the same for tactical skills in chapter 11.

Technical Skills

Of course one of your primary tasks as a coach is to determine the technical skills your players must master to be effective performers, and then to help them learn to perform these technical skills correctly and efficiently.

Assessing Your Technical Skill Knowledge

Take a moment to consider the following questions regarding your knowledge of and ability to coach the technical skills of your sport. Be honest in your assessment.

1. How knowledgeable are you about how to perform all of the technical skills of your sport?

Weak				Strong
1	2	3	4	5

2. How skillful are you at teaching technical skills to your players? Do you know how to break down the skills into the appropriate steps to optimize learning them, and how to guide your players in putting those steps together again to execute the whole skill?

Weak				Strong
1	2	3	4	5

3. How good are you at observing technique, understanding the cause of incorrect execution, and providing cues to your players to correct errors?

Weak				Strong
1	2	3	4	5

4. How knowledgeable are you about the biomechanics of your sport—the science that studies the principles of movement in sport?

Weak				Strong
1	2	3	4	5

Figure 9.1

Celestial Map of Sport Skills

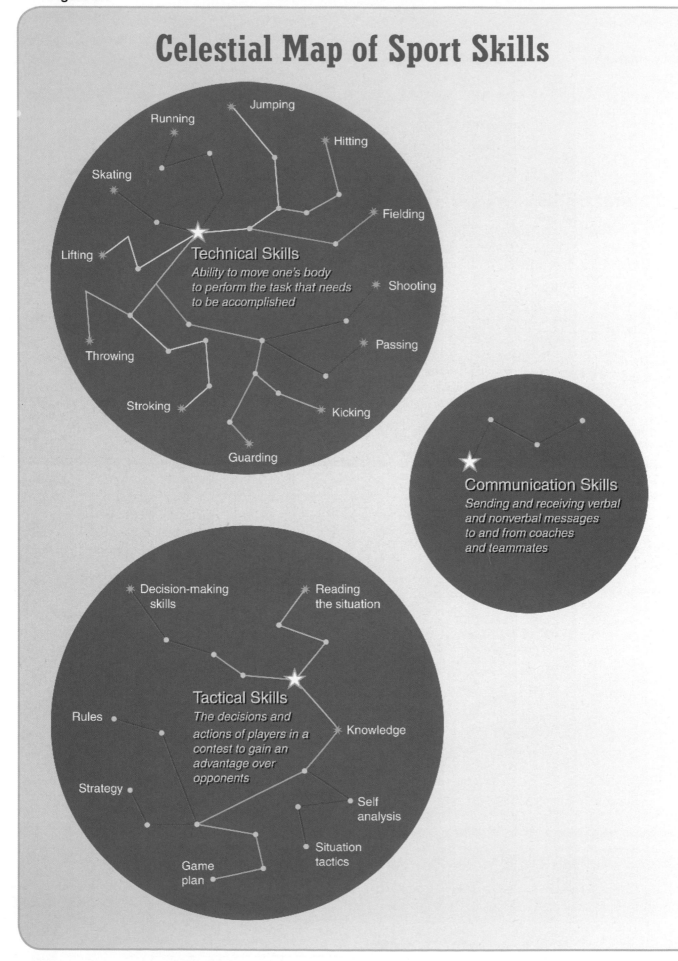

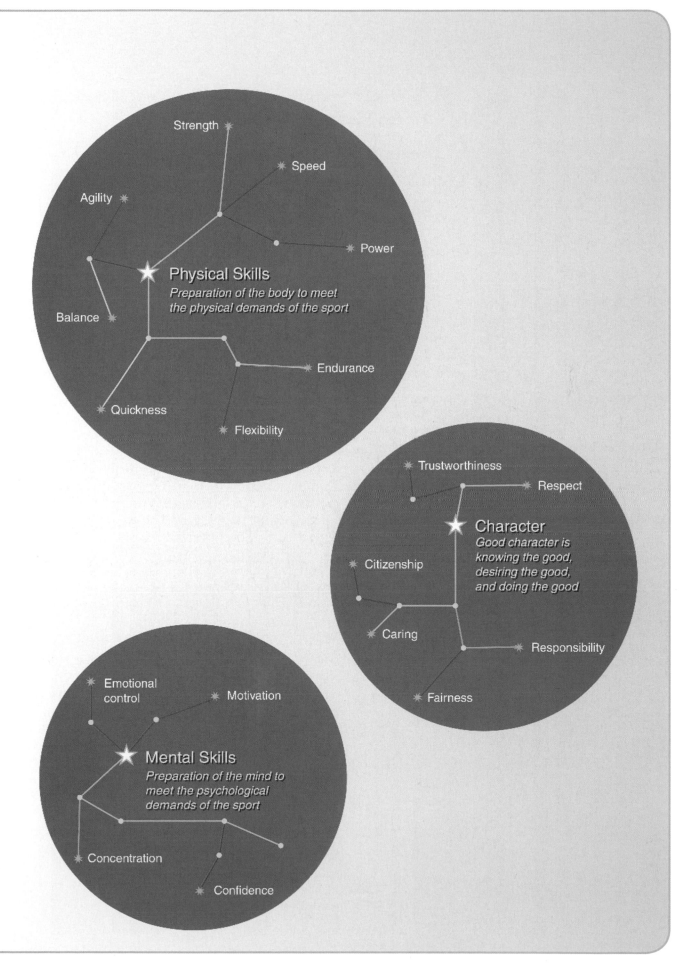

Physical Skills
Preparation of the body to meet the physical demands of the sport

Strength
Speed
Agility
Power
Balance
Endurance
Quickness
Flexibility

Character
Good character is knowing the good, desiring the good, and doing the good

Trustworthiness
Respect
Citizenship
Caring
Responsibility
Fairness

Mental Skills
Preparation of the mind to meet the psychological demands of the sport

Emotional control
Motivation
Concentration
Confidence

Figure 9.2
Tactical triangle.

Part of being a successful coach is being a great teacher of technical skills. If you identified a weakness in your knowledge and ability to teach the technical skills in your sport, take steps to become a better technical coach.

Tactical Skills

Tactical skills are problem-solving skills that are based on

1. an athlete's ability to "read the play," which defines the problem encountered in the contest;

2. an athlete acquiring knowledge about a number of factors to determine the best solution to the problem; and

3. the athlete's decision-making skills to solve the problem effectively.

These three factors, as shown in figure 9.2, form the tactical triangle; together they determine a player's "game sense," which simply means a player's ability to identify and solve the problems encountered when playing the game. Let's look at these three elements of tactical skills more closely.

Reading the Situation

Tactical skills require that athletes have the cognitive skills to "read the situation" to know what is happening during the contest. Reading the situation involves perception, attention, and concentration. To read the situation, athletes must recognize and interpret the stimuli in the sport environment (perception), focus on the important stimuli in the situation (attention), and keep their attention focused on the relevant cues in the situation without being distracted by other stimuli (concentration).

Reading the situation involves recognizing cues such as the opponent's body position and visual focus, interpreting verbal and nonverbal communications among the members of the opposing team, and noticing the pattern of responses or tendencies of the opponent in previous similar situations. It's feeling the balance and weight transfer of the opposing wrestler. It's recognizing the open player on the soccer field. It's seeing the stance of the softball player shift, indicating an intention to hit to right field. Every sport has its complex set of cues that, if read correctly, may give players a tactical advantage.

Tactical knowledge

Acquiring Knowledge

To employ smart tactics during contests, athletes need to know the following:

- ▶ The rules, which determine what players can and cannot do legally in the game
- ▶ The team strategy for the season and for a particular game, the latter being what we call the *game plan*
- ▶ The tactical options for various game situations, including what technical skills are best to use in specific situations
- ▶ The strengths and weaknesses of their opponents
- ▶ Their own strengths and weaknesses

Making Decisions

Armed with accurate perceptions of the immediate situation (reading the situation) and relevant tactical knowledge, players need the decision-making skills to solve the problems posed by the game or the opponents. Often they must make these complex decisions in fractions of a second in the midst of what appears to be chaotic action. In the past we thought that we could drill players to such an extent that all of their actions would be automatic and they would not need to make decisions when they play. We now know better! Developing tactical skills—and thinking athletes—is vital to every sport. Assess your tactical skill knowledge on page 186.

Decision-making skills

Part of being a successful coach is being a great teacher of tactical skills. If you've identified that your knowledge is inadequate or that your teaching of these tactical skills could improve, then plan how you can acquire these coaching skills. You'll learn more about teaching tactical skills in chapter 11.

Other Competencies

Technical and tactical skills are essential, but there are other important skills for athletes to learn, as shown in figure 9.1. Athletes need to be physically and mentally competent to optimize their chances of success; they need good communication skills; and they should learn to play with good character.

Assessing Your Tactical Skill Knowledge

Determine your knowledge of, and ability to coach, the tactical skills of your sport.

1. How competent are you at reading the situation, from the little cues from individual players to the patterns of team play?

Weak				Strong
1	2	3	4	5

2. How skillful are you at teaching your players to read the play?

Weak				Strong
1	2	3	4	5

3. How capable are you of making appropriate tactical decisions?

Weak				Strong
1	2	3	4	5

4. How skillful are you at teaching tactical decision making to your players?

Weak				Strong
1	2	3	4	5

5. To what extent do you plan practices to teach decision making so that your athletes can develop their tactical skills?

Seldom				Usually
1	2	3	4	5

Physical Skills

In part IV you'll learn much more about how to prepare your athletes so that they are in physical condition to meet the demands of the sport—what we call physical fitness. Those demands vary widely from sport to sport, some calling for extraordinary endurance, and others for power, speed, strength, or various combinations of these. When athletes are unfit, their technical skills deteriorate, their decision making falters, and their motivation declines.

As a coach you want to help your athletes not only physically train, but also understand how to physically train so that they can take greater responsibility for their fitness during and after the season. Physical conditioning need not be painful drudgery. We all are willing to work (play) harder when we like what we're doing. Using the principles from the games approach, you can motivate your athletes to train harder through creative games and challenging goals to make physical conditioning more enjoyable.

Mental Skills

Just as athletes need to be physically fit, they also need to be mentally fit to play sports well—to play with confidence, concentration, motivation, and emotional control, or in brief, to be mentally tough. A player is not likely to make good decisions when playing under emotional stress or when lacking confidence and concentration.

Space does not permit me to address the complex subject of mental training in this book, but the American Sport Education Program offers a Silver Level course on how to teach your athletes psychological skills (see the appendix).

Communication Skills

I emphasized the importance of developing your own communication skills in chapter 6, but these skills are also essential for your players. Athletes need to be able to send and receive effective messages for the following reasons:

▶ Communication with teammates during a contest is often vital to facilitate team play—for example, verbal commands; nonverbal signals; and those almost imperceptible movements of the body, face, and eyes that communicate a direction to a player. Most coaches just hope these communication skills develop within their teams, but better coaches direct it to happen.

▶ Outside of the game, how athletes communicate with their fellow teammates plays a huge role in determining the cohesiveness of the team.

▶ Communication is at the heart of the relationship between you and your athletes. Although you may have superb communication skills, if your players do not, then their learning and performance may be limited. Players who can demonstrate listening skills, manage their emotions, resolve conflict, and express themselves are better positioned to be successful.

▶ Athletes need to learn to communicate with the public, especially with the media when being interviewed and possibly when speaking to groups.

Take some time to think about the communication skills your athletes need in your sport. As you work with your players, determine whether you need to help them develop their communication skills on and off the field.

Character Development

Our sixth constellation of skills addresses character education (see chapter 4). Although athletes certainly don't need to be good characters to win in sports, they do need to be good characters to win in life. You can help them achieve this much-needed life skill.

The Collective Skills

Of course all six constellations of skills interact with each other. Technical skills without tactical skills can lose you many games, and tactical skills without the technical skills to execute them can leave you frustrated as well. Technical skills without the physical and mental training to meet the demands of the competitive event can result in physically or mentally fatigued athletes unable to perform at the level you know they can. Communication and character skills are like the glue that bonds a team together to perform well and with "class."

I'm sure you appreciate now the range of knowledge you must have to do your job well. You can see why being a successful coach requires much more knowledge and training than what is acquired from having played the sport, although that is very helpful. You need to be able to take apart and put back together these skills—to see them from different perspectives, to apply, adapt, integrate, and critically evaluate them for each athlete.

Making the Games Approach Work for You

Coaches who are master teachers do far more than just present the technical and tactical skills of the sport; they provide their athletes with real understanding about those skills. They help them understand how each technique and tactic fits into the way the sport is played. They strive to provide them with insight so they can make intelligent decisions about how to perform, and they encourage self-reflection. With better understanding and increased autonomy, athletes are able to take greater responsibility for their own learning.

When I first coached, I used the traditional approach because it was the only approach I knew. Coaches who have used this approach for many years and who have been successful, especially command-style coaches, will be reluctant to try an alternative approach. Also, the traditional approach is certainly efficient in developing some aspects of skilled performance. But the games approach, which is athlete centered, enables you to help your athletes master *all* of the sport skills they need to be successful athletes, and does so in a way that retains the joy of sport participation.

As you prepare for your next season of coaching, reflect on your practices and ask yourself whether adopting the games approach may improve your coaching. Review the drills you use to see how closely they align with what your players do in games. Think about the range of skills that are required to play your sport, and consider how much time you spend on developing each of them. Are you helping your athletes develop tactical skills so that they are thinking athletes with good game sense? Are you helping them to develop their physical and mental skills, and are you helping them to develop character?

Adopt the games approach in whole or in part by trying some of the following ideas:

- ▶ Begin your practice with a game.
- ▶ Redesign some of your drills to make them more gamelike.
- ▶ Study your sport more to identify the tactical principles of the sport, and then design a series of drills to help athletes grasp these principles.
- ▶ Try a freeze replay and ask a question rather than give the answer.
- ▶ Build in time for your athletes to reflect on their actions during the practice.

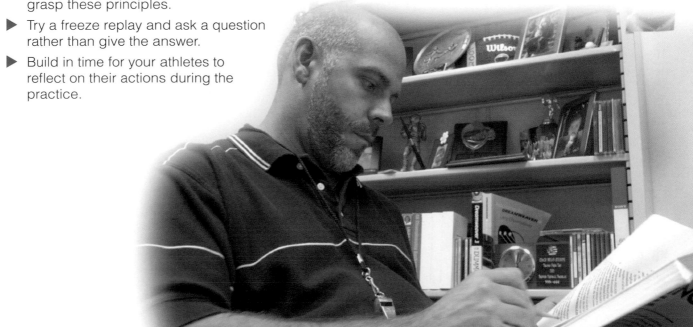

Questions for Reflection

▶ What is the difference between technical and tactical skills? **(p. 169)**

▶ What is the difference between strategy and tactic? **(p. 169)**

▶ Do you use the traditional approach to coaching? What are some of the shortcomings of this approach? **(p. 172)**

▶ What is the value of the guided discovery inherent in the games approach? Are your athletes more engaged when they have more control over their learning? **(p. 175)**

▶ What can you do to "shape" the play of your athletes to create the learning environment you want? **(p. 176)**

▶ How can you focus your players on the key elements you want them to learn? **(p. 177)**

▶ What are some ways you can enhance play to challenge your athletes during practice? **(p. 178)**

▶ What are the three competencies athletes must have to be good tactical players? **(p. 184)**

▶ Do you provide physical training for your athletes along with practice in technical and tactical skills? **(p. 186)**

▶ Do you believe that mental skills training is important for athletes? **(p. 187)**

▶ Why are communication skills important to athletes? Are your athletes good communicators on and off the field? How can you help them improve this skill? **(p. 187)**

▶ What is the value of character education for athletes? **(p. 188)**

Reference

Launder, Alan. 2001. *Play practice: The Games Approach to teaching and coaching sport.* Champaign, IL: Human Kinetics.

10

Teaching Technical Skills

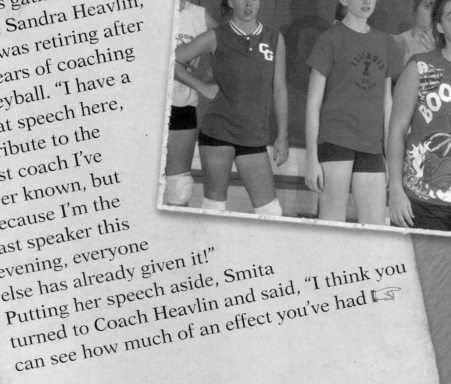

Smita Thakur stood at the podium for a moment looking at the hundreds of former athletes and friends gathered to honor coach Sandra Heavlin, who was retiring after 36 years of coaching volleyball. "I have a great speech here, a tribute to the best coach I've ever known, but because I'm the last speaker this evening, everyone else has already given it!" Putting her speech aside, Smita turned to Coach Heavlin and said, "I think you can see how much of an effect you've had ☞

on our lives, how much you have helped us become better persons. But one thing I've not heard stated this evening is just how you did that. I think it's because you're a great teacher of volleyball skills. You didn't *give* us motivation, self-confidence, or leadership skills. You taught us the game of volleyball very well; and as we learned to serve with power, to block effectively, and to dig skillfully, we *gave ourselves* confidence—we saw that we could achieve more, and that we could be leaders on and off the court. But it only happened because you taught us the game so masterfully."

Coaching is teaching, and teaching is helping your athletes learn. In this chapter we'll focus on teaching your athletes the technical skills to be successful. In chapter 11 we'll look at helping them learn the tactical skills they need to play the game well. I'll use the terms *technique* and *technical skills* interchangeably in this chapter. Many of the teaching principles presented here also apply to teaching the other five constellations of skills discussed in chapter 9.

☛ **If I do a good job of teaching in this chapter, you'll learn**

▶ how athletes learn technical skills by developing motor programs,

▶ the three stages of learning technical skills and your coaching role when players are in each of these stages,

▶ the four steps to teaching technical skills effectively, and

▶ a set of principles for conducting better practices.

Learning Technical Skills

Learning is a relatively permanent improvement in performance as a result of practice. Learning is not directly observable; it is inferred from changes in performance over time. Because things other than learning can cause changes in performance, however, it is not always easy to know whether an athlete has actually learned a technical skill. For example, athletes may perform better because they've matured from the previous season or simply because they've had a lucky day. Athletes sometimes perform poorly because of an injury or illness or loss of concentration. You know learning has occurred when there is a relatively permanent improvement in performance.

Let's look at how athletes learn technical sport skills. That knowledge will be useful when planning and conducting your practices.

Mental Blueprints

Experts used to think that athletes learned technical skills by developing mental blueprints through repeated practice of the task. This explanation worked well for very simple techniques, but as scientists studied highly complex techniques such as shooting in basketball, pitching in baseball, and volleying in tennis, they realized that these tasks actually consist of many different responses of a similar type.

Because each mental blueprint would be useful only under conditions identical to those under which it was developed, you would need millions of blueprints to perform technical skills well. Even if your brain could accommodate so many blueprints, it could not constantly select the right ones to fit the rapidly changing situations in many sports. Thus, the concept of learning through mental blueprints has been debunked.

Abstracting Rules

Today scientists believe that athletes learn complex technical skills in quite a different way. They abstract key pieces of information from each performance to create rules about how to perform in the future. This is a far more efficient way to deal with the many variations that are possible for complex sport skills.

This process of abstracting information from specific experiences to create rules for guiding future behavior is the way we humans learn many things. It is a unique ability of the human brain. For example, when learning language so that you can read this book, you don't learn every possible combination of words to understand their meaning (the blueprint approach). Instead you learn language by coming to understand a set of rules that permits you to use words in a far more functional and creative way.

Each time athletes practice technical skills, their brains seek to abstract the following four types of information about the movement:

- ▶ The condition of the environment (e.g., the playing field or the position of opposing players) and the position of the athlete at the time the technique is initiated
- ▶ The demands of the movement being performed, such as speed, direction, and force
- ▶ The consequences as perceived by the senses during and after the movement
- ▶ A comparison of the actual outcome with the intended outcome based on available feedback (information that tells them how well they are performing the task)

When a wrestler is learning a single-leg takedown, for example, each time he executes the technique, his brain records the position of his opponent and he notes the speed, force, and timing of his movement to execute the move. Then he records his perceptions of the movement—from his visual, tactile, and kinesthetic senses—and whether the takedown was successful. From practicing the single-leg takedown hundreds, maybe even thousands, of times, the wrestler forms rules about executing the technique such as "shoot the takedown when the opponent is moving toward you."

Motor Program

As athletes continue to practice, using feedback to adjust their technique, they synthesize these abstracted pieces of information to mold the general rules into what is called a motor program. A *motor program* is a complex set of rules that, when called into action, permits athletes to produce a movement. Once the movement is initiated, the basic pattern of action is carried out, even though the wrong movement may have been selected. Minor adjustments can be made in the basic movement pattern as it is being executed, but the pattern itself cannot be changed.

For example, in attempting to hit a pitched baseball, once you initiate the swing, you will complete the basic action, even if you later see that the ball is outside the strike zone. We used to think that once the motor program was initiated, minor adjustments in the movement in response to sensory feedback could not be made. Evidence now shows that

minor responses are possible. Thus when hitters see that the ball will be outside of the strike zone, they can adjust their swing to reach out for it.

This motor program, remember, is only a generalized plan of a movement; it enables athletes to make skillful movements. To actually make the correct movement, athletes must add the details of the particular situation. In the baseball example, the hitter's motor program enables him to swing skillfully at a rapidly thrown ball, but to hit a specific pitch, the hitter must determine its exact speed and location.

One of your major responsibilities, then, as a coach is to *help athletes develop good motor programs.* Many factors affect athletes' learning of motor programs: their characteristics such as talent, maturation level, and experience; their motor and cognitive intelligence; their capacity to pay attention and concentrate; and their motivation. Their learning will also be influenced greatly by what you do—how you teach the technique, shape the practice activities, and focus their attention on the important elements of the technique through feedback—in short, how effective you are as a teacher.

Three Stages of Learning

When was the last time you learned a new technical skill? Perhaps it's been a long time, and you've forgotten what it's like to learn. In this section you will become an athlete again, and I'll be the coach teaching you how to juggle.

As you practice, and with my skillful coaching, you will move through three stages of learning—the mental stage, the practice stage, and the automatic stage—to become an expert juggler. These three stages are shown in figure 10.1 as a learning continuum. Keep in mind that each stage of learning requires different instructional strategies.

Mental stage Practice stage Automatic stage

Figure 10.1   The learning road.

Mental Stage

When you are first learning to juggle, your objective is to understand what to do to perform the technique correctly. This requires a great deal of cognitive activity as you search for a mental plan of the correct technique. That's why this beginning stage of learning is called the mental stage. During this stage your brain seeks connections with previous activities you've learned, looks for familiar movement patterns, and begins to build new neural connections.

Characteristics of the Mental Stage

1. Let's assume that you've never juggled before. The first thing you need is an overall picture of the task, which is best provided through demonstration and explanation.

2. Your goal when practicing during this mental stage is to develop a good plan for what you need to do.

Coaching in the Mental Stage

From my experience in coaching juggling, I have learned that some people can get the basics in only a few minutes, but others take quite a bit longer. I must be careful not to teach too much during this mental stage because it is easy to overload your learning circuits. Nevertheless, I'm often tempted to do so because I know juggling so well and it gives me a chance to show what I know. Sometimes I'm impatient and try to go faster than you are able to learn. You may need to remind me to go slowly with you and be patient.

Practice Stage

The next stage of learning is called the practice stage. It doesn't mean that you didn't practice during the mental stage, because you did, but now the emphasis is on the quality of practice to refine the technique. You will spend much more time in this stage than you did in the mental stage.

Characteristics of the Practice Stage

1. During this stage the mental energy required will be less, and your mental activity will shift from an emphasis on learning the sequence of movements to refining the timing and coordination of each phase of the juggling sequence.

2. As you learn the basic fundamentals, or mechanics, your errors decrease and your performance becomes more consistent—a good sign that learning is happening.

3. As you begin to practice juggling, you will benefit from sensory feedback—information from your visual and kinesthetic senses that tells you how well you are performing the task.

4. In the early stages of learning, sensory feedback often is not enough information to optimize learning. Thus, as your coach I can provide you with useful feedback to help you learn faster. For example, I can point out that you should not try to watch any one ball, but maintain an overview of all three balls. (I should also point out that many people learn to juggle without a coach, but with good coaching they learn to juggle better, faster.)

5. I need not give you feedback when your senses already tell you you're making errors. If, for example, you are repeatedly dropping the balls or don't have the feel for how high to throw them, you don't need me yelling in your ear, "Hey, dumb klutz, you're screwing up." You can see that!

6. On the other hand, offering positive reinforcement when your senses tell you you're performing correctly can be helpful.

7. As you continue practicing and learning, you need far less help from me. Increasingly you are able to detect your own errors, and this important ability enables you to make your own adjustments as you practice.

Coaching in the Practice Stage

As I coach you during this phase, I know that it is not just the quantity of practice but also the quality that will increase your rate of learning. Thus, I need to make good judgments about

▶ how often you should practice,

▶ how long each practice should be,

▶ whether the juggling routine should be practiced in parts or as a whole, and

▶ when you should move on to more advanced juggling techniques.

I have learned that my decisions are more effective if I work with you rather than dictate to you. By doing so I am in a better position to consider your capacity to learn, your motivation, and your level of fatigue.

Automatic Stage

As you continue to practice juggling, the technique becomes more and more automatic. Consequently you free up more mental capacity, which you can use to focus on the more critical elements of juggling to achieve superior performance or to add flair or style. You are now ready to learn to juggle more balls, or differently shaped objects, or to juggle while riding a unicycle on a high wire!

Characteristics of the Automatic Stage

1. Now your juggling performance is very reliable, and when you do make an error, you frequently know what to do to correct it.

2. In fact, in the automatic stage, overanalyzing your juggling is likely to hurt your performance. The skill is now so automatic that when you begin analyzing it during execution, you disrupt your performance. That's why at times I may tell you to stop thinking and just let it happen.

3. It's a wonderful feeling to develop a technical sport skill to the automatic stage, but as you likely know, that technique must be practiced continually to keep it in the automatic stage.

Coaching in the Automatic Stage

As you enter the automatic stage of learning, my coaching role changes. Instead of my continuing to decide how you should practice, you take increasing responsibility for your technical skill development. Although most complex sport skills are never totally mastered, and although I may be able to continue to help you *learn* the finer points of juggling, my coaching role shifts to helping you *perform* the skills you know how to do. An example will best make the point.

You enter your first contest and perform poorly. I assume you haven't mastered the technique as well as I thought. Consequently I set up an intensive practice schedule to thoroughly ingrain the technique, perhaps to the point that you become totally bored with juggling. In actuality you performed poorly because you were extremely anxious in your first competition. Practicing juggling more does little to help you manage your anxiety in the future. However, if I recognize that you need help in controlling your anxiety, then my task is to help you further develop your mental skills.

If you employed inappropriate tactics in your first competition, then we need to spend time practicing your tactical skills. If you became verbally abusive when the judges gave you a very low score, then we need to further develop your communication and character skills.

You see the vital point here: When you compete, your technical skills are not the only things that determine your performance; all six of the sport skills discussed in chapter 9 play a part. If I coached you to only learn the technical skill of juggling and didn't coach you to be a complete athlete with effective tactical, physical, mental, and communication skills, I've failed in my job. Part of the art of coaching is knowing when your athletes need help with each of these sport skills.

Teaching Technical Skills

Now I'll let you return to being the coach. Imagine that you begin your practice session with a modified game to emphasize the further development of a technical skill, but as the game progresses you see a pattern of errors that indicates the need to review the fundamentals. So you stop the game and teach the technique using the four steps shown in figure 10.2.

Let's learn more about each of these steps and describe how they are done using the games approach to coaching.

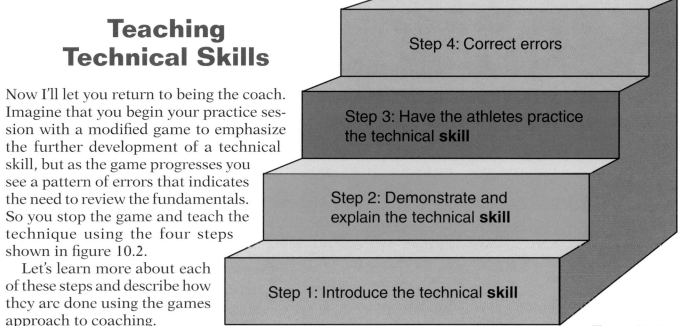

Figure 10.2
Four steps of teaching technical skills.

STEP 1: Introduce the Technical Skill

Introduce the technical skill with enthusiasm expressed in actions and words. Speak clearly and use language your athletes can understand; the younger the athletes are, the simpler your words need to be. Be brief too. Say what you have to say in less than three minutes. Avoid sarcasm, annoying mannerisms, and abusive language; they create a negative learning environment.

A good introduction involves

1. getting the team's attention,
2. arranging the team so all can see and hear you, and
3. naming the technique and explaining how it is used in the game.

Getting the Team's Attention

Develop a regular routine in practice for starting each teaching session. Go to your usual place to begin the session and give a signal, such as blowing a whistle, to get your athletes' attention and bring them into the area. Position yourself to face the team when you speak to them.

If a few athletes are inattentive, look directly at them, move closer to them, and politely but firmly address them by name and ask for their attention. If this fails, have them move to where they cannot disrupt the session. Speak with these athletes either at an opportune time later during the practice or afterward.

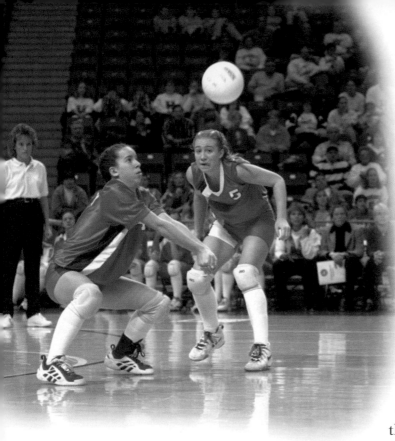

Arranging the Team So All Can See and Hear You

When you speak to your athletes, be sure to organize them so they can see and hear you. If they are milling around or crowding together, you will have more difficulty keeping their attention. Be certain that the background behind you is free of visual distractions and that athletes are not facing the sun. Try also to select a practice area with minimum noise so that athletes can hear you.

Naming the Technique and Explaining How It Is Used

Naming technical skills is important so that you can make quick reference to them. If a skill is widely known by a certain name, use that one. If not, select a short, descriptive title that is easy to remember.

Sometimes the reason for learning a technique is not obvious, especially to athletes with little experience. As I emphasized in chapter 9, the better your athletes understand why they are learning a particular technique and how it fits into the total plan for playing the sport, the easier it is for them to develop a mental plan for learning it. Understanding why they are learning also increases their motivation to learn.

STEP 2: Demonstrate and Explain the Technical Skill

Demonstration and explanation are the primary ways to help your athletes acquire a mental plan for a technique. Someone should do the demonstration who can perform the technique proficiently and whom the athletes respect. If you cannot demonstrate a particular technique, you have several alternatives.

> ▶ Practice the technique until you are able to demonstrate it correctly.
> ▶ Ask someone who is skilled to demonstrate, perhaps a more able player on the team, an assistant coach, or a friend.
> ▶ Show a videocassette to demonstrate the technique.

If none of these alternatives is possible and you cannot give an adequate demonstration, seriously reconsider teaching this technical skill, especially if there is any risk of injury in learning the technique and you don't know how to control this risk.

An effective demonstration and explanation consists of three steps:

1. Demonstrating and explaining
2. Relating the technique to previously learned techniques
3. Checking for understanding

Demonstrate and Explain

Follow these guidelines for giving demonstrations:

▶ Tell them how the demonstration will be given and what to look for.

▶ Make sure you have your athletes' attention during the demonstration.

▶ Demonstrate the whole technique just as it would be performed in a competitive situation.

▶ Demonstrate several times, showing how to perform the technique from different angles.

▶ If the technique is performed from a dominant side, demonstrate it for "lefties" and "righties."

▶ If the technique is complex, demonstrate the major parts separately.

▶ If the technique is performed rapidly, demonstrate it at a slower speed so athletes can see the sequence of movements clearly.

During the demonstration you should also explain how the technical skill is done. However, remember that it is harder for most athletes to convert words into a mental plan for performing the technique than it is to interpret the demonstration. Follow these guidelines for your explanations:

▶ Before the demonstration point out one or two important things to which the athletes should attend.

▶ Keep your explanations simple and brief.

▶ Make certain that the explanation agrees with what is being demonstrated.

▶ Time the explanation to either prepare the athletes for what they will see or to reinforce what they just saw.

Relate the Technique to Previously Learned Techniques

After the technique is initially demonstrated, relate it to any previously learned techniques. Why is this important? As you learned earlier, the motor programs for a technique are generalized rules. Thus it is possible to transfer some of these rules for movement to the new technique being learned. For example, if you are teaching the tennis serve, tell and show your athletes how this skill is similar to throwing a ball.

Check for Understanding

Now check to see if your athletes understand how to perform the technique by inviting or asking questions. If necessary, repeat a question so everyone can hear. Keep your answers short and relevant. Don't begin explaining all the nuances of the technique at this point.

STEP 3: Have the Athletes Practice the Technical Skill

Athletes should begin practicing the technique as soon as possible following the demonstration and explanation. This brings you to a critical decision: Should your players practice the whole technique, or should you break it into parts?

Whole Versus Part Practice

The whole method of practice is obvious: The whole technique is practiced intact. The part method is actually the whole-part-whole method. You teach the whole method as just outlined, practice it in parts, and then recombine the parts back into the whole through practice.

What's the best method to use? When possible, it is best to practice the whole technique to avoid spending time combining the parts back into the whole and to help the athletes learn how to use the technique in the context of the game. However, if the technique is so complex that athletes cannot develop a good mental plan (the first stage of learning), then you should break the technique into parts.

When to Break Techniques Into Parts

To decide whether to break a technical skill into parts, you need to evaluate the task on two dimensions: its complexity and the interdependence of the parts. Two questions will help you determine task complexity, or how difficult it may be for athletes to develop a good mental plan:

1. How many parts are there to the task?
2. How mentally demanding is the task?

Next you need to evaluate how interdependent or independent the parts of the task are. That is, how closely is one part of the technique related to the next? For example, in the tennis serve, you can fairly easily separate the ball toss from the swing of the racket, but you really can't separate the racket swing and contact with the ball from the follow-through.

When the task is low in complexity and high in interdependence, have your athletes practice the whole technique. By contrast, part practice is better when the task is high in complexity and low in interdependence. I've illustrated this in figure 10.3, indicating how I would apply these rules for certain sport skills. You will notice that I've listed only one technique in the part method category. That is because few technical skills are low in interdependence. However, a great many technical skills can be taught by using a combination of the part and whole methods.

Where to Break Techniques Into Parts

Now you have some guidance as to when to break a technique into parts, but how do you know where to make the breaks in the sequence of movements? This is another judgment you must learn to make, perhaps with help from more experienced coaches. In general, the more interdependent the movement, the more it should be left intact. When you analyze a technique, look for points in the movement at which there is less interdependence, or where there is a transition from one type of movement to another. Most technical skills have a preparation

phase, an action phase, and a follow-through phase. Often you can break between the preparation and action phases; it's usually not easy to break between the action and follow-through phases.

Integrating Parts Back Into the Whole

You can teach technical skills many different ways. Just because you are breaking a technique into parts, for example, doesn't mean that you must teach each part independently. If an athlete has mastered a few parts of a technique but still needs work on others, or if an athlete needs work on putting parts together, you might select the *progressive-part method.* Start by having an athlete practice the first part of a technique. Then move on to the next part by having the athlete practice it together with the first part. Continue by progressing through each part of the technique until the athlete is finally practicing the entire technique.

Attention focus is an approach that involves practicing the entire technique, but concentrating on only one aspect of the technique. You might instruct discus throwers, for example, to practice the entire throw, but to focus only on keeping the discus as far as possible from the body as they pull. This method tends to work best with more skilled athletes. Athletes who are still trying to learn the fundamentals of a technique may have difficulty focusing on only one aspect.

Interdependence of task parts

High		Low
Whole method	Whole and part methods combined	Part method
Weightlifting Archery Shooting Heading a soccer ball Cycling	Tennis serve Floor exercise routine Swimming strokes Golf swing Pitching a baseball Basketball layup	Dance sequences
Low		High

Complexity of tasks

Figure 10.3 Complexity and interdependence determine whether skills should be taught in parts or as a whole.

Better Practice Principles

Once you have decided whether you will practice using the whole or the whole-part-whole method, you're ready to plan your practice. Figure 10.4 lists my seven principles for better technical skill practice based on the games approach.

Remember too that formal practice often doesn't provide enough time to master technical skills thoroughly. Teach your athletes how to practice these techniques on their own if they can do so safely. Now let's look at each of the principles in greater depth.

Figure 10.4

Seven Principles for Technical Skill Practice

1. Have athletes practice the right technique.

2. Have athletes practice the technique in gamelike conditions as soon as they can.

3. Keep practices short and frequent when teaching new techniques.

4. Use practice time efficiently.

5. Make optimal use of facilities and equipment.

6. Make sure athletes experience a reasonable amount of success at each practice.

7. Make practice fun.

PRINCIPLE 1: Have Athletes Practice the Right Technique

Suppose you saw me practicing a volleyball serve and said, "Hi there. What are you doing?" and suppose I replied, "Why I'm learning how to play tennis." Now that would make you wonder about my sanity. Suppose I then said, "You know, I've been working hard at this, but my tennis just isn't getting any better. Got any suggestions?" Your reply would be obvious: "If you want to learn how to play tennis, you need to practice tennis!" Of course you would be right—and I'd thank you for not calling me an idiot.

I use this example to overstate the principle. As noted in chapter 9, one of the most common mistakes in designing practice experiences is having athletes perform drills that do not help them learn the techniques required to play the sport. A drill often only teaches the skill unique to that drill. What does running through a series of tires or ropes teach a football player? My answer is, how to run through tires and ropes, but I've never seen tires or ropes on the playing field during a football game.

Many coaches use drills merely because their own coaches used them in the past. Carefully analyze the drills you use. Select only those that you are confident will help your athletes learn the techniques needed to play the sport. Otherwise you may spend time helping your athletes get better at the wrong things.

Practice like you play, and your athletes are more likely to play like they practice.

PRINCIPLE 2: Have Athletes Practice the Technique in Gamelike Conditions

This principle is closely related to principle 1. The purpose of many drills is to limit the variety of choices to be made and responses to be performed. That's useful when athletes are initially learning complex techniques, but when such drills are overused and competitive simulations are few, athletes are not prepared to make choices and responses in the rapidly changing conditions of a game. Thus, as you learned from principle 1, have your athletes practice what is relevant and pertinent when actually playing the sport.

To apply principle 2, athletes should also practice the technique at the speed it is to be performed in competition, provided it can be executed safely and with a reasonable degree of accuracy. This produces more rapid and effective learning than does emphasizing slow, accurate movements and gradually increasing the speed. On the other hand, if the technique requires both speed and accuracy, practice should give equal emphasis to both.

When you adopt the games approach to coaching, you'll be much more likely to apply principles 1 and 2—practicing the right techniques in gamelike conditions.

PRINCIPLE 3: Keep Practices Short and Frequent When Teaching New Techniques

When first learning a technique, athletes are likely to make many mistakes and tire quickly. Therefore, they should practice the technique frequently, but not for too long.

In other words, when athletes must use considerable mental and physical effort to perform a technique, practice should be interspersed with either rest intervals or practice of another technique that uses different muscle groups and demands less effort.

PLEASE WALK

Slower Swimmers

PRINCIPLE 4: Use Practice Time Efficiently

Here are some big practice time wasters and a suggestion or two for improving your use of time:

Time wasters	Time savers
Drills in which most of the athletes' time is spent waiting.	Reorganize drills so athletes are more active.
The coach talks too much.	Keep demonstrations, explanations, and feedback concise.
Moving between activities in the practice schedule.	Be sure you have a practice plan so you know what you'll do next, and develop routines for athletes to follow when changing activities.
Practicing things that don't help athletes play the sport better; selecting useless drills.	Don't spend too much time on techniques athletes already know well; work on those that need the most improvement.
Dealing with athletes' misbehavior.	Separate the misbehaving athlete from the team, have the team continue practicing, and then speak with the misbehaving athlete.
Insufficient facilities or equipment or not having the facilities or equipment ready.	Be sufficiently organized to make the best use of the facilities and equipment available.

Identify the time wasters in your practices and find ways to make your practices more efficient.

PRINCIPLE 5: Make Optimal Use of Facilities and Equipment

Design practice activities to make efficient use of your facilities, equipment, and assistant coaches. Consider not only maximum use, but also best use.

PRINCIPLE 6: *Make Sure Athletes Experience a Reasonable Amount of Success at Each Practice*

If you have set realistic instructional goals and you have helped your athletes set realistic personal goals, as discussed in chapter 7, they will be no strangers to success. An important way to build success into every practice is to select the right progressions for learning technical skills. If you make the steps too difficult, then few athletes can experience success. If athletes are having difficulty performing a technique correctly, you may want to give them a break or have them practice some other aspect of the sport. You may even want to back off from a new technique entirely and approach it afresh another day. Forcing the learning process is likely to produce failure and frustration.

Plan your athletes' success by teaching skills effectively.

PRINCIPLE 7: *Make Practice Fun*

You can avoid boring practice sessions by using a lot of variety around a specific technical theme in practice. Practice games, challenges, and gimmicks to add interest are helpful. Changing your practice schedule occasionally, being enthusiastic, and letting the team help plan practices also are useful ways to make practices more fun.

STEP 4: Correct Errors

Practice alone is not enough to learn a technique correctly. For practice to be productive, you must provide your athletes with two types of information to correct errors:

▶ How the completed performance compared with the desired performance

▶ How to change an incorrect performance to more closely approximate the desired performance

Both types of information are called *feedback*.

Observe and Evaluate Performance

The process of helping your athletes correct errors begins with you observing and evaluating their performances to determine the cause of the errors. Did they not learn the technical skill well, or do they need further development of tactical, physical, mental, or communication skills? This is one of the big challenges in coaching—identifying the correct cause of inadequate performances. If athletes consistently demonstrate good technique in practice, but not in games, then they probably need help with their mental skills. If they demonstrate good technique in practice, but display poor judgment in using those skills in games, then you will want to emphasize tactical skill training.

There is no substitute for knowledge and experience in correcting technical errors. The better you understand a technical skill—not only how it is done correctly but what causes players to err—the more helpful you will be in correcting mistakes. Experience is the most common way to learn to correct errors, but you can expedite the slow process of learning by experience through the study of sport biomechanics and the technical skills in your sport. The use of videotapes to observe your athletes more carefully can also be of great help.

One of the most common coaching mistakes is to provide inaccurate feedback and advice on how to correct errors. Don't rush into error correction; wrong feedback or poor advice will hurt the learning process more than no feedback or advice. If you are uncertain about the cause of the problem or how to correct it, continue to observe and analyze until you are more certain. As a rule, you should observe the error several times before attempting to correct it.

Providing Feedback

Take this short true–false test to check your common sense about giving feedback:

1. Save feedback until the end of practice so as not to disrupt practice time.

   False. The sooner you give feedback, the more likely athletes will remember what the feedback pertains to and to practice correctly.

2. More frequent feedback is better than less frequent feedback.

   True, within reason. The more often athletes get useful feedback, the more they will try to correct their performance, and thus, the faster their learning will be. As athletes' technical skills improve, though, they need to learn to rely more on their own feedback and less on feedback from the coach.

3. When an athlete is making several technical errors, it is best to correct only one error at a time.

   True. Learning is more effective when an athlete attempts to correct only one error at a time, which means that you must decide which error to correct first. To do so, begin by determining whether one error is causing another. If it is, have the athlete try to correct that error first because this will eliminate the other error(s). However, if the errors seem to be unrelated, have the athlete correct the error that you think will bring the greatest improvement when remedied. Improvement will likely motivate the athlete to correct the other errors.

reinforces those aspects for all the athletes in a group. An example of specific positive feedback would be "Nice follow-through on that shot." The same principle holds for negative feedback. If a player performs incorrectly, simply saying "That was a terrible shot" is not helpful. The player already knows the shot was terrible. What is important is how to improve. A more effective approach would be to say, "Your shot was off the mark because you allowed your elbow to swing to the outside. Try keeping the elbow tucked in to your side."

4. You and your assistant coaches should be the only people providing feedback in practice.

False. Athletes, especially those who are a little older, should give feedback to each other. A word of caution, though: If athletes are going to give feedback and suggestions for correcting errors, they must be able to offer accurate information.

5. When giving feedback, you should not tell the athlete what was done incorrectly; only provide feedback about how to do the technique correctly.

False. In fact, feedback means to *feed back* exactly what was done. When athletes perform incorrectly, you should feed back what they did wrong. Then explain how to do the technique correctly.

6. Give simple and precise information about how performance can be improved.

True. Tell and show your athletes what they must do to correct errors. Be careful not to go overboard; give just enough information so that they can concentrate on correcting one error at a time.

7. Frequent positive feedback such as "Nice job!" is more important than lots of technical instruction.

False. Positive feedback is good. However, specific positive feedback is much more valuable. Such feedback specifies what was correct and

8. Use sight and sound in providing feedback.

True. People learn in different ways; some gain most from explanations of how to improve, whereas others need demonstrations. Both explanations and demonstrations should incorporate specific feedback. For example, you might demonstrate how a player performed a skill, explain what was good and what you believe needs more attention for improved performance, and demonstrate the refinement you would like to see. Show and tell your players how they can improve using specific positive and negative feedback.

A Positive Approach to Correcting Errors

Throughout this book I have encouraged you to use the positive approach in coaching your athletes. That is especially applicable when correcting errors. Staying positive when your athletes repeatedly perform a technical skill incorrectly or lack enthusiasm for learning can be a real challenge. It can certainly be frustrating to coach athletes who seemingly don't heed your advice and continue to make the same mistake. When an athlete doesn't seem to care, you may wonder why you should. Please know that it is normal to get frustrated at times when teaching skills. Nevertheless, part of successful coaching is controlling this frustration and continuing to search for a way to help your athletes.

A positive approach to coaching takes the perspective that practice is an opportunity for athletes to make mistakes. Remember, a mistake undetected is a mistake uncorrected. Mistakes tell you the progress your athletes are making in the learning process. Root out errors with patience and enthusiastically help your athletes correct them. Share this perspective with your athletes because they'll appreciate knowing they are permitted to err in the journey to master the sport.

Implementing a positive approach to correcting errors may be easier in individual sports than in team sports. After all, you can focus on individuals more easily in such sports as wrestling, tennis, track and field, and skating. Furthermore, your comments are usually more private, so they do not embarrass the performer.

Team sports provide unique challenges. How do you provide individual feedback in a group setting using a positive, ego-protecting approach? Instead of yelling across the court or field to correct an error (and embarrassing the player), consider substituting for the player who erred. Then you can make the correction individually. This procedure offers three benefits:

- ▶ Players are more receptive to the feedback because they are not being corrected in front of an audience.

- ▶ The other team members remain active so they don't pay attention to the discussion between you and the erring player. Furthermore, they are continuing to practice, which gives them additional technical skill development.

- ▶ Because the rest of the team continues to play, you must make corrective comments simple and concise. This saves both you and athlete from long, drawn-out explanations that lack value because of their complexity.

In a team setting you can also use specific positive feedback to emphasize correct group and individual performances. These performances and the accompanying feedback will serve to reinforce the kinds of behavior and play you want to see. Use this approach only for positive statements. Keep your specific negative feedback for individual discussions.

Questions for Reflection

▶ How can you tell whether an athlete's improvement in performance is a result of learning rather than maturity or a lucky break? **(p. 192)**

▶ What is the currently accepted belief about how athletes learn complex technical skills? **(p. 193)**

▶ What factors can affect athletes' learning of motor programs? Of course, a very important factor is your effectiveness as a coach. **(p. 194)**

▶ What are the three stages of learning? How can you address these stages when teaching technical skills to your athletes? **(p. 195)**

▶ What are the four steps of teaching technical skills? Do you go through these steps when you coach? **(p. 199)**

▶ When you introduce a technique to your athletes, do you get their attention, arrange them so they can all see and hear you, and name the technique? **(p. 199)**

▶ How effective are you at demonstrating and explaining techniques to your athletes? **(p. 200)**

▶ Which techniques that you teach could be broken down into parts, and which should be taught as a whole? How do you decide? **(p. 202)**

▶ Do your athletes practice the right techniques in gamelike conditions? **(p. 206)**

▶ How good are you at using practice time efficiently? **(p. 207)**

▶ Do your athletes have fun and experience success at your practices? How can you ensure that they do? **(p. 208)**

▶ When correcting errors, do you determine the cause of the error, give timely and specific feedback, explain and demonstrate how to improve, and keep a positive attitude? **(p. 211)**

11

Teaching Tactical Skills

"Why did she do it?" mumbled Coach Pohlman after Halstead High School softball team lost the state championship to Hillsboro. In the bottom of the seventh (the last inning), Halstead was down by two runs with one out, a runner was on second, and the team's leading hitter Melissa came to bat. She hit a line drive into the gap between center and right field. The runner on second scored easily, and Melissa appeared to have an easy triple, but as she rounded third she glanced over her shoulder and decided to stretch the triple into a home run. ☞

The second base woman relayed the throw from the outfielder, throwing a strike to home; Melissa was easily out. The next batter hit a long fly ball to the outfield to end the game. "If Melissa would only have stayed at third, she would have been the tying run," muttered Pohlman as the team dejectedly walked off the field. She couldn't help but think about all the hard work the team had done to train physically and mentally, the hours and hours of practicing hitting, fielding, and throwing, only to lose the championship because of a poor base-running decision.

How many games are lost not because of a lack of technical skills, but because of poor decision-making skills—what I call tactical errors—25 percent, 50 percent, 75 percent? Who knows the correct answer, but in some sports I dare to assert that tactical errors lose the game more often than technical errors! And yet, as coaches we are often so focused on physical training and technical skills that we neglect tactical and mental skills. This may be partly because we don't realize how important tactical skills are to playing the sport successfully, and partly because we don't know how to help athletes develop tactical skills.

One of the benefits of using the games approach to coaching is that it places far greater emphasis on developing tactical skills, as noted in chapter 9.

☛ **In this chapter you'll learn**

▶ what tactics and tactical skills are,

▶ what's involved in "reading the situation" during play,

▶ what knowledge your athletes need to make good tactical decisions,

▶ factors that influence tactical decision making, and

▶ how to teach tactical skills.

Tactics and Tactical Skills

Figure 11.1 Terminology for the plans of action in sports.

Let's first review some key terms and then consider the three essential elements of tactical skills.

Tactics, Strategies, and Game Plans

You'll recall from chapter 9 that a *tactic* is a plan to gain an advantage in a contest. That tactic can be at an individual level of play (e.g., the player fakes right and drives left) or at a team level (e.g., using a zone rather than person-to-person defense). A *strategy* is the plan of action for your team for a season or series of contests. Many coaches also refer to a *game plan,* which is the application of the team's strategy to a particular contest, emphasizing the use of a particular set of tactics or the assignment of players to guard or block certain opponents. Figure 11.1 provides a perspective on these definitions.

Tactical Triangle

From a tactical perspective, think of a sport contest as a series of problems to be solved by you and your players. Making good tactical decisions to solve these problems involves a complex set of *tactical skills* consisting of

▶ reading the play or situation,

▶ acquiring the knowledge needed to make an appropriate tactical decision, and

▶ applying one's decision-making skills to the problem.

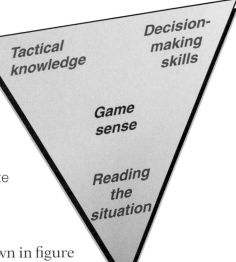

Figure 11.2
Tactical triangle.

These three elements make up the tactical triangle shown in figure 11.2 (we'll examine each of these more closely in a moment). Players with excellent tactical skills have good *game sense,* or what Alan Launder (2001) described as "The ability to use an understanding of the rules; of strategy; of tactics and, most importantly, of oneself to solve the problems posed by the game or by one's opponents" (p. 36).

Tactical skills include the decisions your players make to use various technical skills in certain situations in the contest to optimize their chances of success. For example, it includes the basketball player deciding to shoot a set shot or jump shot; the first baseman deciding to throw overhand or underhand to the pitcher covering the bag; or the hockey player deciding to pass or shoot on goal. Tactical skills also include the decisions you or your players make about the offensive and defensive positions to take prior to the start of play and during the play. For example, the miler deciding to run at the head of the pack, the football defensive line shifting to the right, and the tennis player rushing the net.

Tactical skills also involve making decisions about a set play you or your athletes decide to execute before the action begins as occurs in volleyball, football, and basketball. In football you may decide to fake an off-tackle run and then throw a pass because you notice that the defensive backs are rushing the line hard at the first sign of a run. In basketball you may design a play in which the guard drives the lane and then decides whether to pass to an open player or pull up and shoot a short jumper.

In endurance sports tactical skills involve the pace at which an athlete decides to expend energy by going out hard or laying back for a strong kick at the finish. In wrestling it can be the decision to go all out at the beginning of the match to get a quick pin or to be more defensive initially to fatigue the opponent.

Our focus in this chapter will be on helping you help your athletes make good tactical decisions, but keep in mind that you have tactical decisions to make too. What you learn here can be applied to your own decision making. You'll need to know the rules, decide on a seasonal strategy, and develop a game plan. You'll also need to know the abilities of your players and have as much information about your opponents as possible. And you'll need to accurately perceive what's happening during the contest to help your players make good tactical decisions.

Now let's examine more closely the three elements of our tactical triangle. As we do so, I'll use an example from baseball—stealing second base—throughout, and then summarize that example in a form that will provide you with a model to use in developing your own library of tactical knowledge.

Reading the Situation

To solve the problems in a contest, your athletes first have to recognize what the problems are. That sounds easy enough, but often athletes are so engrossed in the moment-by-moment events of the contest that they fail to perceive the problems. An important but often neglected role of coaches is to help athletes acquire the cognitive skills to recognize the problems they face in the contest. In sport we call these cognitive skills the ability to read the situation, and it's my belief that these skills are among the major factors that separate great athletes from the "almost great."

Reading the situation

Cognitive Skills

Sport scientists have learned that better players learn how to read the situation, which involves the cognitive skills of perception, attention, and concentration. By effectively using these skills to read the situation, athletes gain the knowledge to make the right decision about what technical and tactical skills to use. Moreover they are able to anticipate an action and respond to it much sooner than would a less skilled athlete.

In reading the situation, players gather information from their senses such as vision, audition, tactile or touch, and kinesthetic—the latter being the sensors in our bodies that tell us about the location and movement of our bodies. Then athletes assemble this information to give it meaning. For example, based on the kinesthetic sense a wrestler can feel the pressure applied by the opponent to know when to execute a countermove. From seeing and hearing a ball hit, a baseball player can determines its speed and direction. As the offense snaps the ball and the play develops, the defensive safety can detect the pattern of movements to recognize a pass play in football.

Perception is the term that refers to a person's ability to recognize and interpret

sensory stimuli. In a fast-changing sport situation, there is an enormous amount of sensory stimuli, too much to be processed by the brain. Skillful players learn to direct their *attention* to the important stimuli—the cues—in the flow of action to focus on what is relevant and to filter out the irrelevant to make the appropriate decision. *Concentration* is the ability to sustain one's attention on the relevant cues and not be distracted by all the other stimuli in that situation or by one's own thoughts.

Through practice and coaching, highly skilled players learn to read the situation extremely quickly and make the right response by anticipating what the opponent will do. Highly skilled athletes use the position of the opponent's body, the communication among the opponents, and the probability of succeeding with a certain tactic based on years of experience in similar situations to anticipate an action by an opponent and thus make the right response.

The player with the ball must perceive the position of both his teammates and opponents as he dribbles toward the goal, and then must decide quickly whether to pass or attempt a shot. In the meantime, the opposing goalie must keep a perspective on the position of the nearby opposing players, but concentrate on the attacking player with the ball.

Reading the Situation in Soccer

Two researchers conducted a study in which they took experienced soccer players (13+ years of playing) and less experienced players (4 years of playing) and showed them a series of video clips of soccer plays that ended with a pass by a member of the opposing team. The two groups of players were to imagine themselves as the "sweepers" or defenders trying to stop the advance of the opponents. The players were asked to step on one of four footpads to indicate when and how they would attempt to intercept the opponent's pass. As they did so, the scientists also tracked the players' eye movements as they watched the video clips to learn the cues to which they attended to make their decisions.

The researchers found that the experienced players responded more quickly to the developing play and their attention was focused more on the hips of the opponents, whereas the less experienced players watched the opponents' feet and the ball. The experienced players also spent less time watching the players with the ball, shifting their visual focus more frequently to the nearby opponents who did not have the ball (Williams and Davids 1998).

Stealing Second Base

Meet Sammy Steal, who'll help me illustrate the tactical triangle. While on first base, what should Sammy be aware of or pay attention to with regard to stealing second base?

▶ The first thing is for Sammy to watch his coach for a signal that he should definitely steal or steal only if he sees a good opportunity.

▶ If he is stealing on his own, Sammy needs to know the game situation—the count on the batter, the number of outs, the inning, and the score.

▶ The pitcher's actions are the most important cues for getting a good jump to steal second. Being a smart player, Sammy studies the pitcher's move to home and first base throughout the game to determine when the pitcher will be throwing to first or home.

▶ After the initial break toward second, Sammy should look to home to see what has happened to the ball. If it is hit, Sammy must determine if it will be a base hit or if it will be caught, and quickly decide whether to continue running, stop where he is, or return to first.

▶ If he continues running, Sammy's attention focuses on the infielder covering second base. The infielder's position and movement to catch the ball lets Sammy know whether to slide on the inside or outside of the bag.

Once your players know the cues to attend to, and the possible tactical responses to make in the situation (I'll discuss those later), you'll then want to help them develop their attention and concentration skills. It's one thing to say that you should attend to X, Y, and Z cues in this situation, and it is another thing to do so when there are many distractions and considerable pressure to perform well.

One of the most important factors influencing attention and concentration is the athlete's state of arousal. As discussed in chapter 7, as athletes get optimally "up" for a game, their attention and concentration narrows to focus on the relevant cues in the situation. But when the arousal is too great, especially when the athlete is anxious or threatened, attention narrows too much or turns inwardly with thoughts of self-doubt or fear. The consequence is that the athlete doesn't perceive all the relevant cues in the situation and as a result the athlete's technical and tactical skills suffer.

Improving Attention and Concentration

Here is a list of things you can do to help improve your athletes' attention and concentration when they're playing sports:

▶ Minimize distractions during practice when athletes are first learning skills, but once they have learned technical skills well, introduce gamelike distractions so they can practice focusing their attention and maintaining their concentration.

▶ When your athletes are playing, avoid distracting them with your comments. Save those words of advice for time-outs and practices.

▶ Help your athletes identify what to attend to and what to filter out—creating a "mind-set" or expectation of what to look for in various situations.

▶ Develop and practice pre-event routines that prepare your athletes to concentrate.

▶ Instruct your players to analyze their play only when there is a break in the action. Otherwise they will not have their attention focused on the action.

▶ When players analyze their play, encourage them to keep their focus on the situation or their performance, not on the outcome of the contest.

▶ Athletes who lack confidence and self-esteem are especially vulnerable to distraction. Help these athletes become more confident through positive coaching.

▶ Help athletes develop physical and mental skills to meet the demands of the sport. Attention and concentration falter when athletes are physically and mentally fatigued.

Tactical Knowledge

You might think that the only knowledge needed to make tactical decisions is which tactic to employ in a given situation, but it's not quite that simple. Athletes make better tactical decisions when they have knowledge about these elements:

- ▶ The rules
- ▶ The strategic plan for the season and for that particular game (game plan)
- ▶ The physical playing conditions
- ▶ The strengths and weaknesses of the opponents
- ▶ Their own strengths and weaknesses
- ▶ The tactical options for the various situations within the game

Let's see what your players need to learn about each source of knowledge and how you may be able to help them acquire this knowledge.

Rules

Rules define the boundaries within which athletes are permitted to play so that the contest is equitable. The rules set limits on the tactics players can use. For example, you can't decide to take a safety in football unless you understand the rules about safeties and know when giving up 2 points may be better than giving up 7 points.

Stealing Second Base

What rules does Sammy need to know that are relevant to stealing second?

- ▶ Rules about when runners are safe and out when on and off the bases. For example, Sammy needs to know that when the ball is hit on the ground, he must run to second. When the ball is hit in the air and caught, Sammy must return to first to touch the base after the catch before he can advance to second. When the ball is hit in the air and not caught, he can advance to second without touching first base.

- ▶ Rules pertaining to the pitcher throwing to first and home, especially about balks. This knowledge helps the player get the best start toward second.

- ▶ Rules about interference with the fielders. Sammy must avoid contacting an infielder who is in the base path fielding the ball.

Be sure to review the rules that are infrequently applied in your sport and that your players may misunderstand. In practice games, simulate these situations and describe the correct or preferred action your players should take.

▶ Always have your players play by the rules in practice unless you've modified them for a practice game. Then be sure your players understand that this modification only applies during this practice game. When violations of the rules occur in practice, point them out as a "freeze replay" as described in chapter 9. Players won't avoid violations in games if they don't know they are violations or never had those violations called in practice.

▶ As a backup to teaching the rules in practice games, if your sport has complex rules, consider buying each of your players a copy of the appropriate rulebook. For high school sports the National Federation of State High School Associations publishes rulebooks for each of 14 sports.

▶ In sports in which officials' judgments determine the score an athlete receives, help the athletes understand the criteria officials use to evaluate them.

▶ Rules change periodically. Be sure you know any changes and that you teach these rule changes to your players.

Most players learn the majority of the rules by watching and playing the sport, which is a very good way to learn them. You should expect that your athletes already know many of the rules, and therefore you need comment on them only when a player is in violation. However, many athletes' knowledge of the rules may be incomplete, because some situations occur only rarely, such as the last rule about stealing second base. And sometimes players learn rules incorrectly. Here are some suggestions for making sure your players know the current rules of your sport:

▶ The best way to learn the rules is in practice games in which you explain the rules as they pertain to the technical and tactical skills you are teaching. In this way, your athletes learn the rules in the context of the game rather than in abstraction.

As you plan for your season, be sure to review all of the pertinent rules of the sport you are coaching. As the season progresses, periodically refresh your players' memories about rules you believe they may have forgotten.

Strategic and Game Plans

Your players obviously need to know the strategy, or seasonal plan, you want them to follow as they play. This strategy should be so thoroughly incorporated into your practice plans that it is self-evident and frequently discussed. The team strategy should not be a secret. In individual sports, you may still have a team strategy and then within that plan have specific seasonal goals for each athlete. As we've discussed before, it is far more effective to develop the team strategy with the team and individual goals with each player. When coaches dictate the team strategy and set goals for individuals, the players don't buy into them as readily.

Game plans are formulated by analyzing the strengths and weaknesses of your team and those of the opponents to identify what tactics you may employ to give your team an advantage. Will you charge out hard or lay back initially? Will you keep the ball on the ground or pass? Will you run and shoot or slow down the game? Will you try to run the opposing player in the hope of wearing her down so that your superior conditioning will give you the edge late in the contest?

Stealing Second Base

What does Sammy need to know about the strategic and game plans?

▶ He needs to know if the coach has an aggressive or conservative philosophy about running the bases.

▶ He needs to know whether the plan for this particular game is consistent with the strategic plan or whether it is an exception. For example, the team may have a very aggressive base-running philosophy, but because the pitcher in this game is a left-hander with a very good pickoff move and the catcher has an exceptional arm, the coach directs the team to be more conservative.

Part of being a successful coach is developing your own decision-making skills to develop good strategies and game plans, and then communicating them effectively to your players.

Playing Conditions

You and your players will want to know about any physical playing conditions that may affect your team's play. These conditions vary widely from sport to sport. Part of preparing your team for each contest involves gathering any relevant information about playing conditions and sharing them with your athletes. Here are some factors to consider:

▶ The condition of the playing surface. Does it have good or poor traction? Are there obstacles to avoid?
▶ Weather conditions, including the temperature, humidity, and wind
▶ Altitude
▶ The type of ball and other equipment used to play the game

If there are a lot of physical factors to consider, you may want to develop a checklist for yourself or another person designated to gather this information.

Stealing Second Base

What does Sammy need to know about the playing conditions?

▶ Obviously the quality of the surface between first and second is the primary factor.

▶ Another less likely factor would be a very strong wind, which may affect the speed of the runner and the accuracy of the catcher's throw to second base.

Opponent's Strengths and Weaknesses

Most players want to know as much as they can about their opponents, and in some sports there are elaborate systems for "scouting" the opponents to observe their strengths and weaknesses and their tendencies to employ certain tactics. Most team sports engage in scouting their opponents to assess the strengths and weaknesses of the players and to determine the types of offenses and defenses the opponents use and the opponents' tendencies to employ various tactics in specific situations. It's obviously helpful to know that an opposing team runs the ball to the right 80 percent of the time when the ball is on the left side of the field, or that a wrestling opponent will almost always counter a move with another type of move.

You can obtain information about your opponents by personally observing them play or by watching videotapes of previous games. In sports such as football, basketball, and baseball elaborate systems exist for recording the information about opposing teams. This information is then shared with the team as they prepare for the contest to help them develop the ability to read the situation and therefore have more time to respond to it with a good decision.

Stealing Second Base

What should Sammy know about the opponents?

▶ Does the pitcher have a good pickoff move to first base? If so, Sammy can't take quite as a big a lead, nor can he make as quick a break toward second.

▶ Does the pitcher deliver quickly and throw fast to home? If so, Sammy has less time to get to second.

▶ Does the catcher throw quickly and accurately to second?

▶ How successful have other base runners been at attempting to steal?

Self-Knowledge

To solve the problems in their sports, players must know not only the rules, strategies, game conditions, and strengths and weaknesses of their opponents, but also themselves. They need to know their technical, physical, and mental strengths and weaknesses.

Stealing Second Base

What does Sammy want to consider about himself as he contemplates stealing second base?

▶ How good is he at reading the pitcher's throw to first or home?

▶ How quick is he at getting back to first?

▶ How fast is he at running to second today? Are his legs healthy, or is he nursing an injury?

▶ How skilled is he at sliding into second?

Coaches sometimes comment about players playing "within themselves." What is meant by this phrase is that players should not try to perform beyond their capabilities. Your role as a coach is to help your athletes know their capabilities and make tactical decisions resulting in their playing within themselves. An athlete who is not in good physical condition may want to force the game to a quick conclusion. A player who tends to be a slow starter in a match may want to do more to warm up and get ready to play than others might. A basketball player who is inconsistent from the 3-point line may choose to pass the ball or move in toward the basket before taking a shot.

Tactical Options

Of course athletes need to know the tactical options for the various situations they encounter in their sports. Every sport—running, weightlifting, tennis, lacrosse—has tactics. Generally, the higher the number of players, the more tactics are involved, and the more quickly the situation changes, the more demanding the decision making.

Players can't make decisions about what tactic to use until they know the tactical options available to them. When is it best to hit the ball to the open space? When do you want to play to the opponent's strength, and when do you want to exploit their weakness? When do you want to play it safe, and when do you want to be bold and aggressive? When do you want to stall, and when do you want to hurry?

As part of your coaching duties, you should be teaching your players the tactical options in your sport. You could teach these situation by situation, but for many sports the large number of situations makes this unfeasible. Thus, analogous to the way athletes learn technical skills by creating motor programs or rules that are abstracted from many situations, you can more effectively teach tactical options by teaching tactical principles or rules that are applied in appropriate situations. Examples of tactical principles are as follows:

▶ Move to the open space.
▶ Deny the opponent the open space.
▶ Hit behind the runner.
▶ Reduce the angle of the attack.
▶ Spread the defense.
▶ Get them moving in one direction; then go the other way.
▶ Increase your time to react by reading the play.

Stealing Second Base

What tactical options should Sammy consider as he evaluates his chances of stealing second? The major decision of course is whether to attempt a steal, and that usually is the coach's decision. But at times coaches will instruct players to steal on their own when the opportunity presents itself. Here are some tactical options or guidelines for when Sammy should and should not steal:

▶ Take less risk stealing when your team is behind than when ahead.
▶ Steal more on right-handed pitchers than on left-handed pitchers.
▶ Steal more on pitchers who have a slow motion to home and who throw breaking pitches.
▶ Steal more when catchers have a weak or inaccurate arm.
▶ Steal more as the number of strikes increases against the batter and less as the number of balls increases.
▶ Steal more when a runner is on third because an errant throw may let the third base runner score.
▶ Steal more when the pitcher is dominating the hitters, increasing the chances for a run by means other than base hits.

Decision-Making Skills

Decision-making skills

With the problem in the contest understood, and the appropriate knowledge acquired, your athletes are ready to make the tactical decisions to give them an advantage. In some situations your athletes may have lots of time to decide on the course of action, but in many situations they must process the information and decide very quickly.

The single best way to help your athletes learn to make good, timely decisions is to have them play practice games designed for this purpose, as discussed in chapter 9. In addition Dr. Joan Vickers (no date) described six other methods for teaching what she called decision training. A few of these methods may surprise you.

METHOD 1: Teach the Tactics in Whole, Then the Parts

Consistent with the games approach to coaching, sport scientists (e.g., Doane et al. 1996)

have learned that players develop better decision-making skills when they first are asked to learn complex tactics than when they begin with simple tactics and progress to the more complex. Presumably, once they understand the big picture of the sport, they are challenged immediately to learn to make the decisions necessary to perform well. As they struggle with the complexity of the game, through the use of the decision-making principles discussed in this section, you help them learn the parts of the game that they're having trouble with.

When teaching using this whole–part approach, the bad news is that athletes initially perform more poorly than those who learn the parts only. The good news is that as they continue to practice, athletes begin to sort out the complexities and go on to a higher level of performance. Scientists are not quite sure why those who learn the parts and then are asked to put them into the whole game do not do as well. It may be that they do not see the big picture of how the parts fit in and therefore are unable to integrate the parts into a whole successfully. Or it may be that they underestimate the cognitive effort involved, become bored with the drills, and thus lose motivation to learn.

Determining how in-depth you want to be when presenting the whole sport requires experience and judgment, and is based largely on the ability levels of your players. It also takes experience to develop practice games to work on the parts so they are closely aligned with the whole game.

Team sports, especially, involve complex tactics that players must learn in order to play the game well.

METHOD 2: Have Players Observe Decision Making in Others

How do you help your players understand the whole game and identify the complex problems that they must learn to solve? One way is to observe games with your players, directing their attention to the tactics being employed and the decisions being made. Your goal should be to help your athletes develop their own analytical skills as they observe contests so that they become students of the game independently.

Fortunately it is very easy to observe sport contests. You and your players can attend actual contests in your community, watch them on television, or purchase videocassettes of contests.

Now, what models are best to observe—highly skilled players or those of similar skill to the observer? Actually both are helpful. Observing highly skilled performers helps your athletes learn the correct decisions to make and provides a positive image of what to aspire to. Observing peers is also helpful because the play will be more relevant to them; it also provides a greater opportunity to learn from the mistakes observed. To analyze games independently, however, athletes must be able to recognize errors.

METHOD 3: Have Players Observe Themselves

Just as athletes can learn how to make tactical decisions by observing others, they can learn by observing their own play through video feedback. As with observing other athletes, your athletes should initially observe their own performances with you guiding their observation. You will want to help them identify the tactics being used by the opponent and the tactical opportunities they missed because they didn't recognize the cues. As your athletes develop an understanding of the sport, encourage them to analyze the sport on their own.

METHOD 4: Variable Practice

Based on what you've learned so far, consider the following two methods of practicing hitting baseballs. In option A players hit 15 fastballs, then 15 curveballs, and then 15 change-ups; this is called blocked practice. In option B they hit the same number of fastballs, curves, and change-ups, but the pitcher randomly selects these three pitches for the batter to hit; this is called variable practice.

Would you choose option B? If so, you're right, but why? Are you thinking it's because this type of practice is closer to what happens in the actual game, with the hitter not knowing what pitch is coming? Right again, but why is that important? Part of learning to hit is learning to distinguish between fastballs, curves, and change-ups and then deciding what pitch to swing at. It's about decision making!

Three researchers (see Vickers) actually studied these two practice situations for 12 practice sessions. As you can see in figure 11.3, for the first 8 practice sessions the blocked group performed better, but after the 8th practice they did not improve. The variable practice group continued to improve and eventually went on to hit better than the blocked group, getting three more hits per 45 pitches than the blocked group got during the 12th practice session.

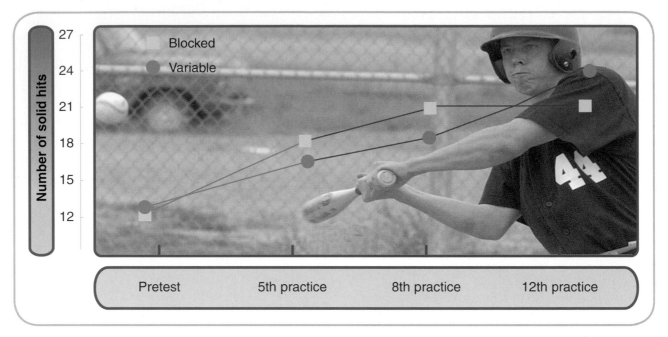

Figure 11.3 Variable practice leads to better long-term practice.

From this study and many others we now know that variable practice, which simulates game conditions, is better than blocked practice, and the primary reason is that it helps players practice making decisions about how to respond to the changing situation. But note that the blocked practice group did better initially, and only after sustained practice did the variable group catch up and pass the blocked group.

The fact that the blocked practice method results in better performances initially seduces many coaches to adopt it. Inevitably, however, players cannot go on to higher levels of performance because they do not learn the decision-making skills they need. Commonly players initially struggle more with variable practice— the games approach— because there is more to learn and thus learning takes longer, but learn they do because they have the opportunity to practice what they must do in the game, and as a result they end up performing at a higher level.

The variability you build into your practices can be within a class of technical skills, among various technical skills, and among various tactics. Variability within a class of skills is like the previous baseball hitting example; it could also be passing in basketball, kicking in soccer, skating in hockey, or many other things.

Design practices so that athletes have the opportunity to practice deciding which technical skill from their repertoire they will want to use in a particular situation. For example, soccer players must have the ability to decide to kick or head the ball to score a goal under various conditions; basketball players must be able to decide to pass, shoot, or drive to the basket; and quarterbacks must be able to choose between passing short or long or keeping the ball and running.

Of course you will also want to design practice games in which your athletes are confronted with the tactical options that they choose among in various game situations.

METHOD 5: Control Feedback

Many years ago I was the sport psychologist for the U.S. Ski Jumping Team. I was watching our team practice with the Canadian team on a very cold day in Thunder Bay, Ontario. The coaches for both teams stood at an observational post and watched each jump. As soon as the U.S. jumpers finished, they picked up a radio to hear the coach's thorough critique of the jump. The Canadian coach, in contrast, would only occasionally comment to his jumpers, and then with only brief remarks. I initially thought the U.S. coach was superior, but then I began to wonder. Which approach do you think is more effective—giving lots of feedback frequently or giving only occasional feedback?

If your answer is occasional feedback, you're right, but why is this better? There are potentially several reasons. With too much feedback athletes may overanalyze during their performances and thus disrupt concentration and flow. In its extreme form it's "paralysis by analysis." Second, think about it from a decision-making perspective. Coaches who provide feedback constantly are doing all of the problem solving, denying their athletes the opportunities to learn to make their own decisions.

What we now know from research (e.g., Lavery 1962; Weeks and Kordus 1998) and experience is that more feedback is better than less feedback when athletes are first learning a skill, and less feedback is better as athletes become more skillful. Part of the art of coaching is knowing when to begin to reduce the amount of feedback and how to encourage your athletes to identify their own problems as they perform and find solutions—in short, helping your athletes become more independent decision makers.

In her decision-training program, Vickers recommends that you identify a range of acceptable performances; when the athlete performs within that range, you need not provide feedback. When the athlete performs outside that range, you provide feedback. We do know that in most cases when feedback is not provided over an extended period of time, performance declines.

Vickers also found that reduced feedback from coaches introduced some problems. First, some athletes misinterpreted the reduction in communication as the coach being displeased with them or ignoring them. Others observing the coach with the athletes—parents and administrators—judged the coach as being less effective than a coach providing more feedback.

Communicate to your athletes that you are reducing the feedback to them so they can develop their own decision-making skills. As you do so, encourage your players to come to you with the problems they encounter when they are unable to find their own solutions. Also, you can prompt their learning by skillfully asking questions about their performance to help them identify the problems they face and find solutions.

If you did not know that it is better to reduce feedback as athletes improve, would you think to reduce feedback? Not likely.

METHOD 6: Ask Questions

Over the years I have observed that highly skilled athletes' knowledge of the technical and tactical skills often exceeds that of their coaches. Some coaches recognize this and shift their role from directing and instructing athletes to "managing" their training and preparation for competition. Others move to a higher level of coaching in which they work very cooperatively with their athletes to solve the problems faced in competition.

This cooperative style of coaching, which I've advocated throughout the book, requires that you shift from constantly giving directions, instructions, and feedback to asking more questions to help your athletes identify and solve the problems that the sport presents. Even if you are not coaching world-class athletes who have more knowledge than you about technical and tactical skills, asking questions is an important tool in developing the decision-making skills of all athletes once they've learned the rudiments of the sport.

Questions have two important purposes:

1. They are probes for you to learn what your athletes need help with.

2. They help athletes think about their experiences to solve the problems they face.

If your athletes already recognize the problem, ask questions to see if they have sufficient information to solve the problem. Do they know the best way to increase strength or build endurance? Do they understand the biomechanics of the skill and how to practice it properly? Are they aware of all of the tactical options in a certain situation?

If they have sufficient information, ask questions to see if they're having trouble making the correct, or a better, decision. Are they having self-discipline problems (e.g., they're unable to perform the training that's necessary)? Are they having trouble reading the play quickly enough to decide what to do? Do they think they need more help practicing decision making?

Ask questions about how a movement felt so the athlete connects the outcome of the response with the kinesthetic sense of making that response. Ask questions about how athletes are feeling physically and mentally as they prepare for competition. Ask how you can help the athlete move to the next level of performance.

Shifting your role to asking more questions is not easy if you've been used to providing all the answers. Asking good questions is challenging, but with practice you can master this important coaching skill if you take the perspective that you're helping your athletes solve the problems they face in competition.

Teaching Tactical Skills

Just as good coaching can shorten the time players need to learn technical skills, good coaching can help reduce the time players need to learn tactical skills. This is no easy task, however. The knowledge of what cues to attend to and what decisions to make based on the cues is not readily available in books or video. Although some coaches and elite athletes have learned these cues and tactical options through years of experience, generally they have not recorded this information so that it is readily accessible. Coaches have a great deal of technical knowledge available to them, but remarkably little tactical knowledge.

So how do you proceed in the absence of a text on how to teach these tactical skills? I've developed a five-step tactical skill development plan that you can use to develop this knowledge. It will help you teach your athletes not only how to read the play, but also how to respond to the situation.

Tactical Skill Development Plan

Develop a plan for teaching a tactical skill in your sport by completing each of the following steps:

STEP 1: Identify the important decisions your players need to make as they play the sport. This is a tremendously valuable exercise that you can use as long as you coach. If you have little experience with the sport, you will still be able to identify the important decisions in several ways. Observe play to see where players make tactical rather than technical errors. Those are the decision-making situations. If you are unable to identify these tactical errors, ask highly experienced players and coaches to do so.

Describe a specific tactical decision athletes must make in your sport.

_____

_____

STEP 2: Determine what knowledge your athletes need to make a good decision regarding the situation described in step 1. What rules do your athletes need to know to make a good tactical decision?

_____

_____

What should your athletes know about your strategic or game plan that is pertinent to this tactical decision?

_____

_____

What playing conditions should your athletes be aware of that may influence their tactical decisions, and how would those conditions influence them?

_____

_____

What particular strengths and weaknesses of the opposing players or team do your players need to know about to make this tactical decision?

_____

_____

What factors should be considered in your athletes' evaluations of their own strengths and weaknesses?

_____

_____

continued ☞

From *Successful Coaching, Third Edition*, by Rainer Martens, 2004, Champaign, IL: Human Kinetics.

Tactical Skill Development Plan (continued)

Step 3: Identify the cues in the situation that your players should and should not attend to, and help them interpret these cues to decide on a likely course of action. This is difficult to do. Becoming a keen observer of the sport, asking your players and more skillful players, consulting with experienced and successful coaches, and reading the technical literature in your sport are all ways you can learn the cues to which players should attend in each decision-making situation.

Cues to which your athletes should attend	Cues to which your athletes should not attend

STEP 4: Identify the appropriate tactical options, guidelines, or rules your athletes should follow to make this tactical decision. When players read the situation in a certain way, what tactical options are available to them? Is there a preferred tactical response? (As in step 2 you can identify these tactical options through your own critical observation or by consulting with highly skilled players and coaches.)

_____

_____

_____

STEP 5: Find or design at least one practice game that gives your athletes the opportunity to work on reading the situation and selecting the appropriate tactic. This is where the games approach is at its best. By learning to identify the decision-making points in step 1, you can design practice conditions to give your players practice in developing their perceptual skills. Often the practice games you design will give players an opportunity to practice more than one decision-making skill. Describe the game here.

_____

_____

_____

From *Successful Coaching, Third Edition*, by Rainer Martens, 2004, Champaign, IL: Human Kinetics.

Depending on your sport, the list of tactical decisions could be very long. You can have offensive and defensive decisions, and those can be position by position and situation by situation. Nevertheless, this is exactly the knowledge your athletes need. You can wait years while your athletes learn these tactical skills through trial and error—but oh how those errors can hurt, as captured in this poetic wisdom:

Experience is a fine teacher, it's true,
But here's what makes me burn;
Experience is always teaching me
Things I'd rather not learn!

Author unknown

Consider this challenge: Prior to the beginning of your next season, identify four to six of the most important tactical decisions your athletes must make. To do so, reflect on the tactical errors your team and other teams have made, or the tactical errors you made when you played the sport. Then prepare your tactical skill development plan for these four to six tactical decisions. As your season progresses, make note of the important tactical errors you and your players make and then develop a tactical skill development plan for each. If you do so and then teach these tactical skills to your players, you'll be a more successful coach.

Questions for Reflection

▶ What are the three cognitive skills athletes need to read the situation in a contest? **(p. 217)**

▶ What can you do to help your athletes improve their attention and concentration? **(p. 219)**

▶ Do you ensure that your players know all of the current rules of your sport? You can help them by teaching skills in gamelike situations using rules, reviewing infrequently applied rules, and giving them rulebooks. **(p. 221)**

▶ Do you involve your athletes in developing team strategies and individual goals? **(p. 221)**

▶ How effective are you at communicating game plans to your athletes? **(p. 222)**

▶ Before a contest do you share with your athletes the expected playing conditions and the opponents' strengths and weaknesses? **(p. 222)**

▶ How can you improve your athletes' self-knowledge so they can play "within themselves"? **(p. 224)**

▶ What are some tactical principles or rules you can teach your athletes to help them improve their tactical play? **(p. 224)**

▶ What are the six methods for teaching "decision training"? **(p. 226)**

▶ What are the five steps to creating a tactical skill development plan? **(p. 231)**

References

Doane, S., D. Alderton, Y. Sohn, and J. Pelligrino. 1996. Acquisition and transfer of skilled performance: Are visual discrimination skills stimulus specific? *Journal of Experimental Psychology: Human Perception and Performance* 22 (5): 1218-1248.

Launder, A. 2001. *Play practice: The Games Approach to teaching and coaching sport.* Champaign, IL: Human Kinetics.

Lavery, J.J. 1962. The retention of simple motor skills as a function of type of knowledge of results. *Canadian Journal of Psychology* 15: 300-311.

Vickers, J. no date. *Decision Training: A new approach to coaching.* Burnaby, British Columbia, Canada: Coaches Association of British Columbia.

Weeks, D.L., and R.N. Kordus. 1998. Relative frequency of knowledge of performance and motor skill learning. *Research Quarterly for Exercise and Sport* 69 (3): 224-230.

Williams, A.M., and K. Davids. 1998. Visual search strategy, selective attention, and expertise in soccer. *Research Quarterly for Exercise and Sport* 69: 111-128.

12

Planning for Teaching

Loaded with speed, the Deland 400-meter relay team was expected to blow away the competition, but the sprinters had trouble with each of the exchanges, almost dropping the baton on the last exchange. The relay team came in a disappointing third, which cost Deland High the chance to win the meet. As the race unfolded, Coach Seyfert realized he had forgotten to teach or practice the relay exchanges, but to those who knew him, that wasn't surprising. ☞

A walking encyclopedia of track and field, Coach Seyfert was probably the most knowledgeable person about the sport in the state. He was brilliant at analyzing the mechanics of running and designing training programs, but if you wanted to meet the stereotypical absent-minded professor, Coach Seyfert stood tall among his peers. Constantly disorganized and frequently late to practice, Coach Seyfert would arrive with no practice plan. He usually began practice by asking the team members what they had worked on the day before, and then for each event he would create a practice plan on the spot.

You've heard the axiom, Failing to plan is planning to fail. Regardless of the competitive level at which you coach, your knowledge of the sport, or your years of experience, you'll benefit from an instructional plan.

☞ **In this chapter, consistent with a games approach to coaching, you'll learn**

▶ how to develop instructional plans for the season, and
▶ how to prepare instructional plans for each practice.

We'll focus only on developing seasonal and daily practice plans, but in today's highly competitive sport world many coaches and athletes develop yearlong and even career-long plans as they seek to excel. Such extended planning, which is beyond the scope of this book, is valuable when working with serious athletes committed to a sport career.

The planning discussed in this chapter pertains entirely to teaching and practicing the skills your athletes need to be successful. In addition to instructional planning, coaches must plan for many other aspects of their work; you'll learn about that in part V, Principles of Management.

Benefits of Planning

Intuitively we all know that planning is a good idea, but often the problem is having the time to plan—or failing to plan to make time! Although planning is time consuming and initially hard work, the benefits are many. A season plan is your road

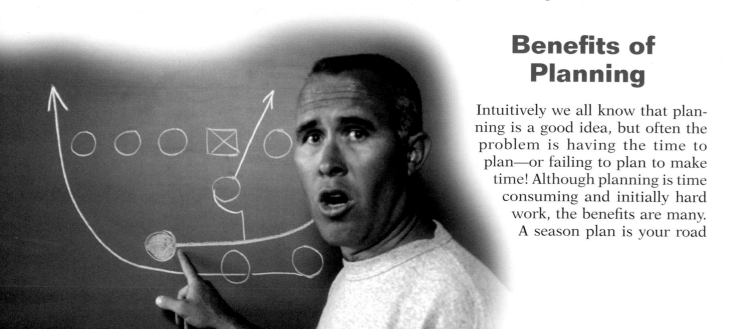

map to ensure that you will teach all that needs to be learned—not only the obvious technical skills and physical training required, but also the tactical, mental, and communication skills that are essential for success. A season plan helps you to keep on track and to sort out what's important. It also pays off over the course of many seasons because it's a framework for evaluating past seasons and developing a better plan for the next season. Think of instructional planning as an investment; it pays big dividends in future time saved.

Through planning you are far more likely to do the following:

▶ Keep your athletes actively involved, resulting in more learning and enjoyment during practices

▶ Provide challenging and relevant learning situations

▶ Teach skills in the appropriate progression to maximize learning and safety

▶ Pace the learning and conditioning so that athletes are not overloaded or overtrained

▶ Make the best use of available time, space, and equipment

▶ Minimize discipline problems

▶ Increase your confidence in your ability to manage the situation

Now that you appreciate the value of planning, let's climb the six-step staircase to effective instructional planning as shown in figure 12.1. If you work through each of the six steps during your forthcoming season, you'll provide more effective instruction than you have in the past.

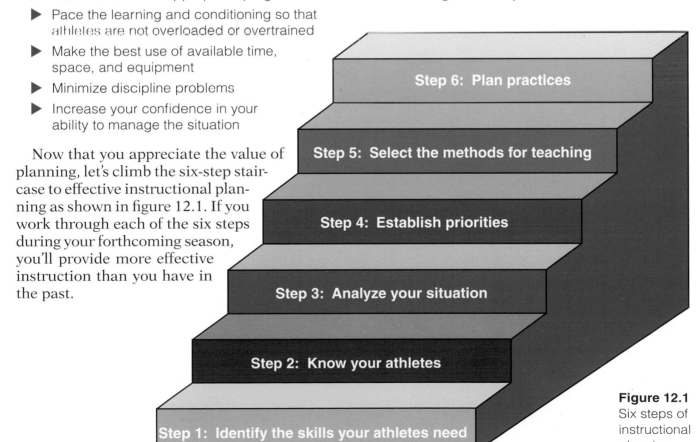

Step 6: Plan practices

Step 5: Select the methods for teaching

Step 4: Establish priorities

Step 3: Analyze your situation

Step 2: Know your athletes

Step 1: Identify the skills your athletes need

Figure 12.1
Six steps of instructional planning.

STEP 1: Identify the Skills Your Athletes Need

It's not just technical and tactical skills we're discussing here, but all the skills that you will want your athletes to learn. The Celestial Map of Sport Skills on pages 182 to 183 in chapter 9 provides an excellent framework for outlining the skills your athletes should master to play the sport successfully. To create your own map of sport skills your athletes will need, list the specific skills in each constellation that are essential or valuable for your athletes to learn. Be as thorough as you can in developing your lists; if you don't plan for it here, you are unlikely to remember to teach it later. This will take some work, but it's good work that is at the heart of coaching and will help you be a much better coach. Your map of sport skills should be your ideal list of competencies to be a successful athlete. As we move through the six-step planning process, we'll adjust the ideal with a healthy dose of reality.

Sources for Identifying Skills

How do you identify the subject matter you will teach? Here are the major sources:

1. Most people who read this book have played the sport and coached before. If this is true for you, draw on your experience to identify the skills you believe are essential.

2. Purchase or borrow books, videocassettes, CDs, and DVDs that explain and demonstrate the skills in your sport.

3. Major sport organizations and individuals conduct clinics and courses in which you can learn more. Contact your national sport organization or search the Internet for courses and information.

4. Consult with more experienced coaches and athletes in your area, asking them to share with you the various skills they teach and how they teach them. Better yet, if you're a beginning coach, try to find a highly experienced coach who will serve as your mentor. It's a great way to learn.

5. Take the ASEP Coaching Technical and Tactical Skills course for your sport (see the appendix).

6. Become a keen observer of the sport. As you watch it in person or on television, at various levels of competition, observe more closely the skills that are essential and how they are taught.

Next I provide some suggestions on how to identify the specific skills in each of the six constellations.

Technical Skills

First identify the basic or core skills that every player must possess to play the sport at your level of competition. Your athletes will likely possess these core skills to varying degrees. Because all sports require that athletes perform the fundamentals well, you'll want to help your athletes develop these skills further and keep them sharp throughout the season. For your sport, consider the skills of each position, or each event, and for various situations in the contest.

After you've identified the core skills, your sport may require that you consider offensive and defensive systems as well. Do you want to adopt one or more of these systems, and if you do, what are the specific skills your athletes will need to execute these systems effectively? Then, keeping in mind any special system you plan to use, identify the advanced skills that you want to teach. In form 12.1 you can see an abbreviated example for a high school basketball team.

Form 12.1

Technical Skills for High School Basketball Team

Primary offensive system: Motion offense, 1-4, 1-3-1 high/low
Primary defensive system: Man-to-man, 2-3 zone

Core Skills for All Players

1. Passing and receiving passes—bounce pass and chest pass
2. Shooting—jump shot, set shot, and free throw
3. Movement and screening—V-cuts, back cuts, on-ball, off-ball
4. Rebounding—positioning, blocking out
5. Dribbling—right and left hand with head up
6. Defense—stance and movement

Core Skills for Specific Positions

Post Players

1. Turnaround jump shots, bank shots, and layups with both hands
2. Screen and roll, up-screens, and down-screens
3. Shot fakes (pump and power up with both hands)
4. Defensive position and footwork on the low and high post

Perimeter Players

1. Crossover, reverse, and change-of-pace dribbles
2. Pass or shoot off the dribble
3. Catch and shoot
4. Force dribbler to use weak hand and to pick up dribble

Advanced Skills by Position

Post Players

1. Outlet passes—two-hand overhead pass and baseball pass
2. Fill the lane—handles pass for layup or jump shot
3. Hook shots and reverse layups
4. Shot blocks

Perimeter Players

1. Fakes to drive, pass, or dribble
2. 3-point shots—around arc on the catch and off the dribble
3. Behind-the-back dribble and between-the-legs dribble
4. Fight through and over the top screens

If you're really serious about coaching as a career, I suggest that you develop a system to catalog information about teaching the technical skills in your sport. One system is to create a folder for each skill, inserting a form such as form 12.2, and then filing articles along with the form in the folder. You can also easily create this form on the computer and catalog these skills as a series of files. It'll be a great resource for you to consult each season.

Form 12.2

Technical Skill Instruction Form

Skill name _____

Position (if any) _____

Skill type: ❑ Core   ❑ Offensive

  ❑ Advanced   ❑ Defensive

Skill description:

_____

_____

_____

_____

Key teaching points:

_____

_____

_____

_____

Common errors and how to correct:

_____

_____

References:

_____

_____

_____

Tactical Skills

As discussed in chapter 11, information is not readily available on the tactical skills to be taught and how to teach them. In that chapter, however, I described the five-step tactical skill development plan and encouraged you to identify the significant tactical decisions in your sport, to describe the knowledge needed to make the appropriate tactical decision, and to determine a way to have your athletes practice these decision-making skills. To do so, as with technical skills, I recommended observing and consulting with other coaches and experienced athletes and working with a mentor coach if possible. You'll also find help in teaching tactical skills in ASEP's Coaching Technical and Tactical Skills courses (see the appendix).

Physical Skills

In sharp contrast to tactical skills, an overwhelming amount of information is available on physical training (e.g., strength, speed, power, and endurance as well as nutrition and weight control). I've described the basics in part IV, Principles of Physical Training, which includes references for more advanced information. You should have no difficulty identifying the physical training skills your athletes will need for your sport.

Mental Skills

You probably recognize the importance to your athletes of self-confidence, mental toughness, concentration, and attention skills along with anxiety and anger control, but you may feel ill equipped to teach these mental skills. You may prefer to call in a sport psychologist—if you can find and afford one. But if you're like many other coaches, you simply ignore these skills, hoping your athletes will acquire them by playing the sport or perhaps through divine intervention.

While a sport psychologist can be of tremendous help in teaching mental skills, on a day-to-day basis you will be the mental skills coach, whether or not you recognize or accept the role. How you demonstrate these mental skills, how you respond under pressure, and how you motivate and provide feedback to your athletes will influence their development of mental skills. You simply can't delegate this coaching function entirely to someone else. To be a successful coach, you must become a student of sport psychology so you will know how to teach the basic mental skills needed for your sport.

Sport psychologists can assist athletes in developing psychological skills, but coaches usually have the day-to-day responsibility of helping athletes develop mental skills.

Oh, yes—there's a bonus in learning these mental skills to teach to your players: It will also improve your mental skills, enabling you to make good tactical decisions during contests.

You learned some of the basics of sport psychology in part II, Principles of Behavior. In addition, I recommend that you seek out advanced courses at universities, attend workshops or conference sessions held by national organizations in your sport, take the ASEP Silver Level Sport Psychology course (see the appendix), and read the sport psychology books listed in the To Learn More section at the end of this chapter.

Communication Skills

You learned the basics about communication skills in chapters 6 and 8, and in chapter 9, page 187, you identified the communication skills you believe your players need to perform well in your sport. Use this list to plan how you'll teach communication skills. Chapter 19 addresses the interpersonal skills you will need to manage your relationships, another facet of communication.

Character Development

Let's not forget about teaching character development, which should be a part of your instructional plan. Revisit chapter 4 to review the Athletes Character Code that we encourage you to teach (page 59), as well as the Teach Principles of Character section (page 60).

Now prepare a form similar to form 12.3. In step 1, list all the skills you've identified in the six constellations. Your technical and tactical skills lists could be very long, depending on your sport. For the other five constellations of skills, I've listed the core skills I discussed previously. You can use these initially, but if you have the knowledge, or when you learn more, replace these with more specific skills for your sport. Disregard the two columns in step 2 and the last section on maturity and experience for now. I'll explain those next when we discuss step 2.

Identifying and Evaluating the Skills You'll Teach

STEP 1	STEP 2						
Skills identified	**Essential skills to evaluate**		**Skill rating** **Weak Strong**				
Technical skills							
Skill 1	Yes	No	1	2	3	4	5
Skill 2	Yes	No	1	2	3	4	5
Skill 3	Yes	No	1	2	3	4	5
Skill 4	Yes	No	1	2	3	4	5
Skill 5	Yes	No	1	2	3	4	5
Skill 6	Yes	No	1	2	3	4	5
Tactical skills							
Ability to read the situation	Yes	No	1	2	3	4	5
Knowledge of the rules	Yes	No	1	2	3	4	5
Knowledge of team strategy	Yes	No	1	2	3	4	5
Knowledge of opponents	Yes	No	1	2	3	4	5
Knowledge of self	Yes	No	1	2	3	4	5
Knowledge of tactical options	Yes	No	1	2	3	4	5
Decision-making ability	Yes	No	1	2	3	4	5
Physical training skills							
Strength	Yes	No	1	2	3	4	5
Speed	Yes	No	1	2	3	4	5
Power	Yes	No	1	2	3	4	5
Endurance	Yes	No	1	2	3	4	5
Flexibility	Yes	No	1	2	3	4	5
Quickness	Yes	No	1	2	3	4	5
Balance	Yes	No	1	2	3	4	5
Agility	Yes	No	1	2	3	4	5
Other	Yes	No	1	2	3	4	5
Mental skills							
Emotional control—anxiety	Yes	No	1	2	3	4	5
Emotional control—anger	Yes	No	1	2	3	4	5

continued ☞

From *Successful Coaching, Third Edition,* by Rainer Martens, 2004, Champaign, IL: Human Kinetics

STEP 1	STEP 2		
Skills identified	**Essential skills to evaluate**	**Skill rating** **Weak**	**Strong**
Mental skills (continued)			
Self-confidence	Yes No	1 2 3 4 5	
Motivation to achieve	Yes No	1 2 3 4 5	
Ability to concentrate	Yes No	1 2 3 4 5	
Other	Yes No	1 2 3 4 5	
Communication skills			
Sends positive messages	Yes No	1 2 3 4 5	
Sends accurate messages	Yes No	1 2 3 4 5	
Listens to messages	Yes No	1 2 3 4 5	
Understands messages	Yes No	1 2 3 4 5	
Receives constructive criticism	Yes No	1 2 3 4 5	
Receives praise and recognition	Yes No	1 2 3 4 5	
Credibility with teammates	Yes No	1 2 3 4 5	
Credibility with coaches	Yes No	1 2 3 4 5	
Character skills			
Trustworthiness	Yes No	1 2 3 4 5	
Respect	Yes No	1 2 3 4 5	
Responsibility	Yes No	1 2 3 4 5	
Fairness	Yes No	1 2 3 4 5	
Caring	Yes No	1 2 3 4 5	
Citizenship	Yes No	1 2 3 4 5	
Maturity and experience			
Physical maturity	1 2 3 4 5		
	Immature Fully mature		
Emotional maturity	1 2 3 4 5		
	Immature Fully mature		
Social maturity	1 2 3 4 5		
	Immature Fully mature		
Playing experience	1 2 3 4 5		
	None Extensive		

From *Successful Coaching, Third Edition,* by Rainer Martens, 2004, Champaign, IL: Human Kinetics.

STEP 2: Know Your Athletes

In planning what you will teach to your athletes, you must consider what they now know and any characteristics about them that may determine what and how much they can learn. As you prepare your instructional plan, you will want to have answers to the following questions about your athletes:

▶ How old are your athletes, and what is their level of physical, psychological, and social maturity?

▶ How much playing experience do your players have, and how wide is that range of experience?

▶ How well do the players know each other, and how well do they work together in groups?

▶ How well do they accept responsibilities?

▶ Are they accustomed to being told what to do (traditional approach), or have they been encouraged to problem solve and think (games approach)?

▶ What are their present skills in each of the six constellations of sport skills?

▶ What are their capabilities in each of the six constellations of sport skills?

Although you may know some or most of your team members well from coaching them in previous seasons, it's beneficial to systematically evaluate your players on the essential skills you've identified in the six constellations of sport skills. Here are four reasons for conducting preseason evaluations:

▶ It helps you establish each athlete's entry level or starting point for instruction, and thus helps personalize instruction to maximize learning and early success.

▶ It helps you assess the improvement your athletes have made over the course of the season.

▶ You may not be able to keep everyone who would like to play on the team. Initial evaluation is a way to select the players you wish to keep.

▶ You can match players by their skills and knowledge and thus organize safe and equitable practice games.

If you find that you avoid preseason evaluation because you're not sure what or how to evaluate, the following are some general guidelines that may help. Also, the ASEP Coaching Technical and Tactical Skills course for your sport introduces a specific evaluation system.

What to Evaluate

In step 1 in form 12.3 you identified the skills for your sport, but it's often not practical to evaluate all the skills you've listed. In fact, some skills may be so advanced that in some sports it would be dangerous to have athletes attempt to perform these skills in order to evaluate them. Thus, evaluate your athletes on the *essential* skills that they can safely perform at the beginning of the season.

How to Evaluate

You can conduct preseason evaluations in one of two ways. You can conduct a formal testing program in which the athletes perform technical and tactical skills, demonstrate their physical conditioning, and complete written or oral examinations to demonstrate other competencies. Alternatively you can have them play one or more practice games and by observing and talking with the athletes, you can make a reasonably accurate rating. Or, as some coaches do, you can use a combination of formal and informal evaluations, formally testing athletes on technical skills and physical conditioning and informally evaluating the other competencies.

If this is the first time you are using an instructional plan, I recommend that you use the informal method to evaluate these skills. The informal method is not the most accurate, but it is reasonably good and practical. It certainly is better than no evaluation at all. After coaching your first season, use more advanced methods of evaluation including the physical training tests in chapters 14 and 15 and the sport-specific skill tests in ASEP's Coaching Technical and Tactical Skills courses.

Now return to form 12.3. First select those skills that you believe are essential to evaluate during the preseason by circling "Yes" in the "Essential skills to evaluate" column. Now make a copy of this form for each athlete on your team and add whatever information you want to obtain from each athlete at the top (e.g., name, age, sex, position, event, and so on). Bingo! Your preseason evaluation form is ready to use.

In the second column of step 2 rate each athlete on each essential skill using the scale shown. At the bottom of form 12.3, I've added three dimensions of maturity to evaluate as well as playing experience because these are important for you to consider as you develop your seasonal plan of instruction.

STEP 3:
Analyze Your Situation

In preparation for developing a season plan you need to collect information specific to your situation. Essentially you're assessing what is available to you and what limitations you will have. To help you make this assessment, answer the questions in form 12.4 as completely as you can.

Evaluating Your Team Situation

How many practices will you have over the entire season, and how long can practices be?

_____

_____

_____

How many contests will you have over the entire season?

_____

_____

_____

What special events (team meetings, parent orientation sessions, banquets, tournaments) will you have and when?

_____

_____

_____

How many athletes will you be coaching? How many assistants will you have? What is the ratio of athletes to coaches?

_____

_____

_____

What facilities will be available for practice?

_____

_____

_____

continued ☞

From _Successful Coaching, Third Edition_, by Rainer Martens, 2004, Champaign, IL: Human Kinetics.

What equipment will be available for practice?

_____

_____

_____

How much money do you have for travel and other expenses?

_____

_____

_____

What instructional resources (videos, books, charts, CDs) will you need?

_____

_____

_____

What other support personnel will be available?

_____

_____

_____

What other factors may affect your instructional plan?

_____

_____

_____

_____

_____

_____

_____

_____

From *Successful Coaching, Third Edition*, by Rainer Martens, 2004, Champaign, IL: Human Kinetics.

If your situation is less than ideal for instruction (e.g., a practice space that is too small, not enough equipment, or not enough assistants), obviously you should first seek to improve your situation. If you cannot, planning becomes even more critical so that you optimize the use of the resources available.

STEP 4: Establish Priorities

Your next step is to establish clear priorities about what skills you will be able to teach and practice given your situation (e.g., time, equipment, facilities, or number of coaches and athletes). You should evaluate each skill in the six constellations on two criteria:

1. The importance or centrality of the skill to playing the sport. Evaluate each skill by answering the following questions:
    —What *must* be taught in the time available to achieve worthwhile outcomes?
    —What *should* be covered if good use is made of the time available?
    —What *could* be taught if time permits?
2. Your athletes' readiness to learn the skill. Ask yourself the following questions:
    —Do they have the strength, endurance, flexibility, and motor coordination to learn the skill?
    —Do they have the mental capacity to learn the skill?
    —Is there a prerequisite skill they must learn before you can teach this skill?
    —Is it safe to teach this skill?

Now look at form 12.5 and complete the following steps:

1. Transfer the list of skills from step 1 in form 12.3.
2. In the "Teaching priorities" column, if the skill *must* be taught, circle "M." If the skill *should* be taught, circle "S." If the skill *could* be taught, circle "C."
3. Based on your preseason evaluations, in the "Readiness to learn" column circle "Yes" if you think the majority of your athletes are ready to learn the skill and circle "No" if they are not.
4. In the "Priority rating" column rate the skills that *must* be taught (and that athletes are ready to learn) an "A." Then go through the list to identify those skills that *should* be taught and identify these as "B" skills. For these B skills note any A skills or prerequisites that your athletes must master before learning these B skills. Then repeat the process for those skills that *could* be taught, marking them as "C" skills and noting any prerequisites.

Identifying and Evaluating the Skills You'll Teach

STEP 1	STEP 4							
Skills identified	**Teaching priorities**			**Readiness to learn**		**Priority rating**		
	Must	**Should**	**Could**	**Yes**	**No**	**A**	**B**	**C**
Technical skills								
Skill 1	M	S	C	Yes	No	A	B	C
Skill 2	M	S	C	Yes	No	A	B	C
Skill 3	M	S	C	Yes	No	A	B	C
Skill 4	M	S	C	Yes	No	A	B	C
Skill 5	M	S	C	Yes	No	A	B	C
Skill 6	M	S	C	Yes	No	A	B	C
Tactical skills								
Ability to read the situation	M	S	C	Yes	No	A	B	C
Knowledge of the rules	M	S	C	Yes	No	A	B	C
Knowledge of team strategy	M	S	C	Yes	No	A	B	C
Knowledge of opponents	M	S	C	Yes	No	A	B	C
Knowledge of self	M	S	C	Yes	No	A	B	C
Knowledge of tactical options	M	S	C	Yes	No	A	B	C
Decision-making ability	M	S	C	Yes	No	A	B	C
Physical training skills								
Strength	M	S	C	Yes	No	A	B	C
Speed	M	S	C	Yes	No	A	B	C
Power	M	S	C	Yes	No	A	B	C
Endurance	M	S	C	Yes	No	A	B	C
Flexibility	M	S	C	Yes	No	A	B	C
Quickness	M	S	C	Yes	No	A	B	C
Balance	M	S	C	Yes	No	A	B	C
Agility	M	S	C	Yes	No	A	B	C
Other	M	S	C	Yes	No	A	B	C

From *Successful Coaching, Third Edition*, by Rainer Martens, 2004, Champaign, IL: Human Kinetics.

Form 12.5 *(continued)*

STEP 1	STEP 4							
	Teaching priorities			**Readiness to learn**		**Priority rating**		
Skills identified	**Must**	**Should**	**Could**	**Yes**	**No**	**A**	**B**	**C**
Mental skills								
Emotional control—anxiety	M	S	C	Yes	No	A	B	C
Emotional control—anger	M	S	C	Yes	No	A	B	C
Self-confidence	M	S	C	Yes	No	A	B	C
Motivation to achieve	M	S	C	Yes	No	A	B	C
Ability to concentrate	M	S	C	Yes	No	A	B	C
Other	M	S	C	Yes	No	A	B	C
Communication skills								
Sends positive messages	M	S	C	Yes	No	A	B	C
Sends accurate messages	M	S	C	Yes	No	A	B	C
Listens to messages	M	S	C	Yes	No	A	B	C
Understands messages	M	S	C	Yes	No	A	B	C
Receives constructive criticism	M	S	C	Yes	No	A	B	C
Receives praise and recognition	M	S	C	Yes	No	A	B	C
Credibility with teammates	M	S	C	Yes	No	A	B	C
Credibility with coaches	M	S	C	Yes	No	A	B	C
Character skills								
Trustworthiness	M	S	C	Yes	No	A	B	C
Respect	M	S	C	Yes	No	A	B	C
Responsibility	M	S	C	Yes	No	A	B	C
Fairness	M	S	C	Yes	No	A	B	C
Caring	M	S	C	Yes	No	A	B	C
Citizenship	M	S	C	Yes	No	A	B	C

From *Successful Coaching, Third Edition,* by Rainer Martens, 2004, Champaign, IL: Human Kinetics.

When you've completed form 12.5, you've established your priorities and your instructional goals for the season. Your A-rated skills are essential to teach, and then you'll want to teach as many of the B-rated skills as you can, depending on the progress of your athletes.

STEP 5: Select the Methods for Teaching

Now that you have established what you want to teach, you need to consider how best to teach and practice each skill to maximize learning. I have advocated that you teach and coach using the games approach, a problem-solving and guided discovery approach to learning. The traditional approach to coaching uses a "directed" method of teaching, in which the coach explains how the skill is used, provides a clear demonstration, creates a drill to practice the skill, observes players practicing, and provides feedback to help players master the skill.

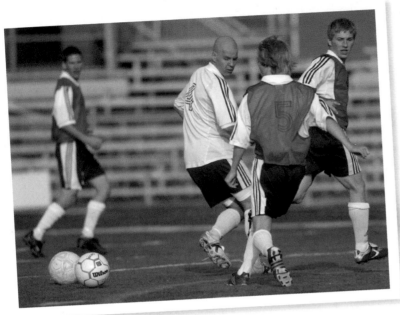

In contrast, the games approach to teaching is an indirect instructional method that is more engaging and enjoyable for athletes because they are actively involved in solving the problem, applying the principles, or discovering the best option. The increased involvement gives the athletes more ownership and responsibility for the knowledge gained, and they are more likely to remember and apply it. As you know from chapter 11, evidence shows that over the long term athletes master skills to a higher level through the games approach than through the directed approach.

There is a place, however, for the traditional approach to instruction, even when adopting the games approach as the overall approach to teaching and practicing. Whether you use a traditional or games approach method of instruction depends on what you're trying to achieve.

Here are some guidelines for selecting one instructional method over the other:

▶ The traditional approach is an efficient means of instruction when there is one clearly accepted best way to perform a technical skill that involves little decision making in its use.

▶ The traditional method of instruction is appropriate when the risk of injury is significant or the skill is too complex to be mastered as a whole.

▶ The games approach is more effective when it is important that athletes learn the principles underlying a technique. For example, in teaching takedowns in wrestling, guided discovery helps the wrestler learn to identify the critical principles (such as balance, center of gravity, misdirection, and leverage) that

must be employed to take an opponent down. Through this approach the wrestler comes to understand takedowns as a dynamic, flexible skill rather than as a series of isolated techniques.

▶ The games approach of course is the most effective way to learn tactical skills, especially in complex, rapidly changing sport environments.

▶ The games approach is superior for helping athletes learn responsibility and leadership, and in helping athletes learn how to learn so that they can function more independently.

As you decide on how you will teach each of the skills in your sport, you will want to begin collecting games, drills, quizzes, stories, videos, and other materials to build your treasure chest of instructional tools.

STEP 6: Plan Practices

OK, you know what you want to teach and practice and the method you want to use to do so for the season. Now you need to take this seasonal plan and develop specific practice plans for each day. This is really one of the fun parts of coaching; you get to orchestrate the learning experience for your athletes!

The basic elements of a practice plan are as follows:

▶ *Date, time of practice, and length of practice session.* Record this information so you know when you taught and how long you practiced certain skills. This information will help after the season when you are evaluating and revising your seasonal plan.

▶ *Objective of the practice.* Obviously you want to have one or more clear objectives of what you want your athletes to know or be able to do as a result of this practice session.

▶ *Equipment needed.* List the equipment needed for the practice (e.g., mats, balls, nets, weights, stop watches). Before practice, check the equipment you plan to use to be certain it is safe, clean, and operational. Also make any special arrangements required for the facility.

▶ *Warm-up.* Every practice should begin with a warm-up that takes 10 to 15 minutes. Its physiological purpose and function in injury prevention are discussed in chapter 13. Warm-ups can be done together by the entire team or individually, depending on the sport and your preference. Warm-ups can easily be made a routine, the value of which we discussed previously, but don't let warm-ups become so routine that they become boring.

▶ *Practice of previously taught skills.* As you plan your practice, you'll usually want to devote some time to previously taught skills. Often the core technical and physical training skills of a sport need to be practiced almost daily, but other skills may need only occasional practice. The time you devote to practicing previously taught skills will depend on the demonstrated skill level and conditioning of your athletes. As you plan the practicing of these skills, consider whether your athletes should practice them individually or as a team, and whether they should practice them through a drill or a game.

▶ *Teach and practice new skills.* Usually you want to teach only one or two new technical or tactical skills in a practice, devoting 20 to 30 minutes to them. The steps for teaching technical skills are explained in chapter 10, and the approach to teaching tactical skills is explained in chapter 11. Mental, communication, and character skills are often best taught in a quiet setting initially, and then reinforced during practice games.

▶ *Cool-down.* Just as every practice begins with a warm-up, the activity portion of practice should conclude with a 10- to 15-minute cool-down. You'll learn about how to properly cool down in chapter 13.

▶ *Coach's comments.* Take 5 minutes at the close of practice to review how the team practiced, directing your comments to the whole team and recognizing any outstanding efforts or performances by individuals. This is not the place to criticize any individual. Point out what skills the team needs to improve further. This is also an opportunity to teach or reinforce a mental, communication, or character skill. Use this time to make any needed announcements about team business, and close by reminding them of the time and place of the next practice and what you plan to do in that practice.

▶ *Evaluation of practice.* Evaluate each practice as soon after its conclusion as possible. With input from your assistant coaches, indicate whether the practice objectives were achieved and make notes of athletes who may need special assistance in future practices. Then file each practice plan in a three-ring notebook or on your computer. You'll find these plans very helpful when planning future practices and next season's plans.

The actual form of practice plans will vary substantially depending on the sport, especially team versus individual sports. Form 12.6 contains an example of a practice plan for volleyball, and form 12.7 is an example for a group of middle-distance runners.

Sample Volleyball Practice Plan

Date: October 20, 2006

Practice start time: 4:00 p.m.

Length of practice: 90 minutes

Practice objectives: (1) Practice core ball-control skills of passing and setting: flat forearm platforms that redirect the ball to the target (minimize swinging) and setting "hands position" at forehead early with contact point on finger pads and thumbs closest to forehead; (2) Enhance player communication: calling first ball ("me" or "mine") and where to attack (line or angle); (3) Continue first opportunity attack emphasis; (4) Develop physical recovery skills with short, intense physical bursts and timed recovery.

Equipment: Bring stopwatches, balls, net, and cones; players need knee pads and court shoes.

Practice Activities			
Time	**Name of activity**	**Description**	**Key teaching points**
4:00-4:07	Warm-up	Shuffle Passing Drill 10 to target and change direction	Emphasize posture and "quiet" passing platform
4:07-4:13	Warm-up	Wall sets—30 low/med/high, finish with jump sets	Emphasize hand shape and wrist position
4:13-4:20	Warm-up	Dynamic stretching	Emphasize full range of motion in stretches
4:20-4:21	Warm-up	Line jumps—forward, side, scissor	Quick feet physical training
4:21-4:22	Water break		
4:22-4:32	Ball control	Weave Passing Drill in teams of 3, 15 to target (both sides)	Emphasize adjusting platform and movement to the ball
4:32-4:42	Ball control	Small court games (pass or set only)	Emphasize ball control to win
4:42-4:52	Ball control	3-on-3 and 3-on-3 backcourt battle drill (winner stays)	Emphasize ball control, reading skills, and communication
4:52-4:55	Ball control	Line races (sprint, shuffle/back)	Physical training

continued ☞

Time	Name of activity	Description	Key teaching points
4:55-5:10	Offensive system 6 on 6	4 before 2 game	Emphasize first opportunity attack, look for best attack in each rotation
5:10-5:15	Transition	Continuous rally game	Emphasize quick recovery from physical and mental errors
5:15-5:23	Cool-down	Mat serving series	Emphasize serving routine and rhythm
5:23-5:25	Cool-down	Main muscle group stretch	Emphasize slow and complete stretch
5:25-5:30	Coach's comments	End-of-practice comments from the coach	General comments on how the whole team practiced Recognize any outstanding efforts or performances Point out what needs to improve Announcements

Evaluation: Ball control is improving with emphasis early in practice on technique. More transition drills are needed to get those proper techniques into more gamelike situations at this point in the season. Hannah and Keily are swinging their arms too much during their forearm pass, but both have good platforms. Setting to our hitters is still our greatest team challenge, but when our setter Michelle handles the ball, our offense runs smoothly.

Communication was much improved and should be reinforced as a positive at our next practice opportunity. Continue to work on our offense and add more serving as we prepare for West High School next Tuesday and some passers we can take advantage of.

Sample Middle-Distance Runner's Practice Plan

Date: March 12, 2005

Practice start time: 3:00 p.m.

Length of practice: 100 minutes

Practice objectives: (1) Reinforce technique skills: lifting the knees high, raising the foot directly under the butt, "pawing" the track on foot strike, avoiding overstriding, and driving the arms powerfully; (2) Develop speed-endurance, or the ability to run fast when tired; (3) Practice concentrating on efficient running form when tired; and (4) Develop the tactical skills of accelerating in the middle of a race and kicking at the end.

Equipment: Workout takes place on a 400-meter track; bring stopwatches and water; runners need their racing spikes.

		Practice Activities	
Time	**Name of activity**	**Description**	**Key teaching points**
3:00-3:07	Warm-up	Easy jogging	
3:07-3:15	Warm-up	Dynamic stretching	Emphasize full range of motion in dynamic stretches
3:15-3:25	Warm-up	5 × 100 meter strides @ 3/4 effort with 100-meter walk recovery	Emphasize technique skills during strides
3:25-3:30	Water break	Everyone drinks 4 to 6 oz	
3:30-3:55	Technique drills	4 × 30 meters high-knee drill with 1-min recovery 4 × 30 meters butt-kick drill with 1-min recovery 4 × 30 meters fast-feet drill with 1-min recovery 4 × 1-min arm-pumping drill with 1-min recovery	Emphasize lifting the knees to be parallel to the track Emphasize keeping the foot close to the body and under the butt Emphasize "pawing" action, landing with the foot moving backward Emphasize "fast hands"
3:55-4:00	Water break	Everyone drinks 4 to 6 oz	

continued ☞

Time	Name of activity	Description	Key teaching points
4:00-4:20	Speed-endurance interval workout	3 sets of 1 × 300 meters and 1 × 200 meters with 1-min recovery between the 300 and 200, and 5-min recovery between sets	For the 300s, keep the runners on 1,600-meter race pace For the 200s, encourage a controlled, building sprint, adding a notch of speed every 50 meters Cue the runners to hold their form on the 200s
4:20-4:25	Water break	Everyone drinks 4 to 6 oz	
4:25-4:35	Cool-down	10-min easy jogging	Cue the runners to attend to any tightness or soreness, for extra stretching, icing, and massage
4:35-4:40	Coach's comments	End-of-practice comments from the coach	General comments on how the whole team practiced Recognize any outstanding efforts or performances Point out what the team needs to improve Announcements

Evaluation: Technique drills—Excellent job by all on high knees, butt kicks, and arm pumping drills, but we're not quite getting the hang of the fast-feet drill, which is a problem because we've still got some overstriders, especially Shawna, Val, Marie, and Kim. Need to help them get the feet down faster so they land under their hips. For Friday, emphasize the fast-feet drill, making it a contest: Whoever has the most foot strikes in 30 meters gets to choose which restaurant the team will stop at on the return trip home from the next meet.

Speed-endurance interval workout: Marie and Val ran together, right on the assigned pace for their 300s (average 64 seconds) and 200s (average 38 seconds). Shawna, Kaella, Sue, and Kim ran the 300s too fast (around 58–61) and the 200s too slow (around 40–42). They didn't get the full effect of improving their acceleration and kicking skills. Next interval session, have Marie and Val set the pace for everyone. Nobody passes them, unless it's on a repetition intended for accelerating or kicking.

The heat was brutal today, and it's going to get worse. For the end of the next track workout, bring watermelon and turn on the infield sprinklers.

Review

There's a fair amount of work in completing these steps, especially if you've never done this type of planning before, but these are the *steps to success* in coaching. Remember that seasonal planning is not something you do at the beginning of the season and put aside. You should consult your seasonal plan regularly as you develop each practice plan.

Instructional planning is not like planning a building. Your plan is not set in stone; it needs to be flexible to adjust to the changing circumstances as your season progresses—the rate at which your players learn, access to facilities, weather conditions, injuries, and a host of other factors. Although your seasonal plans will remain more stable, con-

Step 6: Plan practices

Step 5: Select the methods for teaching

Step 4: Establish priorities

Step 3: Analyze your situation

Step 2: Know your athletes

Step 1: Identify the skills your athletes need

sider planning only a few practices in advance so that you can adjust your practices based on the previous practices, but always with the larger seasonal objectives in mind.

Don't forget to evaluate each practice session. At the end of the season or periodically throughout the season, evaluate how the instructional process is going, recording your thoughts so that you can use them next season in developing even better seasonal and practice plans.

Questions for Reflection

▶ Do you have a seasonal instructional plan, as well as instructional plans for each practice session? What are some benefits of planning? **(p. 236)**

▶ How can you determine the skills your athletes will need to be successful? What are your sources of information? Does your list of skills include technical, tactical, physical, mental, communication, and character skills? **(p. 238)**

▶ How well do you know your athletes? Preseason evaluations can help you create successful instructional plans. **(p. 245)**

▶ What are the assets and liabilities of your situation (practice space, equipment, time, assistants, financial resources)? **(p. 247)**

▶ Have you established your priorities in terms of what skills you will teach your athletes given your situation? **(p. 249)**

▶ In what situations would the traditional, "directed" approach to coaching be more effective than the games approach, and vice versa? **(p. 252)**

▶ Do you consult your seasonal plan when developing individual practice plans? **(p. 253)**

▶ What are the basic elements of a practice plan? **(p. 253)**

To Learn More

Goldberg, Alan. 2001. *Sports slump busting.* Champaign, IL: Human Kinetics.

Jackson, Susan, and Mihaly Csikszentmihalyi. 1999. *Flow in sports.* Champaign, IL: Human Kinetics.

Kauss, David R. 2001. *Mastering your inner game.* Champaign, IL: Human Kinetics.

Martens, Rainer. 1987. *Coaches guide to sport psychology.* Champaign, IL: Human Kinetics.

Orlick, Terry. 2000. *In pursuit of excellence.* 3rd ed. Champaign, IL: Human Kinetics.

Ungerleider, Steven. 1996. *Mental training for peak performance.* Emmaus, PA: Rodale.

PART IV

Principles of Physical Training

In part IV you'll learn the principles of physical training—or the art and science of persuading your athletes' bodies to meet the demands of your sport without asking them to do too much (overtraining). You'll also learn the principles of good nutrition, helping your athletes eat and drink to perform their best. We'll also tackle head-on the difficult problem of drug use by athletes. This part is more technical than other parts of the book because you'll need to understand some physiology, but it's loaded with lots of practical guidelines and tools to help you become a better coach.

13

Training Basics

▶ Larry Brown dominated Ken Ernst in the first two periods of the wrestling match, but as the third period began, Larry tired. Just at the end of the period Ken executed a double-leg takedown to tie the match. In overtime, Ken won easily because of his superior conditioning.

▶ Lakeland High and Peoria Central had played a grueling run-and-shoot basketball game in which the winner was not determined until the last 2 minutes of the game. Lakeland, sensing that the Peoria players were fatigued, turned up the pressure defense and stole the ball three times to make easy layups and win.

▶ Melissa Feld had a batting average of only .121 for the Winslow High School softball team. She was a talented shortstop, but ☞

lacked the power to hit the ball beyond the infielders. Unless she could develop that power, she would likely lose her starting position on the team.

IIIII➡ Swimming in the 100-meter freestyle race, Ming Ming Peng saw Aisha Ansari pass her in the last 30 meters. Although Peng had the endurance, she simply didn't have the speed to keep up with the faster Ansari.

You know the importance of physical fitness in sport, but do you know how to physically train your athletes so they can achieve peak performance? If you direct your athletes' training based on myth or tradition in your sport rather than on the science of sport physiology, you'll deny your athletes the opportunity to be the best they can be.

☞ **In this chapter we begin your journey to become an outstanding physical trainer by**

▶ reviewing how the body works,

▶ teaching the basics about energy and muscular fitness,

▶ explaining your role in developing and conducting physical training programs, and

▶ introducing you to the principles of physical training.

How the Body Works

Our bodies are marvelous moving machines, especially when we train them to move efficiently. Athletes can bench press 683 pounds (310 kilograms), run 125 miles (201 kilometers) in 24 hours, and dive underwater to depths over 400 feet (122 meters) and climb Mount Everest towering at 29,035 feet (8,850 meters), both without the use of oxygen! Let's take a quick excursion of the human body to see how it accomplishes such remarkable feats.

The Framework

Movement begins with our skeleton, which consists of 206 bones that anchor our muscles and protect our internal organs (figure 13.1). Our skeleton was designed for movement, with bones that are very strong yet lightweight and 100 joints connecting our bones with muscle.

Our hands are engineering marvels, permitting us to do many remarkable things. Over millions of years humans' thumbs evolved to oppose the fingers, which gives

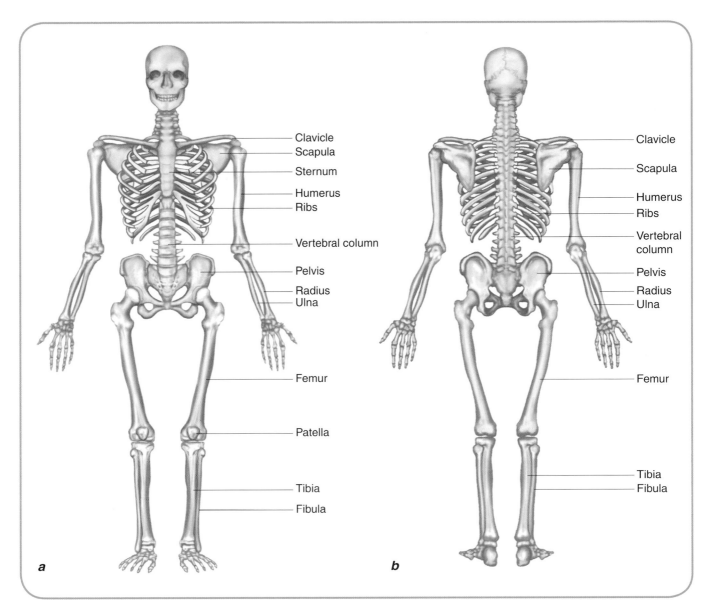

Figure 13.1 Adult male human skeleton: *(a)* front view and *(b)* rear view.
Adapted, with permission, from Harman, 2000.

us the dexterity to make precise movements such as those required in performing eye surgery, playing the piano, and throwing a football or baseball.

The Power

The power to move comes from 640 muscles, which make up about half of our body weight and create movement by pulling on bones as they contract (figure 13.2). Muscles often work in pairs—one muscle contracting to pull a bone and the opposite muscle relaxing. Typically muscles work in teams of 30 or more to return a tennis serve, dismount the pommel horse, or catch a fly ball. As muscles in one part of the body coordinate the movement to execute the technical skill, other muscles respond to maintain balance and correct position.

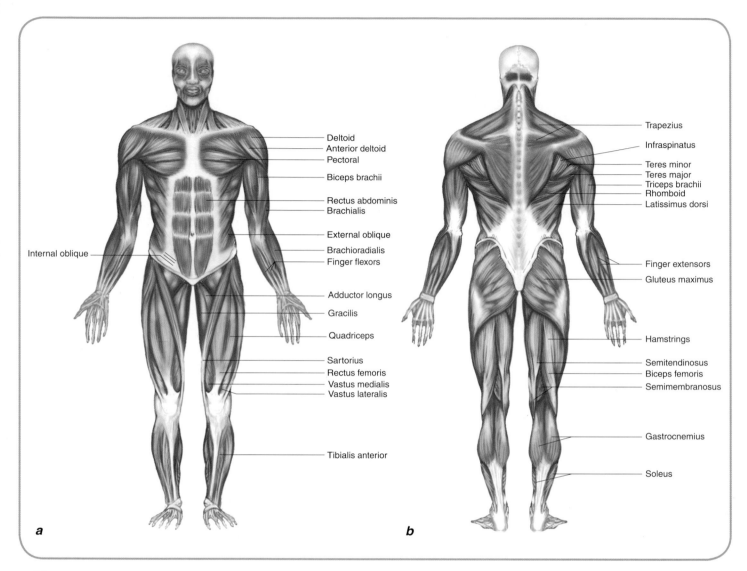

Figure 13.2   Adult male human skeletal musculature: *(a)* front view and *(b)* rear view.

Adapted, with permission, from Harman, 2000.

Muscles can generate tremendous force and have incredible endurance. The world record for push-ups in a 24-hour period is an amazing 46,001! Muscles also can make precise delicate movements very rapidly. For example, a pianist can strike as many as 25 keys per second with varying force and rhythm to interpret the music. We'll take a closer look at muscles in chapter 15.

The Engine

The body has another amazing muscle—the heart. Beating about 100,000 times a day or 2.5 billion times in an average lifetime, the heart pumps blood to every part of the body through the circulatory system, which consists of 60,000 miles of vessels (figure 13.3). That system fuels the muscles and other body parts, removes carbon dioxide and lactic acid (which are by-products of energy production in the muscles) and helps control body temperature similar to coolant circulating in an auto engine.

Long-distance runners and swimmers develop highly efficient circulatory systems. The heart rate of a marathoner is typically 28 to 40 beats per minute, whereas the average young adult has a resting heart rate of 70 to 80 beats per minute. Endurance athletes pump more than twice as much blood per beat than the average person, and the amount of oxygen diffused into their blood may be as much as four times greater. When we begin exercising, our bodies redirect the blood flow to the muscles where it is needed. During rest, 15 to 20 percent of our blood goes to our muscles, but during strenuous exercise it is 80 to 85 percent.

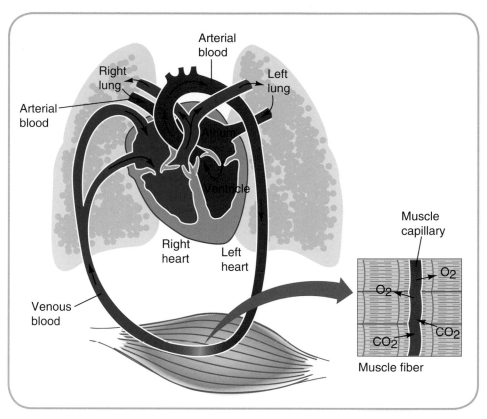

Figure 13.3 Circulorespiratory system.

The Energy

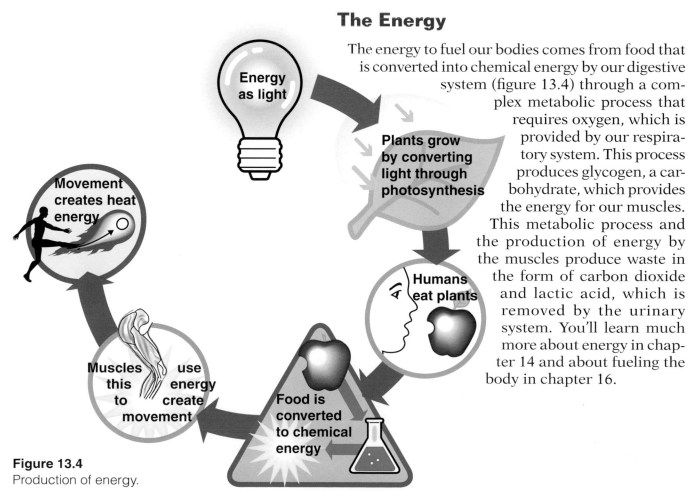

The energy to fuel our bodies comes from food that is converted into chemical energy by our digestive system (figure 13.4) through a complex metabolic process that requires oxygen, which is provided by our respiratory system. This process produces glycogen, a carbohydrate, which provides the energy for our muscles. This metabolic process and the production of energy by the muscles produce waste in the form of carbon dioxide and lactic acid, which is removed by the urinary system. You'll learn much more about energy in chapter 14 and about fueling the body in chapter 16.

Figure 13.4
Production of energy.

The Control

The brain, spinal cord, and a network of roughly 93,000 miles of peripheral nerves, called the nervous system, is the command center for movement. From a stimulus inside or outside the body, the command center in the brain's cortex plans the movement, called the motor program, which we discussed in chapter 10. The plan is sent to the motor center in the cerebellum where feedback from the body about movements in progress is taken into account to create the final motor program. The motor cortex then sends the signals to move through the spinal cord to the muscles. It all happens incredibly fast as shown in figure 13.5.

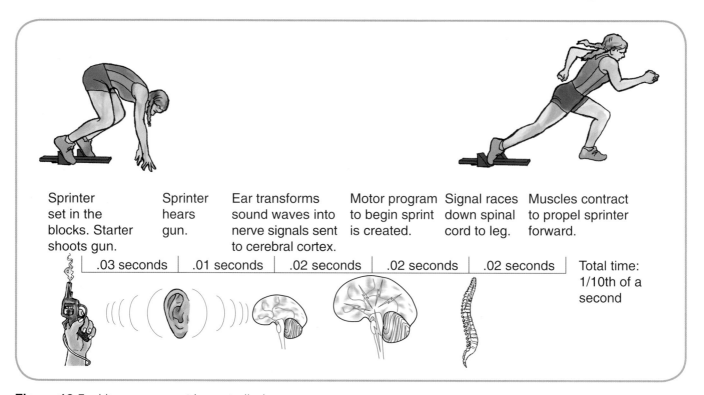

Sprinter set in the blocks. Starter shoots gun.	Sprinter hears gun.	Ear transforms sound waves into nerve signals sent to cerebral cortex.	Motor program to begin sprint is created.	Signal races down spinal cord to leg.	Muscles contract to propel sprinter forward.	
	.03 seconds	.01 seconds	.02 seconds	.02 seconds	.02 seconds	Total time: 1/10th of a second

Figure 13.5 How movement is controlled.

As a coach, you are granted the opportunity to prepare the beautifully engineered bodies of your athletes to move great distances, lift incredible weight, and perform a variety of motor skills with exquisite precision. You can take advantage of this opportunity fully by learning more about the incredible human body and how to train it to be physically fit.

Fitness for Sport and Physical Training

Physical fitness in sport is the ability to meet the physical demands of the sport to perform optimally. Usually the physical demands are substantially greater than what is needed for daily living. At one extreme we have athletes who can run more than 26 miles in just over two hours, a blistering 13-mile-per-hour pace. (If you have a hard time relating to that, get on a bike and pedal at 13 miles per hour for two hours to appreciate the extraordinary feat of running that distance.) To be physically fit for world-class weightlifting, your muscles need to be tuned to lift 650 pounds (295 kilograms) in the bench press.

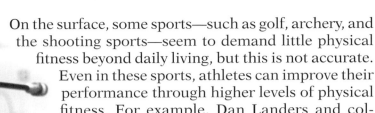

On the surface, some sports—such as golf, archery, and the shooting sports—seem to demand little physical fitness beyond daily living, but this is not accurate. Even in these sports, athletes can improve their performance through higher levels of physical fitness. For example, Dan Landers and colleagues (1980) discovered that the best shooters in the world learned to pull the trigger between heartbeats, eliminating the slight vibration caused by the heart's beating. It didn't take long for shooters to realize that improved physical conditioning lowered their heart rate and thus made it easier to pull the trigger between beats.

Physical fitness is not a permanent condition; it is a state that the body is in at any particular time. As we all know from experience, when we discontinue training, deconditioning occurs quickly and easily—frustratingly so considering the hard work required to achieve a high level of fitness. Recognizing that fitness is transient, coaches often plan training cycles so that athletes are in peak condition for major competitive events.

Practicing technical and tactical skills is a good way to improve physical fitness for your sport, but today's athletes need additional training to be competitive. *Physical training* is a disciplined routine of specialized procedures or steps that are performed by athletes to condition the body for the purpose of improving performance. Physical training is a slow, steady process whereby athletes coax their bodies to adapt to increasingly higher physical demands. The process can't be rushed, but it can be optimized, and that's what you want to learn how to do—optimize the training of your athletes so they can perform at their best.

Benefits of Training

Here are some of the benefits of physical training:

- ▶ Better performance
- ▶ Less fatigue in long-duration contests
- ▶ Quicker recovery after strenuous practice or competitive play
- ▶ Less muscle soreness
- ▶ Greater ability to practice technical and tactical skills longer and better
- ▶ Less susceptibility to injury
- ▶ Quicker recovery from injury
- ▶ Prevention of mental fatigue and improvement of concentration
- ▶ Greater self-confidence knowing that one is physically prepared
- ▶ Greater enjoyment of playing as a result of performing better, winning more, and feeling less fatigued

Components of Physical Fitness

Obviously, different sports require different types of physical fitness. Long-distance events, such as the Tour de France bicycle race or the Boston Marathon, emphasize cardiorespiratory fitness, which is one component of what I'll call *energy fitness*. Sports such as weightlifting and shot putting emphasize *muscular fitness*. Other sports, such as basketball, wrestling, tennis, and field hockey, require both energy and muscular fitness for success. As a physical trainer you need to understand the physiology of these two components of fitness.

Energy Fitness

An athlete's body needs energy to power the muscles to meet the demands of the sport. Physically fit athletes have conditioned their bodies to store and use fuels efficiently and to remove the metabolic waste produced by the working muscles. The cardiovascular, respiratory, and hormonal systems primarily deliver oxygen and fuel to the muscles and remove carbon dioxide and other wastes.

Our elegantly engineered bodies have two energy systems. The *anaerobic system* is for immediate movement and very intense exercise. The *aerobic system* is for more enduring and less intense activity. It's essential that you understand these two energy systems because different sports use these energy systems differently.

When you begin to exercise, the heart, lungs, and a number of other systems jump into action to bring more oxygen to the muscles, but it takes a couple of minutes for this aerobic energy system (*aerobic* means "with oxygen") to respond to your body's request for energy. So how does your body get energy to move in those first couple of minutes? The anaerobic energy system is the answer. Perhaps as an evolutionary survival mechanism to avoid danger, humans have an energy system in which the fuel is stored in the muscle and converted into energy immediately without the need for oxygen (*anaerobic* means "without oxygen"). But this system can produce energy for only a short time—about two minutes—just enough time for the aerobic system to take over (figure 13.6).

The anaerobic energy system is used for fuel not only during the initial demand for energy, but also when the demand for energy is so high that the aerobic energy

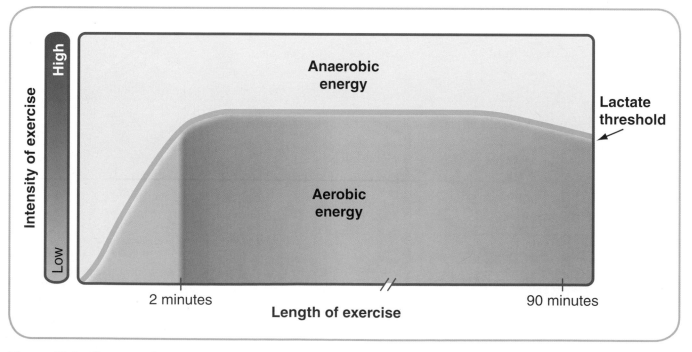

Figure 13.6 Sources of energy.

cannot get enough oxygen to the muscles. The anaerobic energy system is the source of energy for such sport activities as sprinting, power lifting, and hitting baseballs. The aerobic energy system is the source of energy for long-distance and long-duration events. You'll learn much more about these energy systems in chapter 14.

Muscular Fitness

Muscles are the workhorses that create athletic movement. *Muscular fitness* is the ability of muscles to meet the demands of the sport with optimal strength, endurance, speed, power, and flexibility. In planning physical training programs for your athletes, you'll want to know what is optimal for each of these components of muscular fitness and how to train that component. Let's define each of these now.

Muscular strength is the maximum amount of force that a muscle can generate in a single effort. Strength is important in every sport, but you must determine how much is optimal in the sport you coach. Sports such as running and swimming obviously require less muscular strength than do sports such as wrestling and football, where more strength always seems helpful.

Muscular endurance is the ability of a muscle to repeatedly contract or sustain a continuous contraction involving less than maximum force. We typically measure muscular endurance by the number of repetitions a person can perform (e.g., push-ups) or the length of time a person can hold a contraction with a designated force (e.g., holding the "down" position in a push-up).

Speed is the ability to move the body or parts of it very quickly; it's the distance moved divided by time. Speed is a combination of reaction time and movement time. *Reaction time* is the period from when a stimulus is perceived (e.g., the pitcher throws the ball to the batter) to the beginning of the movement (e.g., the batter begins the swing). *Movement time* is the period from the beginning of the movement to the end of the movement. *Quickness* is sometimes used to refer to the reaction time part of the movement, and *speed* to the movement time.

Was it Yogi Berra who said that the three most important qualities of an athlete are speed, speed, and speed? A popular myth is that speed is inherited and can't be trained, but in chapter 15 you'll learn that this is not entirely correct.

Muscular power is the ability to exert muscular strength quickly; it's strength and speed combined. Power is vital in many sports as exemplified in the high jumper, baseball batter, 100-meter sprinter, and tennis server. When you increase strength or speed in your training program, you increase the power of your athletes.

Flexibility is the range of motion through which the body's joints are able to move. It is determined by a combination of the elasticity or suppleness of the muscles, ligaments, and tendons. When I work my muscles hard, they quickly lose their flexibility, and thus I have been prone to muscle pulls and strains. Now I understand the problem so I carefully warm up my muscles before playing and stretch them again after the contest. Improving and maintaining flexibility is a slow process that athletes should work on year-round.

Two other terms are associated with muscular fitness and motor skill development. *Balance* refers to the ability to maintain a certain posture or to move without falling. It's useful to distinguish between *static balance,* or the ability to maintain equilibrium in a stationary position, and *dynamic balance,* or the ability to maintain equilibrium when moving the body. Both are vital in many sports, and they are wonderfully exemplified in sports such as gymnastics, diving, and figure skating.

The other term is *agility,* which is the ability to start, stop, and change speed and direction quickly and with precision. To be an agile athlete, you need strength, endurance, speed, balance, and movement skills.

Although we will study energy and muscular fitness separately to help you learn how to develop training programs for each, they of course work together. Muscles need energy to work, and energy systems depend on muscles to produce skillful movement. Training one helps train the other.

Outcomes of Physical Training

Physical training doesn't guarantee success, but the lack of training almost certainly promises failure. The benefits of physical training on the body are many, as listed here.

▶ Improved use of oxygen in muscle, increasing energy for muscular contraction

▶ Improved ability of the muscles to use fat as a source of energy

▶ Increased size of muscle fibers (unclear if it increases number of fibers), which helps muscle exert more force

▶ Increased number of capillaries serving muscle fiber, which improves blood flow

▶ More efficient respiration, more fully using the lungs' capacity, and greater endurance of the respiratory muscles

▶ Improved blood volume throughout the body and better distribution of blood to the needed body parts

▶ Improved ability of the heart to pump blood with each beat (increased stroke volume) and decreased resting and exercise heart rates

▶ Increased efficiency of the nervous system in controlling movement enabling the body to use less energy to do the same amount of activity

▶ Improved function of the endocrine system by decreasing the amount of insulin needed to metabolize sugar

▶ Improved ability to burn unneeded fat improving body composition so the athlete is not carrying unneeded weight

▶ Stronger bones, ligaments, and tendons, reducing the chance of injury

Coach's Role in Physical Training

Now that you've learned the basic language used in discussing physical fitness in sports, let's consider your role in helping to prepare your athletes to meet the physical demands of your sport. Professional, college, and elite sport coaches often employ professional physical trainers or conditioning coaches to direct the training of their athletes, but most high school and club sport coaches are their team's physical trainer. Even if you have the luxury of a physical trainer, you will still want to know basic sport physiology so you can understand and evaluate the trainer's work and properly plan your practice sessions.

Know Sport Physiology and Training Methods

As a coach one of your duties is to optimize the physical training programs of your athletes so that they are in peak physical fitness. This takes considerable knowledge and skill because in most sports it is very easy to undertrain or overtrain your athletes. Insufficient or incorrect training leaves your athletes underprepared. Working them too hard can actually tear down their bodies rather than build them up. Proper rest, nutrition, and hydration allow your athletes to adapt to the training stress. The more you know about sport physiology and training methods, the more likely you'll be to optimize your athletes' training programs (figure 13.7).

Figure 13.7 The effects of under-, optimal, and overtraining.

Just for fun, review the short test on the following page to check your knowledge of sport physiology.

I hope you answered all of the questions correctly, and if so, congratulations! You're in great position to learn much more. If you didn't know all the correct answers, you need not worry. This is just the start of what I think you'll find to be a most enjoyable learning experience. The human body is a remarkable machine, and learning how to prepare it to achieve outstanding performances will be a source of great satisfaction for you.

Although we'll cover the basics of sport physiology and physical training here in part IV, you can learn much more by taking ASEP's Silver Level Sport Physiology course and by studying the books listed in the To Learn More section at the end of this chapter.

Determine the Physical Demands of Your Sport

In addition to knowing sport physiology well, you will want to understand the physical demands of your sport for each position and function or event. Much of this is common sense, but not entirely. For example, you would emphasize training the aerobic energy system in long-distance swimmers, but just how much strength should endurance swimmers have? You'll want to emphasize strength and power with wrestlers, but how much should you develop their aerobic fitness?

Table 13.1 on pages 276 to 278 shows an estimate of the energy and muscular fitness demands for various sports and positions within some of those sports based on the opinion of exercise physiologists and strength and conditioning experts. Review the table and make your own judgment about the physical demands for your sport. We'll look more closely at the physical demands of sports in the next two chapters.

Sport Physiology Test

True False   **1.** Strength training in prepubescent athletes does not produce appreciable increases in strength.

False. Strength training does improve strength through improved recruitment of muscle fibers and reduced inhibition to lift heavier weights, but it does not produce increased muscle size in prepubescent athletes. That occurs only in postpubescent athletes.

True False   **2.** Lactic acid causes muscle soreness.

False. Although lactic acid is produced when exercising strenuously, and such strenuous exercise often leads to muscle soreness, the lactic acid isn't the cause. The body removes the lactic acid within an hour of exercise. Muscle soreness occurs 24 to 48 hours after the exercise, long after the lactic acid is gone. Soreness is probably due to microtrauma to muscle and connective tissue, which causes swelling thereafter.

True False   **3.** The recommended minimum percentage of body fat for male athletes is 5 to 10 percent.

True. And for female athletes the recommended minimum percentage of body fat is 10 to 15 percent. Note that these are minimum percentages for athletes and are not necessarily ideal for every athlete in every sport. Nonathletes may find higher body fat percentages healthy.

True False   **4.** Plyometrics refers to a set of exercises used to develop strength and endurance in the muscles.

False. Plyometrics are exercises involving explosive movements used to develop power.

True False   **5.** An ideal diet for athletes consists of 20 percent fat, 15 percent protein, and 65 percent carbohydrate.

True. This diet is called the high-performance diet and is recommended not only as a good diet to provide the energy needed in sports, but also as a healthy diet for daily living.

Sport or activity	Energy fitness		Muscular fitness				
	Aerobic	Anaerobic	Flexibility	Strength	Endurance	Speed	Power
Archery	L	L	M	M	L–M	L	L–M
Badminton	M	M–H	M–H	L–M	M	H	M
Baseball (hitting and fielding)	L	M—H	M	M–H	L–M	H	H
Baseball (base running)	L–M	H	M	M	L–M	H	M–H
Baseball (pitching)	L–M	M–H	H	M–H	M	M–H	H
Basketball (offense and defense)	M–H	H	M	M	M–H	H	M–H
Basketball (rebounding)	L–M	H	M	M–H	M	M–H	H
Bowling	L	L	M	L–M	L	L–M	L–M
Cricket	L–M	M	M	M	L–M	M–H	M–H
Cycling (short-distance events)	L–M	H	L–M	M–H	M	H	H
Cycling (middle-distance events)	M–H	M–H	L–M	M–H	H	M	M–H
Cycling (long-distance events)	H	L–M	M	M	H	L–M	M
Diving	L	M–H	H	M–H	L–M	M–H	H
Fencing	M	M–H	M–H	M	M	M–H	M
Field hockey	H	M–H	M	M	M–H	M–H	M–H
Figure skating	M–H	M–H	H	M	M–H	M–H	M–H
Football (linemen)	L–M	H	M	H	L–M	M–H	H
Football (running backs)	M	H	M	H	M	H	H
Football (receivers)	M	H	M–H	M–H	M	H	M–H
Football (punters and kickers)	L	M–H	H	M–H	L–M	M	M–H
Golf	L–M	L–M	M–H	L–M	L–M	L–M	M–H
Gymnastics	L–M	H	H	H	M–H	M–H	H

L = low; M = medium; and H = high.

Table 13.1 *(continued)*

Sport or activity	Energy fitness		Muscular fitness				
	Aerobic	Anaerobic	Flexibility	Strength	Endurance	Speed	Power
Ice hockey (goal keeper)	L–M	M–H	H	M	L–M	M–H	L–M
Ice hockey (other positions)	M–H	H	M	M	M–H	H	H
Judo and karate	M	H	H	M–H	M–H	H	H
Lacrosse (goalkeeper)	L–M	M–H	M–H	M	L–M	M–H	M
Lacrosse (other positions)	M–H	H	M	M	M–H	H	M–H
Netball	M	M	M	M	M	M–H	M
Rowing (short-distance events)	L–M	H	M	H	M	M–H	H
Rowing (middle-distance events)	M–H	M–H	M	M–H	M–H	M	M–H
Rowing (long distance events)	H	L–M	M	M	H	M	M
Rugby	M–H	H	M	M–H	M–H	H	M–H
Skiing—alpine	M	M–H	M–H	M–H	M–H	M–H	M H
Skiing—cross-country (short-distance events)	M–H	M–H	M	M	M–H	M–H	H
Skiing—cross-country (middle-distance events)	H	M–H	M	M	H	M	M
Skiing—cross-country (long-distance events)	H	L–M	M	M	H	L–M	L–M
Skiing—ski jumping	L–M	M–H	M–H	M–H	L–M	M	H
Soccer (goalkeeper)	L	M–H	M–H	M	L–M	H	M
Soccer (other positions)	H	H	M	M	M–H	H	M–H
Softball	Same as for baseball ratings						
Speed skating (short-distance events)	L–M	H	M	M–H	L–M	H	H

L = low; M = medium; and H = high.

continued ☞

Table 13.1 *(continued)*

Sport or activity	Energy fitness		Muscular fitness				
	Aerobic	Anaerobic	Flexibility	Strength	Endurance	Speed	Power
Speed skating (middle-distance events)	M–H	M–H	M	M	M–H	M–H	M–H
Speed skating (long-distance events)	H	L–M	L–M	M	H	M	L–M
Swimming (short-distance events)	M	H	M–H	M–H	M	H	H
Swimming (middle-distance events)	M–H	M–H	M–H	M–H	M–H	M–H	M–H
Swimming (long-distance events)	H	L–M	M–H	M	H	L–M	L–M
Swimming (synchronized)	M–H	M	H	L–M	H	L–M	M
Table tennis	L–M	L–M	M	L–M	M	M–H	L–M
Team handball	M–H	H	M	M	M–H	H	M–H
Tennis	M–H	M–H	M–H	M	M–H	H	H
Track (short-distance events)	L–M	H	M–H	H	L–M	H	H
Track (middle-distance events)	M–H	M–H	M–H	M	M–H	M–H	M
Track (long-distance events)	H	L–M	M	L	H	L–M	L–M
Track and field events	L	H	M–H	H	L–M	M–H	H
Triathlon	H	L–M	M	M–H	H	M	M
Volleyball	M	M–H	M–H	M	M	M–H	H
Water polo	H	M–H	M–H	M–H	M–H	M–H	M–H
Weightlifting	L	H	M	H	L–M	M	H
Wrestling	M	H	M–H	H	M–H	M–H	H

L = low; M = medium; and H = high.

Assess the Fitness of Your Athletes

Just as you can't plan a trip if you don't know where you're starting from, you can't plan a physical training program if you don't know your athletes' current fitness levels. Fitness testing has the following benefits:

▶ It identifies individual differences in each component of physical fitness, helping you to design a specific training program for each athlete.

▶ It helps predict performance potential.

▶ It helps you guide athletes to the best positions or events for them.

▶ It allows you to assess athletes' progress as they train.

Physical testing of elite athletes is the norm and is increasingly common in high school and college sports. The basic components assessed in most physical evaluations of athletes include the following:

Body composition
▶ Body type
▶ Body fat
▶ Muscle fiber type

Energy fitness
▶ Aerobic fitness
▶ Anaerobic fitness

Muscular fitness
▶ Flexibility
▶ Strength
▶ Muscular endurance
▶ Speed
▶ Power

In chapter 14 you'll learn how to test the energy fitness of your athletes as well as their body composition, and in chapter 15 you'll learn how to test muscular fitness.

Guidelines for Testing

▶ Test at least pre- and postseason.
▶ Have athletes warm up properly before testing.
▶ Give special attention to safety.
▶ Use the same equipment for testing all athletes each time you test.
▶ Prepare your athletes for testing with a pretest practice session one to three days before the testing session.
▶ Be well organized and have the testing equipment and facility ready.
▶ Administer the test at the same time of day.
▶ Give the same amount of rest before testing.
▶ Provide clear, concise instructions.
▶ Require proper form in doing the exercises.
▶ Test each function at least twice. Use the best score.
▶ Follow the test procedures and score accurately.
▶ Have a form to record results.
▶ Have athletes cool down after they've been exercising vigorously.
▶ Avoid testing when the weather is extreme if the testing is done outside.
▶ Provide your athletes with results and use those results to plan their energy and muscular fitness programs.
▶ Don't embarrass those who don't score as well as others.
▶ Make the testing fun.

Design a Physical Training Program

You now understand sport physiology, at least the basics. You have a good handle on the physiological demands of your sport, position by position and function by function. You've tested your athletes and know their current fitness levels. The next step is to design a training program. Don't panic. I don't expect you to design a training program yet, but you need to understand what goes into designing a program. You'll learn how to actually design a program in chapters 14 and 15.

Six Decisions

At the basic exercise level you'll need to make decisions about the following six variables:

▶ *Choice of exercise.* Is it long-distance running or sprints? Is it lower body or upper body exercises with moderate weights or heavy weights?

▶ *Order of exercises.* Do you do energy training one day and muscular training the next? Do you alternate muscle groups or exhaust one group?

▶ *Intensity of exercise.* Do you have your athletes go all out or something less?

▶ *Volume of exercise.* How long is the training period? How far do they run or swim? How many repetitions do they do?

▶ *Frequency of training.* Do you train once, twice, or three times a day? Do you train every day or every other day?

▶ *Length of rest period.* How much time do you allow for athletes to recover between sprints or lifts? How much time do you allow between workouts?

Your decisions about these six variables is your training design and will substantially affect the physiological adaptation of your athletes to the training program you plan. In the last section of this chapter I'll introduce you to the major training principles that will help guide you in making choices about the preceding variables.

Annual Training Plan

You'll want to think long term in designing training programs for your athletes. At minimum you'll want to design a training program for the season, but you should try to create an annual plan. Many training programs today are annual plans consisting of four phases as shown in figure 13.8.

In many sports coaches want to prepare their athletes to be in peak condition for major competitive events. Thus they plan the training in cycles and periods, or what is called periodization. A common example of periodization is the "taper" in swimming, which is the marked reduction of regular workouts to let the body not only recover but also accumulate extra energy for the pending competition.

Figure 13.8
Four phases of an annual training cycle.

| Off-season training | Pre-season training | Early season training | Peak season training |

Anatomy of a Workout

Once you've planned the training program, you'll be ready to conduct a workout. Most coaches know the anatomy of a workout—warm up, train or practice skills, and cool down. Chapters 14 and 15 are devoted to training; following are guidelines for warming up and cooling down.

Warm-Up.   The benefits of warming up are as follows:

▶ Increased body and tissue temperature
▶ Increased blood flow through the muscles
▶ Increased heart rate, preparing the cardiovascular system to work
▶ Increased rate of energy release from the cells
▶ Increased speed at which nerve impulses travel, and thus the speed and efficiency with which muscles contract and relax
▶ Decreased viscosity of joint fluids, improving range of motion by as much as 20 percent
▶ Decreased risk of injury to the muscles

The warm-up has three phases, to be done in the order described, each phase lasting 5 to 10 minutes.

▶ *Aerobic warm-up.* Begin with slow aerobic activities such as jogging, cycling, swimming, or skiing, gradually increasing the intensity as the warm-up progresses.

▶ *Stretching.* Always stretch *after* warming up the muscles through aerobic activity, not before. Stretching guidelines and exercises are given in chapter 15.

▶ *Technical skill warm-up.* Practice the activities of the sport to exercise the specific muscle groups to be used and to review the motor program for the technical skill.

Cool-Down.   After a vigorous workout athletes should cool down for 10 to 15 minutes by light jogging, walking, and stretching. Doing so helps remove the lactic acid to speed recovery for the next workout.

The benefits of cooling down are as follows:

▶ Decreased chance of blood pooling in the lower body causing lightheadedness or dizziness
▶ Removal of lactic acid from the muscles, which speeds recovery
▶ Reduced muscle soreness

The cool-down has two phases.

▶ *Aerobic phase.* The body's engine is gradually brought down to idle speed through low-intensity exercise, often the same aerobic exercise done to warm up.

▶ *Stretching phase.* Muscles that have been contracting repeatedly during exercise remain partially contracted afterward. Stretching them helps return them to their optimal length and is thought to reduce muscle soreness.

Educate Your Athletes About the Training Program

In work and sport people are much more willing to do the work assigned when they are told the reason for the work and how it will benefit them or others. Athletes especially will work hard to physically condition their bodies if you explain to them the purpose of each component of the training program.

When you explain the reasons for various exercise routines, you are in fact teaching your athletes sport physiology and how to design their own training programs. This educates athletes about how to continue their training outside of the formal practice setting. Moreover, as athletes become more experienced, they come to "read" their own bodies better, and thus can often better determine when they should make adjustments in their training program. Thus, your role is not to prescribe the training program, but to work with your athlete to develop a training program together.

By explaining the logic behind the training program you've designed for athletes, you engender in them confidence in you and in their preparation for competition. As a bonus, they'll know how to maintain a fitness program for the rest of their lives.

Conduct the Training Program

Of course the last step is to conduct the training program. For some sports this typically occurs before and after the technical and tactical parts of a practice session (e.g., team sports), and in other sports much of the practice session is the training program (e.g., track, swimming, or cycling).

One of the training principles you'll read about on page 285 is the individual differences principle, which states that you will obtain better results from your training program if you account for individual differences. Invariably athletes differ in their preseason fitness levels, and, depending on many factors, will respond differently to the same physical training program. Thus, your training program should be designed and conducted for individual athletes, not for the team as a whole.

If you have 5 to 10 athletes on your team, individualizing workouts is not so difficult, but if you're a football coach with 40 to 60 players or more, designing a personal training program for each player and meeting all of your other responsibilities may be nearly impossible. So what can you do?

▶ Using your preseason physical fitness testing results, group players by similar fitness levels and then conduct the training program specifically for each group.

▶ If the physical fitness demands vary by position (e.g., football linemen as compared to backs), conduct the training program in groups by those positions.

▶ Create even smaller groups by using differences in position and fitness levels.

▶ After you've taught your athletes the basics of fitness training, let them become responsible for their own training, consulting with you when they need help.

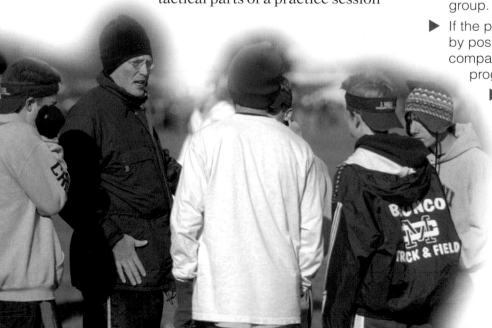

Overweight and Out of Shape

I can vividly recall Darrell showing up for his first practice on my high school football team. He was very overweight and had done no preseason training. Just getting through the warm-ups and practice drills was a Herculean effort for Darrell. At the end of that first practice our coach made him run wind sprints with everyone else. Of course Darrell came in last each time, and each time our coach pointed this out to the rest of us. In the midst of the third wind sprint Darrell stopped to vomit. The coach chided him for being so out of condition. Darrell never came to practice again.

My coach missed an opportunity. If he had recognized Darrell's physical status and designed a physical training program for Darrell to give him a chance to lose the weight and catch up with the physical condition of the other players, Darrell could have become an accomplished football player. Instead Darrell was turned away from sport, and he may have been turned off to physical activity for the rest of his life.

Training Principles

Follow these eight cardinal training principles and you will be well on your way to designing effective fitness programs.

Specificity Principle

The specificity principle asserts that the best way to develop physical fitness for your sport is to train the energy systems and muscles as closely as possible to the way they are used in your sport. Thus, the best way to train for running is to run, for swimming is to swim, and for weightlifting is to lift. In sports such as basketball, baseball, and soccer, the training program should not only overload the energy systems and muscles used in that sport, but should also duplicate similar movement patterns. For example, in strengthening a quarterback's throwing arm, design the exercise to simulate the throwing movement. Warning: This principle can be taken too far. Ample evidence suggests that cross training, or doing another sport or activity, can help improve performance (see the variation principle).

Overload Principle

To improve their fitness levels, athletes must do more than what their bodies are used to doing. When more is demanded, within reason, the body adapts to the increased demand. You can apply overload in duration, intensity, or both. If you increase a cross country runner's long-distance run by five minutes, you've added an overload of duration. If you instead ask the runner to run her normal distance but in a shorter amount of time, you've added an overload of intensity.

Progression Principle

To steadily improve the fitness levels of your athletes, you must continually increase the physical demands to overload their systems. If the training demand is increased too quickly, the athlete will be unable to adapt and may break down. If the demand is not adequate, the athlete will not achieve optimal fitness levels.

Diminishing Returns Principle

When unfit athletes begin a training regime, their fitness levels improve rapidly, but as they become fitter, the diminishing returns principle becomes law. That is, as athletes become fitter, the amount of improvement is less as they approach their genetic limits (figure 13.9). A corollary to this principle is that as fitness levels increase, more work or training is needed to make the same gains. As you're designing training programs, remember that fitness levels will not continue to improve at the same rate as athletes become fitter.

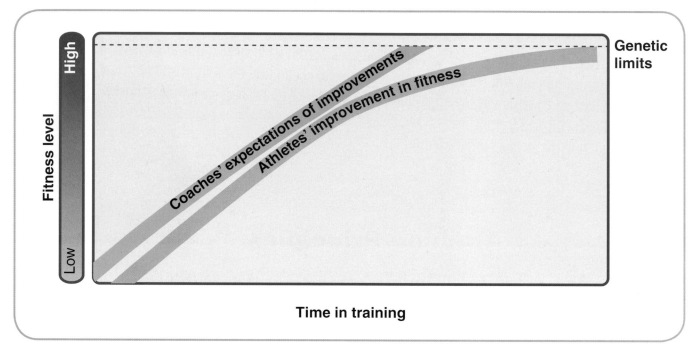

Figure 13.9   The diminishing returns principle: As athletes reach their genetic limits, their improvement becomes less marked.

Variation Principle

This principle has several meanings. After your athletes have trained hard for several days, they should train lightly to give their bodies a chance to recover. Over the course of the year use training cycles (periodization) to vary the intensity and volume of training to help your athletes achieve peak levels of fitness for competition. This principle also means that you should change the exercises or activities regularly so that you do not overstress a part of the body. Of course changing activities also maintains athletes' interest in training.

Perhaps you're thinking that the specificity principle and variation principle seem to be incompatible. The specificity principle states that the more specific the training to the demands of the sport, the better; and the variation principle seemingly asserts the opposite—train by using a variety of activities. The incompatibility is resolved by the degree to which each principle is followed. More specific training is better, but it can become exceedingly boring. Thus some variety that involves the same muscle groups is a useful change.

Reversibility Principle

We all know the following adage: Use it or lose it. When athletes stop training, their hard-won fitness gains disappear, usually faster than they were gained. The actual rate of decline depends on the length of the training period before detraining, the specific muscle group, and other factors. A person confined to complete bed rest is estimated to lose cardiovascular fitness at the rate of 10 percent a week. Smart coaches and athletes today recognize that maintaining a moderately high level of fitness year-round is easier than detraining at the end of the season and then retraining at the beginning of the next.

Individual Differences Principle

Every athlete is different and responds differently to the same training activities. As discussed in chapter 5, the value of training depends in part on the athlete's maturation. Before puberty, training is less effective than after puberty. Other factors that affect how athletes respond to training include their pretraining condition; genetic predisposition; gender and race; diet and sleep; environmental factors such as heat, cold, and humidity; and of course motivation. As discussed previously, it's essential to individualize training as much as possible.

Moderation Principle

Here is another familiar adage: All things in moderation. Remember that training is a slow, gradual process. Give athletes time to progress. Your challenge as a physical conditioning coach is to design a training program that progresses optimally using the principles just discussed. You want to gently coax your athletes' bodies into superior condition, not beat them up by overtraining.

Make training fun. Design games and activities that challenge athletes to do the same work but without the drudgery of monotonous exercises. Be encouraging and promote a positive attitude about training. By all means don't use training activities as punishment for misbehaviors.

Coaching Yourself:
Being Physically Fit

What would you think if while your doctor was lecturing you to stop smoking, he had a cigarette in his mouth? How much confidence would you have in an obese dietician counseling you on losing weight? At minimum, you'd see the irony in the contradiction of "do as I say, not as I do," and more likely you'd completely disregard the advice because of a lack of credibility. You can probably see where I'm going here. How credible would you seem to your athletes if you promoted physical conditioning and advocated it for a lifetime for your athletes, but were physically inactive and perhaps substantially overweight partly because of the inactivity?

Coaches tell me they are not physically active for the following reasons:

▶ I'm too busy coaching and working.

▶ I don't like training after all those years of training as an athlete.

▶ I've had the mind-set that you only exercise to be in shape to play sports and haven't thought about exercising for my health and to be a good role model.

▶ I want to be in better shape, but I just can't get myself started with an exercise program.

Many coaches are excellent physical role models, exercising regularly and keeping themselves in good physical condition. They are models of an active lifestyle not only to their athletes but also to the community. You are to be applauded if you are among these coaches. If you are not, I encourage you to become physically fit—foremost for your own health but also to serve as a positive role model for your athletes and all those who observe you. As you get into better shape, you'll find that you have more energy for coaching and the other things you like to do. You'll also see in subtle ways that your athletes and others will have more respect for you.

You have a significant advantage over many other people in getting off the couch and starting a daily exercise program. You know about fitness (and if you don't, you will when you finish this part of the book), you likely have ready access to fitness equipment, and you're in an environment in which fitness is part of the daily culture. Here are some steps to help you get moving:

1. Decide that you want to become fit. Just as you direct your athletes to achieve goals, decide that you want to achieve a fitness goal and set out the steps to get started. Your goal should be at minimum to maintain good health. The U.S. government recommends at least 30 minutes of moderate exercise a day, such as a brisk walk, biking at 10 mph or faster, or playing a moderately vigorous game of tennis. Another guideline is to accumulate at least ten thousand steps a day, which you can check by wearing a pedometer.

2. Set aside a time to exercise regularly so that it becomes a habit. Try not to let other activities interfere with your exercise, but if they do, be flexible and find an alternative time.

3. Determine whether you prefer to exercise with others or alone. If you like to exercise with others, they can be great social support to keep you going on the days you would rather not exercise.

4. If you're finding changing your sedentary behavior difficult, I recommend that you read Steven Blair and colleagues' book *Active Living Every Day* (2002). The book takes you through 20 steps to help you change your behavior from inactivity to healthy and enjoyable activity.

Questions for Reflection

▶ What is physical training, and what are its benefits? **(p. 269)**

▶ Which energy system (anaerobic or aerobic) do your athletes primarily use ? **(p. 270)**

▶ Do you have a program for training your athletes' muscular fitness, including strength, endurance, speed, power, and flexibility? **(p. 271)**

▶ What are some physiological outcomes of physical training? **(p. 273)**

▶ Do you assess the fitness of your athletes both pre- and postseason? **(p. 279)**

▶ What are the six basic decisions you must make when designing a physical training program? **(p. 280)**

▶ What are the benefits of warming up and cooling down? Do you have your athletes go through all of the phases of both? **(p. 281)**

▶ How well do you communicate to your athletes the purpose behind the various components of the training program? Are they partners with you in creating their workouts? **(p. 282)**

▶ Are you able to individualize your training program to account for differences among your athletes? **(p. 282)**

▶ Do you understand the eight cardinal training principles and consider them when designing training programs for your athletes? **(p. 283)**

▶ Are you a good role model of physical fitness for your athletes and your community? **(p. 286)**

References

Blair, S.N., A.L. Dunn, B.H. Marcus, R.A. Carpenter, and P. Jaret. 2002. *Active living every day.* Champaign, IL: Human Kinetics.

Landers, D.M., R.W. Christina, B.D. Hatfield, F.S. Daniels, M. Wilkinson, and L.A. Doyle. 1980. Research in shooting sports: A preliminary report. *The American Rifleman* April, 36-37; 76-77.

To Learn More

Brown, Lee, Vance Ferrigno, and Juan Santana. 2000. *Training for speed, agility, and quickness.* Champaign, IL: Human Kinetics.

Foran, Bill, ed. 2001. *High-performance sports conditioning.* Champaign, IL: Human Kinetics.

Hoffman, Jay. 2002. *Physiological aspects of sport training and performance.* Champaign, IL: Human Kinetics.

Lockette, Kevin F., and Ann M. Keyes. 1994. *Conditioning with physical disabilities.* Champaign, IL: Human Kinetics.

Moran, Gary T., and George H. McGlynn. 1997. *Cross-training for sports.* Champaign, IL: Human Kinetics.

National Strength and Conditioning Association. 2000. *Essentials of strength training and conditioning.* 2nd ed. Champaign, IL: Human Kinetics.

Wilmore, Jack H., and David L. Costill. 2004. *Physiology of sport and exercise.* 3rd ed. Champaign, IL: Human Kinetics.

Training for Energy Fitness

A small group of us were having dinner with Sir Roger Bannister during a pre-Olympic scientific congress at Skidmore College prior to the 1980 Olympic Games. I asked Sir Roger why he thought he was the first person to break the four-minute-mile record when so many before him had failed and so many after him had succeeded. A modest person, Sir Roger didn't attribute the achievement to his running ability or superior training, but to his knowledge of physiology. Because he was studying to become a medical doctor and understood the energy systems of the body, Sir Roger recognized that the four-minute mile was not a physiological impossibility but a psychological barrier.

W've learned much in the last 50 years about how to physically train athletes so they have the energy to run a mile in record time or perform other phenomenal physical feats.

☞ **In this chapter you'll learn**

▶ the basic physiology of the body's energy systems,

▶ how to determine the energy demands of your sport,

▶ how to assess and monitor energy fitness, and

▶ how to design an energy fitness training program.

You'll recognize these four parts of this chapter as addressing four of the six duties coaches have as physical trainers that I described in chapter 13. First, let's look closer at what *energy* and *energy fitness* are.

Energy and Energy Fitness

Your body continuously needs energy to power your muscles to move and sustain your life-supporting systems. *Energy,* which means the capacity for work, comes from food, which is converted to fuel in the body's cells through a complex chemical process called *metabolism* (figure 14.1).

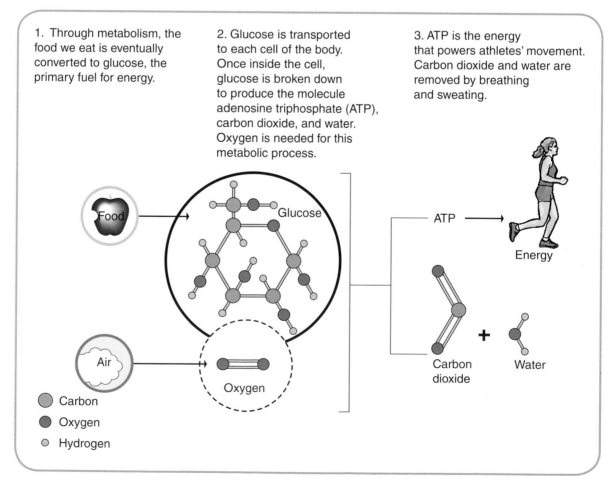

1. Through metabolism, the food we eat is eventually converted to glucose, the primary fuel for energy.

2. Glucose is transported to each cell of the body. Once inside the cell, glucose is broken down to produce the molecule adenosine triphosphate (ATP), carbon dioxide, and water. Oxygen is needed for this metabolic process.

3. ATP is the energy that powers athletes' movement. Carbon dioxide and water are removed by breathing and sweating.

Food • Glucose • ATP → Energy

Air • Oxygen • Carbon dioxide + Water

● Carbon
● Oxygen
○ Hydrogen

Figure 14.1
Metabolism.

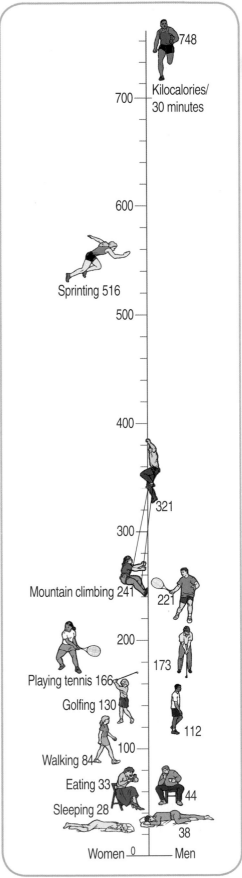

748

700 — Kilocalories/
30 minutes

600 —

Sprinting 516

500 —

400 —

321

300 —

Mountain climbing 241   221

200 —
                         173

Playing tennis 166
Golfing 130
                              112
100 —
Walking 84
Eating 33   44
Sleeping 28
                              38
Women — 0 — Men

Figure 14.2 Approximate calories used for various activities.

Reprinted, by permission, from Whitfield, 1995.

The amount of energy used over a period of time is the metabolic rate. The average woman who is not active uses about 2,000 calories per day, and the average man about 2,500 calories per day. At rest the muscles use about 20 percent of the body's energy and the brain uses another 20 percent. Athletes in intensive training will use as much as 4,000 to 5,000 calories per day, with the muscles consuming 80 to 90 percent of the body's energy during exercise. In figure 14.2 you can see the approximate calories used to perform a variety of activities. (A calorie is a measure of energy in the form of heat. It is the amount of heat required to raise the temperature of 1 kilogram of water 1 degree centigrade.)

Energy fitness is the ability of the anaerobic and aerobic energy systems to use the energy the body has stored. As fitness improves, the body is better able to convert stored energy in the form of carbohydrates and fat into ATP and to more efficiently use ATP within the cells to generate energy. Let's see how incredibly well the human body works to provide us with the energy needed to accomplish amazing feats.

Physiology of Energy Systems

In chapter 13 you learned that our bodies have two systems to provide energy to the muscles—anaerobic and aerobic energy systems. When first starting to exercise or when exercising intensively, the body uses the anaerobic system (without oxygen), but the supply of fuel for this system is very limited. As soon as the body begins demanding more and continuous energy, the aerobic system (with oxygen) jumps into action, but it takes a couple of minutes for the heart and lungs to bring oxygen and fuel to the muscles. Once the aerobic system is engaged, and as long as the energy demands are not too high, it is the primary source of energy. If the

body needs a little extra power, the anaerobic system kicks in to provide more energy, but it can't do so for very long.

The preceding explanation of the aerobic and anaerobic energy systems is accurate, but incomplete. You need to know more. There are actually two systems that work anaerobically: the ATP-PCr system and the anaerobic glycolysis system.

ATP-PCr System

Adenosine triphosphate (ATP) is the only fuel a cell can use to contract muscle, build new tissue, and transport minerals and waste through the body. When the body needs an immediate burst of energy for power or speed, it uses ATP stored in the cells. The ATP teams up with phosphocreatine (PCr) in a complex process to create a very high rate of energy. That's the good news. The bad news is that the cells of the body can only store about 80 to 100 grams of ATP, enough to fuel a one-minute walk or a five- to six-second sprint. As ATP and PCr are depleted, lactic acid—a by-product of ATP breakdown—accumulates in the cells, which signals its teammate, the anaerobic glycolysis system, to step in to help.

Anaerobic Glycolysis System

As the ATP is depleted and the body calls for more energy, the anaerobic glycolysis system jumps in to replenish the ATP. It does so by using carbohydrates as fuel, which are stored in the liver and muscles in the form of glycogen or as glucose in the bloodstream. *Glycogen* is simply a group of glucose molecules joined together.

Creatine Supplement

Phosphocreatine (PCr), or simply creatine, is essential to produce ATP. Athletes in power and speed sports don't want to run out of this essential amino acid. Studies have found that consuming up to 20 grams of creatine supplement per day for five days increases the PCr in muscles and improves performance. Thus, many athletes today take creatine. As a food supplement it is legal, and current scientific data show no harmful health effects on athletes when taken in recommended doses (20 grams per day). However, because creatine supplementation has only been practiced since the early 1990s, the long-term effects are not yet known. Should you recommend or condone the use of creatine? See chapter 16 for the answer and more information about creatine.

Glycolysis

The chemical process of breaking down glycogen to glucose is called *glycolysis*. Thus *anaerobic glycolysis* means to break down glycogen into glucose without oxygen. Glycolysis also occurs with oxygen, as you'll see when we discuss the aerobic system. Anaerobic glycolysis is not a very efficient source of energy: It produces only two molecules of ATP, whereas aerobic glycolysis produces 38 molecules of ATP.

The anaerobic glycolysis system provides energy for only about 60 to 80 seconds when a person is engaged in intense exercise. But it's not the fuel supply of carbohydrates in the form of glucose and glycogen that limits the production of energy. It's our nemesis, lactic acid, the accumulation of which is the price we pay when producing energy without oxygen.

Lactic Acid

As lactic acid builds up, it hinders ATP production, impedes the force generated by muscle, and impairs coordination. It's a pain, literally, causing that burning sensation in muscle. It is also the source of both physical and mental fatigue, but as you learned in chapter 13, it is not the source of muscle soreness after exercise. The good news is that by training the aerobic energy system, athletes can delay the production of lactic acid, and by training the anaerobic glycolysis system, they can clear lactic acid from muscle and blood more quickly.

Just what happens to lactic acid in the body? The majority of it is removed from the muscles through the bloodstream very quickly, and it is amazingly converted to fuel for the aerobic energy system. When sport physiologists learned this, they recognized that light exercise after intense exercise—called active recovery—keeps the blood moving and thus helps remove the lactic acid

from the body, an important reason to have a proper cool-down.

When the intensity of exercise is high, the body produces lactic acid faster than it can clear it. Lactic acid then rapidly builds up in the blood. The point at which blood lactate begins an abrupt increase is called the *blood lactate threshold* or anaerobic threshold. Highly conditioned athletes experience this threshold at 70 to 80 percent of their maximum aerobic exercise capacity compared to untrained athletes, who do so at 50 to 60 percent of their maximum aerobic capacity. The lactate threshold is important to understand because it is an indicator of when an athlete is shifting from predominantly aerobic to predominantly anaerobic energy systems. We'll address this further in our discussion of designing training programs.

Aerobic Energy System

For long-term efficient use of the body's stored energy, the aerobic energy system wins hands down. This system uses carbohydrates and fats, combined with oxygen, to produce glucose, which is converted to ATP. Carbohydrates are in limited supply in the body, providing about 1 to 2 percent of the energy needed for daily living. But fat, as most of us know, is in abundant supply and is the primary source of stored energy.

Note that only the aerobic energy system uses fat for energy. As long as the body has enough oxygen, it burns fat and minimizes the use of the limited supply of carbohydrates,

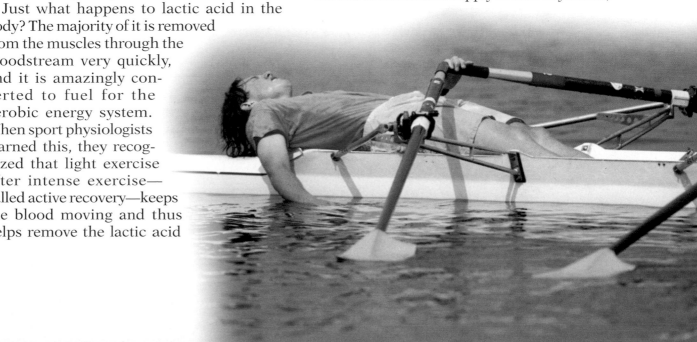

which are stored in the form of glycogen. In this way, the body cleverly keeps the glycogen available in reserve for intense periods of exercise. As a twist, though, when the aerobic energy system uses fat as a fuel, it needs carbohydrates to convert the fat to glucose, and therefore is dependent on the anaerobic glycolysis system to keep a supply of carbohydrates available for this purpose.

We are inclined to think negatively about fat because many of us store an overabundance of it as a result of eating too much and exercising too little. However, fat is an excellent energy source, producing 9 calories of energy per gram compared to only 4 calories per gram from carbohydrates. If an athlete weighs 90 kilograms (198 pounds) and has body fat of 15 percent, he would have 13.5 kilograms (30 pounds) of fat. If he could burn all the fat, he would have 121,500 calories of energy or enough to run 1,350 miles at a slow pace or play tennis for 225 hours.

Perhaps you've noticed that I haven't mentioned protein as a source of energy. It's used for tissue maintenance, repair, and growth mostly. However, protein can be used for production of glucose if glycogen stores are too low, which can occur when training is too hard and the body has inadequate rest and diet to recover. You don't want to let athletes use protein as an energy source. When they do, they cannibalize their muscle tissue and work their kidneys excessively.

Muscle Fiber Types and Energy Systems

Sport physiologists are famous for sticking huge needles in athletes' muscles to rip out muscle fibers in the name of science (these are called muscle biopsies, and they hurt). These sport physiologists have discovered that humans have three types of muscle fiber—one type of slow-twitch and two types of fast-twitch fibers. Most muscles have both fast- and slow-twitch fibers; the percentage of distribution of each fiber type is determined primarily by genetics. Slow-twitch fibers take about 110 milliseconds to reach their maximum tension, and fast-twitch fibers take only 50 milliseconds.

You need to understand muscle fiber types because each type relies more on one of the three energy systems and therefore influence your training design. For slower movements such as jogging, the nervous system recruits the slow-twitch fibers, and for sprints and explosive movements, it recruits both slow- and fast-twitch fibers. Slow-twitch fibers have more endurance than the quickly fatiguing fast-twitch fibers. That's because they have a rich network of capillaries (small blood vessels) to supply them with oxygen and remove lactic acid. Consequently athletes with large amounts of slow-twitch fibers have higher lactate thresholds. As you would surmise, slow-twitch fibers primarily use the aerobic energy system to produce ATP.

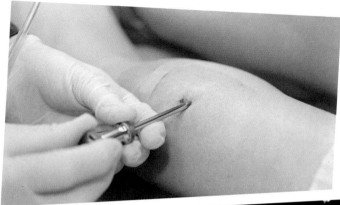

Muscle biopsy.

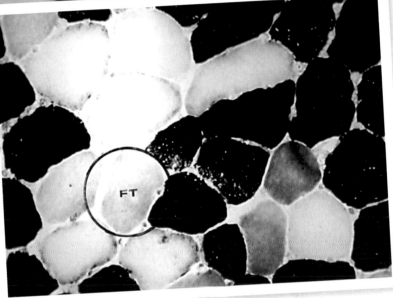

Cross-sectional view of slow-twitch and fast-twitch muscle fibers.

The two types of fast-twitch fibers are *fast oxidative glycolytic (FOG)* and *fast glycolytic (FG)* fibers. Fast oxidative glycolytic fibers twitch fast; they use oxygen and thus can produce energy through the aerobic system; and they're glycolytic, meaning that they can produce energy through the anaerobic system as well. Fast glycolytic fibers are the fastest twitching fibers, and they have the greatest capacity to produce energy via the anaerobic energy systems. FOGs, although helpful for fast, explosive movements, can also be trained to improve performance in endurance sports. A summary of the properties of these three fiber types is shown in table 14.1.

Table 14.1—Properties of Muscle Fiber Types			
Fiber type properties	**Slow twitch**	**Fast oxidative glycolytic (FOG)**	**Fast glycolytic (FG)**
Contractile speed	Slow	Fast	Fast
Aerobic capacity	High	Moderately high	Low
Anaerobic capacity	Low	High	Highest
Endurance	High	Moderate	Low

World-class marathoners have between 80 and 95 percent slow-twitch fibers, and world-class sprinters have only 25 percent slow-twitch fibers. The latest view among sport physiologists is that a person's muscle fiber composition is mostly genetically determined, but through extensive training it may be changed to a limited extent—perhaps 5 percent. Through strength training, fast-twitch fibers will increase their fiber size and thus improve the muscles' performance, but it's not clear whether strength training produces new fast-twitch fibers.

Let's briefly review the key points here. Humans have three energy systems. The ATP-PCr system provides immediate energy from ATP stored in the muscle cells and does so anaerobically. As this energy system runs out of fuel, the anaerobic glycolysis system jumps in, providing enough energy for another one to three minutes from carbohydrates stored as glycogen in the muscles and from blood glucose, which is converted to ATP. Lactic acid, the by-product of energy produced by the anaerobic systems, limits these systems' ability to continue providing energy. The aerobic energy system uses fat and carbohydrates for fuel, which, combined with oxygen, provides more enduring and efficient fuel for the body. Review table 14.2 for a summary of the energy systems used based on the duration and intensity of exercise.

Table 14.2—Effect of Event Duration on Primary Energy System Used

Duration of event	Intensity of event	Primary energy system
0–6 sec	Very intense	ATP-PCr
6–30 sec	Intense	ATP-PCr and anaerobic glycolysis
30 sec–2 min	Heavy	Anaerobic glycolysis
2–3 min	Moderate	Anaerobic glycolysis and aerobic
> 3 min	Light	Aerobic

We also know that we have three types of muscle fibers—slow-twitch, fast oxidative glycolytic, and fast glycolytic fibers. Slow-twitch fibers are used for endurance work and obtain their energy primarily from the aerobic energy system, whereas fast-twitch fibers are used for power and speed work and obtain their energy from the anaerobic energy systems.

Energy Demands of Your Sport

The three energy systems are not used sequentially, with the ATP-PCr system first, the anaerobic glycolysis system next, and the aerobic system third. All three systems are usually used simultaneously to provide athletes with energy, with the relative contributions from each determined mostly by the intensity of exercise and amount of carbohydrates and fat available for use.

Although the aerobic energy system provides energy for the long term, its rate of energy production is only 10 to 15 calories per minute, whereas the anaerobic glycolysis system's rate is 15 to 20 calories per minute. When an athlete needs that explosive power to execute a takedown in wrestling or hit a home run in baseball, the ATP-PCr system provides a whopping 35 to 40 calories per minute.

Figure 14.3 shows estimates of the aerobic and anaerobic (the ATP-PCr and anaerobic glycolysis systems combined) sources of energy for a number of sports. The estimates are based on some research, but mostly on the opinions of sport physiologists and myself. These estimates are based on the overall demands of the sport as we see them, not on the specific functions or positions within the sport. You'll want to do a more specific analysis for your sport.

Complete form 14.1 on the next page to help you estimate the energy demands of your sport. Begin by writing in the various positions (e.g., goalie and forwards), various events (sprints and pole vaulting), and different functions (fielding and hitting) in the left column. Then for each position, event, or function, rate the importance of anaerobic and aerobic fitness by circling the letter you think is appropriate for the activity. "L" means low importance, "M" is medium importance, and "H" is high importance. Make copies of this form if you have more than 10 different types of activities to rate.

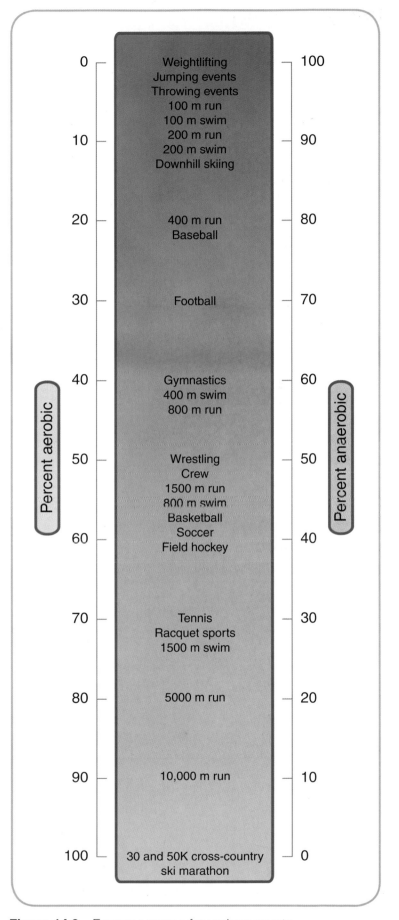

Figure 14.3 Energy sources for various sports.

Energy Demands of Your Sport

Position, event, or function	Anaerobic fitness			Aerobic fitness		
	L	M	H	L	M	H
	L	M	H	L	M	H
	L	M	H	L	M	H
	L	M	H	L	M	H
	L	M	H	L	M	H
	L	M	H	L	M	H
	L	M	H	L	M	H
	L	M	H	L	M	H
	L	M	H	L	M	H
	L	M	H	L	M	H

L = low importance; M = medium importance; H = high importance.

From *Successful Coaching, Third Edition,* by Rainer Martens, 2004, Champaign, IL: Human Kinetics.

Measuring Energy Fitness

Now you know much more about how the body generates energy to power the movements of athletes. The next step in developing your training program is to assess your athletes' fitness. In this section you'll learn how to measure body composition and energy fitness, and in chapter 15 you'll learn about a variety of muscular fitness tests. See table 14.3 for the components of fitness to be tested and the tests to be used.

Table 14.3—Body Composition and Energy Fitness Tests	
Fitness component	**Test name**
Body type (ectomorph, mesomorph, or endomorph)	Weight/height index
Body fat	Skinfold test or bioelectrical impedance
Muscle fiber type	Vertical jump
Aerobic fitness	1.5-mile run
Anaerobic capacity	30-second max test

At the end of this chapter is the Fitness Assessment for SporT, or FAST, form (see pages 316 to 318), which you can use to record the results for all tests in this chapter and chapter 15.

Body Type

The weight/height index is a simple test to confirm your observation of a person's body type. Proceed through the following steps, record your results on the FAST form, and interpret the results by looking at table 14.4.

1. Measure the person's weight using a good quality scale.

2. Measure the person's height using the scale (if it has a height scale as shown in the photo) or a yard stick taped to the wall.

3. Divide the weight in pounds or kilograms by the height in inches or centimeters.

Table 14.4—Evaluation of Weight/Height Index Scores

Body type	Females	Males
Ectomorph (lean)	Under 1.9 lb/in. (Under 0.339 kg/cm)	Under 2 lb/in. (Under 0.357 kg/cm)
Mesomorph (muscular)	1.9–2.5 lb/in. (0.339–0.446 kg/cm)	2–2.8 lb/in. (0.357–0.500 kg/cm)
Endomorph (heavy)	Over 2.5 lb/in. (Over 0.446 kg/cm)	Over 2.8 lb/in. (Over 0.500 kg/cm)

Body type is one factor that may help you direct athletes into sports and positions within sports for which they are physically better suited (figure 14.4). Ectomorphs are slender athletes. They are well suited for endurance sports and lower weight classes in wrestling and judo. Mesomorphs, often synonymous with "athletic build," do well in a wide variety of individual and team sports. Endomorphs, with round body builds, may excel in lifting and throwing sports and in the upper weight classes in wrestling and judo. Even though body type is moderately related to body fat, you should measure body fat separately.

Figure 14.4
General body types:
(a) mesomorphs,
(b) endomorphs, and
(c) ectomorphs.

Reprinted, by permission, from Faigenbaum, 2000.

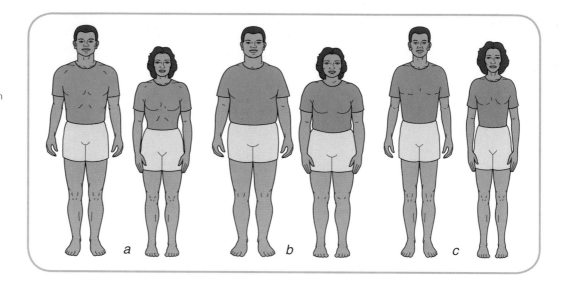

a   *b*   *c*

Body Fat

Low body fat and high muscle mass helps athletes perform better in most sports. Consequently you and your athletes will want to know how much body fat the athlete has. Too much or too little fat will impair performance in sports and can be harmful to the athlete's health. By measuring body fat and suggesting a diet and exercise program, you can help your athletes achieve an optimal percent body fat.

The two most practical ways to measure the percent body fat of your athletes is to measure the thickness of skinfolds or to use a bioelectrical impedance analyzer. Descriptions of the procedures for both of these tests are beyond the scope of this book, but I'll tell you how these tests work and where to get the information you need to conduct them.

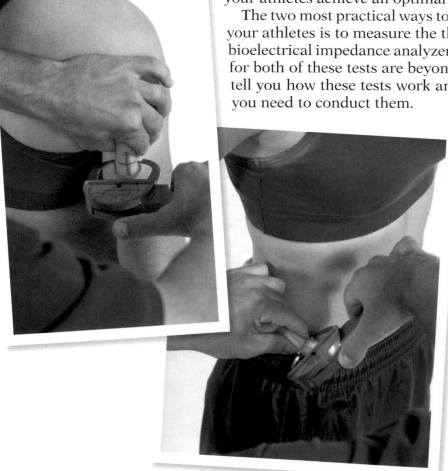

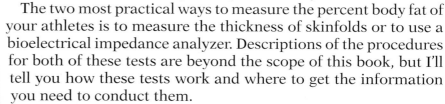

Skinfold Test

The skinfold test uses inexpensive skin calipers to measure the thickness of skin folded or pinched at selected sites on the body. Then a series of calculations are made to estimate the percent of body fat. It's easy to learn to use the calipers, but it takes some practice to get reliable results. If you are interested in doing skinfold testing, I recommend that you purchase the Practical Body Composition Kit (see the To Learn More section at the end of this chapter).

Bioelectrical Impedance Analyzers

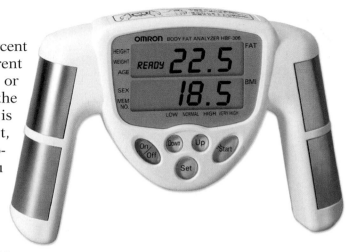

Bioelectrical impedance analyzers measure the percent of body fat by running a low-level electrical current through the body and measuring the resistance or impedance to the current. The more fat there is, the more resistance will be measured. This method is easy, less time consuming than the skinfold test, safe, and inexpensive, but not as accurate. It provides a good general idea of body fat, but if you need more accuracy, use skin calipers (see the To Learn More section about the Omron analyzer).

Once you've obtained an estimate of the percent body fat, record the results on the FAST form and compare them with the recommendations for the percent body fat for athletes in various sports presented in table 14.5.

Table 14.5—Percent Body Fat Recommendations for Athletes						
	Females			Males		
Sport category	Under 11 years	11–15 years	Over 15 years	Under 11 years	11–15 years	Over 15 years
High energy, low weight (wrestling, distance running, gymnastics)	13–15%	12–14%	11–13%	7–9%	6–8%	5–7%
Medium energy, medium weight (team sports, tennis)	15–17%	14–16%	13–15%	9–11%	8–10%	7–9%
Low energy, high weight (football, weightlifting, shot putting, discus throwing)	17–19%	16–18%	15–17%	11–13%	10–12%	9–11%

If your athletes' percent body fat is higher than that recommended, encourage them to lower it through improved nutrition, which you'll learn more about in chapter 16. If your sport does not involve a great deal of physical activity, they may benefit from a good aerobic training program. Why aerobic? Because it burns fat! Athletes also may have too low percent body fat, especially in sports such as gymnastics, swimming, wrestling, and distance running. Proper nutrition can solve this problem unless the athlete has an eating disorder, which makes the issue much more complicated. We'll also discuss eating disorders in chapter 16.

Muscle Fiber Type

The most accurate method to determine muscle fiber type is the muscle biopsy, but your athletes will appreciate you selecting the vertical jump as a simple and far less painful method to get an approximate measure of fast-twitch muscle fiber composition.

Here's how to conduct the vertical jump test to determine fiber type. Follow the steps and record the results on the FAST form.

1. If your budget allows, you can purchase a vertical jump testing apparatus like the one shown on the left.

2. The athlete leaps as high as possible and flips the moveable arm.

3. Alternatively, the athlete reaches (does not jump) as high as possible next to a wall. Mark the spot.

4. The athlete then puts chalk on the fingers, takes two steps, and jumps as high as possible, marking the wall with the chalked fingers.

5. Each athlete gets three tries; use the best jump. Measure to the nearest half inch.

6. The score is the difference between the standing reach and the highest jump.

7. Interpret the scores by using table 14.6.

Table 14.6—Evaluation of the Vertical Jump Test to Determine Muscle Fiber Type			
Age and sex	Low percent of fast-twitch fibers	Medium percent of fast-twitch fibers	High percent of fast-twitch fibers
14 and under males	Under 15 in. (38 cm)	15–20 in. (38–51 cm)	Over 20 in. (51 cm)
14 and under females	Under 8 in. (20 cm)	8–12 in. (20–30 cm)	Over 12 in. (30 cm)
15 and over males	Under 17 in. (43 cm)	17–23 in. (43–58 cm)	Over 23 in. (58 cm)
15 and over females	Under 10 in. (25 cm)	10–15 in. (25–38 cm)	Over 15 in. (38 cm)

This test is a rough approximation of fiber type and is substantially influenced by athletes' percent body fat. Scores on the 1.5-mile run will help corroborate these results. Those who run slower over a long distance are more likely to have a higher percentage of fast-twitch fibers, and those who run faster are more likely to have a higher percentage of slow-twitch fibers. With these test results in hand, you'll be better able to direct your athletes into positions or events with demands that are more in line with their muscle fiber types, and to design training programs that meet the demands of your sport.

Aerobic Fitness

The 1.5-mile run is used most often to measure aerobic fitness for athletes ages 13 and older. Use the mile run for younger athletes.

1. A quarter-mile track is ideal for this test.
2. Have your athletes warm up properly.
3. With up to 25 athletes at a time start the run and use a stopwatch to time them.
4. As they cross the finish line, yell out the time and name of the person and have an assistant record the time on the FAST form.
5. Compare the results with scores from the general population shown in table 14.7.

Table 14.7—Aerobic Fitness Categories for the 1.5-Mile Test				
Fitness category	Males 13–19 yr	Females 13–19 yr	Males 20–29 yr	Females 20–29 yr
High	< 9:40	<12:29	<10:45	<13:30
Average	9:41–12:10	12:30–16:54	10:46–14:00	13:31–18:30
Very Poor	>12:10	>16:55	>14:00	>18:31

Adapted, by permission, from Cooper, 1982.

How much aerobic fitness do your athletes need in your sport? The National Strength and Conditioning Association offers the guidelines shown in figure 14.5.

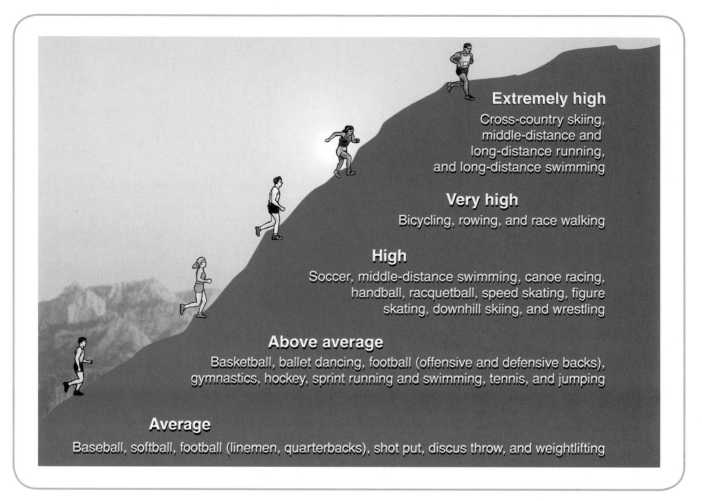

Figure 14.5 Aerobic fitness levels for various sports.

Anaerobic Capacity

Anaerobic capacity is the maximum rate of energy produced by the ATP-PCr and anaerobic glycolysis systems. It can be inferred from a 30-second maximum effort test. You can do the test as a running test, a cycling test, or a swimming test.

Running Test

1. Find a moderately upward sloping road or golf fairway.

2. Mark a line "A" from where the athlete starts and then another line "B" 10 yards (or meters) from that point (figure 14.6).

3. The athlete uses the first 10 yards to get up to maximum speed. Start the stopwatch as the athlete crosses line B.

4. Record the distance traveled at the end of 30 seconds on the FAST form.

5. Oh yes, be sure to let the athlete know when the 30 seconds are up!

Figure 14.6   Running test.

Cycling Test

1. Find a moderately upward sloping road to mark out a course.
2. Mark a line "A" from where the athlete starts and then another line "B" 100 yards (or meters) from that point (figure 14.7).
3. Then, using high gear, the athlete uses the first 100 yards to get up to maximum speed. Start the stopwatch as the athlete crosses line B.
4. Record the distance traveled at the end of 30 seconds on the FAST form.

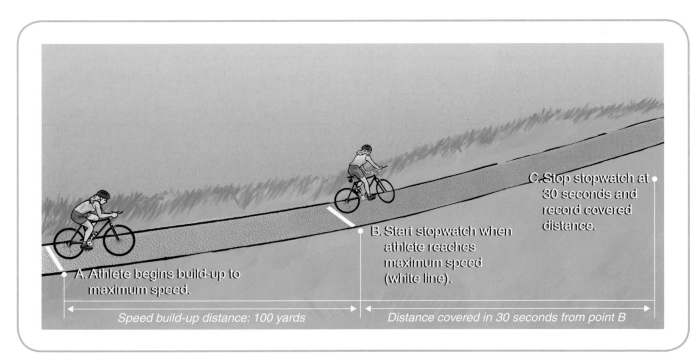

Figure 14.7   Cycling test.

Swimming Test

1. Find an upward sloping pool so the swimmers can swim up a slight grade. (Just checking to see if you're paying attention.)
2. Have the athletes start by pushing off from the end of the pool rather than diving in. There is no "flying" start for this test.
3. Record the distance covered in 30 seconds on the FAST form.

I cannot provide comparative scores because the test conditions are not standardized. You'll need to collect scores among your athletes, comparing them to each other and to the changes they make as you guide them through their anaerobic training program.

The greater the distance covered in 30 seconds, the higher the athlete's lactic acid capacity. This capacity is a major factor in determining success in moderately short, intense events such as the 200- and 400-meter races in track, moderate distances in swimming and cycling, and team sports such as soccer and basketball in which the pace is very high.

Designing an Energy Fitness Training Program

You have now learned the essentials of sport physiology. You've determined the physical demands of your sport, and you know how to assess the aerobic and anaerobic fitness levels of your athletes. Now we're ready to design an energy fitness training program.

Training Pyramid

Remember the overload principle and the progression principle to achieve adaptation from chapter 13? They are the foundation of our training design for energy fitness. Figure 14.8 shows the training pyramid, a four-phase training plan for developing energy fitness that was developed by Brian Sharkey.

All athletes should first develop their aerobic foundation, preferably during the off-season and then move on to lactate threshold training, anaerobic training, and speed training, depending on the demands of their sport. As

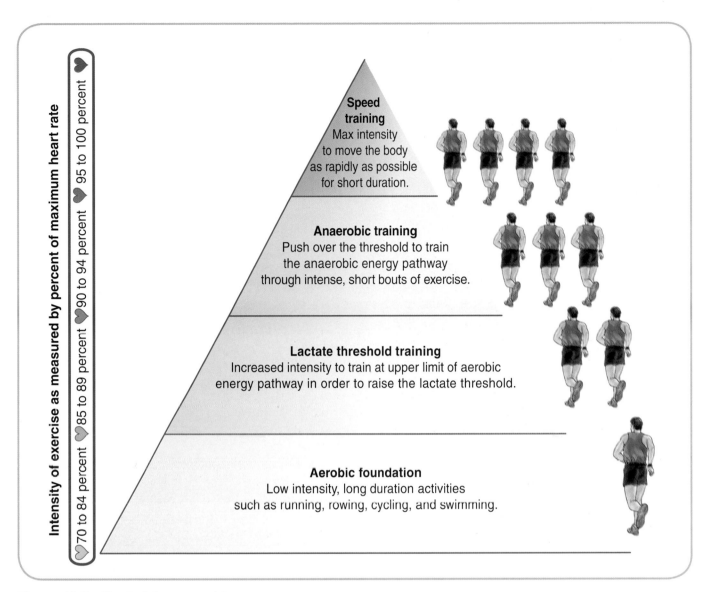

Figure 14.8 The training pyramid.

athletes progress from one level of training to the next, the training becomes more intense but of shorter duration.

The most important factor in designing and monitoring an energy training program is the intensity of exercise. Sport physiologists measure exercise intensity by using complex and expensive instruments to measure the oxygen inspired, carbon dioxide expired, and blood gases. That type of instrumentation is only available to a few, however, and requires specialized training to use. What you need is a practical way to measure exercise intensity, and fortunately we have it in *heart rate (HR)*. Once you know your athletes' resting heart rates and their maximum heart rates, you can guide their training as a percent of their maximum heart rates. Look again at figure 14.8. On the left side it shows the intensity as the percent of maximum HR within which to exercise for the four phases of energy training. See page 308 to learn how to use heart rate as an easy measure of exercise intensity.

Target Heart Rate

Heart rate is controlled by the autonomic nervous system whose command center is in the brain's hypothalamus. Resting heart rate is a good indicator of a person's general fitness level, and a person's HR when exercising is a good indicator of the amount of work being done by the body.

To use HR as a practical tool in your physical training program, you need to determine the target training heart rate (TTHR) for each athlete. Here's how.

STEP 1: Have your athletes take their resting HR before rising in the morning.

During exercise it may be easier to take the pulse at the carotid artery at the neck. Remember, though, that the HR taken in step 1 should be taken at rest, before rising in the morning.

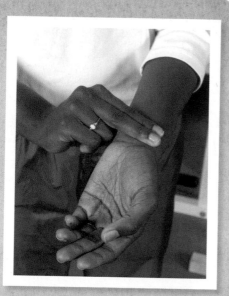

Place two fingers lightly on the thumb side of the wrist in the position shown.

Place two fingers lightly along the throat just to the side of the windpipe. Apply only light pressure; too much pressure at this location may artificially slow the HR. A third and increasingly popular way to measure HR is to use a heart rate monitor, during both rest and exercise. These monitors are widely used today in training for endurance sports (see the Burke book in the To Learn More section).

STEP 2: Estimate the maximum HR of each athlete with the following formula:

Max HR = 220 − age in years

If you're coaching a highly conditioned endurance athlete, you should use the following formula:

Max HR = 210 − age in years

STEP 3: Select the percent of training intensity as measured by percent of maximum HR at which you want the athlete to train. These percents are shown as the "Intensity" range to the left of the four training phases in figure 14.8.

STEP 4: Calculate the training target HR (TTHR) as follows:

220 − _____ = _____ − _____ = _____ × _____ + _____ = _____

(Age in years) (Max HR) (Resting HR) (Exercise HR) (% of training intensity as measured by % of max HR) (Resting HR) (TTHR)

Table 14.8 shows examples of calculated TTHR for athletes of different ages.

Max HR (220 – age) (Step 2)	Minus resting HR (Step 1)	Equals exercise HR	Times % of max HR (Step 3)	Equals max HR – resting HR	Plus resting HR	Equals TTHR
(Age 14) 206	60 60	146 146	70% 84%	102.2 122.6	60 60	162.2 182.6
(Age 16) 204	50 50	154 154	85% 89%	130.9 137.1	50 50	180.9 187.1
(Age 18) 202	46 46	156 156	90% 94%	140.4 146.6	46 46	186.4 192.6
(Age 20) 200	40 40	160 160	95% 99%	152 158.4	40 40	192 198.4

Table 14.8—Estimates of Training Target Heart Rate for Athletes of Different Ages

Seasonal Training Plan for Aerobic Fitness

Today's athletes cannot achieve the fitness levels they need for success by beginning a training program a few weeks before the competitive season. They need to stay in shape all year long with a training plan that brings them to peak condition for the competitive season and the major contests in your sport.

Figure 14.9 shows a general seasonal training plan with the percentage of peak performance that athletes should train at for the four training seasons. Of course the length of each season and the specific type of training will depend on your sport and the fitness level of each athlete. Remember that some athletes who come to you at the beginning of the season may require weeks of skillful conditioning to reach 70 percent of maximum heart rate. Use this general plan to design your specific annual training plan.

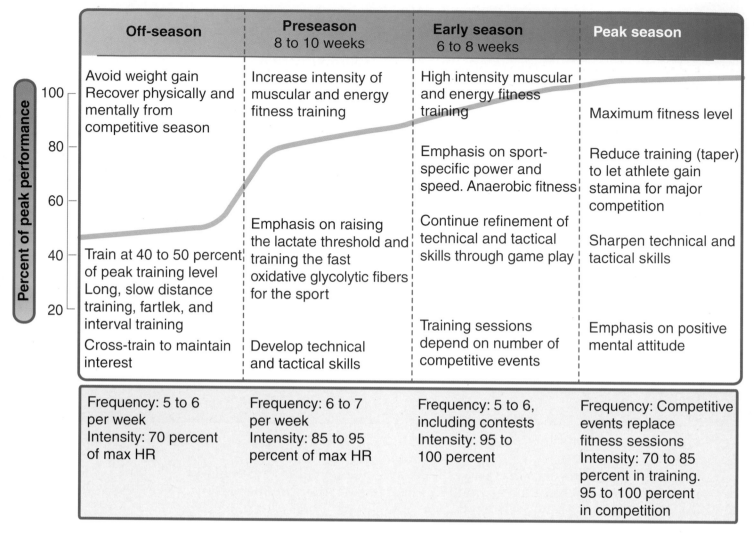

Figure 14.9
Seasonal training plan.

Types of Exercise

Now that you know about the intensity of exercise to develop the energy pathways, and you have a general idea of a seasonal training plan, let's consider the types of exercises you may want to select for your training program. As we do so, I'll also provide you with recommendations on the volume and frequency of exercise and the length of rest. The order of exercise is not much of an issue in energy fitness training; you usually want to do your physical training after doing your technical and tactical skill training because you don't want your athletes fatigued for these technical and tactical skill training sessions.

Sport-Specific Training

The specificity principle tells us that the best training is achieved by playing your sport. To apply the overload principle to improve aerobic fitness, however, you may need to modify how you practice your sport to increase the intensity. For example, in basketball you can increase the intensity by having your athletes play three-on-three, disallowing dribbling, or permitting players to hold the ball for only one second before passing. In wrestling, in which matches last only 5 to 6 minutes, you can increase the intensity by having one wrestler wrestle 12 to 18 minutes, with a fresh opponent rotated in every minute.

One difficulty with training only by playing your sport, especially with team sports, is the inability to control the intensity level so that each athlete is working at the desired percent of maximum heart rate (max HR). Thus alternative forms of training are usually beneficial to obtain optimal energy fitness levels. Let's look at five forms of energy training, each intended to help develop one or more of the four phases of training shown in figure 14.9.

Long, Slow Distance Training

This form of exercise, whether it be running, rowing, cycling, swimming, skiing, skating, or paddling, is appropriate for developing the aerobic foundation. The intensity is between 70 to 85 percent of the max HR, a pace at which athletes can be talking with each other while exercising. The duration of the exercise depends on the amount of continuous movement in your sport as shown in table 14.9.

Table 14.9—Exercise Duration for Developing Aerobic Foundation

Continuous movement in the sport	Exercise duration in miles per week[a]	Exercise duration in hours per week[b]
Under 10 seconds	10–15 miles	1–2 hours
10 seconds–2 minutes	15–20 miles	2–3 hours
2–15 minutes	20–30 miles	3–5 hours
15–30 minutes	30–40 miles	5–7 hours
Over 30 minutes	Over 40 miles	Over 7 hours

[a] Use miles for sports that are played on foot such as basketball, soccer, tennis, and track.
[b] Use hours for sports such as swimming, skiing, cycling, and rowing.

Adapted, by permission, from Sharkey 1986.

Pace/Tempo Training

Pace/tempo training is an increase in the intensity of long, slow distance training, moving from 70 percent of max HR toward 85 percent of max HR, and thus shifting from training the aerobic foundation to training the lactate threshold. Pace/tempo training can be steady, continuous exercise for about 20 to 30 minutes or intermittent training consisting of alternate exercise and recovery periods. An athlete might row steadily for 30 minutes gradually increasing the tempo so that the max HR increases from 70 to 85 percent. Pace/tempo training improves both the aerobic and anaerobic energy pathways and is specifically intended to raise the lactate threshold.

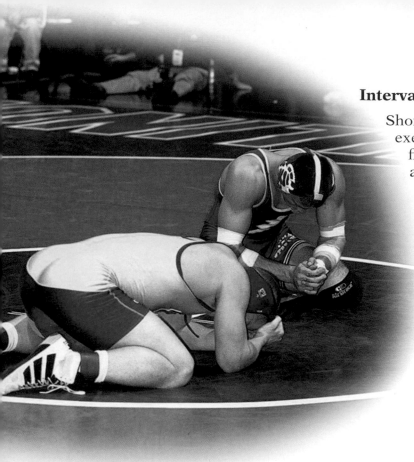

Interval Training

Shorter distances or time and higher intensity exercise describes interval training. Two to five minutes of exercise followed by an equal amount of time to recover at an intensity level of 85 to 89 percent of max HR trains the aerobic energy system and lactate threshold. Thirty to ninety seconds of exercise followed by a recovery period of four times longer than the exercise period working at 90 to 95 percent of the max HR trains the anaerobic energy system.

Fartlek Training

This training method does not refer to energy derived from flatulence; *fartlek* is a Swedish word meaning "speed play." Gosta Holmer is credited with inventing fartlek training, which consists of continuous exercise with intervals of speed followed by slower exercise to recover. Holmer emphasized the playfulness of this form of exercise by having athletes run through the trails in Sweden, enjoying the scenery while alternating bursts of speed and running up hills more slowly as a form of active recovery. Fartlek training is a nice change of pace for training the anaerobic energy pathways and developing speed.

Sprints

Sprints are usually for speed training and thus done at 95 to 100 percent of max HR. Because speed training primarily involves power and neuromuscular development, we'll discuss it further in chapter 15.

Table 14.10 provides a summary of the types of training methods; the energy systems trained; and the recommended intensity, frequency, and duration of training in general. You'll need to adapt these general recommendations to your specific sport and to each of your athletes.

Table 14.10—Training Methods for Energy Fitness					
Training method	Intensity (% max HR)	Frequency	Duration	% develops aerobic energy	% develops anaerobic energy
Long, slow distance	70–80%	1–2 times per week	See table 14.9	95%	5%
Pace/ tempo	85–89%	1–2 times per week	20–30 min	80%	20%
Interval: aerobic	85–89%	1–2 times per week	2–5 min with equal rest intervals	70%	30%
Interval: anaerobic	90–95%	1 time per week	30–90 sec with 4× rest intervals	30%	70%
Fartlek	70–90%	1 time per week	20–60 min	75%	25%
Sprints	95–100%	Depends on sport	10–15 sec with 6× rest intervals	5%	95%

Reprinted, by permission, from Sharkey, 1986.

Overtraining

Overtraining is the result of excessive training and inadequate recovery and causes long-term physical and mental fatigue. It's a serious problem in many sports because many coaches and athletes alike embrace the "more is better" attitude. More isn't better; it's not just the quantity of training that counts, but the quality as well. Your role as physical trainer is to help your athletes achieve optimal fitness for your sport, finding that zone between under- and overtraining.

How do you determine when athletes are overtraining? Some common signs are listed next. Taken individually they are not very indicative of overtraining, but if you see several of these signs, you should suspect overtraining and work with the athlete to find the right balance of training and rest.

- ▶ Sudden or gradual decline in performance
- ▶ Inability to train at levels previously reached
- ▶ Loss of coordination
- ▶ Increased muscle soreness
- ▶ Increased resting heart rate
- ▶ Insomnia
- ▶ Loss of appetite
- ▶ Headaches

- ▶ Decreased body fat
- ▶ Increased susceptibility to illnesses, cold, and flu
- ▶ Depression, apathy
- ▶ Loss of self-esteem
- ▶ Emotional instability
- ▶ Fear of competition

The most effective cure for overtrained athletes is rest.

Questions for Reflection

▶ What is the role of adenosine triphosphate (ATP) in the body? **(p. 291)**

▶ What are the three energy systems of the human body? What is the function of each? **(p. 292)**

▶ What can your athletes do to remove lactic acid from their bodies after exercise? **(p. 293)**

▶ What types of activities use slow-twitch muscle fibers, and which use fast-twitch muscle fibers? What are the two types of fast-twitch fibers? **(p. 295)**

▶ Which energy system (anaerobic or aerobic) is more important in the sport you coach? **(p. 297)**

▶ Do you test your athletes' fitness levels, including body type, body fat, muscle fiber type, aerobic fitness, and anaerobic capacity? **(p. 299)**

▶ Do you know the resting, maximum, and target training heart rates for each of your athletes? This is a good tool for helping you design effective individualized physical training programs. **(p. 308)**

▶ Does your training program include regimens for all four training seasons—the off-season, the preseason, the early season, and the peak season? **(p. 309)**

▶ What are some exercises you can include in your athletes' physical training programs (such as sport-specific; long, slow distance; pace/tempo; interval; fartlek; or sprints)? **(p. 310)**

▶ Do you monitor your athletes for signs of overtraining? **(p. 314)**

References

Moran, Gary T., and George H. McGlynn. 1997. *Cross-training for sports.* Champaign, IL: Human Kinetics.

National Strength and Conditioning Association. 2000. *Essentials of strength training and conditioning.* 2nd ed. Champaign, IL: Human Kinetics.

Sharkey, Brian J. 1986. *Coaches guide to sport physiology.* Champaign, IL: Human Kinetics.

To Learn More

Burke, Ed. 1998. *Precision heart rate training.* Champaign, IL: Human Kinetics.

Human Kinetics. *Practical body composition kit.* The kit includes a guide that explains how to conduct the test, a video to show how to pinch the skin and use the calipers, the calipers and a tape measure, and software to do the calculations.

Omron Hand-held Bio-Analyzer (model HBF-306). At the time of printing, it is priced at $99 (see www.omronhealthcare.com).

Williams, Melvin H., Richard B. Kreider, and J. David Branch. 1999. *Creatine: The power supplement.* Champaign, IL: Human Kinetics.

Fitness Assessment for SporT (FAST) Form

Body Composition

Body Type Assessment

Weight/height index

Weight _____ / height _____ = _____
                                    (score)

Body type evaluation
(Circle rating from table 14.4)

Ecto (lean)
Meso (muscular)
Endo (heavy)

Body Fat Assessment

❑ Skinfold
❑ Bioelectrical impedance

Body fat evaluation
(Circle rating from table 14.5)

Below recommendation
Within recommendation
Above recommendation

Percent body fat _____

Muscle Fiber Type Testing

Vertical jump test

Standing reach _____
                (nearest ½ in)

Fiber type evaluation
(Circle rating from table 14.6)

Low percent of fast-twitch fibers
Medium percent of fast-twitch fibers
High percent of fast-twitch fibers

Jump score _____ _____ _____
           (test 1) (test 2) (test 3)

Highest jump _____ minus reach _____ = _____

Energy Fitness

Aerobic Fitness Testing

1.5-mile run

Run time_____

Aerobic fitness evaluation
(Circle rating from table 14.7)

High
Average
Low

Anaerobic Capacity Testing

30-second max test

Activity _____
(run, swim, bike, row, skate)

Anaerobic evaluation
(no comparison scores)

Low
Average
High

Distance traveled _____

From *Successful Coaching, Third Edition,* by Rainer Martens, 2004, Champaign, IL: Human Kinetics.

Muscular Fitness

Flexibility Testing

Sit-and-reach test (hip and low back)

Test scores _____ _____ _____
             (test 1)   (test 2)   (test 3)

Hip/back evaluation
(Circle rating from table 15.3)
Low
Average
High

Back scratch test (arm and shoulders)

	Right arm over right shoulder	Left arm over left shoulder
Test 1	_____	_____
Test 2	_____	_____
Test 3	_____	_____

Arm/shoulder evaluation
(no comparison scores)
Low
Average
High

(Scoring: If fingers do not touch, the score is minus the inches the fingers are apart. If fingers just touch, the score is 0. If fingers overlap, the score is plus the inches overlapped. Score to nearest half inch or centimeter. Use the best score of the three tests.)

Strength Testing

Exercise	10 rep estimate	Weight lifted	Reps (between 6 and 15)	Estimated 1RM (from table 15.5)	Strength evaluation (from table 15.6)
Chest and shoulder Bench press (fw) Chest press (rm)					Low Avg High Low Avg High
Upper back Bent-over row (fw) Seated row (rm)					Low Avg High Low Avg High
Shoulder Standing press (fw) Seated press (rm)					Low Avg High Low Avg High
Upper arm Biceps curl (fw) Low pulley biceps curl (rm)					Low Avg High Low Avg High
Upper arm Triceps extension (fw) Triceps press-down (rm)					Low Avg High Low Avg High
Upper leg Squat (fw) Leg press (rm)					Low Avg High Low Avg High
Upper leg Leg curl (rm)					Low Avg High
Abdomen Twisting trunk curl (fw) Crunch (rm)					Low Avg High Low Avg High

continued

From *Successful Coaching, Third Edition,* by Rainer Martens, 2004, Champaign, IL: Human Kinetics.

Endurance Testing

Push-up test (arm/shoulders)

      Push-ups completed _____
      (to muscular failure)

Arm/shoulder evaluation
(Circle rating from table 15.7)

Low
Average
High

Curl-up test (arm/shoulders)

      Curl-ups completed _____
      (in 1 minute)

Abdominal evaluation
(Circle rating from table 15.8)

Low
Average
High

Speed testing

50-yard test

      50-yard score _____ _____ _____
            (test 1) (test 2) (test 3)
            (select best time)

Speed evaluation
(Circle rating from table 15.9)

Low
Average
High

Power testing

Vertical jump test (see muscle fiber type test)

      Best test score _____

Power evaluation
(Circle rating from table 14.6)

Low
Medium
High

Stair sprint test

      Time _____ _____ _____
          (test 1) (test 2) (test 3)
         (select fastest time)

Power evaluation
(Circle rating from table 15.10)

Low
Average
High

      Formula _____ $\times$ _____ /_____ = _____
           (body   (distance in ft) (time   (power)
           weight in lb)   in sec)

From *Successful Coaching, Third Edition,* by Rainer Martens, 2004, Champaign, IL: Human Kinetics.

15

Training for Muscular Fitness

Milo of Crotona, the legendary Greek wrestler of the sixth century, was known for his phenomenal strength, which as Greek lore would have it, was acquired by training with a newborn calf. Each day Milo would pick up the calf, place it across his shoulders, and walk around the stadium. As the calf grew, Milo grew in strength, which he claimed helped him win six Olympic titles. Whether or not Milo knew it, he effectively applied the overload and progression principles that you learned about in chapter 13.

Muscles are athletes' tools of the trade, and athletes are more likely to be successful when their muscles are fit.

☞ **In this chapter you'll learn the essentials about muscular fitness, including**

▶ what muscular fitness is,

▶ how muscles work and the effect training has on muscles,

▶ how to determine the muscular demands of your sport and assess muscular fitness, and

▶ how to design a muscular fitness training program.

Muscular Fitness Defined

Muscular fitness is having enough strength, endurance, speed, power, and flexibility to meet the demands of the sport, recognizing that each sport has its own unique requirements.

Muscular strength is the maximum amount of force that a muscle can generate in a single effort. Strength is the foundation of muscular fitness because it's essential for endurance, speed, and power. Strength is increased through resistance training, which involves lifting a load greater than that to which the muscle is accustomed.

Muscular endurance is the ability of a muscle to contract repeatedly or sustain a continuous contraction involving less than maximum force. Sports vary in the muscular endurance they require from short term to long term, as shown in figure 15.1. We now recognize that strength is very beneficial in endurance sports because stronger muscles can produce the same force with less effort.

Speed is about moving from point A to point B quickly; it consists of reaction time and movement time. Reaction time is the time from when the stimulus signals the athlete to move to the beginning of the movement, and movement time is the time from when the movement begins to its completion. Reaction time can be improved by training the neuromuscular system to respond to the stimulus more quickly. Movement time is partly determined by the athlete's inherited fiber type, but it can be improved through strength, speed, and power training.

Power, which is strength and speed combined, is sometimes called speed-strength. It is force produced quickly—a football lineman blocking a defender, a forward leaping high to rebound the basketball, or a swimmer exploding off the blocks to start a race. Increase strength or speed, or both, and you increase power.

Flexibility is the ability to move the joints in the needed range of motion demanded by the sport. Inflexibility limits movement, decreases speed, and increases chances of tearing muscle. Flexibility is improved primarily through stretching.

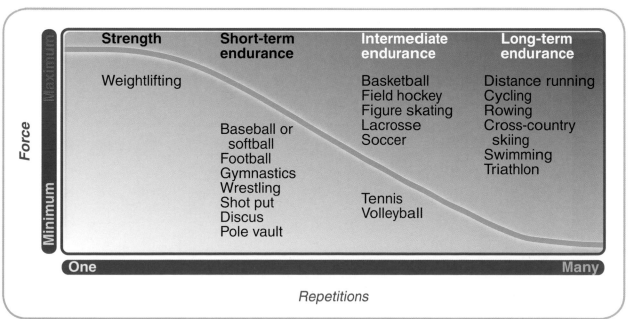

Figure 15.1 Note the relationship between force and repetition. As more force is required, the sport requires fewer repetitions. As the sport involves more repetitions, the force required for each repetition decreases.

How Muscles Work

Let's strengthen your knowledge about the working of muscles before we tackle the design of muscular fitness programs.

Muscle Mechanics

The typical muscle has a bulging body that tapers at each end into a narrow tendon that is attached to a bone, as shown in figure 15.2. Tendons are inelastic and much stronger than muscles, which are elastic. Thus when something has to give, the muscle usually tears before the tendon.

All muscles are "pullers"—they shorten or contract, moving the bone to which they are attached and creating a powerful lever. Muscles usually work in pairs around a joint. When one contracts, the other relaxes. In figure 15.3 you see the biceps muscle attached to the lower arm bone (radius) and the triceps muscle attached to the other lower arm bone (ulna). When the biceps contract and the triceps relax, the arm is pulled upward. When the triceps contract and the biceps relax, the arm is pulled downward. When these muscles contract, they shorten only a small amount, but with the elbow joint as a fulcrum for the lever, the biceps and triceps can move the lower arm a considerable distance with substantial force. A clever engineering job, I'd say!

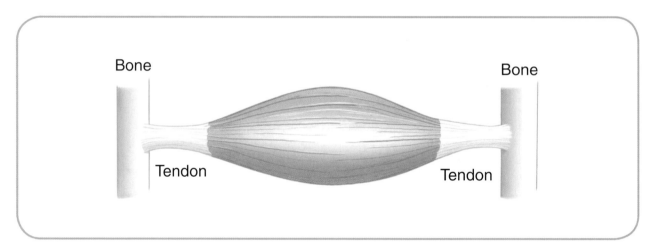

Figure 15.2 Basic muscle anatomy.

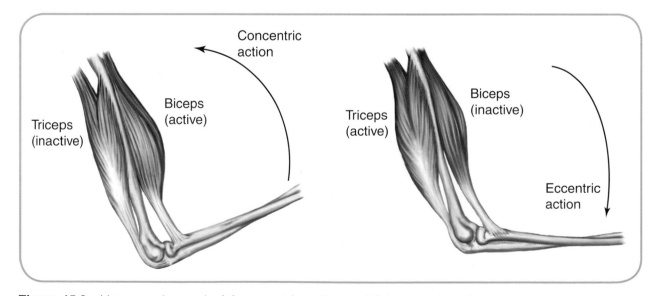

Figure 15.3 How muscles work: *(a)* concentric action and *(b)* eccentric action.

Muscles produce three types of action.

▶ *Concentric action* is when the muscle shortens, as seen in the biceps muscle when a weight is lifted in a biceps curl (see figure 15.3a). This movement is also called flexion because it decreases the angle of the joint.

▶ *Eccentric action* is when the muscle lengthens, as seen in the biceps muscle when a weight is lowered in a biceps curl (see figure 15.3b). This movement is also called extension because it increases the angle of the joint.

▶ *Isometric or static action* is when tension develops in the muscle but no movement occurs. Push your two hands together in front of your chest, counteracting the force of each, and you have an example of an isometric contraction.

Muscle Physiology

A basic understanding of muscle physiology is useful. Each muscle contains thousands of stringy muscle fibers grouped into bundles, as shown in figure 15.4. Within these fibers, contractile proteins called actin and myosin create movement.

To understand how actin and myosin work, place your hands palm down on a table with your fingertips touching each other. Now slide your fingers between each other. The fingers of one hand are actin and the fingers of the other are myosin. Now imagine thousands of tiny flexible bands or cross-bridges connecting your actin fingers to your myosin fingers. These connectors reach out and pull like oars. This microscopic movement is powered by ATP (discussed in

chapter 14), and when thousands of these tiny bands move, visible motion occurs.

Muscles are told to contract by the nervous system. As nerves come out of the spinal cord, they branch out to the muscles, with each major muscle having hundreds to more than a thousand slender nerves activating a group of muscle fibers. The nerve and the fibers it controls are called a motor unit; when the nerve is told to contract, all the fibers it controls contract. Some nerves control a small number of fibers, others a large number, with the average being about 150 fibers per nerve.

How do athletes produce strong contractions to generate a lot of force (such as when powering down the ice in hockey), and how do they produce weak contractions to produce fine, delicate movements (such as in the shooting sports)? Athletes learn—we all learn—to recruit motor units with many fibers for powerful movements and those with few fibers for delicate movements. As they develop technical skill, athletes learn how many motor units they need to make a driving layup or shoot a shot from outside the 3-point line in basketball.

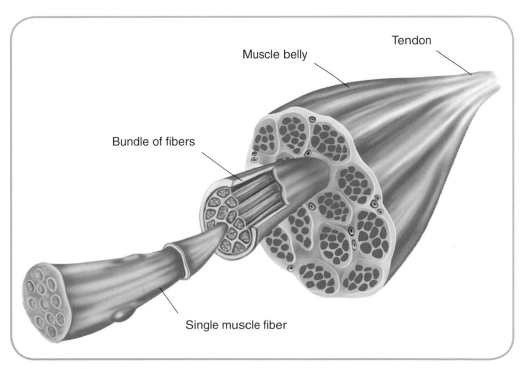

Figure 15.4 Muscle fibers.

Muscle Soreness

All athletes know about muscle soreness. When first overloading muscles (whether from resistance training or aerobic exercise), athletes experience muscle soreness. In resistance training, scientists have discovered that muscle soreness does not occur from concentric movement (lifting the resistance) but only from eccentric movement (lowering the resistance). They don't know why, however.

When muscles are slightly strained, the soreness is thought to be a result of microtears in the muscle fibers. When severely strained, many muscle fibers are torn and the muscle is likely to bleed. With slight or severe strains, muscles quickly respond by releasing fluid to produce swelling or inflammation to immobilize the damaged tissue. The inflammation causes pain and in some cases muscle spasm. After the initial inflammation, the body begins to repair itself by releasing collagen in the area to form scar tissue. As scar tissue ages, it contracts and reduces flexibility.

When athletes train too hard and experience a lot of muscle soreness, they damage their muscles. Your goal is to design training programs that follow the progression principle to minimize muscle soreness and maximize muscular fitness.

Training for Muscular Fitness

Now let's focus on the two most important methods for developing muscular fitness:

▶ Stretching for flexibility training
▶ Resistance training for strength, muscular endurance, speed, and power

Following the introduction here, similar to the steps in chapter 14, we'll consider

▶ the muscular demands of your sport,
▶ tests to assess your athletes' muscular fitness, and
▶ the principles for designing a muscular fitness training program.

Flexibility Training

Physical training and sport performances can be very hard on athletes' muscles, often decreasing flexibility. Proper care of them is vital to long-term success. Athletes should work at improving or maintaining their flexibility every day of the year because flexibility increases range of motion and improves performance.

Muscles appreciate being warmed up with light activity before they are exercised hard. Warming up by increasing blood flow to the muscles improves flexibility by 20 percent, and proper stretching will increase the flexibility further. Muscles also like to be cooled down after a hard workout with slow stretching so they can return to their relaxed, elongated state.

Decreased flexibility from hard training and playing and a lack of proper flexibility training are leading causes of muscle injuries. The less flexibility an athlete has, the more likely that athlete will develop a muscle strain. A lack of flexibility in the back and hamstring muscles, along with weak abdominal muscles, is a common cause of back pain that humbles the toughest of athletes.

Resistance Training

Resistance training is the primary means for developing muscular fitness, so it is essential that you understand the basics, which we'll cover here. I use the term *resistance training* rather than *strength training* because resistance training can be done to develop not only strength, but also endurance, power, and speed.

For many years the sport world believed that resistance training made athletes muscle-bound, inflexible, and slow. Just the opposite is true. Strength, endurance, power, and speed can all be improved through resistance training without decreasing flexibility when the overload and progression principles are effectively applied. Resistance training builds strength in two ways.

► It increases the size of the muscle fibers, especially the fast-twitch ones.
► It trains the nervous and muscular systems to recruit more muscle fibers at just the right time to produce greater force.

The latter reason accounts for initial improvements, and the former for later improvements.

Resistance training improves muscular endurance by increasing the ability of muscles to work anaerobically and by reducing the number of muscle fibers used in early periods of exercise, holding some back in reserve for later work. Short-term endurance training adds strength and power, whereas long-term endurance training improves the aerobic energy pathways.

Methods of Resistance Training

There are many ways to do resistance training, as shown on page 326. We'll focus on free weights and fixed resistance machines because they are commonly used, widely available, and effective.

Resistance Exercise Systems

Free weights.

Fixed resistance machine.

Variable resistance machine.

Partner-resisted training.

Elastic resistance training.

Variable resistance machines are designed to create a consistent stress on muscles throughout the range of movement. That's not the case with free weights and fixed resistance machines. For advanced training, variable resistance machines may be superior, but for a basic resistance training program free weights and fixed resistance machines work well. If your team doesn't have access to free weights or machines, partner and elastic resistance training methods are a good alternative (see the To Learn More section at the end of the chapter for references on using these methods).

Know Your Muscles

Suppose you read an article recommending that soccer players strengthen their biceps femoris. Which exercises do that? You might be tempted to answer, the biceps curl.

Oops! Wrong answer. The biceps femoris is not the biceps in the front of the upper arm. It's part of the hamstrings in back of the upper leg. To design effective resistance training programs, you should know the names and locations of the major muscles in the body. I've narrowed the list from the 640 muscles in your body to the 25 major ones. Go back to chapter 13, figure 13.2, to learn these muscles and their location.

Know the Lingo

You probably know the language associated with resistance training, but let's quickly review it just in case.

▶ *Resistance* is the weight or "load" a muscle works against.

▶ *Repetition* (reps) is one complete movement of an exercise, usually involving a concentric action (in which the muscle shortens) of lifting the weight and an eccentric action (in which the muscle lengthens) of lowering the weight.

▶ A *set* is a number of repetitions done continuously without stopping followed by a rest.

You may say to an athlete that you want him to do three sets of eight reps of a leg press with a resistance of 200 pounds (91 kilograms).

Muscular Demands of Your Sport

How important are flexibility, strength, endurance, speed, and power in your sport? For some sports, the answer is obvious. In competitive weightlifting, you can't have too much strength or power. In marathon racing, you can't have too much aerobic and muscular endurance.

Complete table 15.1 to assess the muscular fitness requirements for your sport. Consider each position on your team, the different events of your sport, or the different types of functions. For example, if you're a baseball coach, you may want to list positions such as catchers, pitchers, infielders, and outfielders, and then also list fielding, throwing, hitting, and baserunning. If you're a track or swimming coach, you would list each event in your sport. As you complete the form, ask yourself, How important is this muscular component in my sport? Circle the appropriate letter, with "L" indicating low, "M" moderate, and "H" high.

Table 15.1—Estimating the Muscular Demands of Your Sport

Position, event, or function	Flexibility	Strength	Endurance	Speed	Power
	L M H	L M H	L M H	L M H	L M H
	L M H	L M H	L M H	L M H	L M H
	L M H	L M H	L M H	L M H	L M H
	L M H	L M H	L M H	L M H	L M H
	L M H	L M H	L M H	L M H	L M H
	L M H	L M H	L M H	L M H	L M H
	L M H	L M H	L M H	L M H	L M H
	L M H	L M H	L M H	L M H	L M H
	L M H	L M H	L M H	L M H	L M H
	L M H	L M H	L M H	L M H	L M H

L = low demand; M = moderate demand; H = high demand.

This evaluation gives you a good starting point, but just how much strength do your athletes need? For endurance sports, strength should be at least 2.5 times the resistance encountered. In rowing, let's say the resistance is 40 pounds (18 kilograms) as the rower pulls on the oar. The muscles used in rowing should be able to produce a maximum force of 100 pounds (45 kilograms).

For power sports strength should be five times the force required to perform the action. Let's say it takes 20 pounds (9 kilograms) of force for the muscles (mostly the triceps) to pull a bat through the swing. Those muscles should have 100 pounds (45 kilograms) of strength.

The challenge for you is to find a way to estimate the force generated in the movements in your sport. That's often not easy. One way to do so is by using a weight machine or pulleys to simulate the movement to determine the force needed to make the movement. When it's not possible or practical to use weights, make the movement yourself and have several of your athletes also do so without weights and arrive at your best estimate.

Testing Muscular Fitness

In this section you'll learn how to test your athletes' flexibility, strength, endurance, speed, and power. The tests we'll use are summarized in table 15.2. Review the guidelines for testing in chapter 13, page 279, before you begin testing. You can record your test results on the FAST form on pages 316 to 318.

If you have a very large group of athletes or a limited amount of time, you may need to select only the most pertinent tests. In such cases, you may want to use one test each for flexibility, muscular endurance, speed, and power and the two most pertinent strength tests for your sport or certain sport positions.

Flexibility Testing

I recommend two flexibility tests, one for hip and low back flexibility, called the sit-and-reach test, and the other for the arms and shoulders, called the back scratch test.

Table 15.2—Muscular Fitness Tests

Muscular fitness component	Test name
Flexibility	Sit-and-reach test Back scratch test
Strength	Essential eight resistance test
Muscular endurance	Push-up test Curl-up test
Speed	50-yard test
Power	Vertical jump test Stair sprint test

Sit-and-Reach Test

1. You'll need a yardstick or meter stick. Tape the yardstick to the floor by placing a piece of tape about 2 feet (61 centimeters) long across the yardstick at the 15-inch (38-centimeter) mark as shown.

2. Have each athlete complete a regular warm-up as described in chapter 13.

3. With shoes off, position the athlete to sit so that the yardstick is between the legs with the zero end toward the body. The heels should be on the tape exactly at the 15-inch line. The feet should be 12 inches (30 centimeters) apart, and pointed up as shown.

4. Instruct the athlete to reach forward, sliding both hands as far forward as possible on the yardstick. Tell the athlete to exhale and lower the head between the arms to get the best stretch. To prevent injury, advise the athlete not to "bounce" forward. The stretch should be slow and gradual.

5. Make sure the athlete does not bend the knees; you may need to place a hand on the knees to keep them straight. Do not permit one hand to lead. The hands should be parallel and touching each other through the stretch.

6. Give each athlete three tries, and use the best score. Score to the nearest quarter inch or half centimeter and record the results on the FAST form found at the very end of chapter 14. A score of less than 15 inches (38 centimeters) means that the athlete could not reach the bottom of the feet (see table 15.3 for comparative scores).

Table 15.3—Evaluation of the Sit-and-Reach Test Scores

Sex	LOW		AVERAGE		HIGH	
	in.	cm	in.	cm	in.	cm
Females	< 18	< 44	18–20	44–50	21+	51+
Males	< 15	< 38	15–18	38–47	19+	48+

Back Scratch Test

1. Have the athlete stand and place the left arm behind the back and the right hand over the right shoulder as shown.
2. The left hand is palm out, with the fingertips reaching up the spine as far as possible.
3. The right hand is palm in, with the fingertips reaching down the spine as far as possible.
4. Align the middle fingers if possible. If not possible, measure the distance between the middle fingers, even though they are not aligned.
5. If the fingers do not touch or overlap, measure the distance to the nearest half inch (or centimeter) and record the score as a minus number. If the fingers overlap, measure the distance the middle fingers overlap and record as a positive number. If the middle fingers just touch, the score is 0.
6. Give the athlete three tries, recording the results on the FAST form, and selecting the best score.
7. Now repeat the test with the left arm coming over the left shoulder with the right arm behind the back. Record the results, selecting the best of the three tries.

Unfortunately, norms for young athletes are not available for this test. As you test your athletes, you'll soon get a reasonable idea of what good flexibility is for this test.

Testing by Doing

Another approach to evaluating the flexibility of your athletes is to have them do the 14 all-star stretches shown on pages 340 to 343. If your athletes can do all of the exercises to the full range of motion shown, they have sufficient flexibility and should continue these stretching exercises as part of their warm-up and cool-down routines to maintain their flexibility. If any athletes are unable to complete the stretching exercises to the full range of motion, then additional stretching is called for.

Strength Testing

Now let's look at the four major steps for conducting strength tests.

STEP 1: Select Resistance Exercises

First you need to select the muscles you want to strengthen and the exercises you want to use to test the strength of these muscles. After consulting with resistance training experts, I've selected the essential eight resistance exercises (table 15.4). These exercises involve the major muscle groups of the body that are essential to success in most sports.

Table 15.4—Essential Eight Resistance Exercises		
Exercise name*	**Body part**	**Muscles used**
Bench press (fw) Chest press (rm)	Chest and shoulder	Pectorals and anterior deltoid
Bent-over row (fw) Seated row (rm)	Upper back and back of shoulders	Rhomboid, trapezius, latissimus dorsi, teres major deltoid, infraspinatus, teres minor
Standing press (fw) Seated press (rm)	Shoulder	Deltoids and triceps
Biceps curl (fw) Low pulley biceps curl (rm)	Upper arm	Biceps
Triceps extension (fw) Triceps press-down (rm)	Upper arm	Triceps
Squat (fw) Leg press (rm)	Upper leg	Quadriceps and gluteus muscles
Leg curl (rm)	Upper leg	Hamstrings
Twisting trunk curl (fw) Crunch (rm)	Abdomen	Rectus abdominis, external and internal obliques, quadriceps

*fw = free weights; rm = resistance machine.

You can test using free weights if you're experienced in spotting (positioning to catch the weights if the athlete loses control), but I recommend the safer fixed resistance machines. If you're unfamiliar with these exercises and if your physical condition permits, practice these exercises—safely please—so you know how to do them and can better teach them. You can see how to do these exercises with free weights and fixed resistance machines on pages 345 to 349.

STEP 2: Determine How Much Weight Athletes Can Lift 6 to 15 Times

We test strength by finding out the maximum weight a muscle or group of muscles can move one time. This is called the one repetition maximum or 1RM. The classic 1RM test, however, can be dangerous to athletes who have not been weight training regularly. Therefore I recommend a safer, indirect method of determining 1RM.

Start your resistance training with three practice sessions over a week's time in which you teach athletes the proper technique and safety and they practice the various exercises using resistance they can readily move. In this way

they experience initial success and avoid excessive muscle soreness.

After a week of training, use an indirect method of determining 1RM by having your athletes do between 6 and 15 reps to muscle failure (inability to complete a repetition). Then from table 15.5 on page 333 you can estimate the 1RM. But how do you estimate the resistance for muscle failure between 6 and 15 reps? During those first three practice sessions, work with each of your athletes to estimate the resistance they can move 10 times for each exercise by considering the following factors. Record the estimate on the FAST form.

▶ The heavier athletes are, the more strength they are likely to have.

▶ The greater muscle definition or hypertrophy athletes have, the more strength they are likely to have.

▶ Determine whether athletes have had previous weight training experience and have some idea of their strength.

▶ Review the norms (the average strength of athletes as a percent of their body weight) shown in table 15.6 on page 334 for the essential eight exercises and judge whether athletes are likely to be below or above the norm.

Based on your best estimate have your athletes try each exercise at the weight you have determined for that exercise. If they realize in the first or second rep that they've selected far too much resistance to complete 6 reps, have them stop immediately and adjust the weight. Do the same if they recognize immediately that they've selected too light a weight and will be able to exceed 15 reps. At the end of the three practice sessions each athlete should know a resistance he or she can move about 10 times for each exercise.

STEP 3: Test Your Athletes on Each of the Essential Eight Exercises

If the athlete completes between 6 and 15 reps, then proceed to step 4. If an athlete fails to reach 6 reps, decrease the load to an amount you think the athlete can lift 10 times. If an athlete exceeds 15 reps, increase the load based on the number of reps completed to an amount you think the athlete can lift 10 times. A guideline is to add 5 pounds (2.3 kilograms) for each additional 2 reps completed over 15. Allow at least 15 minutes between tests of the same muscle group. Use the FAST form to record results.

STEP 4: Determine the 1RM

Once you know the load the athletes can move between 6 and 15 reps for each exercise, then go to table 15.5 to look up the estimated 1RM. Using table 15.5, you can get the athlete's estimated 1RM by finding the weight the athlete lifted in the far left column of the table. Then locate the number of repetitions the athlete lifted in the row above the table. Find the corresponding number where the row and column of weight and repetitions meet. This is the athlete's estimated 1RM. For example, your athlete completes 10 repetitions of the chest press with a load of 100 pounds (45.4 kilograms). The table indicates that 133 pounds (60.3 kilograms) is the best estimate of 1RM. If the athlete completes 7, 9, 11, 13, or 14 reps, simply extrapolate the number between the two columns on either side of that number of reps. Record the results for each test on the FAST form.

You've accomplished two things by conducting these strength tests. First, you now know the 1RM, which is needed to design a resistance training program for your athletes. Second, you can compare your athletes' strength with each other and with the benchmarks shown in table 15.6. For each of the eight exercises a panel of experts has provided an estimate of low, average, and high strength levels based on the percent of an athlete's body weight. For the bench press, if a female athlete weighs 150 pounds (68 kilograms), a low strength score would be 60 pounds (27 kilograms) (150 × .40 = 60 pounds), an average strength score would be 82.5 pounds (37 kilograms), and a high score would be 120 pounds (54 kilograms).

Table 15.5—Estimating 1RM From the Essential Eight Test

Weight lifted in pounds (kg)	Maximum repetitions (% 1RM)				
	6 (85%)	8 (80%)	10 (75%)	12 (67%)	15 (65%)
10 (4.5)	12 (5.2)	13 (5.9)	13 (5.9)	15 (6.8)	15 (6.8)
15 (6.8)	18 (8.2)	19 (8.6)	20 (9.1)	22 (10)	23 (10.4)
20 (9.1)	24 (10.9)	25 (11.3)	27 (12.3)	30 (13.6)	31 (14.1)
25 (11.3)	29 (13.2)	31 (14.1)	33 (15)	37 (16.8)	38 (17.2)
30 (13.6)	35 (15.9)	38 (17.2)	40 (18.1)	45 (20.4)	46 (20.9)
35 (15.9)	41 (18.6)	44 (20)	47 (21.3)	52 (23.6)	54 (24.5)
40 (18.1)	47 (21.3)	50 (22.7)	53 (24)	60 (27.2)	62 (28.1)
45 (20.4)	53 (24)	56 (25.4)	60 (27.2)	67 (30.4)	69 (31.3)
50 (22.7)	59 (26.8)	63 (28.6)	67 (30.4)	75 (34)	77 (34.9)
55 (25)	65 (29.5)	69 (31.3)	73 (33.1)	82 (37.2)	85 (38.6)
60 (27.2)	71 (32.2)	75 (34)	80 (36.3)	90 (40.8)	92 (41.7)
65 (29.5)	76 (34.5)	81 (36.7)	87 (39.5)	97 (44)	100 (45.4)
70 (31.8)	82 (37.2)	88 (39.9)	93 (42.2)	104 (47.2)	108 (49)
75 (34)	88 (39.9)	94 (42.6)	100 (45.4)	112 (50.8)	115 (52.2)
80 (36.3)	94 (42.6)	100 (45.4)	107 (48.5)	119 (54)	123 (55.8)
85 (38.6)	100 (45.4)	106 (48.1)	113 (51.3)	127 (57.6)	131 (59.4)
90 (40.8)	106 (48.1)	113 (51.3)	120 (54.4)	134 (60.8)	138 (62.6)
95 (43.1)	112 (50.8)	119 (54)	127 (57.6)	142 (64.4)	146 (66.2)
100 (45.4)	118 (53.5)	125 (56.7)	133 (60.3)	149 (67.6)	154 (69.9)
110 (49.9)	129 (58.5)	138 (62.6)	147 (66.7)	164 (74.4)	169 (76.7)
120 (54.4)	141 (64)	150 (68)	160 (72.6)	179 (81.2)	185 (83.9)
130 (59)	153 (69.4)	163 (73.9)	173 (78.5)	194 (88)	200 (90.7)
140 (63.5)	165 (74.8)	175 (79.4)	187 (84.8)	209 (94.8)	215 (97.5)
150 (68)	176 (79.8)	188 (85.3)	200 (90.7)	224 (101.6)	231 (104.8)
160 (72.6)	188 (85.3)	200 (90.7)	213 (96.6)	239 (108.4)	246 (111.6)
170 (77.1)	200 (90.7)	213 (96.6)	227 (103)	254 (115.2)	262 (118.8)
180 (81.6)	212 (96.2)	225 (102.1)	240 (108.9)	269 (122)	277 (125.6)
190 (86.2)	224 (101.6)	238 (108)	253 (114.8)	284 (128.8)	292 (132.4)
200 (90.7)	235 (106.6)	250 (113.4)	267 (121.1)	299 (135.6)	308 (139.7)
220 (99.8)	259 (117.5)	275 (124.7)	293 (132.9)	328 (148.8)	338 (153.3)
240 (108.9)	282 (127.9)	300 (136.1)	320 (145.1)	358 (162.4)	369 (167.4)
260 (117.9)	306 (138.8)	325 (147.4)	347 (157.4)	388 (176)	400 (181.4)
280 (127)	329 (149.2)	350 (158.8)	373 (169.2)	418 (189.6)	431 (195.5)
300 (136.1)	353 (160.1)	375 (170.1)	400 (181.4)	448 (203.2)	462 (209.6)

You can get the athlete's estimated 1RM by finding the weight the athlete lifted in the far left column of the table. Then locate the number of repetitions the athlete lifted in the row above the table. Find the corresponding number where the row and column of weight and repetitions meet. This is the athlete's estimated 1RM.

Adapted, by permission, from Baechle and Earle, 2000.

Table 15.6—Average Strength of Athletes As a Percentage of Their Body Weight for the Essential Eight Strength Test Scores

Exercise	LOW		AVERAGE		HIGH	
	Female	Male	Female	Male	Female	Male
Bench press (fw) Chest press (rm)	40% 50%	65% 90%	55% 70%	90% 115%	80% 90%	120% 150%
Bent-over row (fw) Seated row (rm)	20% 25%	30% 35%	30% 35%	40% 50%	40% 45%	50% 60%
Standing press (fw) Seated press (rm)	15% 20%	25% 35%	25% 35%	35% 50%	35% 45%	50% 60%
Biceps curl (fw) Low pulley biceps curl (rm)	10% 15%	20% 25%	20% 25%	25% 30%	25% 30%	33% 40%
Triceps extension (fw) Triceps press-down (rm)	10% 15%	10% 15%	15% 20%	20% 25%	20% 25%	30% 35%
Squat (fw) Leg press (rm)	40% 60%	60% 100%	65% 80%	90% 125%	80% 110%	125% 150%
Leg curl (rm)	15%	20%	20%	25%	25%	30%
Twisting trunk curl Crunch (rm)	10 reps 10 reps	15 reps 15 reps	20 reps 15 reps	30 reps 20 reps	25 reps 20 reps	40 reps 25 reps

Muscular Endurance Testing

You can test muscular endurance by determining the number of reps athletes can do at something less than maximum. Push-ups are commonly used for upper body endurance testing, and partial curl-ups or crunches are used for abdominal muscles. Here's how to do these tests.

Push-Up Test

Traditionally males have done "regular" push-ups (described next) and females have done modified push-ups, but many females are capable of doing standard push-ups, and some males may need to do modified push-ups. You'll need to decide which form of push-ups is right for each of your athletes.

1. For regular push-ups the athlete places the hands on the floor just slightly outside the shoulders, then pushes onto the toes, keeping the body in a straight line with the head forward.

2. A repetition is completed by starting in the "up" position, bending the arms to touch the chin to the floor without the abdomen touching the floor, and returning to the up position.

3. The athlete does as many correct repetitions as possible until muscular failure. Record the results on the FAST form.

4. Modified push-ups are done the same way, but the knees provide the base of support rather than the toes.

In table 15.7, we have norms for comparing scores for males doing regular push-ups and females doing modified push-ups. Norms for females doing regular push-ups or males doing modified push-ups don't exist. If you

Table 15.7—Evaluation of Push-Up Test Scores (Ages 15–19)			
Sex	**Low**	**Average**	**High**
Females (modified push-ups)	< 15	16–26	27+
Males (regular push-ups)	< 20	21–34	35+

decide to use standard push-ups for females, and if some of your male athletes need to use modified push-ups, you can create your own unofficial norms by recording results over several seasons. Alternatively you can compare the results of your female athletes with the norms of the males in table 15.7, but keep in mind the cross-sex comparison.

Curl-Up Test

The curl-up test has replaced the sit-up test, which can place stress on the neck and back, for measuring abdominal endurance. The curl-up test consists of doing as many curl-ups in one minute as possible. Here's how to do this test.

1. Place a piece of tape across the mat as shown. Then place a second piece of tape parallel with the first so that the front edge of the second piece is 3.5 inches (9 centimeters) from the front edge of the first piece.

2. The athlete lies on the mat face up with the knees bent to 90 degrees. Position the athlete so that when the arms are at the side and fully extended with the palms down, the middle finger touches comfortably the front edge of the first piece of tape as shown.

3. A correct repetition is to curl the body up toward the knees, sliding the fingers from the first piece of tape to the front edge of the second piece of tape, and then returning the body so the shoulders touch the mat. The head does not need to touch the mat, however.

4. With the athlete's back on the mat, give the "Go" command and start the stopwatch. The score is the number of correct curl-ups done in one minute. Record the results on the FAST form.

See table 15.8 for comparative scores of the general population ages 18 to 25.

Table 15.8—Evaluation of Curl-Up Test Scores (Ages 18–25)			
Sex	**Low**	**Average**	**High**
Females	< 35	36–55	56+
Males	< 40	41–59	60+

As an alternative to these two general tests, you can design tests that are more specific to the muscular endurance demands of your sport. Here's how:

1. Review figure 15.1, which shows the relationship between force and repetitions. Analyze your sport to determine if short-, intermediate-, or long-term muscular endurance is needed.
2. Next decide what muscle groups are involved and select one or more of the eight resistance exercises in table 15.4 as a test.
3. If the task is a short-term endurance activity, estimate 80 percent of the athlete's 1RM to see how many repetitions can be done. If the activity is of intermediate endurance, then estimate 60 percent of the 1RM, and if it is of long-term endurance, estimate 40 percent of the 1RM to test the athlete's endurance.

Speed Testing

Speed is often tested over distances of 40 and 50 yards (or meters). We'll use the 50-yard test because we have norms with which you can compare results. Here's how to do the test:

1. Mark off a 50-yard course with sufficient space to slow down after crossing the finish line. Make sure the surface is clean and not slippery. A track of course is ideal.
2. Pair up athletes you believe have about the same speed and test them at the same time. Have two assistants keep time, one for each athlete.
3. Have athletes complete a proper warm-up.
4. Start the race with your arm above your head and give the commands, "Are you ready?" followed by a two-second pause, and "Go." Simultaneously bring your arm down to signal the timers standing at the finish line.
5. Give each athlete three tries with five-minute rests between trials.
6. The score is recorded in seconds, to the nearest 10th, counting the best time of the three.

You can compare the results of your athletes with the norms in table 15.9, which are based on the AAHPERD Youth Fitness Test for the general population. Athletes are likely to be in the "high" category.

	LOW		AVERAGE		HIGH	
Age	**Female**	**Male**	**Female**	**Male**	**Female**	**Male**
12	8.7	8.3	8.1	7.8	7.3	7.1
13	8.5	8.0	8.0	7.5	7.1	6.7
14	8.3	7.7	7.8	7.2	7.0	6.5
15	8.2	7.3	7.8	6.9	7.1	6.2
16	8.3	7.0	7.9	6.7	7.2	6.2
17+	8.4	7.0	7.9	6.6	7.1	6.1

Table 15.9—Evaluation of 50-Yard Sprint Test Scores

Power Testing

The two most widely used tests of muscular power are the vertical jump test and the stair sprint test.

Vertical Jump Test

The vertical jump test is the most widely used power test, and you'll remember that I described it in chapter 14, page 302, for determining muscle fiber type. Review table 14.6 to interpret scores, but now interpret the scores as measures of low, medium, and high power.

Stair Sprint Test

This test requires athletes to run up stairs as fast as possible—but caution is required. Warn your athletes of the risk of injury should they trip and fall on a stair, and allow them to practice the test slowly in previous practice sessions to get the "feel" of the stairs. You'll need a stopwatch that keeps time to 100ths of a second. Here's how to conduct the test.

1. Find a staircase with at least 10 steps, with a 7- or 8-inch (18- or 20-centimeter) rise per step, and at least a 10-foot (3-meter) approach and enough space to stop after the 10th step.

2. Mark step 2 and step 10 visually so you can time the athlete (figure 15.5).

3. The athlete starts 10 feet (3 meters) from the first stair and runs as fast as possible, stepping on the second stair and every other stair through the 10th stair. You begin the time when the athlete's foot hits stair 2 and stop it when it hits stair 10.

4. After a warm-up and demonstration, give the athlete two practice trials at moderate speed. Then give each athlete three tries, counting the fastest time. Record the results on the FAST form.

Figure 15.5   Setup for stair sprint test.

5. To obtain a score, first determine the vertical rise of the stairs from step 2 to step 10. For example, if the stairs have a 7-inch rise, you multiply 7 inches by 8 stairs to obtain 56 inches or 4.67 feet. Then calculate the following formula:

$$\text{Power} = \frac{\text{Body weight (lb)} \times \text{distance (ft)}}{\text{Time (sec)}}$$

For example, a football lineman weighs 210 pounds and runs 7-inch stairs in 1.1 seconds.

$$\text{Power} = \frac{210 \times 4.67}{1.1} = 892$$

You can evaluate your athletes' power by comparing their scores with those in table 15.10.

Table 15.10—Evaluation of Stair Sprint Test Scores

Age and sex	Low	Average	High
Males 14 and under	Under 600	600–800	Over 800
Females 14 and under	Under 400	400–600	Over 600
Males 15 and older	Under 700	700–900	Over 900
Females 15 and older	Under 500	500–750	Over 750

Adapted, by permission, from Sharkey, 1986.

Designing a Muscular Fitness Program

Much like a chef, you now have the ingredients for designing an effective muscular fitness program for your athletes. All you need is the recipe describing how to prepare those ingredients. First, we'll prepare a gourmet appetizer in the form of flexibility training, followed by the main course—resistance training for strength, endurance, and power—and closing with a mouthwatering dessert of speed.

Flexibility Training

Stretching is your primary ingredient for developing flexibility, and although it comes in many forms, we'll stick with the basics here. If your athletes follow these 10 commandments for stretching, they will maintain or improve their flexibility.

10 Commandments for Stretching

1. Before stretching, do an aerobic warm-up to get muscles warm.

2. Stretch before every workout.

3. Stretch daily, and if you are especially tight, stretch twice a day.

4. Stretch within 10 minutes after every workout.

5. Stretch to the edge of discomfort in the muscle, but not to the point of pain.

6. Breathe normally as you stretch.

7. Move into each stretch slowly, hold it for 30 seconds, and slowly return to the starting position.

8. Repeat each stretch three times.

9. Perform all one-sided stretches on both sides.

10. Don't bounce to increase the range of motion. This is called ballistic stretching, and it is not safe.

The 14 all-star stretches on pages 340 to 343 cover the major muscle groups.

All-Star Stretches

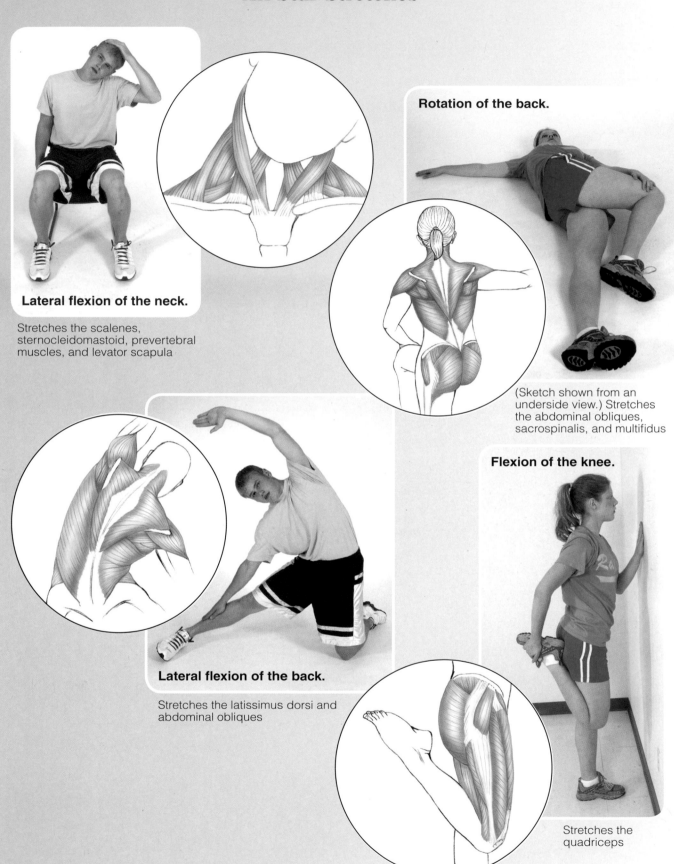

Lateral flexion of the neck.

Stretches the scalenes, sternocleidomastoid, prevertebral muscles, and levator scapula

Rotation of the back.

(Sketch shown from an underside view.) Stretches the abdominal obliques, sacrospinalis, and multifidus

Lateral flexion of the back.

Stretches the latissimus dorsi and abdominal obliques

Flexion of the knee.

Stretches the quadriceps

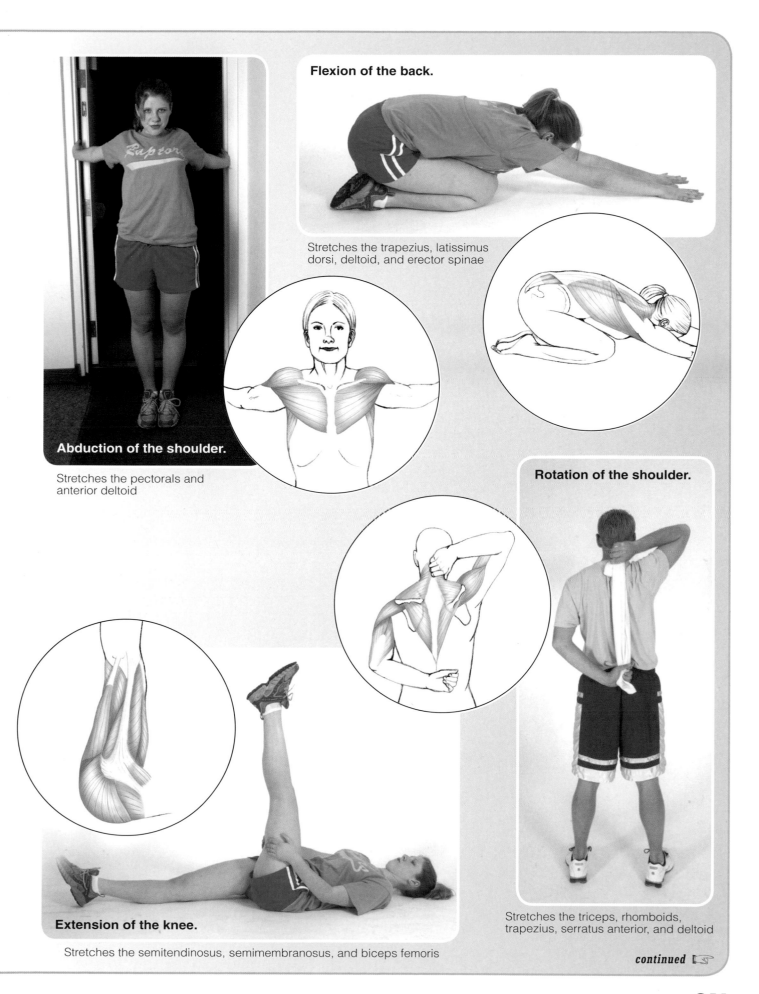

Abduction of the shoulder.

Stretches the pectorals and anterior deltoid

Flexion of the back.

Stretches the trapezius, latissimus dorsi, deltoid, and erector spinae

Rotation of the shoulder.

Stretches the triceps, rhomboids, trapezius, serratus anterior, and deltoid

Extension of the knee.

Stretches the semitendinosus, semimembranosus, and biceps femoris

continued ☞

All-Star Stretches (continued)

Abduction of the hip.

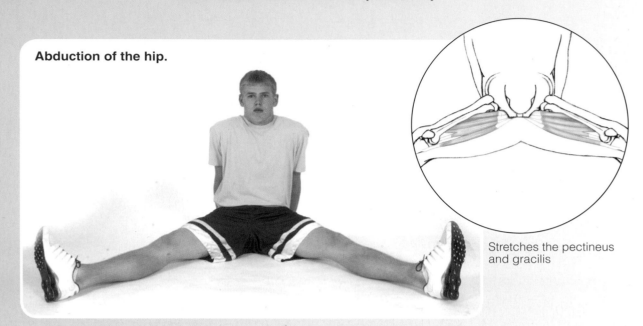

Stretches the pectineus and gracilis

Flexion of the shoulder.

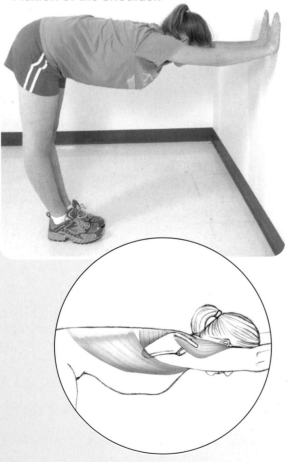

Stretches the latissimus dorsi, trapezius, and rhomboids

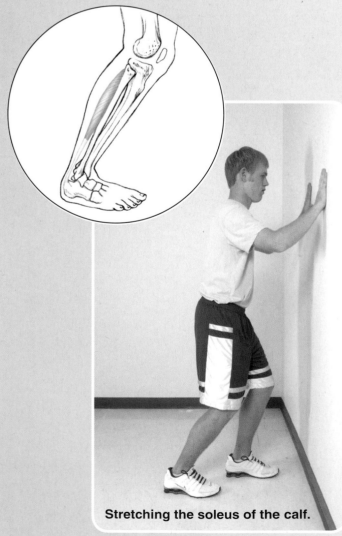

Stretching the soleus of the calf.

Stretches the soleus

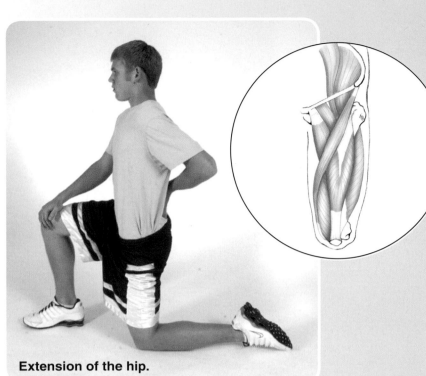

Extension of the hip.

Stretches the rectus femoris and iliopsoas

Adduction of the hip.

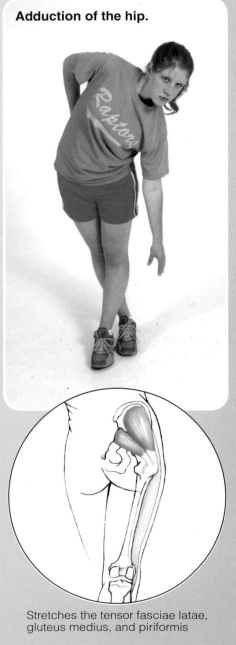

Stretches the tensor fasciae latae, gluteus medius, and piriformis

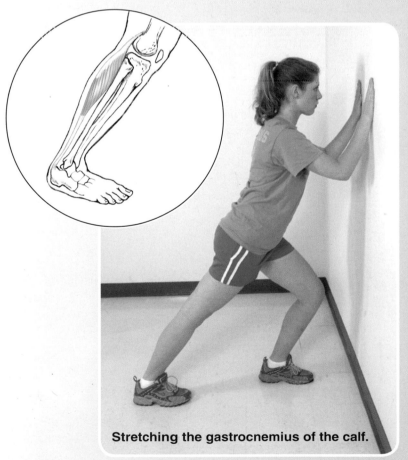

Stretching the gastrocnemius of the calf.

Stretches the gastrocnemius

Resistance Training

We know a great deal about resistance training for strength, endurance, power, and speed. I'll give you the basics to get started here, but when you're ready for more advanced information, see the references in the To Learn More section at the end of the chapter.

Training Objective

Your first decision in designing a training program is what muscular fitness objective you want to help your athletes achieve. Select from the following four objectives (review figure 15.1, which is repeated below):

▶ Developing strength as a foundation for your sport or for competitive weightlifting

▶ Developing short-term endurance or power (activities with few repetitions)

▶ Developing intermediate-term endurance or power (activities with a moderate number of repetitions)

▶ Developing long-term endurance (activities with many repetitions)

Exercises

The exercises are the essential eight you were introduced to in the testing section on pages 330 to 334. These exercises are shown on pages 345 to 349 using free weights and fixed resistance machines. As your athletes progress and you learn more, you'll want to add other exercises that may more specifically fit the muscular demands of your sport.

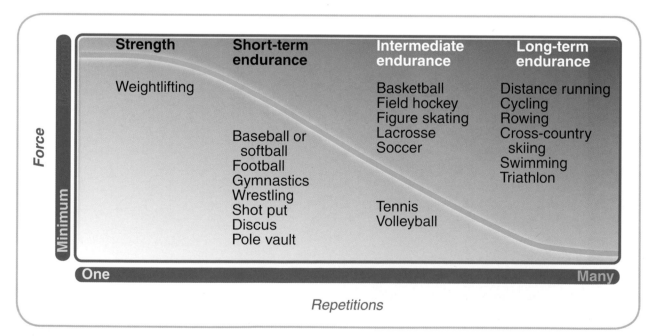

Figure 15.1 Note the relationship between force and repetition. As more force is required, the sport requires fewer repetitions. As the sport involves more repetitions, the force required for each repetition decreases.

Essential Eight Resistance Exercises

BENCH PRESS

beginning position

downward movement position

CHEST PRESS

beginning position

backward movement position

BENT-OVER ROW

beginning position

upward movement position

continued ☞

Essential Eight Resistance Exercises *(continued)*

SEATED ROW

beginning position

backward movement position

STANDING PRESS

beginning position

upward movement position

SEATED PRESS

beginning position

upward movement position

BICEPS CURL

beginning position

upward movement position

LOW PULLEY BICEPS CURL

beginning position

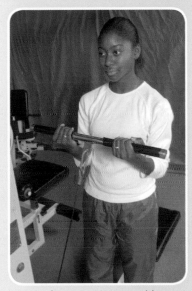

upward movement position

TRICEPS EXTENSION

beginning position

downward movement position

continued ☞

Essential Eight Resistance Exercises (continued)

TRICEPS PRESS-DOWN

beginning position

downward movement position

SQUAT

beginning position

downward movement position

LEG PRESS

beginning position

downward movement position

LEG CURL

beginning position

upward movement position

TWISTING TRUNK CURL

beginning position

upward movement position

CRUNCH

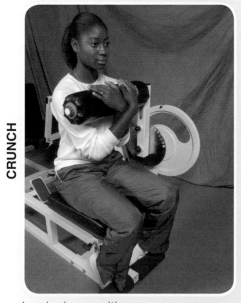

beginning position

downward movement position

Which is better—free weights or machines? I recommended machines for testing athletes who have little experience with weightlifting, but for regular training both free weights and fixed or variable resistance machines are good, each having some advantages and disadvantages.

Don't forget safety in supervising your resistance exercise program. Here are some key tips to keep in mind:

▶ Instruct your athletes on the proper technique for doing each resistance exercise.

▶ Always have adult supervision in the exercise area.

▶ Be sure to use trained spotters when exercising with free weights.

▶ Insist that collars are always used on bars.

Exercise Order

The key principle here is to alternate between muscle groups to provide time for adequate recovery. One of two approaches is commonly used: Alternate exercises between the upper and lower body, or alternate between pushing and pulling exercises. When doing more than one set, do one set of each exercise and then do the second set of each exercise.

Determining the Starting Weight

This step is easy. You've already established the 1RM for each exercise. Now turn to table 15.11, select the row with your objective, and from the "Resistance" column obtain the percent of 1RM. As an example, John Klein is a high school sophomore who lacks basic strength. So for this objective you see that the resistance or exercise load for the essential eight exercises should be 85 percent of the 1RM. John's bench press test estimated his 1RM at only 75 pounds, so the recommended starting weight for him is 64 pounds (75 × .85 = 63.75). In addition, you can see that John should do two to six sets of fewer than six repetitions, with a two- to five-minute rest between sets.

Volume

It's better when starting a resistance training program to use less resistance, fewer sets, and higher repetitions. It gives your athletes a chance to learn the correct techniques for doing the exercises (especially if you're using free weights) and to experience success. One set of 8 to 12 reps performed to muscular failure is good for beginners. But after four to six weeks, move to the recommendations in table 15.11.

Beginners should train two to three times per week, intermediates three to four times per week, and advanced athletes four to six times per week. For advanced athletes, resistance training should be done year-round. Have your athletes work out four to six times per week during the off-season; this is a great time to make gains in strength and power. During the preseason your athletes should train three to four times per week, during the in-season only

Muscular fitness objective	Resistance (% 1RM)	Repetitions	Sets	Rest interval
Strength	85%	< 6	2–6	2–5 min
Power—single effort event and short-term endurance	80–90%	1–2	3–5	2–5 min
Power—multiple effort event and intermediate-term endurance	75–85%	3–5	3–5	2–5 min
Endurance—long-term	60%	>12	2–3	1 min

Table 15.11—Determining the Starting Resistance or Load for Strength Training

one to two times per week, and during the post-season recovery period one to three times per week. Remember, more is not always better. Resting to let muscles recover is an important part of resistance training programs.

Load Adjustments

How do you know when to increase the weight? Use the two-for-two rule: If an athlete can do two or more reps over the target number of reps in the last set in two consecutive workouts, increase the load. For smaller, weaker, or less trained athletes increase the weight by 2.5 percent for upper body exercises and 5 percent for lower body exercises. For larger, stronger, and more trained athletes, increase the weight by 5 percent for upper body exercises and 10 percent for lower body exercises.

Muscular Endurance Training

Training muscular endurance follows the same program design principles as described for resistance training, but as you can see in table 15.11, the greater the endurance, the lower the resistance and the greater number of repetitions. And don't forget the specificity principle. A great way to train muscular endurance is to practice the specific technical skill of the sport.

Muscular endurance increases rapidly with training, as much as 30 percent per week. Short-term endurance is easier to maintain, but long-term endurance is lost rapidly with inactivity.

Speed Training

Although speed training can involve more than running, here we'll focus on improving running speed, as this is applicable to many sports. Consider the football wide receiver who must run a certain route and then sprint to the goal line or the basketball player making a fast break up the court.

The best way for athletes to obtain speed is to select parents who endow them with a high percentage of fast-twitch muscle fibers. After that, they have five ways to improve speed:

1. Improve reaction time to the stimulus, or what is often referred to as quickness.
2. Improve acceleration time to reach full speed faster.
3. Increase the length of the stride while maintaining the pace of the strides.
4. Increase the pace or number of steps taken per unit of time.
5. Improve speed endurance or the ability to maintain speed for the distance required.

Athletes can improve their reaction time by developing anticipation skills, which help them focus on the cues to trigger the decision to move. Acceleration, stride length, and number of steps are all developed through strength and power training. Speed endurance can be improved through short- to intermediate-term endurance training and the development of anaerobic endurance.

Three special training methods are used for developing speed.

▶ *Speed resistance training.* This involves adding weights or resistance to athletes' bodies as they move as fast as possible. Athletes can wear weighted vests or weighted belts. They can wear harnesses tied to a rope to pull a weighted sled, pull an open parachute, or have another person provide some resistance. They can also run up hills, climb stadium stairs, and run in the sand.

Speed resistance training with harness and elastic tubing.

▶ *Improving running form.* Through training athletes can develop more efficient mechanics in their stride and arm movements, learning to relax the opposite muscle when the active muscle is working.

Overspeed training with high-speed running on a treadmill.

▶ *Overspeed training.* The emphasis here is on training the neuromuscular system to work at a faster pace by increasing stride rate. The methods used include sprinting downhill, towing with surgical tubing, and high-speed running on a treadmill.

A common mistake in speed training is to provide too much resistance or too much assistance. Follow the 10 percent rule: Athletes should train with no more than a 10 percent decrease in their usual time (an increase in speed) when training with assistance and no more than a 10 percent increase in time (a decrease in speed) when training with resistance. See the To Learn More section for additional references on speed training.

Power Training

Remember that power is moving a resistance as fast as possible. It's speed and strength combined; improve either one and you improve power. Follow these two steps to increase your athletes' power:

1. First develop strength in your athletes along with aerobic and anaerobic fitness as a foundation for power training.

2. Then, with experienced, resistance trained athletes, you may move on to power weightlifting exercises such as cleans, snatches, push presses, and jump squats. These lifts are done with near maximum resistance and require near maximal effort. These are definitely advanced training methods and should be done only when you and your athletes are ready. See the To Learn More section for more information on these techniques.

Power Weightlifting

Popularized by a Russian sprinter in the 1960s, plyometrics are widely used to increase power. Plyometric exercises are those in which the muscle is stretched initially followed by immediate maximum contraction. Plyometric exercises for the lower body involve bounding, hopping, and jumping exercises, and those for the upper body involve catching and throwing medicine balls. Plyometrics have a higher risk of injury if athletes are not physically fit or if they perform them incorrectly or too frequently. Strong caution should be used with athletes under age 14. Before adding plyometrics to your training schedule, learn more about this advanced method of training by checking out the references in the To Learn More section.

Plyometric Exercises

DOUBLE-LEG VERTICAL JUMP

countermovement

upward movement

DOUBLE-LEG HOP

countermovement

forward movement

take-off position

forward bound

start position

ball thrust forward

355

Questions for Reflection

▶ Do you have a general understanding of muscle mechanics and physiology? It will help you develop an effective muscular fitness program. **(p. 323)**

▶ What is the physiology of muscle soreness? How can you help your athletes train progressively to avoid damaging their muscles? **(p. 324)**

▶ What are the muscular demands of your sport? Do your athletes primarily need flexibility, strength, endurance, speed, power, or a combination of these? **(p. 327)**

▶ What are the best methods for testing your athletes for flexibility, strength, endurance, speed, and power? **(p. 328)**

▶ What are the 10 commandments of stretching? Do your athletes know them? **(p. 339)**

▶ What is your resistance training objective—short-term, intermediate-term, or long-term endurance or power? **(p. 344)**

▶ What are the essential eight resistance exercises? How can you modify them to fit your training objectives? **(p. 345)**

▶ How can you help your athletes improve their speed? **(p. 351)**

▶ What are the two steps to increasing power? **(p. 353)**

References

Baechle, Tom, and Barney Groves. 1998. *Weight training: Steps to success.* 2nd ed. Champaign, IL: Human Kinetics.

National Strength and Conditioning Association. 2000. *Essentials of strength training and conditioning.* 2nd ed. Champaign, IL: Human Kinetics.

Sharkey, Brian. 1986. *Coaches guide to sport physiology.* Champaign, IL: Human Kinetics.

To Learn More

Alter, Michael J. 1998. *Sport stretch.* 2nd ed. Champaign, IL: Human Kinetics. This book shows 311 stretches and describes stretching programs for 41 sports.

Bompa, Tudor, Mauro Di Pasquale, and Lorenzo Cornacchia. 2002. *Serious strength training.* 2nd ed. Champaign, IL: Human Kinetics. An advanced text by the world's leading authorities on periodized training.

Brown, Lee, Vance Ferrigno, and Juan Santana. 2000. *Training for speed, agility, and quickness.* Champaign, IL: Human Kinetics. Contains 180 drills for developing these three athletic qualities.

Chu, Donald A. 1998. *Jumping into plyometrics.* 2nd ed. Champaign, IL: Human Kinetics. An excellent introduction to this popular method of power training. There is also a companion video available.

Dintiman, George, and Bob Ward. 2003. *Sports speed.* 3rd ed. Champaign, IL: Human Kinetics. The most comprehensive book on the subject.

Faigenbaum, Avery, and Wayne Westcott. 2000. *Strength & power for youth athletes.* Champaign, IL: Human Kinetics. Provides instructions for 82 exercises, as well as including proven training programs.

Fleck, Steven J., and William J. Kraemer. 2004. *Designing resistance training programs.* 3rd ed. Champaign, IL: Human Kinetics.. Excellent for designing advanced training programs; it explains many different types of resistance training systems.

Foran, Bill, ed. 2001. *High-performance sports conditioning.* Champaign, IL: Human Kinetics. Explains advanced training programs for power, quickness, balance, agility, and speed, and shows how to incorporate sport-specific skills into conditioning. Also shows how to design periodized training programs.

National Strength and Conditioning Association. 2000. *Essentials of strength training and conditioning.* 2nd ed. Champaign, IL: Human Kinetics. Comprehensive text on all aspects of resistance training. Used as a text in college courses and to prepare for certification as a strength and conditioning coach.

Partner-resistance strength training video. 1998. Champaign, IL: Human Kinetics. Demonstrates 23 exercises for developing strength through resistance provided by a partner.

Spector-Flock, Noa. 2002. *Get stronger by stretching with Thera-Band.* 2nd ed. Hightstown, NJ: Princeton Book Company. The book shows and explains many strength exercises for the lower body in part II and upper body in part III, using elastic resistance bands.

16

Fueling Your Athletes

When I was coaching college and high school wrestling, our prematch meal consisted of steak and eggs. That's what my coach had fed me, explaining that the high protein content provided the fuel my muscles would need, and I dutifully carried on his tradition. I know better today. As you learned in chapter 14, protein is not a desirable fuel for muscles. I also encouraged my athletes to lose weight by whatever means—mostly starvation and dangerous dehydration. It was what everyone did then, but I know better today.

We've learned much about sport nutrition and weight control since the 1960s.

With this knowledge you can help your athletes

▶ consume the fuel required to improve their performance,

▶ decrease their recovery time from strenuous workouts,

▶ minimize injuries from fatigue,

▶ control weight and body fat, and

▶ improve their health so they'll be able to play for many years and live longer.

As a bonus you may find the motivation to improve your own diet and, if necessary, shed a few pounds.

Coach's Role

As a coach you want to help your athletes fuel their bodies so that they have the energy to play at their best and to achieve or maintain an optimal weight. In doing so, you also teach them healthy eating habits for a lifetime. But teaching athletes how to "eat to win" is no easy task. Eating habits are hard to change, and your athletes live in a junk food society popular with their peers. So what can you do? Quite a bit, actually.

1. *Educate.* Your athletes are making a substantial investment in their sport. Explain to them that fueling their bodies to play well is a vital part of making that investment pay. Create an athlete's guide to nutrition based on the content of this chapter and other reading you do, and include it in your player handbook. Reinforce the content of the guide in your team meetings with wall posters, through brief comments to the team, and informally to individuals.

2. *Encourage.* Changing habits is hard to do, but by reminding athletes of the positive consequences, you'll provide encouragement.

3. *Involve parents.* At the preseason meeting with parents (see chapter 19), explain the importance of good nutrition, give them a copy of your athlete's guide to nutrition, and ask them to provide well-balanced diets.

4. *Special help.* Identify athletes who may need special help to eat better, such as those who run out of energy in practices and games, those who are under- and overweight, and those who come from impoverished homes or homes where parental guidance is weak. You can do this best by conducting a systematic nutritional analysis with every athlete using nutritional software (see the To Learn More section at the end of this chapter).

5. *Role model.* Remember that you are a powerful role model. The food you select for your athletes when you're feeding them and how you eat and manage your weight speak louder than your words! Even if you're overweight or feel uncomfortable about advocating good nutrition, don't ignore this vital subject with your athletes.

Six Basic Nutrients

You may know the six basic nutrients, but a refresher will be useful as we proceed through the chapter.

▶ *Carbohydrates.* Carbohydrates provide energy for the muscles from starches and sugars in the form of glycogen. The fiber in these foods helps digestion and the control of fat and cholesterol.

▶ *Protein.* Protein is essential for developing new tissue and maintaining existing tissue, including muscles, red blood cells, and hair. The body needs protein to produce essential enzymes, antibodies, and hormones. Protein also helps control the water level inside and outside the cells.

▶ *Fat.* Fat is a primary source of stored energy that is used when the body is resting and in long-term aerobic activity. Fat from animals (meat, butter) tends to be saturated and contributes to cardiovascular disease and cancer. Fat from plants (corn oil, canola oil, olive oil) is unsaturated and healthier.

▶ *Vitamins.* These nutrients are catalysts that regulate metabolic reactions within the body. Vitamin A helps the eyes work correctly. A and C are needed for the immune system. B vitamins help the cells burn energy, and folic acid and thiamin (also B vitamins) help the nervous system. D vitamins help calcium and phosphorous go from the food you eat to your bloodstream, and antioxidants help protect the cells from damage arising from their production of energy.

▶ *Minerals.* These elements help form structures in the body and regulate body processes. Calcium, phosphorus, and magnesium help keep bones strong, and fluoride strengthens teeth. Iron is essential in oxygen transport, and sodium and potassium are vital in controlling blood volume. Zinc helps derive energy from fuel, and iodine helps control the rate energy is used.

▶ *Water.* Water is essential for temperature control through sweating, and for carrying nutrients to cells and removing waste from the cells. It's also an important constituent of muscle and in processes inside cells. Water constitutes 60 to 70 percent of the body's weight.

Athletes derive energy from foods that contain carbohydrates, protein, and fat. Vitamins and minerals are not direct sources of energy, but are needed to derive energy from carbohydrates, protein, and fat.

Now let's answer the three big questions:

▶ What should your athletes eat?

▶ How much should they consume?

▶ When should they eat?

The Athlete's Diet

For most athletes, the best diet consists of eating 55 to 65 percent carbohydrates, 25 to 30 percent fat, and 15 to 20 percent protein. It's no magic diet; it's the same diet the U.S. government recommends as a healthy diet for the entire population. A well-balanced diet will almost always provide the energy your athletes need. But just what is a well-balanced diet? The U.S. government's Food Guide Pyramid, shown in figure 16.1, provides the answer. Take a moment and study it.

The Food Guide Pyramid is valuable for making good daily food choices. It shows five food groups and the recommended number of servings for each food group. The apex of the pyramid shows fats, oils, and sweets without recommending a number of servings. You'll also notice that, at a glance, you can see how much fat and sugar are in each food group.

Serving Size

To use the Food Guide Pyramid, you and your athletes need to know what a serving size is. No, it's not how much you can pile on your plate! You'll find the answer in table 16.1.

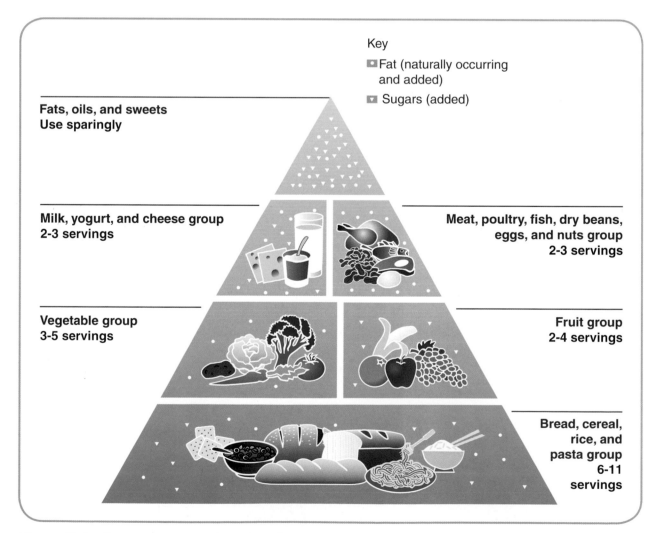

Key
◾ Fat (naturally occurring and added)
▾ Sugars (added)

Fats, oils, and sweets
Use sparingly

Milk, yogurt, and cheese group
2-3 servings

Meat, poultry, fish, dry beans, eggs, and nuts group
2-3 servings

Vegetable group
3-5 servings

Fruit group
2-4 servings

Bread, cereal, rice, and pasta group
6-11 servings

Figure 16.1 Get an electronic copy of the Food Guide Pyramid by downloading it from www.usda.gov/cnpp/pyramid.html and have it enlarged into a poster. Place several of them in the locker room and other strategic places to remind athletes of the athlete's diet.

U.S. Department of Agriculture/U.S. Department of Health and Human Services.

Table 16.1—Serving Sizes for the Food Guide Pyramid

Food	Servings for 1,600 cal/day[a]	Servings for 2,200 cal/day[b]	Servings for 2,800 cal/day[c]	Servings for 3,500 cal/day[d]
Bread, cereal, rice, and pasta				
1 slice of bread 1/2 bun or bagel 1/2 medium doughnut 1 cup of ready-to-eat cereal 1/2 cup of cooked cereal, rice, or pasta 3–4 small plain crackers 2 medium-sized cookies	6	9	11	20
Vegetables				
1 cup of raw leafy vegetables 1/2 cup of other vegetables (cooked or chopped raw) 3/4 cup of vegetable juice	3	4	5	6
Fruit				
1 medium apple, banana, or orange 1/4 cup of dried fruit 1/2 cup of chopped, cooked, or canned fruit 3/4 cup of fruit juice	2	3	4	10
Meat, poultry, fish, dry beans, eggs, and nuts				
Cooked lean meat, poultry, or fish (in total oz per day) 1/2 cup of cooked dry beans, or 1 egg, or 2 tbsp of peanut butter, or 1/3 cup of nuts count as 1 oz of lean meat (about 1/3 serving)	5 oz (142 grams)	6 oz (170 grams)	7 oz (198 grams)	7 oz (198 grams)
Milk, yogurt, and cheese				
1 cup of milk or yogurt 1 and 1/2 oz of natural cheese (e.g., cheddar) 2 oz of processed cheese (e.g., American) (1 oz is about the size of your thumb)	2–3	2–3	2–3	5
Fats, oils, and sweets				
This category of foods includes full-fat salad dressing, cream cheese, sour cream, butter, margarine, shortening, lard, sugars, soft drinks, fruit drinks, candies, and sweet snack foods. Limit these foods because they provide calories but few vitamins and minerals.				

[a] 1,600 calories per day is appropriate for very sedentary women and inactive older adults.

[b] 2,200 calories per day is about right for children, teenage girls, moderately active women, and sedentary men.

[c] 2,800 calories per day is appropriate for teenage boys, many active men, and very active women.

[d] 3,500 calories per day is about right for active teenage boys, active men, and extremely active women. Very active men will need more than 3,500 calories per day.

Adapted from the Food Guide Pyramid, USDA, 1992.

Help your athletes recognize serving sizes and make sure they know the number of recommended daily servings from each food category. Put up a poster of the Food Guide Pyramid and consider replacing the slogan "When the going gets tough, the tough get going" with the slogan "Eat right! Without energy, inspiration wilts into exasperation." Now let's look at these five food groups more closely.

Breads, Cereals, Rice, and Pasta

Athletes should eat 11 to 20 servings of these high-carbohydrate foods, which provide much of the energy muscles need. Most foods from grain that are not processed or lightly processed are excellent choices. They include cereals without sugar coatings, oatmeal, bagels, muffins, whole grain and dark breads, and stoned wheat and whole grain crackers. Rice, preferably brown and long grain, as well as many pasta dishes, are good foods that can be prepared to be very tasty. Popcorn is also a great snack food that fits into this food group. The trick with this food group is not adding lots of fats to them in the form of butter, cream cheese, or lunch meats (in sandwiches).

Vegetables

Feed your athletes spinach so they can be like Popeye—strong and courageous. Veggies are low in calories and fat, so you can eat a lot of them, and high in nutrients, providing many of the vitamins and minerals athletes need. Athletes should have five to six servings of vegetables a day. There aren't any bad vegetables, but the darker and more colorful ones, in general, have more nutrients. Broccoli, green peppers, brussels sprouts, cauliflower, cabbage, tomatoes—and of course spinach—are excellent choices. Fresh vegetables are the best for taste, but frozen and canned vegetables are good too.

Fruits

Athletes should eat 4 to 10 servings a day of fruits, which are high in carbohydrates, fiber, potassium, and many vitamins. Fruits are particularly helpful in aiding recovery from intense exercise and healing injuries. Bananas, containing 100 calories, are great energy boosters and widely used by athletes as a snack food. Citrus fruits and juices are high in vitamin C and potassium and should be a vital part of an athlete's diet.

Meats, Poultry, Fish, Dry Beans, Eggs, and Nuts

Athletes should eat about 7 ounces (196 grams) of these high-protein foods a day, but in the American diet athletes often eat much more—for example, a 12-ounce (336-gram) steak. Lean beef is healthy in moderation, and skinless chicken is better for people than red meat because it has less saturated fat. Nutritionists recommend that we eat three fish meals a week, with the best fish being the oilier ones, such as salmon, tuna, and swordfish.

Eggs are another source of high protein, but they have lots of cholesterol. We often eat more eggs than we recognize because they are a hidden ingredient in other dishes. A few tablespoons of peanut butter on bread and crackers provide lots of protein, vitamins, and fiber, but have no cholesterol. Cholesterol comes only from animal products.

Milk, Yogurt, and Cheese

These foods are also high in protein and are especially rich in calcium, an important mineral for female athletes in particular. Athletes should eat three to five servings of this food group a day, preferably selecting low-fat and skim milk and low-fat yogurt and cheeses. Don't confuse frozen yogurt with regular yogurt. Although frozen yogurt is fat free, it contains lots of calories without nutrients. It fits in the "sweets" category of foods.

Fats, Oils, and Sweets

Fats and sugars are nutrient poor, but they add spice to life and rightfully sit on top of the Food Guide Pyramid. Think of these foods as something you and your athletes get to eat after eating your way through the lower levels of the food pyramid. You're likely to run into athletes who have turned the pyramid upside down, eating a junk food diet. It's no easy task to change this rich and tasty diet, but try to do so by encouraging athletes to eat foods from the lower three levels of the Food Guide Pyramid whenever they get hungry.

Seven Rules for Eating Right

The Food Guide Pyramid is not a rigid prescription of what to eat each day. Instead, it provides a general guide to you and your athletes. If your athletes follow these seven rules, which are based on the food pyramid, they will be eating right:

1. Eat a variety of foods from the five food groups. No one food provides all the nutrients an athlete needs, and variety makes eating interesting.

2. Eat a diet high in whole grain products, vegetables, and fruits. It provides the complex carbohydrates needed for energy and the essential vitamins, minerals, and fiber—and it's low in fat. In short, such a diet provides the energy athletes need and is good for their health.

3. Eat a diet moderate in fat, saturated fat, and cholesterol. Foods high in fat can be high in calories and can lead to unwanted weight gain. More important, such a diet reduces the risk of cardiovascular disease and cancer.

4. Eat a diet moderate in sugars. A diet with lots of sugars has too few nutrients and too many calories.

5. Eat a diet moderate in salt or sodium. Athletes can lose a lot of sodium when they sweat, and they need to replace that sodium to maintain proper fluid balance. On the other hand, today's youth get an overabundance of salt in their normal diets. Lowering salt intake may also reduce the risk of high blood pressure. In essence, your athletes should not take in too little or too much salt.

6. Drink lots of fluids. Water is essential to all body functions, and intense physical activity increases the risk of dehydration.

7. Avoid alcohol, or if of age, drink alcohol in moderation. Alcohol contains lots of calories and almost no nutrients, increases the likelihood of dehydration, and decreases the efficiency of energy metabolism.

More About Carbohydrates, Protein, and Fat

As you'll remember, carbohydrates, protein, and fat supply the body with energy. Let's learn more about these three essential nutrients.

Carbohydrates

Carbohydrates are the foundation of a high-octane diet to meet athletes' energy needs. No less than 55 to 65 percent of calories should come from carbohydrates. The typical diet for a 150-pound (68-kilogram) nonactive person should include about 1,350 calories from carbohydrates per day. Athletes of the same weight need about 1,900 to 2,700 calories from carbohydrates per day, and even more when they are training intensely.

Carbohydrates may be simple or complex, and complex carbohydrates may be either digestible or indigestible. Simple carbohydrates include sugars, glucose, dextrose, fructose, sucrose, and lactose, and are found in fruits, vegetables, and processed foods such as candies and sport beverages. Simple carbohydrates are converted to glucose for energy. Digestible complex carbohydrates are found in starchy foods, including potatoes, pasta, bread, cereal, and beans. Indigestible complex carbohydrates, which provide fiber to the diet, are found in the bran portion of cereals, in fruit, and in vegetables. Both types of carbohydrates provide energy, but complex carbohydrates contain many more nutrients. Note that fruit, a simple carbohy-drate, also contains many valuable vitamins and minerals.

I used to tell the athletes I coached to eat complex rather than simple carbohydrates in pregame meals because I was taught that simple carbohydrates would give athletes a sugar high, making them hyperglycemic (large and rapid rise in blood glucose and insulin), followed by a sugar low (hypoglycemic). Now we know that we cannot classify foods as producing low or high glycemic responses by whether they are simple or complex carbohydrates. Instead, nutritionists have developed an index of how quickly foods produce a glycemic response (table 16.2).

Table 16.2—Glycemic Index (GI) of Some Common Foods*

High glycemic index foods (GI > 85)

Angel food cake	Cornflakes	Maltose	Rye flour bread
Bagel, white	Cornmeal	Melba toast	Shredded wheat
Barley flour bread	Couscous	Millet	Soda crackers
Brown rice	Cream of wheat	Molasses	Soft drinks
Cake doughnut	Crispix cereal	Müeslix	Sport drinks
Carrots	Croissant	Muffins	Sucrose
Cheerios	Glucose	Oatmeal	Total cereal
Cheese pizza	Grape-Nuts	Potatoes	Waffles
Corn bran cereal	Hard candy	Raisins	Watermelon
Corn Chex cerea	Honey/syrups	Rice cakes	White bread
Corn chips	Ice cream	Rice Krispies	Whole wheat bread

Moderate glycemic index foods (GI = 60–85)

All-Bran cereal	Durum spaghetti	Mixed grain bread	Rye kernel bread
Banana	Fruit cocktail	Oat bran bread	Special K cereal
Basmati rice	Grapefruit juice	Oat bran cereal	Sponge cake
Bran Chex cereal	Grapes	Orange (whole or juice)	Sweet corn
Buckwheat	Ice cream, low fat	Parboiled rice	Sweet potato or yams
Bulgur	Kiwi fruit	Pastry	Wheat, cooked
Bulgur bread	Linguine	Pita bread, white	White rice, long grain
Cracked barley	Mango or papaya	Popcorn	Wild rice

Low glycemic index foods (GI < 60)

Apples	Cherries	Milk	Rice bran
Apricots (dried)	Dried peas	Peaches (fresh)	Spaghetti
Barley	Fructose	Peanuts	Tomato soup
Barley kernel bread	Grapefruit	Pears (fresh)	Wheat kernels
Beans (all types)	Lentils	Plums	Yogurt (all types)

*White bread (50g) was used as the reference food and has a GI of 100.

Low and moderate glycemic foods such as spaghetti, yogurt, and bananas are best to eat as a pregame food because they provide energy over a longer period, whereas high glycemic foods such as potatoes and muffins are better to eat during or after strenuous exercise to help refuel the body. You and your athletes should know which foods to select for pre- and postgame meals.

Protein

Protein used to be a substantial part of athletes' diets because coaches thought it built muscle. It doesn't; well, not directly. When we eat protein, it is digested into amino acids, which are used to build and repair all types of tissue—muscle, bones, ligaments, tendons—as well as produce needed hormones and enzymes. Although proteins are the building blocks for muscle, you build strength not by eating protein, but through resistance training.

In the well-balanced athlete's diet, protein should be about 15 to 20 percent of the calories consumed. Table 16.3 shows the recommended protein intake for athletes.

Because protein is not stored in the body, athletes need to consume the amount needed daily. This is easy to do if they eat a well-balanced diet according to the Food Guide Pyramid. Of course, not all athletes eat a well-balanced diet. Athletes who are trying to lose weight or are on a restricted diet for other reasons need to pay attention to eating enough protein. Also, the foods that are high in protein are often high in fat (e.g., meats or dairy products), and so in an effort to reduce fat in the diet, athletes may also consume inadequate amounts of protein. Athletes who eat a vegetarian diet with no meat, fish, poultry, eggs, or milk must make sure they get enough protein. Beans, rice, corn, corn tortillas, refried beans, peanut butter, and bread are good protein sources for vegans.

Athletes can also eat too much protein, which can create serious problems. First, when athletes eat diets high in protein, they are less likely to be eating enough carbohydrates. As we discussed in chapter 14, when muscles cannot obtain energy from fat and carbohydrates, they'll burn protein for energy. This is undesirable because it uses the protein needed for tissue maintenance. Second, because protein can't be stored and produces more metabolic waste that must be removed through the urine, the risk of dehydration is greater with a high-protein diet. This is why athletes' diets should be high in carbo-

Table 16.3—Recommended Protein Intake for Athletes		
Type of athlete	**Daily calories of protein per pound of body weight**	**Daily calories of protein per kilogram of body weight**
Athletes in endurance events	2.2–2.6	4.8–5.6
Athletes in strength training programs	2.9–3.1	5.6–7.2
Growing teenage athletes	3.6–4.0	7.2–8.0

hydrates; you don't want them to deplete this more efficient burning fuel and begin the destructive process of consuming their own muscle tissue.

There's a booming business in protein supplements, especially among bodybuilders and power athletes. We'll discuss these supplements later, but in general your athletes will be better off getting their proteins from food rather than from pills.

Fat

Fats are a highly concentrated fuel that provides 9 calories of energy per gram versus just 4 calories per gram from protein and carbohydrates. Fats in our diet provide essential fatty acids and fat-soluble vitamins and add flavor to the foods we eat. Many people, including athletes, consume 40 to 50 percent of their calories in the form of fat by eating lots of meats, dairy products, and foods from the tip of the food pyramid, or junk foods. A healthy diet calls for only 25 to 30 percent fat.

The fats or lipids we commonly consume are called triglycerides. When we overeat, our body stores the excess energy in the form of triglycerides. When we burn fat, the triglycerides are taken out of storage and converted into glycogen for the muscle to burn as fuel.

You've surely heard of fats categorized as *saturated fats,* those found in foods from animals and palm and coconut oil, and *unsaturated fats,* those found mostly in plant foods. Athletes who have high-fat diets should especially reduce the saturated fats, because in many people they increase artery-clogging cholesterol levels. They can do so by reducing their intake of red meats, chocolate (which contains saturated tropical oils), fried foods, and high-fat dairy products. When athletes reduce the fats they eat, they should replace the calories not with foods from the tip of the food pyramid but with complex carbohydrates from the base of the pyramid.

Because fats contain 9 calories per gram and carbohydrates only 4 calories per gram, athletes will need to eat nearly twice the volume of complex carbohydrates compared to the fats they had been eating. If athletes are training extensively and consuming 4,000 or more calories per day, they may need to consume more unsaturated fats simply because they can't consume the volume of complex carbohydrates to meet their daily energy needs.

To improve athletes' performance in endurance events, researchers have studied how to improve the ability of the body to burn fat during exercise. Carnitine, caffeine, and other supplements have all been tried, and they continue to be promoted to athletes. The scientific evidence shows no benefits from these supplements in improving fat metabolism. As you'll see in a moment, caffeine can be beneficial to sport performances, but not by increasing fat metabolism. Instead, the best way to improve fat oxidation during exercise is to improve the athlete's level of fitness.

We'll look at nutritional supplements next, and in chapter 17 we'll look at pharmacological supplements when we consider drugs in sport.

Nutritional Supplements

Most athletes do not need to take nutritional supplements if they eat a balanced diet. But some don't eat a balanced diet, so a supplement may help. However, you should do all you can to encourage athletes to improve their diets rather than pop a pill to compensate for insufficiencies.

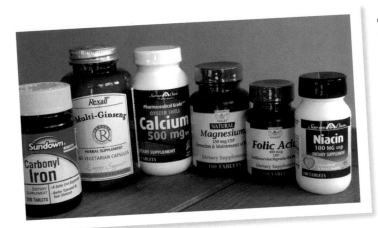

It's reported that the majority of high school, college, and professional athletes take some type of supplement, not because it will make up for some dietary deficiency but because athletes believe it will give them a competitive edge. These ergogenic—which means "work-enhancing"—nutritional supplements are purported to increase muscle tissue, improve muscle energy supplies, and increase the rate of energy production in the muscles. There is a multibillion-dollar industry that encourages this belief, but just how effective and safe are these supplements?

Review of Nutritional Supplements Used in Sport

Supplements are available for all six nutrients—carbohydrates, protein, fat, vitamins, minerals, and water. In table 16.4 I've identified the more popular supplements being used in sport and summarized what we know about their effectiveness as ergogenic aids and their benefits or risks to health. I've also identified those supplements that have been banned by any prominent national or international sport organizations.

Consult table 16.4 when you hear or read about these supplements in the media or when your athletes ask you about them. As you can see, most of these supplements have not been proven to improve performance; although most are safe, a few are unsafe. For some, the risk to health is unknown. Of course, consuming excess amounts of any supplement may be harmful to an athlete's health.

If athletes have a deficiency in a nutrient, then a supplement will help, but it is far preferable to try to improve the diet to eliminate the deficiency than to take supplements. The more-is-better mentality lacks scientific support for enhancing performance.

Next we'll look at the three most popular nutritional supplements used by athletes—vitamins, creatine, and caffeine.

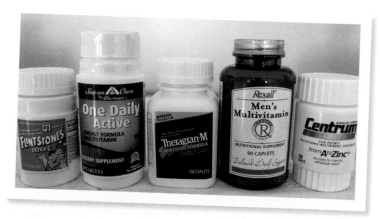

Vitamin Supplements

It's reported that 75 percent of athletes take vitamin supplements, most believing it can't do any harm and it might do some good. Most athletes don't understand that vitamins do not provide energy to muscles, but are catalysts that regulate metabolic reactions. Extensive training doesn't increase the need for more vitamins than what is obtained through eating balanced meals.

Table 16.4—Nutritional Supplements in Sport

Supplement name	What it claims to do	Scientific evidence of effectiveness	Banned	Health risks
Anabolic phytosterols	Increases muscle mass; decreases body fat	No evidence	No	Unknown
Androstenedione	Increases muscle mass and strength	Inconclusive	Yes	Unknown
Antioxidants (beta-carotene, vitamin C and E, selenium, coenzyme Q10)	Physical power by preventing tissue damage during strenuous training	Inconclusive	No	Safe
Aspartates (potassium and magnesium)	Improves aerobic power and endurance	Inconclusive but some support	No	Safe
Bee pollen	Improves anaerobic and aerobic power	Evidence refutes claim	No	Safe unless allergic
Boron	Natural testosterone booster; increases muscle mass; decreases body fat	Evidence refutes claim	No	Safe
Branched-chain amino acids (BCAA)	Prevents fatigue; increases aerobic endurance	Inconclusive	No	Safe
Caffeine	Increases energy, endurance, and fat loss; mental stimulant	Evidence supports claim	Yes (in high doses)	Safe
Calcium	Increases power from all three energy systems	Evidence refutes claim	No	Safe
Carbohydrate supplements	Increases aerobic power and endurance	Effective for events lasting longer than 60 mins	No	Safe
Carnitine (L-Carnitine)	Increases anaerobic and aerobic power and endurance	No evidence to support claim	No	Safe
Choline (lecithin)	Increases aerobic endurance	Inconclusive	No	Safe
Chromium	Increases muscle mass, strength, and power; decreases body fat	Evidence refutes claim	No	Safe
Coenzyme Q10	Increases aerobic power and endurance	Evidence refutes claim	No	Safe
Conjugated linoleic acid (CLA)	Increases lean mass; decreases fat mass	Inconclusive	No	Safe
Creatine	Increases energy for speed and power sports; increases muscle mass	Evidence supports claim for males, not females	No	Short term safe; long term unknown
Dehydroepiandrosterone (DHEA)	Increases muscle mass for strength; decreases body fat	Inconclusive	Yes	Unknown
Echinacea	Decreases risk of respiratory infection and symptoms of cold	No evidence	No	Safe
Ephedrine or ma huang	Improves physical power and mental strength	No evidence	Yes	Unsafe
Folic acid	Increases aerobic power and endurance	No evidence	No	Safe
Ginseng	Increases physical power from all three energy systems	Evidence refutes claim	No	Unclear

continued ☞

Table 16.4 *(continued)*

Supplement name	What it claims to do	Scientific evidence of effectiveness	Banned	Health risks
Glucosamine or chondroitin	Protects against joint destruction; heals tendons, ligaments, and cartilage	Inconclusive	No	Safe
Glutamine	Increases immune function; prevents overtraining	Inconclusive	No	Safe
Glycerol	Enhances aerobic power and endurance; improves temperature regulation	Inconclusive	No	Unclear
HMB (Beta-hydroxy-beta-methylbutyrate)	Increases strength and power; increases muscle mass; decreases body fat	Preliminary evidence positive, more study needed	No	Safe
Inosine	Increases aerobic power and endurance	Evidence refutes claim	No	Safe
Iron	Increases aerobic power and endurance	Evidence refutes claim except when iron deficient	No	Safe
Magnesium	Increases muscle mass and power in ATP-PC energy system	Evidence refutes claim	No	Safe
Medium chain triglycerides (MCT)	Increases energy, prolonging endurance; spares muscle glycogen; decreases body fat	Inconclusive	No	Safe but causes GI distress
Niacin	Increases anaerobic and aerobic power and endurance	Evidence refutes claim; may impair performance	No	Safe
Omega-3 fatty acids	Increases muscle mass and aerobic power and endurance	No evidence to support claim	No	Safe
Pantothenic acid	Increases aerobic power and endurance	Evidence refutes claim	No	Safe
Phosphate salts	Increases aerobic power and endurance	Inconclusive	No	Safe
Protein supplements (amino acids arginine, lysine, ornithine)	Increases muscle mass; decreases body fat	No evidence	Yes	Safe
Pyruvate and dihydroxyacetone	Increases aerobic endurance and metabolic rate; decreases fat mass	Preliminary study positive, more evidence needed	No	Safe
Riboflavin (vitamin B2)	Increases aerobic power	Evidence refutes claim	No	Safe
Sodium bicarbonate	Increases power through the anaerobic system	Evidence supports claim	No	Safe
St. John's Wort	Improves mood; reduces anxiety	Inconclusive	No	Safe
Thiamin (vitamin B1)	Increases aerobic power and endurance	No evidence to support claim	No	Safe
Tryptophan	Decreases perception of pain from intensive training	Inconclusive	No	Unclear
Vanadium	Increases muscle mass for power and strength	No evidence to support claim	No	Safe but side effects
Yohimbine	Increases muscle mass for strength and endurance; decreases body fat	No evidence to support claim	No	Safe but side effects
Zinc	Increases muscle mass and power	Inconclusive	No	Safe

If athletes have vitamin deficiencies, however, a vitamin supplement will help, but it doesn't provide all the other nutrients athletes need from a balanced diet. In general, athletes are much better off spending their money on fruits and vegetables than on vitamin supplements. There's not a shred of scientific evidence that extra vitamins improve performance!

Creatine

Next to vitamins, creatine, used mostly by young males, is the most popular nutritional supplement in sport. Considerable evidence shows that creatine increases power and speed in short-duration, high-intensity sport events that derive their energy from the ATP-PCr system, as we discussed in chapter 14. Creatine, taken in dosages of 20 to 30 grams per day spread out over the day in four doses of 5 grams each, increases muscle by as much as 20 percent. If creatine is supplemented with resistance training, it improves strength significantly.

The ergogenic effect of creatine diminishes rapidly for events lasting longer than 30 seconds, and from the little evidence available, appears to be far less effective with females. Creatine appears to be safe, although we don't know about its long-term effects on the body. There are some anecdotal reports of cramping, dehydration, and muscle strain associated with its use. To learn more about creatine see the Williams reference in the To Learn More section at the end of the chapter.

Caffeine

This popular stimulant, found in coffee, tea, and chocolate, has been shown to improve performance in endurance events by as much as 20 percent. Caffeine stimulates the central nervous system and increases the force of muscle contractions, thereby making it an effective ergogenic aid for some athletes. Caffeine also has been shown to increase the resting metabolic rate.

The effect of caffeine, however, varies from person to person. For some people, caffeine perks them up; for others, it makes them overanxious. For those who find it beneficial, the recommended dose is 2.25 milligrams per pound of body weight (5 milligrams/kg), which is obtained in 2 to 3 cups of coffee. A higher dose is not of greater value, and it risks exceeding the limit allowed by International Olympic Committee drug regulations. The downside of caffeine is that it makes some athletes jittery and may create gastrointestinal distress.

Should Coaches Recommend Nutritional Supplements?

In one survey 71 percent of coaches encouraged supplement use among athletes. But what's the right thing to do? Should you recommend vitamins, creatine, caffeine, or any other nutritional supplement to your athletes, or should you actively discourage their use?

At this time we have no consensus among national sport organizations on the matter of coaches recommending or providing athletes with nutritional supplements. The National Federation of State High School Associations (NFHS) advises coaches not to recommend any supplements to athletes, but that then excludes vitamins and sport drinks. The United States Olympic Committee (USOC) takes no position on coaches recommending supplements other than those that are banned by the International Olympic Committee. After consulting with the NFHS, USOC, NCAA, and numerous experts, here are my guidelines for you to consider.

1. Foremost, encourage athletes to eat a balanced diet and train properly so that they have no need for nutritional supplements.

2. You should not recommend any supplement that is banned by any national or international organization (see table 16.4).

3. You should not recommend any supplements where there are known health risks or the health risks are unknown.

4. You should not recommend supplements that lack considerable scientific evidence of their health benefits or ergogenic powers. That eliminates most nutritional supplements.

5. You should recommend safe nutritional supplements—e.g., vitamins and sport drinks (a nutritional supplement)—when athletes have known deficiencies.

6. You may recommend nutritional supplements that are proven effective and safe as ergogenic aids to enhance performance, not just remedy a deficiency.

With regard to creatine, the only national sport organization that provides guidance on the use of this supplement is the NCAA. It states, "An institution may provide only nonmuscle-building nutritional supplements to a student-athlete at any time for the purpose of providing additional calories and electrolytes, provided the supplements do not contain any NCAA banned substances." (NCAA 2002). Thus, it would be imprudent as a coach at any level to provide athletes with creatine. Instead, you should share with athletes the facts about this nutritional supplement.

Hydration

The stereotypical coach of yesteryear was infamous for depriving athletes of fluids during strenuous exercise, even in extreme heat and humidity. My high school and college football coaches were from that school, believing that training without drink breaks made athletes tough. We practiced two to four hours per day in the humid 100-plus-degree heat of a Kansas August, and never once took in fluids during practice. The risk of serious heat illness was great, but our coaches didn't know better then. Now we do!

Dehydration

Hydration is critical to every function in the body. Insufficient fluid intake before, during, and after exercise is the most common nutritional problem of athletes. When you think of all that you invest in helping athletes perform better, you'll get more return for the time invested by helping them properly hydrate. Dehydration hurts performance in many ways. For each 1 percent of body weight lost by dehydration in endurance events, the ability to work is reduced by 2 percent. When dehydration exceeds 2 percent of body weight, heart rate and body temperature rise, impairing performance by fatiguing athletes physically and mentally. Dehydration can also increase the risk of injury and lead to increased risk of heat illness, which I discuss next.

When athletes exercise, their muscles can generate as much as 20 times more heat than when resting. Sweating is the primary way this heat is dissipated, working in much the same way an auto cools its engine. It's not the sweat itself that cools the body, but the sweat evaporating on the skin; it cools the blood near the surface, which then cools the inner body when it circulates.

Heat Illness

When athletes are dehydrated, the flow of blood to the skin is reduced, which then limits the body's ability to sweat and therefore cool itself. Body temperature rises rapidly, and serious heat illness becomes more likely. Table 16.5 lists the warning signs of serious dehydration and heat illness. Know these symptoms and teach them to your athletes. Especially note the warning signs for heatstroke.

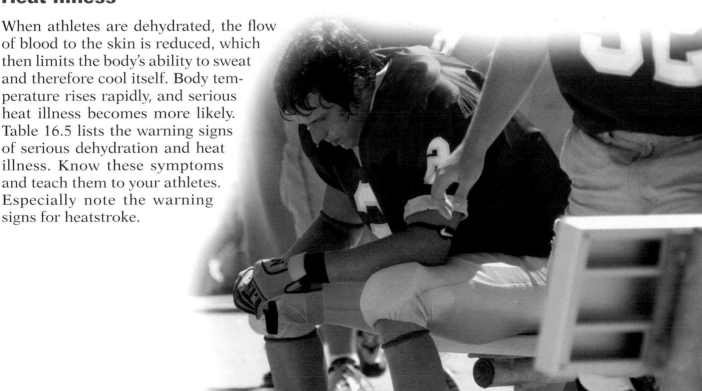

Table 16.5—Warning Signs of Heat Illness

DEHYDRATION	HEAT EXHAUSTION	HEATSTROKE
Symptoms		
• Thirst • Dry lips and mouth • Flushed skin • Irritability • Headache or dizziness • Apathy • Nausea or vomiting • Dark urine • Feeling weak or unusual fatigue • Decreased performance	• Difficulty continuing to play • Temperature below 104 degrees F (40 degrees C) • Profuse sweating • Pale skin • Dizziness or fainting • Coordination problems • Rapid, weak pulse • Headache • Nausea • Vomiting • Chills • Fatigue • Thirst • Diarrhea • Stomach cramps • Muscle cramps	• Temperature above 105 degrees F (40.6 degrees C) (rectal temperature 104 degrees F or more) (40 degrees C) • Confused, disoriented, or irrational • Altered consciousness, coma • Hot and wet or dry skin[a] • Nausea, vomiting, diarrhea • Headache or dizziness • Increased heart rate, rapid breathing
Treatment		
STOP the activity immediately. MOVE to a cool environment. DRINK fluids immediately (sport drinks containing carbohydrates and electrolytes are preferred).	STOP the activity immediately. MOVE to a cool environment. REMOVE excess clothing and equipment. COOL athlete until rectal temperature is 101 degrees F (38.3 degrees C). Cold-water bath or shower, or ice and cold towels applied to as much of the body as possible. REST on back with legs elevated above heart (unless athlete is vomiting; then place on side). DRINK fluids if conscious and not nauseated or vomiting. TRANSPORT to an emergency medical facility if the athlete does not recover quickly or condition worsens.	STOP the activity immediately. MOVE to a cool environment. REMOVE excess clothing and equipment. COOL entire body immediately by immersion or alternatives if possible. SEND for emergency medical assistance. (Cool first, then transport if cooling on site is possible.) DRINK fluids if conscious and not nauseated or vomiting.
Return to play guidelines		
• Athlete is symptom free. • Athlete maintains hydration (see page 376). • Monitor athlete closely for recurrence of symptoms.	• Physician clearance to return to play is recommended. • If physician not consulted, athlete should be symptom free. • Athlete maintains hydration. • Avoid return to play for at least one day.	• Physician clearance to return to play is essential.

[a] It is important to note that athlete's skin may be wet or dry at time of incident.

Based on recommendations from NATA, Inter-Association Task Force on Exertional Heat Illness Consensus Statement, June 2003.

Sodium Loss

With profuse sweating, you may have noticed the thin layer of salt on your skin or the white ring of salt on your hat or clothing. The loss of salt, or more accurately sodium and chloride, when sweating may limit the ability of water molecules to flow between cell membranes, which impairs the function of muscles and other tissues. This is called an electrolyte imbalance.

In the "old days" coaches used to dispense salt tablets indiscriminately to replace the lost sodium. Today athletes usually do not need salt tablets because they consume adequate amounts of salt in their diet. However, you should be aware of how much sodium or salt athletes can lose during a practice or game. When athletes are training or competing for hours at a time, they will need to replace sodium to promote fluid retention and can typically do so by salting foods and drinking sport beverages that contain a small amount of sodium.

What Athletes Should Drink

Water used to be the preferred choice, if for no other reason than it's free. But bottled water has become a big business, costing as much in some cases as other beverages. Nevertheless, water remains an excellent choice.

If your practices or competitive events have the potential to deplete your athletes' carbohydrates or electrolytes, however, then sport drinks before, during, and after training and competing are a preferred choice. Sport drinks contain about 50 to 80 calories of carbohydrates per 8 fluid ounces (240 milliliters) and a small amount of electrolytes (usually sodium and potassium) to replace what is lost in sweat.

What about other beverages?

▶ Soft drinks contain water and sugar, which helps fuel the muscles but provides no other nutrients.

▶ Diet soft drinks contain water without any nutrients.

▶ Juices are a good refreshment beverage, containing more nutrients, but are not absorbed into the body as quickly as sport drinks.

▶ You may not like hearing this. It's a myth that beer is a good sport drink. Drinking a lot of alcohol after a strenuous workout impairs rehydration. Also, alcohol is a poor source of nutrients and doesn't help athletes recover for the next exercise event.

Athletes should balance what is good for them with what tastes good to them. The more they like the taste of a beverage, the more they're likely to drink it.

Educate your athletes about hydration.

Have athletes weigh themselves before and after practices and competitions.

Preventing Dehydration

How do you and your athletes know if they are drinking enough fluids? The body's thirst mechanism is not a good guide of the need for fluids; it's too slow in telling athletes to drink. When athletes sweat, they lose water from their blood, making the blood more viscous and raising the concentration of sodium. This triggers the thirst mechanism, but by then athletes have lost 1.5 liters of water and may find it difficult to drink enough fluid to avoid becoming dehydrated. That's why athletes are advised to begin drinking before they feel thirsty, and to drink on a schedule rather than rely on their thirst mechanism.

What can you do to make sure your athletes are well hydrated? Plenty.

1. Educate your athletes about staying well hydrated and recognizing the symptoms of dehydration listed in table 16.5.

2. Have athletes weigh themselves before and after practices and competitive events to monitor their water loss. Educate them to drink at least 2 cups of fluids for every pound (about 480 milliliters for every .46 kilograms) of weight lost during exercise. When they return for the next practice, they should weigh the same as their usual pre-exercise weight.

3. Teach athletes to monitor the color of their urine using the urine color chart in figure 16.2 to determine their level of dehydration.

4. Teach athletes to drink fluids before, during, and after exercise. Figure 16.3 provides guidelines for doing so from the American College of Sports Medicine and sport nutritionists.

You can help make certain that athletes are adequately hydrated and that no one ever experiences a heat illness by educating

1
2
3
4
5
6
7
8

An athlete should match the color of the athlete's urine sample to a color on the chart. If the urine sample matches #1, #2, or #3 on the chart, the athlete is well hydrated. If the urine color matches # 4, #5 or #6, the athlete is beginning to show signs of dehydrating and should begin drinking liquids. If the urine color is #7 or #8, the athlete is dehydrated and should consume fluids.

Figure 16.2 Urine color chart.

Reprinted, by permission, from Armstrong, 2000.

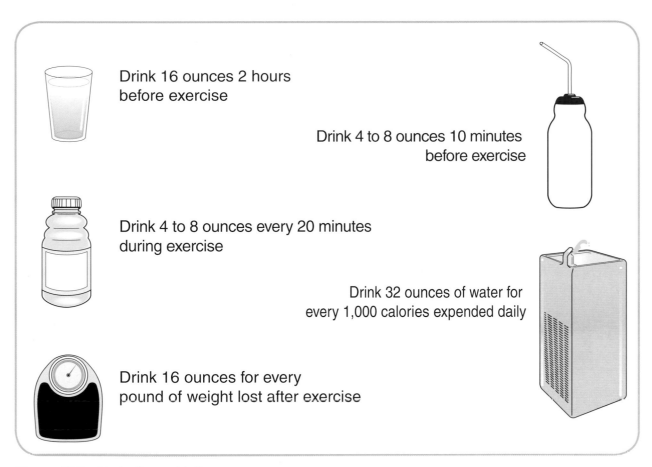

Drink 16 ounces 2 hours before exercise

Drink 4 to 8 ounces 10 minutes before exercise

Drink 4 to 8 ounces every 20 minutes during exercise

Drink 32 ounces of water for every 1,000 calories expended daily

Drink 16 ounces for every pound of weight lost after exercise

Figure 16.3   Hydration guidelines.

them, making sure drinks are readily available, building in drink breaks, and encouraging athletes to drink whenever they feel thirsty.

How Much to Eat

How much should your athletes eat to maintain weight, lose weight, or gain weight? If you want your athletes to maintain their weight, they need to eat enough calories to equal the calories they expend each day. If you want them to lose weight, they need to eat fewer calories. To gain weight, athletes need to eat more calories than they burn. This may sound simple, but it actually isn't.

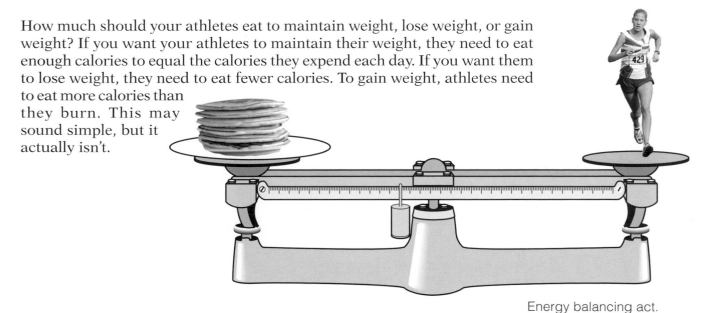

Energy balancing act.

Energy Balance

Energy balance (energy intake versus energy expenditure) is also determined by body composition—percent body fat and lean mass. Muscles use more energy to maintain themselves than fat does, and thus expend more energy even at resting rates.

Energy balance is also influenced by what happens when extra energy is stored as fat. For example, if you ate an extra 100-calorie chocolate chip cookie every night for 40 years, how much weight would you gain? Theoretically, you would add 1.5 million calories to your intake, and at 3,500 calories per pound of fat, you would gain an astounding 417 pounds (189 kilograms). But in reality, this doesn't happen. You would only gain about 6 pounds (2.7 kilograms) because the extra calories would lead to initial weight gain, but your larger body size would increase energy expenditure to balance the extra calories consumed. This works in reverse too. When people lose weight, they burn fewer calories because of the smaller body size, all other things being equal. This doesn't mean that you should take overeating lightly!

Energy balance is affected not just by the amount eaten, but also by the proportion of carbohydrates, fat, protein, and alcohol consumed and how these nutrients are burned as energy. Usually when we consume more carbohydrates, protein, and alcohol, the body increases the rate at which these nutrients are burned. Consequently these nutrients are not easily converted to body fat. Fat as a nutrient, however, doesn't work this way; it is easily converted to adipose tissue.

Here's more bad news about alcohol: The body burns the alcohol immediately after it is consumed until it is all cleared from the body. When the body is busy burning alcohol, it does not burn dietary fat, which is then stored as adipose tissue. Alcohol also suppresses the burning of carbohydrates and protein, but to a lesser degree.

To maintain weight and body composition, athletes must not only balance energy intake and output, but also eat carbohydrates, protein, and fat in the right proportions. That's achieved best through the athlete's diet described earlier.

Weight Loss

When athletes have too much body fat, they have to do more work to move the extra weight, which may impair performance. In aesthetic sports such as figure skating and diving, excess weight may bias judges adversely. Helping your athletes achieve ideal body weight is a desirable goal, but you need to proceed with some caution. In Western societies females' weight is a sensitive issue, and pressure from coaches to lose weight is one cause of eating disorders among female athletes. Also, in sports with weight categories, you should be careful not to encourage or allow athletes to "cut" weight too rapidly or go below the recommended ideal body weight guidelines given in chapter 14.

Athletes who want to lose weight have several options.

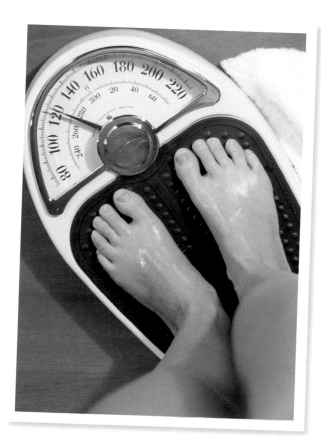

Changing eating habits is difficult. The person must cognitively want to make the change. Through education and positive encouragement, you can help athletes reach that cognitive state.

Weight Gain

Just as losing weight is beneficial for some athletes, gaining weight is beneficial for others. More mass, especially muscle mass, is beneficial (up to a point) for athletes such as football players and centers in basketball. But be careful not to promote too much weight gain too rapidly, especially if it creates undesirable long-term eating habits.

For most of us, gaining weight is much easier than losing it, but for some athletes who are growing rapidly and training intensely, maintaining and gaining weight can be a big challenge. Here are some guidelines for helping your athletes gain weight:

▶ Set realistic goals about gaining weight.

▶ Increase the total energy consumed. About 1 pound (.5 kilogram) per week, or 500 extra calories daily, is a good rate of increase.

▶ Eat the athlete's diet so the weight gain is not fat, but lean muscle mass.

▶ Incorporate resistance training.

▶ Use sport supplement drinks and bars between meals to increase intake.

▶ *Reduce the calories consumed.* There are 3,500 calories in a pound of body fat. If athletes cut the calories by 500 per day (say, from 3,000 to 2,500), they will lose 1 pound (about .5 kilogram) in seven days. Athletes should not try to lose more than 2 pounds (.9 kilogram) per week.

▶ *Increase the calories expended.* More physical activity is probably the easiest factor to control, but of course there is a commonsense limit here.

▶ *Eat the athlete's diet.* This lower-fat, higher-carbohydrate diet will provide more energy and decrease the storage of body fat.

▶ *Receive motivational support.* As a coach, you can encourage athletes to monitor their energy intake and output. Help them learn to control the triggers that lead them to eat when they're not truly hungry. Teach them to use positive reinforcement for progress they make. And provide them with positive reinforcement and support in their weight loss efforts.

When and What to Eat

When should athletes eat before competition or strenuous exercise, and what should they eat? Should they eat during endurance events? Does it make a difference when and what athletes eat after strenuous exercise? You'll find the answers to these questions in this section.

Pre-Event Eating

The goal in pre-event fueling is to eat enough carbohydrates that the muscles are fully loaded with glycogen and the body is well hydrated, but not so much as to cause any gastrointestinal distress. There isn't any one right way to eat before an event, but here are some helpful guidelines on what to eat and when.

What to Eat

▶ Eat the athlete's diet every day to fuel and refuel the muscles.

▶ If exercising for more than 60 to 90 minutes, choose carbohydrates with low to moderate glycemic ratings (these raise the blood sugar levels at a slower rate). Apples, yogurt, bananas, bean soup, and lentils are examples of such foods (see table 16.2 for others).

▶ Limit high-fat proteins such as cheese, steak, hamburgers, and peanut butter.

▶ Eat foods you are familiar with and that you digest easily.

▶ Use caution with foods that have a high glycemic rating. They may give you a sugar high followed by a sugar low. You should know how these foods affect you.

When to Eat

▶ Allow the following times for food to digest before being physically active:
—One hour for a small snack
—One to two hours for a blended or liquid meal
—Two to three hours for a small meal
—Three to four hours for a large meal

▶ Allow more digestion time before intense exercise than before low-level activity.

▶ If you tend to get nervous or highly aroused before competition and don't tolerate food well the day of a competitive event, don't eat. But eat well the day before with a bedtime snack.

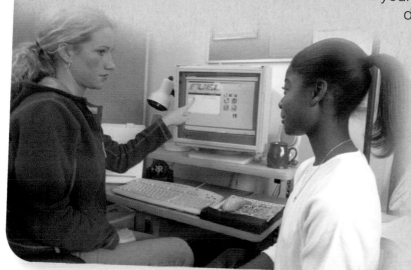

Nutritional Analysis

Helping your athletes with proper nutrition and weight management is an important part of your coaching job, but potentially could be very time consuming. It's not difficult to determine an athlete's energy intake and energy expenditure and to analyze the nutrients in the diet, but it takes time. That's why I highly recommend the use of software for this purpose. A good sport nutrition software package will help you determine the nutrients in your athletes' diets, estimate daily energy expenditure, and recommend dietary changes to meet their daily activities. More comprehensive programs will also provide recommendations on precompetition, competition, and postcompetition menus, taking into account the athletes' food preferences. See the To Learn More section for my software recommendation.

Eating During Endurance Events

For events lasting an hour, sport nutritionists recommend that athletes eat 100 to 300 calories of carbohydrates per hour of endurance exercise or .5 grams of carbohydrates per pound of body weight. For a 150-pound (68-kilogram) person that's 75 grams or 300 calories (4 calories per carbohydrate). Sport drinks and sport bars, juices, and watery foods such as melons and grapes are excellent fuels for these events.

Tournaments and Daylong Events

Many sports involve intermittent competitive events spread out over a day or several days. Nutrition is especially important during these events, and you should provide clear guidelines for your athletes on how to fuel themselves if you don't provide the food for the team. Many athletes just eat what's available, often from concession stands that offer hot dogs, chips covered with cheese, hamburgers, and candy bars. Some eat nothing between events.

The goal during these events is to eat to meet the energy demands of the sport, maintain good hydration, and keep blood sugar levels even. Sport drinks and bars, fruits of all types, and juices are good snacks between competitive events. If there is at least a couple of hours between events, an easily digested snack or light meal is recommended. To keep athletes from eating junk foods, have them bring healthy foods to the competition site.

Postevent Eating

After hard workouts and competitive events, the goal is to replace the lost glycogen in the muscles and to rehydrate in preparation for the next event or workout. Glycogen is replaced at the rate of 5 percent per hour; thus 20 hours are required to fully replenish the muscles when they are completely depleted. However, if athletes begin eating within 15 to 20 minutes after strenuous exercise, when enzymes responsible for making glycogen are most active, depleted glycogen will be replaced at a 7 to 8 percent rate. Therefore, athletes should eat .5 grams of complex carbohydrates per pound of body weight every two hours for six to eight hours, beginning 15 to 20 minutes after strenuous exercise.

Eating Disorders

She was a superb cross-country skier, ideally built for the sport, and a member of the U.S. Olympic cross-country ski team when I met her. On my first trip with the team as its sport psychologist, Angela Snyder confided in me her perception of being fat and her vicious cycle of dieting to the point of starvation, then bingeing, followed by feeling guilt and shame, then purging followed by feeling relief, and dieting again. Angela had anorexia nervosa and bulimia nervosa, both serious eating disorders.

Anorexia is characterized by

▶ a refusal to maintain a normal weight for one's age and height,

▶ a distorted body image,

▶ an intense fear of gaining weight or becoming fat, and

▶ amenorrhea (lack of menstrual periods) in women.

Bulimia is characterized by

▶ an uncontrollable desire to overeat or binge on food;

▶ feeling a loss of control about eating; and

▶ purging food by inducing vomiting or using laxatives, enemas, diuretics, or even excessive exercise.

Eating disorders are 10 times more common among females than males, and they are more prevalent among athletes in aesthetic and weight-dependent and endurance sports, but they can occur among athletes in any sport. The causes of eating disorders are complex and rooted in negative perceptions about body image associated with low self-esteem. Five factors are known to increase the risk of eating disorders among athletes:

1. Dieting at an early age or attempting to make a certain weight class

2. Personal attributes of perfectionism, high self-expectations, and tenaciousness

3. A traumatic experience with a weigh-in or unfavorable comments from coaches, peers, or family members

4. Stressful events such as an injury or loss of a revered coach

5. Extreme pressure from coaches to make weight or look thin

Of course you do not want to contribute to an athlete developing an eating disorder; instead, you want to be able to recognize the signs of these disorders and help your athletes deal with these abnormal behaviors. The following are some signals to look for in your athletes.

- Weight loss to the point of being 10 to 15 percent below ideal body weight
- Lack of energy in practices and contests that is reflected in a decline in performance
- Expressing perceptions of being fat when that is not the case
- Sudden increase in training volume
- Avoiding eating with others

If you suspect that one of your athletes has an eating disorder, you'll need professional help to address the problem. A physician, clinical psychologist or psychiatrist, or nutrition therapist who specializes in eating disorders should be consulted. In the meantime, what can you do? Here's what the Anorexia Nervosa and Related Eating Disorders, Inc., recommends:

- When you suspect one of your athletes has an eating disorder, arrange a private meeting with the athlete.
- Express support for the athlete and concern for the athlete's best interests. Stress that health and happiness transcend the athletic arena. Be empathic and caring.
- In an objective, nonpunitive way list what you have seen and what you have heard that have led you to be concerned.

Let the athlete respond fully. Expect denial and rationalization.

- Emphasize that the athlete's place on the team will not be endangered by an admission that the athlete has an eating disorder *unless* the eating disorder has compromised the person's health or put the athlete at risk of injury.
- If the athlete admits having an eating disorder, try to determine if the athlete can voluntarily abstain from the behaviors.
- If, in the face of compelling evidence, the athlete refuses to admit that a problem exists, or if it seems that the problem has been long-standing and cannot be corrected readily, consult a clinician with expertise in treating eating disorders.
- Remember that most athletes with eating disorders have tried repeatedly, and failed, to correct the problem on their own. Failure is especially demoralizing to athletes who are always oriented toward success.
- Let the person know that eating disorders are treatable, and people do recover from them. Almost always, though, professional help is necessary. Needing help should not be regarded as a sign of weakness, inadequacy, or lack of effort.
- Arrange for regular, private follow-up meetings apart from practice times.
- If the athlete is working with a physician or counselor, ask for permission to ask that resource person how best you can help. Then do it.
- Remember that many athletes who develop eating disorders have been told that they need to lose weight. Realize that past or present coaches or trainers may have contributed to the eating disorder. Let the athlete know that you know the demands of the sport may have played a role in the development of the problem.

Here are some things you should not do:

▶ Don't question teammates or talk to them about the athlete. Talk directly to the athlete.

▶ Don't hope the problem will go away if you ignore it. It won't. If you have evidence that a problem exists, intervene.

▶ Don't tell the athlete that you know there is a problem without giving the athlete your reasons and evidence. The athlete will only become defensive.

▶ Don't tell the athlete to straighten up. Don't threaten to keep checking on the athlete. The athlete will experience increased stress, which will only make the eating disorder worse.

▶ Don't conclude that if the athlete really wanted to stop the behaviors, she or he would. Don't make the mistake of believing that failure to improve shows a lack of effort. Even the fastest of recoveries, facilitated by mental health professionals, take several months to years to achieve.

▶ Don't refuse to admit that you, and the demands of the sport, may have contributed to the eating disorder.

▶ Don't try to keep the problem hidden by attempting to deal with it yourself when professional intervention and treatment are clearly appropriate.

▶ Don't nag, bribe, threaten, or manipulate. These tactics don't work; they only make matters worse.

▶ Don't try to rescue the athletes from the eating disorder single-handedly. Anorexia nervosa and bulimia are complex medical and psychological challenges. Unless you are a physician or mental health clinician, you do not have the training or skills to provide the treatment that is needed. Help the person connect with appropriate professionals.

Lists on pages 383 and 384 from pg. 83, with permission from Rosen, McKeag, Hough, et al, 1986.

Coaching Yourself:
Eating Healthfully

In this chapter you've learned how to coach your athletes about proper nutrition and weight management. But are you eating right and controlling your weight, or do you also need to coach yourself? In our fast-food world it's easy to slip into poor eating habits—eating meals on the run, nibbling between meals, and consuming junk food with empty calories. If you're not exercising (see sidebar, page 286 in chapter 13) and finding your life full of stress (see sidebar, page 138 in chapter 7), you also may be gaining undesirable fat weight.

Some coaches lament that when their athletic careers ended and they became coaches, they continued eating the way they did when they were athletes, consuming 4,000 calories a day. Now as coaches they are burning only 2,500 calories a day. At the rate of 1,500 extra calories a day, they would gain about 3 pounds (1.4 kilograms) of fat a week. Notice how many ex-professional athletes balloon in weight one to two years after they retire. They failed to reduce the calories consumed when they markedly decreased the calories burned.

Eating right is not only about balancing the energy you're consuming with the energy you're burning so that you don't gain weight; it's also about eating foods that are good for your body. A healthy diet for you is the same diet I've described in this chapter for your athletes.

Take some time now to look at your eating and weight. How well do you follow the seven rules for eating right on page 364? Are you happy with your weight? Are you a good role model for healthy eating and weight control for your athletes and your community of supporters? If the answer is no to any of these questions, then now is the best time to start making changes. Take that discipline you learned when training for your sport and apply it to training for healthy living by eating right.

Questions for Reflection

▶ What can you do to help your athletes improve their nutritional knowledge and habits? **(p. 358)**

▶ What are the six basic nutrients, and what are their roles in the body? **(p. 359)**

▶ Are you aware of the recommendations for a healthy diet? Do your athletes understand the Food Guide Pyramid and how to translate it into a healthy diet for themselves? **(p. 360)**

▶ What are the seven rules for eating right? **(p. 364)**

▶ What percentage of your athletes' diets should come from carbohydrates, protein, and fat? **(p. 364)**

▶ What advice can you give your athletes about nutritional supplements? **(p. 368)**

▶ What can you do to prevent dehydration in your athletes? **(p. 376)**

▶ Are your athletes aware of how many calories they need to maintain an ideal body weight? **(p. 378)**

▶ Do you instruct your athletes how to eat before, during, and following competitions? Software can help you keep track of your athletes' weight and nutrition. **(p. 380)**

▶ What are the signs of eating disorders? Do you have a plan for addressing this issue if it arises? **(p. 382)**

▶ Are you a good role model of healthy eating for your athletes and your community? **(p. 385)**

References

Armstrong, Lawrence E. 2000. *Performing in extreme environments*. Champaign, IL: Human Kinetics.

Foster-Powell, K., and J. Brand Miller. 1995. International tables of glycemic index. *American Journal of Clinical Nutrition* 62:871S-893S.

National Collegiate Athletic Association. June 2002. NCAA Guideline 2J. Nutritional Ergogenic Aids, p. 43. Indianapolis: NCAA.

Rosen, Lionel, Douglas McKeag, David Hough, and Victoria Curley. 1986. "Pathogenic weight-control behavior in female athletes." *The Physician and Sportsmedicine* (14):79-86.

To Learn More

Benardot, Dan. 2000. *Nutrition for serious athletes*. Champaign, IL: Human Kinetics.

Clark, Nancy. 2003. *Nancy Clark's sports nutrition guidebook*. 3rd ed. Champaign, IL: Human Kinetics.

Eberle, Suzanne G. 2000. *Endurance sports nutrition*. Champaign, IL: Human Kinetics.

Fuel Standard Version Software. 2002. Champaign, IL: Human Kinetics.

Kleiner, Susan M. 2001. *Power eating*. 2nd ed. Champaign, IL: Human Kinetics.

Williams, Melvin H. 1998. *The ergogenics edge: Pushing the limits of sports performance*. Champaign, IL: Human Kinetics.

Williams, Melvin H., Richard B. Kreider, and J. David Branch. 1999. *Creatine: The power supplement*. Champaign, IL: Human Kinetics.

Anorexia Nervosa and Related Eating Disorders (ANRED) Web site: www.anred.com. An excellent source for a more in-depth discussion of eating disorders.

17

Battling Drugs

Janis Meyer was a promising golfer on Shayna Pyrtel's high school golf team until the accident. Coach Pyrtel had being hearing rumors that Janis was drinking a lot, and by making a few inquiries learned that Janis's mother was an alcoholic and her father a traveling salesman. Janis had missed several practices, her performance was lackluster, and her interest and commitment to golf were in remission. Coach Pyrtel was contemplating talking with Janis about what she was observing but was reluctant to confront her. Then she received the report that Janis had been in an auto accident. Driving intoxicated, Janis had run a red light and smashed into a car, killing an elderly woman. Janis survived, but she will live the rest of her life in a wheelchair.

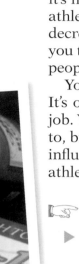

et's face it. Alcohol and drugs are everywhere and are a huge problem in our society, especially among young people—the people you coach. You may be tempted to ignore the problem of substance abuse, to pretend it's not there. After all, who wants to be a cop policing the behavior of their athletes? Or you may decide to deal with the alcohol and drug problem by decree: Athletes who consume alcohol or drugs will be cut from the team. If you take either of these approaches, you abdicate your role of helping young people become responsible adults.

You need to be prepared to address the issue of substance abuse in sport. It's one of the many responsibilities that come with this most challenging job. You can't solve this problem alone of course, nor does anyone expect you to, but you can be part of the solution. Because you are in the powerful and influential position of coach, you just may be in the best position to help an athlete on your team who has a drug or alcohol problem.

☞ **In this chapter you'll learn what you realistically can do.**

▶ You can become sufficiently knowledgeable about drugs so that you are in a position to help.

▶ You can develop and enforce a drug-free participation policy.

▶ You can and should provide your players with preventive education about substance abuse.

▶ You can learn to detect the signs of substance abuse among your athletes.

▶ You can counsel your athletes and, when necessary, help them obtain professional help.

Drugs 101

In this chapter our focus will be on tobacco, alcohol, and illegal drug use. Rather than always saying "tobacco, alcohol, and drugs," I'll often use the term *drugs* to refer to all three substances, although technically alcohol is not a drug.

Drugs You Should Know About

As a coach you need to be concerned about the use of drugs that violate not only the law, but also the rules of sport and the ethics of fair play—what is commonly called "doping" in sport. You also need to be concerned about the use of drugs that are illegal for everyone, as well as those that are legal for adults but illegal for minors (tobacco and alcohol). In addition, you must address not only the immediate effects of drugs on your athletes' behaviors, but also the long-term health consequences. Although "performance-enhancing" drugs are intended to do just that—improve the performance of your athletes—illicit drugs almost always impair performance. Both performance-enhancing and illicit drugs may also impair athletes' ability to learn in school and increase their chances of engaging in risky behaviors such as driving under the influence of alcohol, having unsafe sex, and committing crimes to obtain money to purchase drugs.

It's helpful to know as much as you can about the drugs that your athletes may use. Figure 17.1 lists some facts about alcohol, tobacco, and common drugs found on the street, or what are called illicit drugs. Figure 17.2, on page 393 contains information about performance-enhancing drugs that are banned by most major sport governing bodies.

Figure 17.1

Illicit Drugs

Alcohol

Product names: Beer, gin, vodka, bourbon, whiskey, tequila, liqueurs, wine, brandy, champagne, rum, sherry, port, coolers

Street names: Booze, sauce, brews, brewskis, hard stuff, juice

Symptoms of use: Impaired judgment and motor skills, slurred speech, loss of coordination, confusion, tremors, drowsiness, agitation, nausea and vomiting, respiratory ailments, depression

Potential consequences: Impaired judgment can result in inappropriate sexual behavior, sexually transmitted diseases, injuries, and auto accidents. Habitual use can lead to alcoholism, blackouts and memory loss, interference with personal relationships, cirrhosis of the liver, vitamin deficiencies, damage to the heart and central nervous system, sexual impotence, weight gain.

Legal status: Legal drinking age in all states is currently 21.

Cannabis (marijuana)

Product names: Delta-9-tetrahydrocannabinol, cannabis sativa, marijuana, hashish, hashish oil

Street names: Weed, pot, grass, reefer, Mary Jane, joint, roach, nail, blunt

Symptoms of use: Mood swings, euphoria, slow thinking and reflexes, dilated pupils, increased appetite, dryness of mouth, increased pulse rate, delusions, hallucinations

Potential consequences: Lack of motivation, memory impairment, weight gain, increased risk for cancer, lower sperm counts and lower testosterone levels for men, increased risk of infertility for women, psychological dependence requiring more of the drug to get the same effect. Marijuana serves as a barrier against self-awareness, and users may not be able to learn key developmental skills.

Legal status: Illegal

continued ☞

Figure 17.1 *(continued)*

Cocaine

Product names: Cocaine, crack cocaine

Street names: Cocaine—coke, snow, blow, toot, nose candy, flake, dust, sneeze. Crack cocaine—crack, rock, base, sugar block, Rox/Roxanne.

Symptoms of use: Excitability, euphoria, talkativeness, anxiety, increased pulse rate, dilated pupils, paranoia, agitation, hallucinations

Potential consequences: High risk for addiction, violent or erratic behavior, hallucinations, cocaine psychosis, eating or sleeping disorders, impaired sexual performance, ongoing respiratory problems, ulceration of the mucous membrane of the nose, collapse of the nasal septum, death from cardiac or respiratory arrest

Legal status: Illegal

Depressants

Product names: Sleeping pills and tranquilizers (Seconal, Nembutal, Smytal, Quaalude, Miltown, Norcet, Placidyl, Valium, Librium, Tauxene, Ativan, Xanax, Serax)

Street names: Downers, ludes, blues, goofball, red devil, blue devil, yellow jackets, yellow bullets, pink ladies, Christmas trees, phennies, peanuts

Symptoms of use: Drowsiness, confusion, loss of coordination, tremors, slurred speech, depressed pulse rate, shallow respiration, dilated pupils

Potential consequences: Anxiety, depression, restlessness, psychotic episodes, chronic fatigue, insomnia, changes in eyesight, irregular menstruation, stopped breathing, suicide, dependence requiring more of the drug to get the same effect, severe withdrawal symptoms

Legal status: Prescription only

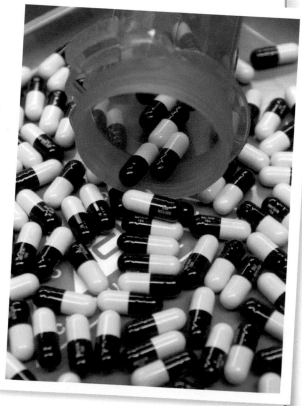

Hallucinogens

Product names: LSD (lysergic acid diethylamide), PCP (phencyclidine), DMT (dimethyltryptamine), mescaline, MDA (methylenedioxyamphetamine), STP (dimethoxymethamphetamine), psilocybin, Rohypnol, GHB (gammahydroxybutyric acid), MDMA (methylenedioxymethamphetamine)

Street names: LSD—A, acid, blotter, microdots, windowpane. PCP—angel dust, angel mist, animal tranquilizer. Psilocybin—mushrooms, magic mushrooms, shrooms. MDMA—ecstasy, E, X, XTC. Rohypnol—R-2, roofies, roaches, "the date rape drug." GHB—liquid ecstasy, liquid X, Georgia home brew, Georgia home boyz.

Symptoms of use: Trancelike state, excitation, euphoria, increased pulse rate, insomnia

Potential consequences: Impaired judgment and coordination can result in greater risk for injury, self-inflicted injury, violent behavior, paranoia, depression or anxiety, unpredictable flashbacks.

Legal status: Illegal

Inhalants

Product names: Organic solvents, nitrous oxide, nitrites, aerosols, airplane glue, nail polish remover, lighter fluid, gasoline, paints, hair spray

Street names: Glue, kick, bang, sniff, huff, poppers, whippets, Texas shoeshine

Symptoms of use: Slurred speech, loss of coordination, nausea, vomiting, slowed breathing

Potential consequences: Brain damage; pains in chest, muscles, and joints; heart trouble; severe depression; toxic psychosis; nerve damage; fatigue; loss of appetite; bronchial tube spasm; sores on nose or mouth; nosebleeds; diarrhea; nausea; bizarre or reckless behavior; sudden death; suffocation

Legal status: Most products available in retail stores

continued ☞

Figure 17.1 *(continued)*

Narcotics

Product names: Heroin, morphine, codeine, Dilaudid, Demerol, Percodan, Methadone, Talwin

Street names: Heroin—smack, junk, horse, H, tar. Morphine—mojo, mud, Mary, Murphy, M, Miss Emma, Mister Black. Codeine—schoolboy, Cody, Captain Cody. Methadone—dollies, fizzies.

Symptoms of use: Lethargy, drowsiness, euphoria, nausea, constipation, constricted pupils, slowed breathing

BLACK TAR HEROIN

Potential consequences: HIV infection, heart or respiratory problems, mood swings, chronic constipation, tremors, toxic psychosis, high potential for addiction

Legal status: Illegal except by prescription

Tobacco

Product names: Smoking forms—cigarettes, cigars, and pipes. Smokeless forms—chewing tobacco and dipping snuff.

Symptoms of use: Loss of smell, coughing, bad breath, dulled taste, stimulant to the brain and depressant to respiratory system, change in moods, increased pulse and blood pressure

Potential consequences: Highly addictive; decreases life expectancy; major cause of various cancers, coronary artery disease, and stroke. Also increases likelihood of erectile dysfunction, infertility in men and women, and osteoporosis. Primary cause of emphysema, an irreversible and usually deadly lung disease.

Legal status: Illegal for minors; legal for adults. Age when a person is an adult varies from state to state (usually 18 to 21 years of age).

Figure 17.2

Performance-Enhancing Drugs
Banned by IOC, NCAA, and USOC

Anabolic Agents

Examples of anabolic agents used by athletes: Anabolic steroids, androstenedione, dehydroepiandrosterone (DHEA), stanozolol, and testosterone

Potential performance effects: Increased muscular size, strength, power, and endurance

Potential health consequences: Acne, baldness, premature growth plate closure in adolescents, masculinization of females, testicular atrophy, reduced sperm production, altered cholesterol levels, increased blood pressure, liver dysfunction, increased aggressiveness and violence, HIV infection

Legal status: Illegal except by prescription

Diuretics

Examples of diuretics used by athletes: Furosemide, chlorothiazide, acetazolamide, and triamterene

Potential performance effects: Weight loss and masking of other unauthorized drug use

Potential health consequences: Dehydration, muscle weakness and cramping, irregular heartbeats

Legal status: Legal with prescription

Peptide Hormones

Examples of peptide hormones used by athletes: Human growth hormone (HGH, somatotrophin), corticotrophin, and erythropoietin (EPO)

Potential performance effects: Growth hormone—increased muscle mass and decreased body fat resulting in improved strength, power, and appearance. Corticotrophin—mobilized energy stores, elevated blood sugar levels, and anti-inflammatory effect. Erythropoietin—increased aerobic power and endurance.

Potential health consequences: Growth hormone—acromegaly. Corticotrophin—muscle tissue, tendon, and ligament atrophy. Erythropoietin—increased hematocrit, blood viscosity, and blood pressure.

Legal status: Legal with prescription

Stimulants

Examples of stimulants used by athletes: Amphetamine, caffeine, and cocaine

Potential performance effects: Increased mental alertness and energy output, weight loss

Potential health consequences: Increased anxiety, nervousness, and tension; irregular heartbeats; weight loss; death

Legal status: Illegal except by prescription—amphetamine, cocaine. Legal—caffeine. Caffeine is illegal if the concentration in the urine exceeds 12 micrograms per milliliter, which is more than three cups of black coffee.

You can obtain a current and complete list of banned substances from the following organizations by going to the Web site addresses provided:

▶ The United States Olympic Committee created the United States Anti Doping Agency, which publishes the *Guide to Prohibited Classes of Substances and Prohibited Methods of Doping*. The guide is free by downloading it at www.usantidoping.org/files/USADA_ Guide.pdf.

▶ The National Collegiate Athletic Association's list of banned drugs is located at www.ncaa.org/sports_ sciences/drugtesting/banned_list.html.

▶ The International Olympic Committee's list of banned drugs is found on page 16 at http://multimedia.olympic.org/pdf/ en_report_21.pdf.

Use of Drugs

In figures 17.3, 17.4, and 17.5, you'll find the percent of the U.S. population 12 years and older that reported using alcohol, tobacco, and illicit drugs, respectively, in the past month, as well as the percent of 12- to 17-year-olds who reported using these substances in the past month.

Because alcohol and tobacco are legal for people of majority age, but not minors, they are readily available to consumers and easily obtained by minors. Thus it is not surprising that alcohol is the most widely used and misused drug from 8th graders through college students. As shown in figure 17.3, 20.5 percent of 12- to 17-year-olds reported using alcohol in the past month, 8 percent reported binge drinking (five or more drinks at one occasion), and 3 percent reported being heavy or daily drinkers. Stainback (1997) reported that 51 percent of high school seniors drank alcohol in the past 30 days, and 28 percent were heavy drinkers.

Tobacco use is the second most common substance used by 12- to 17-year-olds. As seen in figure 17.4, among this age group 15.1 percent use some form of tobacco products, predominantly cigarettes. Because professional athletes often use smokeless tobacco, the use of chewing tobacco and snuff has increased 15-fold among 17- to 19-year-olds in the last 20 years.

Alcohol in Moderation

Alcohol is similar to tobacco in that it is legal for adults, but it is very different in other ways. Alcohol does not have the negative health effects that tobacco has when used in moderation. In fact, more and more studies are finding that drinking one or two alcoholic beverages a day may even have positive health consequences. The problem with alcohol is that it can be difficult to consume moderately and responsibly. Just as you teach your athletes to be disciplined in their training and play, you can help teach your athletes that they should use alcohol only when they are of legal age and then with discipline.

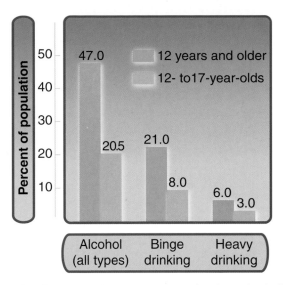

Figure 17.3 Percent of U.S. population that reported using alcohol in the past 30 days.

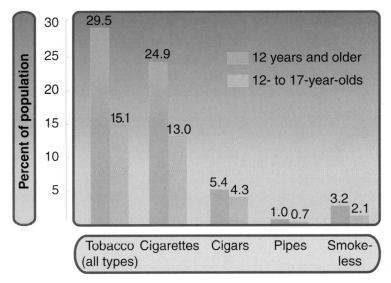

Figure 17.4 Percent of U.S. population that reported using tobacco products in the past 30 days.

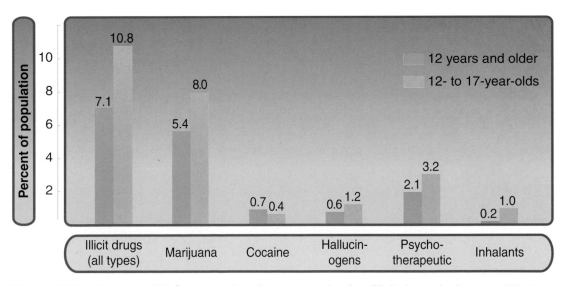

Figure 17.5 Percent of U.S. population that reported using illicit drugs in the past 30 days.

Why Would Anyone Smoke?

Smokers compared with nonsmokers are 16 times more likely to get emphysema, 15 times more likely to get cancer, 10 times more likely to get bronchitis, and two times more likely to have heart attacks. Get this: Experts estimate that cigarette smokers lose 15 minutes of life expectancy for every cigarette they smoke.

Recently a series of reports showed the danger of using ephedra, a diet supplement. After a professional baseball player died and a few hundred people reported other serious health consequences, a huge outcry was heard to ban the supplement, and a federal law was passed doing so. Yet an estimated one thousand Americans die each day from tobacco use, and our lawmakers don't consider banning tobacco.

Smokeless tobacco is not a safe alternative, contrary to what 60 percent of high school students think; it can lead to nicotine addiction and increases the chance of getting oral cancer by a whopping 400 percent. Some athletes believe that smokeless tobacco will give them a competitive edge, but there is no evidence to support that view. So know this, Coach—tobacco kills.

Many sources indicate that athletes in the 12- to 17-year-old age group appear to use alcohol, tobacco, and illicit drugs at about the same rate that their nonathletic peers do. Thus, the notion that sports help prevent drug abuse unfortunately doesn't hold up well.

The prevalence of performance-enhancing drugs is not well known, although many have speculated on it. The exception is anabolic steroids. From several studies (see Yesalis 2000), usage among high school students is reported to be from 7 to 12 percent. It's speculated to be somewhat higher in collegiate sports, and much higher in professional sports. It's also speculated to be much higher in sports in which strength and power are critical to success.

Gateway Drugs

How concerned should we be about young people using alcohol and tobacco? Soon enough they will be adults and can consume these substances legally. *Be concerned!* Alcohol and tobacco, along with marijuana, are known as "gateway" drugs—meaning that they are drugs young people use that can lead to the use of illicit drugs. Consider these statistics for 12- to 17-year-olds:

► Those who smoke cigarettes are over 9 times more likely to use illicit drugs and over 15 times more likely to drink heavily than nonsmoking youth.

► Those who use marijuana weekly are nine times more likely than nonusers to experiment with illicit drugs or alcohol, six times more likely to run away from home, five times more likely to steal, four times more likely to be violent, and three times more likely to have thoughts of committing suicide.

► The younger people are when they start smoking, the more likely they will be to smoke throughout their lives. The longer they smoke, the greater the risk of serious health problems (see the sidebar on page 396).

Why Athletes Use and Do Not Use Drugs

Athletes use performance-enhancing drugs for obvious reasons—to perform better, to look better, and to hasten recovery from strenuous workouts. They seek to gain a competitive advantage—unfairly—and convince themselves that doing so is OK because "everyone else is doing it and I'll be at a disadvantage if I don't." Athletes choose not to use performance-enhancing drugs primarily because they believe it is cheating, and they are concerned about the long-term effects on their health.

Athletes choose to use or not use illicit drugs for the same reasons nonathletes do. This can be illustrated as a tug-of-war, with reasons for using drugs on the left side and reasons not to use drugs on the right side.

Reasons Athletes Use Drugs

They derive pleasure from them.
They enjoy the thrill of taking a risk.
They are curious about the effects of drugs others are talking about.
They want to be part of their peer group.
They believe drugs help them cope with stress.
They want to escape their problems.

Reasons Athletes Do Not Use Drugs

Their parents will object.
Drugs may harm their sport performance.
They fear being out of control.
They do not like the effects of drugs.
They are concerned about the effect on their health.
They hold strong moral or religious beliefs against using drugs.

We've reviewed some basic information about drugs and their use. You can learn more by checking out the references in the To Learn More section at the end of this chapter. Now let's see how you can help prevent drug use and abuse among your athletes and those young people they influence.

Your Role in Prevention

The drug problem is too big a fight for you to take on alone. It's a societal problem that must be addressed by parents, educators, religious leaders, community health workers, law enforcement officers—and you. See yourself as part of a team helping youth fight this insidious malady.

There's no simple solution to this complex problem, but there are some realistic and useful things you can do to reduce the likelihood of your athletes becoming substance abusers. These are shown in the Wall of Drug Prevention.

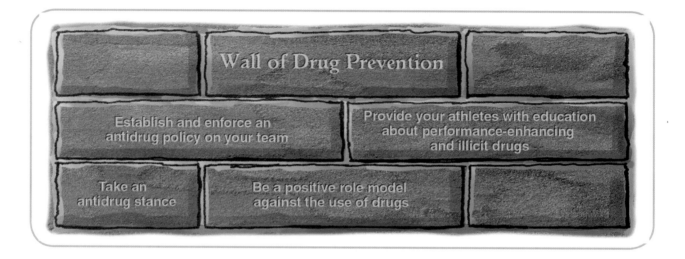

Wall of Drug Prevention

Establish and enforce an antidrug policy on your team

Provide your athletes with education about performance-enhancing and illicit drugs

Take an antidrug stance

Be a positive role model against the use of drugs

Let's consider each of these four steps more closely now.

Take an Antidrug Stance

If you have credibility with your athletes, you can be exceptionally influential in discouraging them from using drugs. You can be a powerful role model, a paragon of virtue—well, maybe that's going too far—but you can be influential. That influence is seeded in your attitude about drugs. Take a moment now to examine your position about drugs in sport by completing the following survey.

Coach's Attitude Toward Drugs Survey

Circle the response that best represents your attitude about each issue with regard to athletes' use of alcohol, tobacco, and illicit drugs in sport.

1. Athletes' use of illicit drugs at any time

1	2	3	4	5
Not opposed		**Opposed**		**Strongly opposed**

2. Athletes receiving special consideration from coaches, administrators, and law enforcement officers if caught using illicit or performance-enhancing drugs

1	2	3	4	5
Not opposed		**Opposed**		**Strongly opposed**

3. Athletes' use of drugs that are banned by a regulating sport governing body

1	2	3	4	5
Not opposed		**Opposed**		**Strongly opposed**

4. Athletes' use of these banned substances even when participating in competitive events in which no rules against the use of these drugs exist

1	2	3	4	5
Not opposed		**Opposed**		**Strongly opposed**

5. Use of tobacco when an athlete is a minor

1	2	3	4	5
Not opposed		**Opposed**		**Strongly opposed**

6. Use of tobacco when an athlete is an adult

1	2	3	4	5
Not opposed		**Opposed**		**Strongly opposed**

7. Allowing the use of tobacco and alcohol by adults at sport events in which minors are participating

1	2	3	4	5
Not opposed		**Opposed**		**Strongly opposed**

8. Use of alcohol when an athlete is a minor

1	2	3	4	5
Not opposed		**Opposed**		**Strongly opposed**

9. Use of alcohol when an athlete is an adult

1	2	3	4	5
Not opposed		**Opposed**		**Strongly opposed**

Think about your position. Are you strongly opposed to drug use by your athletes, or are you less concerned as long as it doesn't interfere with your athletes playing the sport? Let's move beyond your attitudes about drug use to your actions. Are you silent on the use of drugs with your athletes, or are you willing to speak out against them? Do you condone or even actively encourage the use of performance-enhancing drugs? Are you hypocritical by being opposed to your athletes using drugs but then use one or more forms yourself?

We know that when authority figures—parents, coaches, and teachers—take a firm position against drugs, they influence young people positively. We also know that when these same adults are not hypocritical and avoid using these substances themselves, the message is even more powerful.

Be a Role Model

Your actions speak volumes to your athletes. By modeling healthy behaviors, you help athletes see that life can be full and productive without the use of tobacco and illicit drugs, and by using alcohol responsibly. Coaches with high expectations for their athletes are more likely to have athletes who meet those expectations.

Establish and Enforce Rules

You'll recall that we discussed sportsmanship and moral behavior in chapter 4, and guidelines for developing and enforcing rules in chapter 8. We now apply that information to the use of drugs in sport. Although establishing and enforcing rules regarding drug use is not *the* solution to preventing drug use, it is part of the solution.

Recommended Coach's Position on Athlete Drug Use

If you are unsure about your position on athletes' use of drugs, consider ASEP's position:

▶ Athletes should not use illicit drugs. Not only are they illegal, but they are also dangerous to your athletes' health. Moreover, illicit drugs don't solve problems. They create problems.

▶ Athletes should not use tobacco. It's very harmful to their health, is highly addictive, and is a gateway to using illicit drugs.

▶ Athletes should not use alcohol when under age, and when of legal age, they should use alcohol in moderation and responsibly.

▶ Athletes should not use performance-enhancing drugs that are banned by the IOC, NCAA, or USOC because it is cheating and is likely to be harmful to their health. Even if these drugs are not banned by your sport governing body, athletes should not use them. Help your athletes improve their performance through safe and fair training methods.

American Sport Education Program

Coaching Yourself:
Substance Abuse

Let's talk straight about your use of tobacco, alcohol, and illicit drugs. Without regard to your role as a coach, the use of tobacco, the excessive use of alcohol, and the use of illicit drugs are dangerous to your health, and when you are under the influence of alcohol and drugs, you may be dangerous to others. Surely you know this by now. The bottom line is that if you have a substance abuse problem, you need to seek professional help before becoming a coach.

When you become a coach, the expectations and standards for your behavior with regard to drugs are high. Many sport organizations have policies about your use of tobacco, alcohol, and illicit drugs. You should know what they are and abide by them. If your organization doesn't have a policy, I urge you to follow these guidelines:

▶ If you use illicit drugs, you must stop if you are going to coach. If you can't stop, stop coaching and seek help.

▶ Although it is legal for you to use tobacco products, I urge you to quit for your own health and so you'll be a better role model for your athletes. If you choose not to quit, don't smoke in the presence of your athletes. Even if you don't smoke in their presence, they'll know you're a smoker. When you discuss tobacco with them, admit that you use. Explain how addictive nicotine is and let them know that when you started you thought you could stop easily, but you've found that's not the case. Encourage your athletes not to do as you do!

▶ If you use alcohol, drink in moderation and avoid drinking in front of your athletes. Government guidelines recommend not more than one drink for women and two drinks for men per day. (Is this discrimination against or in favor of women?) When you discuss alcohol with your athletes, clarify the line between use and misuse. If you have an alcohol problem, do not coach and seek help.

If you've used drugs in the past, should you tell your athletes? That's a tough decision to make. You need to decide if telling them would be instructive and help prevent them from using or if it would send a message that it's OK to try it and then later quit.

Drug Testing

It's easy to create rules against the use of drugs in sport, and it's not difficult to establish penalties for breaking these rules (see Team Policy for Drug Use, page 403). What can be very difficult is detecting the use of both illicit and performance-enhancing drugs and having sufficient evidence to invoke penalties. Thus, to ensure that their sport programs are drug free, many national and international sport governing bodies have turned to drug testing.

Testing adolescent athletes for drugs is controversial. In many sport organizations the decision to test is not the coach's, but that of the school, state, or governing body for that sport. Nevertheless, you may be a part of the decision-making team that is considering a drug testing program.

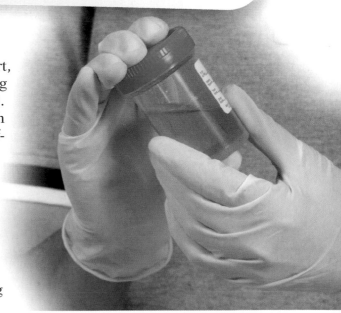

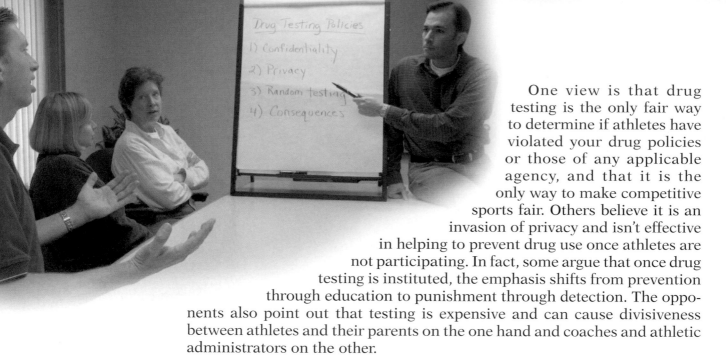

One view is that drug testing is the only fair way to determine if athletes have violated your drug policies or those of any applicable agency, and that it is the only way to make competitive sports fair. Others believe it is an invasion of privacy and isn't effective in helping to prevent drug use once athletes are not participating. In fact, some argue that once drug testing is instituted, the emphasis shifts from prevention through education to punishment through detection. The opponents also point out that testing is expensive and can cause divisiveness between athletes and their parents on the one hand and coaches and athletic administrators on the other.

Many national and international sport governing bodies have mandatory and random drug testing. Drug testing is mandatory at the collegiate level, but currently is not mandated by any state high school activity association, and only a small percent of the high schools have mandatory testing programs. The National Federation of State High School Associations takes no position on drug testing. Prior to 1995 schools were fearful of testing, but the 1995 U.S. Supreme Court ruling in the case of *Vernonia School District 47 v. Acton* (515 U.S. 646, 1995) declared that drug testing of athletes was legal and reasonable.

The decision to test athletes for drugs is a difficult one, but when weighing the pros and cons, I recommend testing. To have drug-free sports, we need effective enforcement, and testing is the only way to achieve that. I believe most athletes are willing to give up privacy to make competitive sports fair, and when they know the playing field is fair through random drug testing, they won't feel forced to use drugs to even the playing field. School administrators who have implemented drug testing consistently report that it is an effective deterrent to drug use and gives athletes a reason to say no when pressured to use drugs. Drug testing and enforcement, however, must be done uniformly and fairly, and should be supported with strong educational and counseling programs. (See the To Learn More section for additional information on this subject.)

Drug Policy

You may coach within an organization that has rules regarding drug use by athletes. If such rules exist, obviously you'll want to abide by them, but you may want to augment these rules with your own team policies. Consider the sample team policy that follows on the next page. Adopt it or modify it to meet your needs.

Drug education experts recommend that you do the following:

▶ Discuss your policies and expectations with your team in advance.

▶ When the policies are violated, administer the consequences fairly and consistently.

▶ Praise your athletes when they follow the policies, especially when you know they have made a deliberate choice to do so.

Team Policy for Drug Use

To make participation on [your team name] a safe, positive, and healthy experience, your coaches will enforce the following team policy with regard to the use of alcohol, tobacco, illicit drugs, and performance-enhancing drugs.

1. All members of the team are prohibited from using, purchasing, possessing, manufacturing, or selling any

   a. illicit drugs;

   b. performance-enhancing drugs banned by the International Olympic Committee, United States Olympic Committee, or National Collegiate Athletic Association; or

   c. any drugs banned by [insert the name of any sport governing body regulating competition in your sport].

2. All members of the team are prohibited from using alcohol and tobacco at any team facility or function. This includes locker rooms, practice and contest facilities, meeting rooms, eating facilities, and transportation vehicles. It also includes not only competitive events, but also team meetings, awards banquets, and official team events.

3. Athletes of minority age are not permitted to use alcohol and tobacco products at any time because they are illegal.

4. Athletes of majority age are not denied the right to smoke when not participating in a team event because it is legal to do so, but they are highly encouraged not to smoke because of the negative consequences to their health.

5. Athletes of majority age are not denied the right to use alcohol when not participating in a team event because it is legal to do so, but they are highly encouraged to use alcohol responsibly and in moderation. Athletes who use alcohol irresponsibly are subject to the same penalties as for illegal and banned substance use.

6. All members of the team are required to attend the annual Drug-Free Sport seminar prior to the beginning of the season and to carefully review and sign the Athlete Code of Conduct (see chapter 8) and to abide by the code throughout the season.

7. If an athlete violates any of these team rules, the following actions will be taken:

   a. *First offense:* The athlete is not permitted to participate in the next two consecutive contests or two weeks of the competitive season, whichever is greater. The athlete's parents or guardian will meet with the coach to receive notification of the violation and to agree to the athlete's participation in [describe available counseling or educational session]. The athlete must also comply with any legal or other disciplinary action mandated by the law or applicable authority.

   b. *Second offense:* The athlete is not permitted to participate in any contests for six weeks. The athlete's parents or guardian will meet with the coach to receive notification of the violation. If the athlete wishes to return to the team, the athlete must agree to participate in [describe available counseling or educational session]. The athlete must also comply with any legal or other disciplinary action mandated by the law or applicable authority.

   c. *Third offense:* The athlete is not permitted to participate in any contests for the remainder of the competitive season, including postseason tournaments. The athlete's parents or guardian will meet with the coach to receive notification of the violation. If the athlete wishes to return to the team the next season, the athlete must agree to participate in [describe more intensive counseling available or educational session]. The athlete must also comply with any legal or other disciplinary action mandated by the law or applicable authority.

8. Any athlete who is subject to the corrective action of the team policy by the coach has the right to appeal to [title of position overseeing the sport program].

9. Athletes will continue to participate in practices while disciplinary action and rehabilitation are occurring.

If your sport organization does not now test for drugs, I advocate that you supplement the Team Policy for Drug Use with a testing program. The tests should check for all illegal and banned substances in your policy, and the tests should be unannounced and conducted throughout the year, not just during the sport season. Coaches should have the right to request athletes to be tested at any time. If you need assistance in setting up a drug testing program, see www.drugfreesport.com or www.sportsafe.com, the latter posting a sample drug testing policy for athletes.

Educate Your Athletes

Although knowledge about drug use is not sufficient to prevent it, evidence shows that it is an essential part of the solution. Thus you need to see that your athletes receive appropriate drug education, which should be provided during at least one formal session each season and reinforced through your informal educational efforts.

Formal Education

Many schools and some national sport organizations offer drug education sessions for their athletes. If your team does not have access to such a session, you should organize one. Below are some guidelines for organizing and conducting a Preseason Drug-Free Sport Seminar.

Informal Education

An annual formal educational session is useful, and yet it may be those unplanned, spontaneous opportunities to discuss drugs in sport that will have the greatest impact on your athletes. Throughout this book I've advocated your use of those "teachable moments" that come your way as a coach. They often are more influential with athletes because you're not seen as playing a formal role. Look for opportunities like these to ask questions and initiate discussions.

Preseason Drug-Free Sport Seminar

Who should attend: All athletes, assistant coaches, and student trainers should be required to attend. Invite parents or guardians and consider making their attendance mandatory.

Time and length of program: Schedule the meeting for one evening during the preseason at a time that avoids conflicts with other community events. Announce the meeting well in advance so everyone can plan to attend. Schedule the session for one to two hours.

Agenda:

1. Use of drugs in sport. The session should present facts about the use of illicit drugs, performance-enhancing drugs, and alcohol and tobacco. A local drug expert may be available in your community who can speak authoritatively on the subject. Alternatively, you may choose to show a video on the subject. See the To Learn More section at the end of the chapter for references.

2. Review the team drug policies and those of any other applicable governing body.

3. Review drug testing policies if drug testing is done.

4. Discuss nutritional supplements and their inherent risks.

Direct the speakers to avoid the negative approach or the use of "scare tactics" in discussing drugs in sport. This approach is ineffective with young people. Instead present the facts about drugs, both positive and negative. For example, for years, sport administrators and the medical community denied the positive effects of steroids, which diminished their credibility when athletes could readily see the positive results.

Design the session so that it is not just a presentation or lecture, but an opportunity for athletes and parents to ask questions and discuss the use of drugs. Consider breaking into small groups, athletes and parents together, to discuss selected issues.

- ▶ When you see a billboard advertising cigarettes or alcohol while traveling with the team.

- ▶ When a newspaper story appears about an athlete abusing drugs.

- ▶ When watching a movie with the team and substance use is shown.

- ▶ When alcohol is promoted on television in conjunction with sport events.

- ▶ When athletes ask you about nutritional supplements and other performance-enhancing substances.

- ▶ When you hear about a big party coming up. Ask your athletes how they will deal with the presence of alcohol, tobacco, and illicit drugs.

- ▶ When a member of the team violates the drug policy. Discuss the purpose of the team rule and how you feel about the violation.

When Athletes Have a Drug Problem

When you suspect that an athlete has a drug problem, the first task is to determine whether the athlete indeed has a drug problem and whether the athlete has violated your drug policy. It's far easier to do so if you test for drugs, but in this section we'll outline how to respond regardless of whether you drug test. Of course, once you've determined that an athlete has a drug problem, you need to enforce your penalties for violating the rules and provide the appropriate help. We'll first look at how you can detect when athletes have drug problems in the absence of a drug testing program, and then we'll discuss how to respond.

Recognizing the Signs

Actually you're in a good position to detect athletes with a drug problem because you observe your athletes regularly and often see them performing at their optimum. Because drugs change people's behavior, you'll likely notice differences from your athletes' usual behaviors and performances.

Substance abuse occurs in all segments of our society, but some people are at greater risk than others. Table 17.1 lists some common risk factors and buffers against drug use that may help you identify athletes who are at risk.

Table 17.1—Risk Factors for and Buffers Against Drug Use

Risk factors for drug use	Buffers against drug use
Dysfunctional families and family histories of substance abuse	Parental disapproval of drug use
Low self-esteem	High self-esteem
Inability to turn down a drug offer	Ability to turn down a drug offer
Belief that drug use will win peer approval	Belief in peer intolerance to drug use
Belief that many are using drugs	Understanding actual drug use prevalence

Here are some of the common warning signs of alcohol and drug use. Study these, be alert to these changes in behavior, and recognize that not one sign, but a combination of signs, usually signals a problem.

Physical Signs

▶ Looks tired and run down
▶ Glassy, red, or dull eyes
▶ Skin tone is pale or grayish
▶ Walking and body movements are sort of aimless
▶ Wearing sunglasses at inappropriate times
▶ Pupils larger or smaller than usual; blank stare
▶ Smell of substance on breath, body, or clothes
▶ Change in speech patterns
▶ Deterioration and change in dress and physical appearance
▶ Tremors or shakes of hands, feet, or head

Emotional Signs

▶ Personality change with no other identifiable cause
▶ Avoiding responsibility
▶ Inappropriate overreaction to mild criticism or simple requests
▶ Extreme mood swings
▶ Irritability
▶ Low self-esteem
▶ Apathy or depression
▶ Verbally abusive

Family Signs

▶ Argumentative and hostile toward family members
▶ Breaking family rules
▶ Unexplained change in financial position (more or less money)
▶ Loss of interest in family and family friends
▶ Excessive need for privacy
▶ Chronic dishonesty and deception

School Signs

▶ Loss of interest in school and consequent decline in grades
▶ Problems concentrating; short attention span
▶ Doesn't listen well
▶ Mental deterioration, disordered thinking, "spaciness"
▶ Forgetfulness
▶ Negative attitude toward school
▶ Unexplained absences

Sport Signs

▶ Loss of conditioning
▶ Decline in performance
▶ Noticeable loss of weight
▶ Missing practices because of frequent sickness
▶ Decreased interaction and communication with coach and other players
▶ Loss of motivation and enthusiasm to play
▶ Trouble looking you in the eye
▶ Less receptive to coaching; more defensive

Social Signs

▶ New and different friends; defensiveness when asked about these friends
▶ Uncooperativeness and hostility
▶ Strong denial of drug use and defending drug use and abuse
▶ Persistent lateness
▶ Secretive behavior
▶ Aggressive behavior

Although different drugs produce different symptoms (see figure 17.1), you don't need to be an expert on each of these drugs. You just need to detect that something is wrong and that your player needs help.

Choosing to Respond

Even without a drug testing program, you may see the signs of drug abuse in one of your athletes. You know something is wrong; perhaps not exactly what, but something. What should you do? Talk to your athlete? Leave the athlete alone? Get someone else to help? In the sidebar below you'll see the reasons coaches give for not responding weighed against the reasons to respond. Which way does the scale tilt for you?

Weighing Your Decision to Respond to an Athlete Demonstrating Signs of a Drug Problem

Reasons not to respond:

▶ Not my problem
▶ Makes me uncomfortable
▶ Parents may get angry
▶ Will take a lot of time
▶ I could be wrong
▶ Afraid of lawsuit
▶ Afraid I won't be supported

Reasons to respond:

▶ It will help the team
▶ It's the right thing to do
▶ You care about the athlete

As the opening story in this chapter portrayed, failing to respond can be catastrophic. Remember that your duties as a coach are broader than just teaching athletes the technical and tactical skills of the game. You're teaching and guiding them to become better human beings. If a player on your team broke an arm, you wouldn't leave the player lying on the field, saying, "That's not my problem." It's no different when an athlete has a drug problem. By the way, the courts are supportive of coaches seeking help for their athletes and less supportive when they fail to act.

It's hard being a coach of people who are substance abusers because they often behave erratically, are unreliable, and perhaps are loaded with talent but unmotivated to use it. The easy solution would be to cut them from the team, get rid of the problem. I am not being overdramatic, however, when I say that you may be the very one that can help a drug-abusing athlete turn his or her life around. Isn't that as rewarding as winning a game or championship?

Sharing Your Concern

You're committed to helping your athlete. You've investigated sufficiently that you have reasonable cause for concern. Now it's time to meet with the athlete privately and share your concern. Be sure the athlete is sober or clearheaded when you meet. This meeting is *not* a time to accuse, blame, judge, lecture, demand, or threaten the athlete. Ringhofer (1996) offers these useful guidelines for sharing your concern:

Sharing Your Concern With the Athlete

I Care . . . . Let the athlete know that he is important to you and to the rest of the team. You may be comfortable telling him directly that you care about him, or you may let him know indirectly by a smile, a gesture, or by telling him how important he is to the team.

I See . . . . Focus on observable behavior. What tipped you off that something was wrong? What did you see or hear that caused you to be concerned in the first place? Focusing on observable behavior helps you avoid labeling, being judgmental, or accusing the athlete. .

Try saying . . .	Do not say . . .
You missed three practices.	You are not living up to your commitment.
You decreased your speed from . . . to	You are slacking off.
You do not look at me when I talk to you.	You are disrespectful.
You were late twice this week.	You are irresponsible.
You are doing the minimum . . .	You are lazy; you are not giving 100%.
You yelled at the manager yesterday.	You are an angry person.
Your eyes are red.	What are you on, anyway? Drugs?

I Feel . . . . Tell the athlete how you feel about her behavior. Express feelings in a few words: "I feel angry," or "I feel worried." This lets the athlete know that what she is doing is affecting someone else. It can also reduce the chance of raising defenses and getting into an argument.

Listen . . . . Listen to what the athlete has to say. Ask questions. Pay attention to him by resisting other distractions. Use good nonverbal listening skills. Be prepared for silence. You have picked the time and place to talk about this issue. Recognize that he may not be prepared to talk at this time. Also be prepared for anger, a sad or tragic story, or an emotional outpouring. When confronted, most people do not just say "thank you" and immediately change their behavior.

I Want . . . . Once you have heard her perspective, let her know what you would like to have happen. Do you want her to follow team expectations? Seek help? Talk to someone else? Stay on the team? This is an opportunity to reinforce your standards and to state how you want the behavior to change.

I Will . . . . Then let the athlete know how you will provide support. What are you willing to do? Go with the athlete to seek help from someone else? Be available to talk at another time? This lets the athlete know that he is not alone. You have a stake and a role in helping him change. It can be very threatening to be asked to change behavior; your support can reinforce your bond with the athlete and make it possible for him to change.

Reprinted, by permission, from Ringhofer, 1996.

Here is one other suggestion for you to consider: Coaches are used to "coaching" their athletes, directing them about what to do. Know your limits with drug abuse problems; don't expand your coaching role into a therapist role.

Getting Help

At the conclusion of the meeting with the athlete you have some decisions to make.

▶ Do you need to take action immediately? The answer should be yes if the athlete is a risk to him or herself or others, or is violating the law by using or selling drugs.

▶ Do you need to notify the athlete's parents? If you determine that the athlete has violated your drug policy or needs outside assistance, then you need to involve the parents immediately.

▶ Who else do you need to notify—the school, the sport governing body, a law enforcement agency?

▶ Do you judge the problem to be one that requires outside assistance at this time? If yes, what type of assistance do you need, and where can you get it?

Here are some common sources where you can obtain help:

▶ School and college student assistance programs

▶ School counselors or nurses

▶ Local medical centers

▶ County mental health society

▶ Local religious leaders (pastors, priests, or rabbis)

▶ Alcohol and drug treatment services found in the yellow pages under "alcoholism" and "drug abuse and addiction"

▶ The Internet can be very helpful. Check these Web sites:

www.drughelp.org offers a comprehensive referral service for the entire country.

www.whitehousedrugpolicy.gov/treat/index.html is an excellent site that explains types of treatment, where to locate treatment providers, and how to evaluate treatment effectiveness.

Once Athletes Have Been Referred for Help

You may decide to refer an athlete to a formal drug treatment program. Being referred for drug treatment can be extremely threatening to a young person. You or the athlete's parents, or both, should accompany the athlete to the program and express your continued support. The athlete may not express appreciation at the moment. In fact, the athlete may be very resentful that you've exposed the problem. Later, though, the athlete will likely appreciate the support you showed.

If the referral requires that the athlete not continue to practice with the team, rejoining the team can be difficult. Prior to the athlete returning discuss briefly with your team how you want them to help the athlete rejoin the team. Then demonstrate to the athlete and the team your openness to him or her returning.

Questions for Reflection

▶ How prevalent is substance use among athletes of the age that you coach? **(p. 394)**

▶ What are your attitudes about drug use? Do you communicate a clear antidrug stance? **(p. 398)**

▶ Are you a positive role model for your athletes in terms of tobacco, alcohol, and drug use? **(p. 400)**

▶ What rules have you established regarding drug use in your sport program? Make sure to communicate your drug policy clearly and to enforce it consistently and fairly. **(p. 402)**

▶ Do you have a formal drug education session for athletes and their parents before the start of the season? **(p. 404)**

▶ How can you capitalize on "teachable moments" regarding drug use? **(p. 404)**

▶ What are the signs of a drug problem? **(p. 406)**

▶ What would you do if you suspected that an athlete you coach has a drug problem? What outside sources are available to help you? **(p. 407)**

References

Ringhofer, Kevin. 1996. *Coaches guide to drugs and sport*. Champaign, IL: Human Kinetics.

Stainback, Robert D. 1997. *Alcohol and sport*. Champaign, IL: Human Kinetics.

Yesalis, Charles. 2000. *Anabolic steroids in sport and exercise*. Champaign, IL: Human Kinetics.

To Learn More

Bahrke, Michael S., and Charles E. Yesalis. 2002. *Performance-enhancing substances in sport and exercise*. Champaign, IL: Human Kinetics.

Reents, Stan. 2000. *Sport and exercise pharmacology*. Champaign, IL: Human Kinetics.

Wilson, Wayne, and Edward A. Derse. 2001. *Doping in elite sport*. Champaign, IL: Human Kinetics.

Yesalis, Charles, and Virginia Cowart. 1998. *The steroids game*. Champaign, IL: Human Kinetics.

CNS Productions, Box 96, Ashland, OR 97520-1962, 800-888-0617, or www.cnsproductions.com, offers a video titled *Sports and Drugs* and has many other educational videos on alcohol and illicit drugs.

www.drugfreesport.com. This is the Web site of the National Center for Drug Free Sport. Its mission "is to help high schools, colleges, universities, and other athletic organizations ensure drug free environments." It provides help in setting up policies and testing services.

www.whitehousedrugpolicy.gov/pdf/drug_testing.pdf. This site has a free copy of *Drug Testing in Schools*.

U.S. Department of Health and Human Services, Alcohol and Drug Information, at www.health.org, is an excellent source for further information on the subject.

PART V

Principles of Management

You've developed a sound coaching philosophy, you understand the psychology of coaching, you're becoming a master teacher of technical and tactical sports skills, and you're gifted in training and fueling your athletes' bodies. Now you are ready to coach so you can put this knowledge to use. But wait. Before you leap up and race to the playing field, gymnasium, or pool, you need to learn how to *manage* your team—how to plan, organize, staff, and direct all of the functions you have responsibility for as a coach. In chapter 18 you'll learn about the seven team management functions you have as a coach. In chapter 19 you'll learn how to manage relationships with your fellow coaches, administrators, medical personnel, officials, parents, and the media. And in chapter 20 you'll learn how to fulfill your nine legal duties to manage the risk of injury to your athletes, and reduce your risk of litigation. Once you've mastered management, you're ready to be a *successful coach!*

18

Managing Your Team

He was an ingenious technical skills teacher, a master tactician, and an inspirational leader loved and respected by his team, but Coach Wikgren couldn't organize his way out of a wet paper bag. His last two assistant coaches quit because they never received any direction from him. Coach Wikgren doesn't plan before the season, fails to organize effective practices, forgets to schedule the practice field, tells the players the wrong departure time for a trip, and is constantly late for practices and games. This discombobulated coach would be humorous if he weren't so frustrating to all who depend on him to manage the team.

How effective are you in managing your team? Do you sometimes feel overwhelmed, disorganized, or out of control?

The saying "The devil is in the details" is never more apropos than in coaching. You can be a terrific teacher of technical skills and a masterful game tactician, but you're unlikely to be successful if you fail to plan for the team, if you fail to effectively organize team activities, and if you fail to direct and control team events. By managing the myriad details of your team effectively, you will provide the foundation for your team's success.

You may wish that you had fewer management responsibilities so that you would have more time to actually coach. Most coaches do. Unfortunately, though, team management functions are part and parcel of the job. The more efficiently you manage your team, the more time you will have to coach your athletes.

In this chapter I'll help you identify your management responsibilities and provide you with assistance in preparing to fulfill these responsibilities through helpful lists and probing questions. I won't discuss *how* to manage the many functions for which you are responsible, but will focus instead on *what* you have to manage (or delegate). The *how* of management in coaching is the same as that of any position. It consists of planning, organizing, staffing, directing, and controlling—and there are many books, courses, and workshops available on how to perform these skills effectively. See the To Learn More section at the end of the chapter for recommendations.

☞ **In this chapter you'll learn about your management responsibilities in the following seven categories:**

▶ Policy management

▶ Information management

▶ Personnel management

▶ Instructional management

▶ Event and contest management

▶ Logistics management

▶ Financial management

In chapters 19 and 20, we'll focus on two other management responsibilities: relationship management and risk management.

Now let's meet seven managers and learn about the vital team management functions they perform. As a coach you will need to master each of their jobs or prudently delegate the responsibilities to assistant coaches, parent boosters, or responsible adults. Carefully review table 18.1 to get an overview of these seven managers' functions during the preseason, in-season, and postseason, and then read further about each. As you do so, determine which functions are relevant to

Table 18.1—The Seven Managers You Need to Be

Manager category	Preseason functions	In-season functions	Postseason functions
Policy manager	Review organization policies and establish team policies	Apply and enforce team policies	Evaluate policies
Information manager	Create information system and set policies on its use	Collect, store appropriately, and disseminate information as needed	Update records, evaluate system, store safely
Personnel manager	Determine staff needs; select and train staff; recruit, select, and prepare players for season	Organize and control staff and player activities	Recognize, reward, and evaluate staff and players
Instructional manager	Set instructional goals; select subject matter; create season and practice plans	Organize instruction; adjust plans based on performance	Evaluate season plans
Event and contest manager	Plan events and schedule contests	Conduct events and pre- and postcontest functions; coach at games	Evaluate events and schedules; evaluate game coaching
Logistics manager	Plan for facilities, equipment and uniforms, supplies, and transportation	Monitor for cleanliness, availability, and safety; replace as needed	Evaluate each logistical function
Financial manager	Obtain funds; prepare budget; know approval process for expenditures	Make or approve purchases as needed and within budget; keep records	Compare actual versus budgeted income and expenses

your coaching situation and use the lists and questions provided to help you prepare to manage these functions. If these functions are not your responsibility, be sure you know who is responsible for them because if they are not managed well, your team is likely to be adversely affected.

As we look at the work of each of these managers, keep in mind that the foundation for successful coaching is built during the preseason. The more planning and preparation you do during this less pressured time, the fewer management hassles you will have during the season. In-season is the time to put the plans to work by skillfully organizing, directing, and controlling activities. Postseason is the time to recognize and thank those who helped you, complete and archive records, and evaluate the season.

Policy Manager

Preseason functions	In-season functions	Postseason functions
Review organization policies and establish team policies	Apply and enforce team policies	Evaluate policies

You'll recall that I described how to create team policies and provided an outline of team rules to be developed along with an athlete code of conduct in chapter 8. Let's briefly consider your policy management responsibilities here.

Preseason

If you have written team policies, you will want to review and update them during the preseason. If you don't have written team policies, take the time to develop them during the preseason. As you develop or revise your team policies, you should also review any applicable policies from the organization governing your team's participation in competitive events.

In-Season

As the season begins, you'll want to present the team policies to your athletes in their player handbook (we'll discuss this document later) and in one of your preseason team meetings. As a team policy manager, your task through the season is to apply the team policies to the many situations that arise and to enforce the consequences described in the policies when they are violated.

Postseason

Immediately after the season, while your memory of the season's events is fresh, write down any "critical incidents" that occurred that tested your team policies. Make notes to remind yourself later that you may need to add or modify a policy based on these events. Then use that information in revising your team policies during the next preseason.

Information Manager

Preseason functions	In-season functions	Postseason functions
Create information system and set policies on its use	Collect, store appropriately, and disseminate information as needed	Update records, evaluate system, store safely

A well-planned and well-maintained information system is an important part of being a successful coach.

Preseason

The preseason is the time to create or improve your information systems. You'll need a plan for collecting, accessing, disseminating, and archiving information. Here's the typical information coaches need to manage:

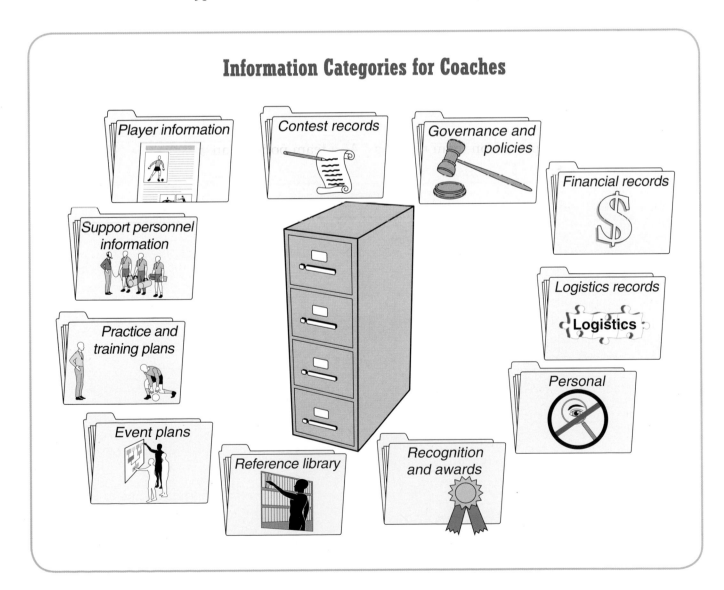

Information Categories for Coaches

Player information

Contest records

Governance and policies

Financial records

Support personnel information

Logistics records

Logistics

Practice and training plans

Personal

Event plans

Reference library

Recognition and awards

Player Information

Contact and emergency contact information
Playing history
Medical history
Preparticipation examination results
Proof of eligibility
Signed waivers and release forms
Signed code of conduct forms
Injury report forms
Team policy violation reports
Fitness Assessment for SporT (FAST)
    evaluations
Technical and tactical skill evaluations

Support Personnel Information

Contact and emergency contact information
Job description
Résumé
Performance evaluations
Letters of recommendation

Practice and Training Plans

Seasonal instructional plans
Practice schedules
Practice plans
Physical training and conditioning plans

Event Plans

Team meeting agendas
Support staff meeting agendas
Plans for other special events

Reference Library

Rule books
Technical and tactical skill books, tapes, and
    articles
Physical conditioning and nutrition articles
Mental training articles
Character development articles

Recognition and Awards

Press releases
Press clippings
Player awards
Support personnel awards

Personal (for the coach)

Résumé
Win–loss records
Recognitions and awards
Job description
Job contract

Logistics Records

Equipment records
Facility records
Supply records
Transportation records

Financial Records

Income sources
Expense sources
Receipts
Reimbursement requests and receipts

Governance and Policies

Policies from national, state, and local
    governing bodies
Team policies
Risk management plan
Insurance records
Accident and injury reports

Contest Records

Contest schedule(s)
Scouting reports
Postcontest evaluations
Team win–loss records

You may not have responsibility for all of these records, but for many you will. Develop your preseason plan by answering these questions:

▶ What information do you need to coach this team effectively?

▶ How will you obtain this information, whether it is rules and policies for competition, contest schedules, or player and support staff information?

▶ How will you organize this information so you can readily access it, and how will you permit others to access information they need, but retain the confidentiality of certain information?

▶ What information will you want to disseminate to players, support staff, administrators, and the media? Will you do this through written or verbal channels?

Many of your responsibilities as a coach will involve managing information. A good filing system is essential. Using the computer to help you manage your information can be very beneficial. Some sports even have software programs to help coaches with some of the information tracking functions discussed. You may also use a PDA (personal digital assistant) to help manage team information.

In-Season

During the season you want to shift from developing your information system to using it. Your system should give you quick access to the information you and your support team need and be easy to update as events occur throughout the season. In this section we'll consider two special informational tasks—gathering information through the process of "scouting" the opposing teams, and providing information to the media in the form of publicity and news.

Scouting

The sport you coach, or the level at which you coach, may not be so competitive that you will scout your opponents, but this activity is common in many sports. Here are some questions to consider if you plan to scout:

▶ Who will do the scouting?

▶ What contests will you scout?

▶ Do you have a standard scouting form?

▶ How will you use the information you collect?

▶ Will you scout by observing opponents directly or by watching videos?

▶ What is the cost of scouting? Is it a justified expense? Do you have the money to scout?

▶ Are there regulations or unwritten ethics that impose restrictions on scouting?

Publicity

Most sport teams want publicity. Sport information directors coordinate publicity at the collegiate and professional levels of sport, but for many teams publicity is the coach's responsibility. If you want publicity, answer these questions:

▶ How much and what type of publicity do you want for your team?

▶ Should you appoint a publicity manager?

▶ How do you get media coverage? (We'll discuss this in chapter 19.)

▶ Do you desire additional publicity, such as speaking to local groups, a team brochure or media kit, posters, and so on?

▶ How do you provide information to the appropriate sources to get the media you desire for your team?

Postseason

I saw a cartoon once of a fellow coming out of an outhouse on which a sign was posted, saying, "You're not done until you're finished with the paperwork!" That's true for coaches too. Once the season has ended, you need to make certain that the records are complete and then submitted to the right person or filed safely. Consider these questions in performing this management function:

▶ Are your player records complete, including current addresses, so you can communicate with players during the off-season?

▶ Have you retained all medical examination records?

▶ Have you made copies of all accident reports?

▶ Do you have copies of all requests for fixing unsafe facilities or damaged equipment?

▶ Have you updated all eligibility records?

▶ Have you summarized and organized all participation, individual performance, and team outcome records?

▶ Have you recorded an accurate inventory of all equipment and supplies?

▶ Have you balanced the budget and prepared all needed financial reports?

▶ Do you need to update any other records?

▶ How will you safely store your records?

Personnel Manager

Preseason functions	In-season functions	Postseason functions
Determine staff needs; select and train staff members; recruit, select, and prepare players for season	Organize and control staff and player activities	Recognize, reward, and evaluate staff and players

Besides managing all the players on your team, you may have assistant coaches, a team manager, athletic trainers, and other support staff to manage as well. In this section we'll look at your personnel manager functions for support staff and players, a vital part of being a successful coach.

Preseason

First we'll look at managing your support staff, if any, and then we'll consider player management issues not previously addressed.

Support Staff

Your first task is to decide what support positions you need or want. I recommend that every team have a minimum support staff of at least one assistant coach, a team manager, and an athletic trainer. You need at least one assistant in case you can't be there, and more if you have a large number of players on your team. A team manager who helps with informational, event and contest, logistical, and financial management tasks can save you enormous time—time that you can devote to coaching. And it's essential that your team have a certified athletic trainer, student athletic trainer, or some other professional for medical support.

I'll discuss your relationship with these three positions further in chapter 19, but for now consider these questions:

▶ How many assistant coaches should you have, and what qualifications will you look for in each assistant?

▶ What duties will you assign to a team manager, and what qualities should this person have?

▶ How will you arrange for medical assistance?

▶ What other support staff do you need or want? Consider a financial manager, publicity manager, team scorekeeper and statistician, and transportation coordinator.

▶ Are you responsible for recruiting and selecting your support staff?

▶ Will you provide your support staff with written job descriptions and training?

Through written documents—including a job description, your team policies, and player handbook—as well as one or more preseason staff meetings, you can communicate the essen-

tial information support staff will need to fulfill the duties of their assigned positions.

Player Recruitment

Consider the following questions about recruiting and selecting players for the upcoming season:

▶ Are you responsible for promoting participation or finding your players?

▶ How do you let potential athletes know about your team?

▶ What can you do to encourage participation?

▶ Are there recruiting regulations you must follow?

Player Evaluation and Selection

During the preseason you will want to prepare the tools you'll use to evaluate the knowledge, motor skills, and physical attributes of your players (see chapters 9, 14, and 15 for recommendations), and then determine how you will select the players for your team. Here are some other important questions to answer:

▶ Will you conduct tryouts for the team, and if so, what procedures will you use to select players?

▶ When will you conduct tryouts?

▶ Will you evaluate your players for other purposes such as to plan their instruction, to classify them into categories, or to assign them to positions?

▶ Do you document your evaluations so you can justify selection decisions?

Player Communication

Setting up systems for communicating with your players is important, not only for routine matters but also for when plans change or emergencies occur. Consider these questions:

Preparing Your Support Staff

Here's an agenda of topics to be communicated to your support staff during the preseason:

❑ *Staff introductions*
❑ *Team philosophy and policies*
❑ *Organizational structure of staff*
❑ *Staff responsibilities*
❑ *Staff conduct*
❑ *Budget (funds, salaries, equipment, and so on)*
❑ *Problem-solving procedures*
❑ *Athlete roster and eligibility*
❑ *Emergency medical procedures*
❑ *Athlete–staff relations*
❑ *Athletes' conduct*
❑ *Parental issues*
❑ *Plans for initial preseason team meeting with players*
❑ *Plans for meeting with athletes' parents*
❑ *Season practice and game schedules*
❑ *Travel procedures*
❑ *Technical and tactical skills to be taught*

▶ How will you communicate with players throughout the season?

▶ What team meetings will you schedule for the season?

▶ Will you use the phone, e-mail, a Web site, or bulletin boards to communicate with your team?

▶ How will you notify players of rainouts, cancellations, or other changes in plans?

▶ Are you prepared with emergency contact information for each player and for various emergency services?

Player Eligibility

Prior to the season you also need to consider the eligibility of your players to participate. Here are some questions to which you should have answers:

▶ Do you have eligibility requirements for your players?

▶ Do your players know and understand them?

▶ Do you need verification of players' ages?

▶ Must players or their parents (or both) sign release forms, and are you responsible for collecting them?

▶ If your players must meet academic requirements, do you have a way to monitor their grades during the course of the school year?

Team Captains

It's common for individual and team sports to have one or more team captains. Here are some questions for you to answer about team captains prior to the season:

▶ Should you have any team captains?

▶ Who should make the selection, you or the team, and what procedures will be used?

▶ What are the responsibilities of a team captain? See the following list of possible team captain duties:

Sample Topics for Team Meetings

- ☐ Overview of program
- ☐ Introduction of coaches and their responsibilities
- ☐ Coaching philosophy
- ☐ Introduction of players
- ☐ Eligibility requirements
- ☐ Team rules
- ☐ Expectations for player conduct
- ☐ Risks of the sport
- ☐ Importance of following staff directions
- ☐ Season goals and objectives
- ☐ Training and practice routines and content
- ☐ Player selection (for team and starting positions)
- ☐ Season practice and competitive schedules
- ☐ Contingency plans for bad weather for outdoor sports
- ☐ Keeping hydrated during hot weather
- ☐ Maintaining equipment
- ☐ Safety rules—for example, no sliding head first; no spear tackling
- ☐ Team social functions
- ☐ Pregame meals
- ☐ Fund-raising events (needs and options)

Sample Duties of Team Captains

▶ Discuss player concerns with the coach
▶ Represent the players to the coaches, presenting their ideas and suggestions
▶ Organize team activities away from athletic environment
▶ Show leadership on and off the field, helping the team make decisions
▶ Model hard work, academically and athletically
▶ Demonstrate sportsmanship and positive attitude and encourage other players to do the same
▶ Abide by team rules and code of conduct and influence other players to do the same
▶ Help resolve conflicts between team members
▶ Serve as the team's spokesperson with officials

Player Recognition

Another preseason task is to make decisions and preparations with regard to how you'll recognize and distribute awards to your players. Here are some questions to help you prepare.

▶ Will you have one or more award systems?
▶ How will the award systems work?
▶ What publicity will you seek for the team or for individual players?

To the right, you'll find some ways coaches recognize players.

Sample Award Systems

☐ Decals given to players for various types and levels of achievement
☐ Player of the game, week, or month recognition
☐ Award letters for team members meeting certain criteria over the course of the season
☐ Specific performance honors for each game, match, or meet (e.g., the highest percentage of good first tennis serves)
☐ Publicly spotlighting the athlete who demonstrates the most effort in practice each week
☐ Publicizing the most valuable reserve player in the school newspaper each week
☐ Allowing a "practice player of the day" to have input into the next practice session

Player Handbook

I highly recommend that you prepare a player handbook to provide your team with essential and valuable information in written form. The player handbook, and a preseason team meeting in which you review the contents of the handbook, will go a long way in helping you, your support staff, and your players work together. Here is an outline of topics to be included in a player handbook:

Player Handbook Table of Contents

PART I About the Team

▶ Sport administrator welcome
▶ Coach and staff welcome
▶ Staff contact information (instructions for contacting you and all support staff)
▶ Player contact information
▶ Team history (championships won, recognitions earned, individual accomplishments, summary of the preceding season results)
▶ Coaching philosophy (your statement about your coaching objectives and your approach or style to coaching)
▶ Season goals (what you want to accomplish as a team)
▶ Team captains (explanation of captains' duties and how captains are selected)

PART II Player Guidelines

▶ Team policies
▶ Eligibility requirements
▶ Preparticipation physical examination requirements (see chapter 20)
▶ Player insurance requirements (see chapter 20)
▶ Inherent risks of participation (see chapter 20)
▶ Participation fees
▶ Purchase or rental of uniforms, equipment, and supplies
▶ Practice schedule and practice routines (when and where practices are held, prepractice preparation—e.g., taping, warm-ups, or skill work)
▶ Contest schedule
▶ Schedule of special events
▶ Player selection criteria (explanation of how players are selected for the team or for starting assignments)
▶ Travel policies (if not covered under team policies)
▶ Awards and recognition (awards and criteria for earning them)

PART III Rules of the Sport

(Include a rule book or reprint of the rules for your sport.)

PART IV Technical and Tactical Skills

(In this section you can provide your players with information about the technical and tactical skills you will be teaching and practicing. This could be in the form of descriptions and photos of specific skills, offensive and defensive plays, and copies of articles you've collected about the technical and tactical skills of your sport.)

PART V Player Preparation

▶ Physical conditioning (Provide information on energy and muscular fitness training for your athletes pre-, in-, and postseason. For example, you may include the essential eight resistance training exercises and the 14 all-star stretches described in chapter 15.)
▶ Injury prevention guidelines (information on the importance of warming up and cooling down, proper use of equipment, unsafe practices, and personal hygiene)
▶ Athlete guide to nutrition (discussed in chapter 16)
▶ Mental training guidelines (articles on various aspects of mental training)

PART VI Player Forms

(Insert a copy here of all the forms that players and their parents need to complete and return to you or a designated person.)

▶ Contact and emergency contact information
▶ Player participation history
▶ Player code of conduct
▶ Medical release form
▶ Parental approval form
▶ Others

In-Season

You have a number of ongoing responsibilities in managing your staff and players during the season. Here are some questions that will help you think about your management duties during the season:

- ▶ Are you communicating effectively with your staff regarding their work?
- ▶ Are you monitoring your staff's work, encouraging and recognizing them when the work is well done, and helping them improve their work when it falls short of your expectations?
- ▶ Do you know your legal duties for supervising your athletes? (You'll find them in chapter 20.)
- ▶ Are you fulfilling your supervisory duties appropriately during practices and contests?
- ▶ Are you keeping the team organized and motivated to achieve your team goals?

Postseason

When the season comes to an end, you'll likely be eager for a break, but your work is not quite done. The following questions will help you plan for completing your postseason duties:

- ▶ Will you have a final team meeting to review the season's goals; recognize players and staff; and recommend off-season camps, clinics, and conditioning programs?
- ▶ Will you have an awards dinner or banquet? What other method will you use to recognize the team and players appropriately (see Awards Banquet Program Ideas below)?
- ▶ When will players return their uniforms and equipment?
- ▶ How will you evaluate your players and staff after the season, and will you provide them with a written report?
- ▶ Will you ask players to evaluate the program?
- ▶ Will you help graduating players obtain scholarships?
- ▶ What records do you need to update and properly file?

Awards Banquet Program Ideas

- ▶ Host the team and support staff at your home.
- ▶ Have parents and members of the community put on a potluck dinner.
- ▶ Hold a catered buffet funded by a civic or booster organization with the team and coaches as guests of honor.
- ▶ Schedule a popular speaker, such as a college coach.
- ▶ Plan a reunion with former team members.
- ▶ Sell tickets to pay for trophies, food, a guest speaker, and the use of a facility.
- ▶ Barter with a favorite restaurant to use its banquet room in exchange for free advertising the following season.
- ▶ Create a videotape of season highlights.
- ▶ Have the captain or another team member recap the season.
- ▶ Combine with other teams for an all-sports banquet.
- ▶ Develop a tradition for passing responsibilities from the seniors to the other players (such as a senior will or legacy).

Instructional Manager

Preseason functions	In-season functions	Postseason functions
Set instructional goals; select subject matter; create season and practice plans	Organize instruction; adjust plans based on performance	Evaluate season plans

We've covered this subject extensively in part III. In this section I simply want to remind you of your instructional responsibilities pre-, in-, and post-season.

Preseason

Regardless of how long you have coached, you'll be a better coach if you approach the season with a solid instructional plan. To develop your season plan, you need to answer three questions:

▶ What are your instructional goals for the season?

▶ What subject matter will you teach to achieve each goal?

▶ What's the best way to organize this subject matter for instruction?

In-Season

You know about the need for developing practice plans, but now that you are into the season, are you allocating sufficient time to develop them? Consider these questions as you plan:

▶ Are you following your season plan but making adjustments based on the progress of your players?

▶ Are you seeking input from your players and assistants?

▶ Are you developing practice plans that work?

▶ Are you filing those plans for future reference?

Postseason

After the season is over, go through your instructional plan for the season and evaluate the effectiveness of the plan and how well you and your assistant coaches executed it. Make notes of what worked well and not so well to assist you when revising the plan prior to next season. Then file your season and practice plans away for safe-keeping.

Event and Contest Manager

Preseason functions	In-season functions	Postseason functions
Plan events and schedule contests	Conduct events and pre- and postcontest functions; coach at games	Evaluate events and schedules; evaluate game coaching

An "event" may be a team meeting, a pep rally, team preparticipation physical examinations, or a presentation by you to the Optimist Club. An event can be hosting the opposing team for a home contest or conducting a tournament for hundreds of participants. Some events are quite simple to plan, organize, and conduct, whereas others are complex and very time consuming. In this section we'll consider your management functions with regard to planning, organizing, conducting, and evaluating various events, including contests.

Preseason

During the calm of the preseason, determine the events you want to conduct and those that you are expected to conduct. The schedule of contests and tournaments of course takes precedence in your planning, whether you or someone else schedules these events. Even if scheduling isn't your job, you'll want to double-check that it is complete. If scheduling is your job, here are some questions to guide you:

▶ Are there any regulations governing the length of the season and the number of contests?

▶ How many contests do you want to schedule, and with whom, when, and where?

▶ How soon should you start the scheduling process?

▶ Do you need contracts, or are verbal agreements sufficient?

▶ Do you need to schedule contest facilities?

▶ Are you responsible for scheduling preseason contests?

▶ If you are responsible for scheduling officials, how do you identify officials who are qualified? You might want to begin by checking with your optometrist to see who meets the minimum qualifications!

▶ Do you need contracts with officials? Are they volunteers or paid? What records do you need to keep?

Once you know your competitive schedule, you can plan your practice schedule. Then decide on the noncontest and practice events that you want to conduct, considering such events as the following:

▶ Staff meetings

▶ Team meetings

▶ Parent meetings

▶ Team preparticipation physical examinations

▶ Uniform and equipment distribution and collection
▶ Pep rallies
▶ Public speaking
▶ Coaching education courses
▶ Meetings with the press

Of course you're responsible for planning, organizing, and conducting your team's practices and participation in the competitive contests. You'll also want to be clear about who is responsible for planning, organizing, and conducting the other events that you've scheduled. Is it your job, or will you delegate certain events to your assistant coaches or team manager? Also, with your daily planner in hand, identify all of the events that you will have the pleasure of attending before, during, and after the season that you do not need to organize.

In-Season

Your focus during the season will be on conducting practices, participating in contests, and making certain the other scheduled events are organized and conducted effectively. Of course you'll also need to organize and conduct unexpected events because of a special need or circumstance.

Now let's examine your management responsibilities associated with a contest. I'm not referring here to your tactical wizardry, but to the planning, organizing, and controlling functions associated with your team participating in a competitive event. If you're fortunate, you'll have a sport administrator to manage many of these functions for you. If not, the following questions will help you determine your level of preparedness:

Contest Preparation

▶ Have you arranged for the facility?
▶ Have you verified the attendance of officials and arranged for someone to greet them and take them to their dressing area?
▶ Have you arranged for janitorial service, ticket takers, ushers, scorekeepers, announcers, and any other personnel needed to conduct the contest?
▶ Have you made arrangements to assist the press in covering your contest?
▶ Have you arranged to have programs prepared for the contest?
▶ Have you briefed your staff on their duties?
▶ If your sport is a collision sport, have you arranged for a physician and ambulance to be present?
▶ Have you made arrangements for the visiting team, including someone to greet them and take care of their needs?
▶ If you expect a large crowd, what crowd control steps do you need to take?
▶ Is all contest equipment ready for use?

Precontest Team Management

Consider your responsibilities in preparing your team for the contest by asking yourself these questions:

▶ Do you need to arrange for a pregame meal or provide your players with directions about pregame nutrition?

▶ Have you arranged for fluid replacement during the contest?

▶ Have you selected the starting lineup and planned for substitutes?

▶ Have you developed your tactical plan for the contest?

▶ Have you prepared your players for the precontest routine you want to follow, including the warm-up?

▶ Will you meet with your team before the contest? If so, what is the purpose of the meeting?

Contest Management

During the contest you will have many team management responsibilities. The following questions should help you feel more prepared for the many responsibilities you will face during contests:

▶ Are you prepared to manage your own behavior so that it positively influences your players and represents your organization favorably?

▶ Are you prepared to manage your staff and players' behavior so they represent your organization well?

▶ What will you do if an official makes an error? if a player is hurt? if players get in a fight? if the crowd is acting ugly?

▶ How will you observe the contest to make the best tactical decisions?

▶ When should you substitute, and how will you handle the substitution process?

▶ When do you call time-out, and what do you do during the time-out?

▶ How will you record your observations about the team and individual players for later instructional use?

▶ What will you do with the team between periods?

Postcontest Management

Your management responsibilities don't end with the contest. Consider the following questions:

▶ What postgame routine do you and your team want to follow, especially with the opposing team and coaches?

▶ What messages do you want to communicate to players after a win? a loss?

▶ What do you want to say, and refrain from saying, to officials, and who will pay them?

▶ Who will supervise the locker rooms?

▶ Do you need to do anything with the departing visiting team?

▶ Whom do you need to thank?

▶ What responsibilities do you have with the media?

Postseason

When the season is over, you will have time to reflect and evaluate the season's activities so that you can make the next season even better. Here are some questions to ask yourself:

▶ Was the practice schedule effective? Were there too few or too many practices? Was the length of each practice about right?

▶ Was the schedule of contests appropriate for your team? If not, can you do anything to change the schedule next season?

▶ Was the schedule of noncontest and practice events appropriate? Do you need to add or delete some events?

▶ Did you organize and conduct effective practices? What can you do to improve your organization of practices next season?

▶ Did you manage the team well during contests? Did you and your players demonstrate the sportsmanship you wanted?

▶ How effective were you in the tactical decisions you made during the contests? What would you do differently next time?

Logistics Manager

Preseason functions	In-season functions	Postseason functions
Plan for facilities, equipment and uniforms, supplies, and transportation	Monitor for cleanliness, availability, and safety; replace as needed	Evaluate each logistical function

As a logistics manager, you may have responsibility for the facility in which you practice and compete, for the uniforms and equipment used in your sport, and for various supplies. You may also have responsibility for the transportation of your players to and from practices and contests. We'll consider all of these logistical duties in this section.

Preseason

During the preseason you will want to arrange for and delegate as many of your logistical responsibilities as possible so that you're not encumbered with them during the season.

Facilities

You may or may not be responsible for the facilities in which you practice and compete. Just to make certain that you are meeting your logistical management duties, answer these questions:

▶ What facilities will you need for practices and contests?

▶ Are you responsible for scheduling them?

▶ Must you prepare and maintain the practice facility for your use?

▶ If you rely on outdoor facilities for regular practice, what alternatives do you have during bad weather, if any?

▶ Do you regularly inspect facilities for hazards? (See the facility inspection checklist in chapter 20.)

▶ Are you responsible for preparing the contest facility? If so, what must you do to prepare it? If not, whom do you contact if it is not properly prepared?

Equipment and Supplies

Coaches often purchase their equipment, or they give considerable input into the process. Consider the following questions in managing equipment and supplies:

▶ Are you responsible for purchasing equipment and supplies?

▶ What is the present inventory and state of repair of your equipment?

▶ Are there existing procedures for uniform rotation, equipment replacement, or large equipment purchases?

- ▶ What equipment and supplies do you expect to need for the season?
- ▶ Do you have a sufficient budget to buy them?
- ▶ Do you need someone's approval to make the purchase?
- ▶ What equipment must athletes buy?
- ▶ Do you need to give them instructions on what to buy, where to buy it, and how much to spend?
- ▶ Where will you buy the items you need?
- ▶ Are there any factors to consider besides quality, cost, and service in making purchases?
- ▶ Is your equipment properly identified and inventoried?
- ▶ Do you have procedures for issuing equipment and uniforms?
- ▶ How will you ensure that equipment is properly fitted and that athletes know how to use it correctly?
- ▶ What audiovisual equipment will you need during the season? How do you arrange to have it available?
- ▶ What supplies will you need? How large a stock of supplies do you need on hand?
- ▶ Do you have adequate record-keeping systems for equipment and supplies?

Transportation

Transporting athletes and others associated with your team is one of several activities that carry considerable risk. You'll learn more about how to manage this risk in chapter 20. As you identify your team management functions, answer these questions about transportation:

- ▶ Are you responsible for arranging transportation?
- ▶ Will you use privately owned vehicles or public transportation?
- ▶ Who will drive? Are the drivers properly licensed and insured?
- ▶ Are people other than the players permitted to travel with the team if you use public transportation?

- ▶ Are you aware of your legal responsibilities when transporting athletes?
- ▶ Will you allow players to travel to or from games with family or friends? If so, what procedures will you follow?

In-Season

Here are a few more management concerns for dealing with equipment and supplies as the course of the season progresses. Make sure you have answers to these questions:

- ▶ Who is responsible for maintaining equipment?
- ▶ Do you regularly inspect protective equipment and other equipment that may cause injury?
- ▶ Who is responsible for cleaning uniforms and other equipment, and how often do they do so?
- ▶ What are the procedures for replacing broken, lost, or stolen equipment?
- ▶ Who monitors the use of supplies and determines when to reorder?

Postseason

If you have responsibilities for facilities, equipment and supplies, and transportation, then here are some postseason tasks to consider:

- ▶ What do you need to do to close the facility?
- ▶ To whom do you report any needed repairs?
- ▶ What is the procedure for returning equipment?
- ▶ Who is responsible for checking the equipment for damage and recording what needs to be done?
- ▶ Who is responsible for repairing equipment?
- ▶ Where are supplies and equipment stored?
- ▶ Who prepares the final inventory of equipment and supplies, and where is it kept until needed next season?

Financial Manager

Preseason functions	In-season functions	Postseason functions
Obtain funds; prepare budget; know approval process for expenditures	Make or approve purchases as needed and within budget; keep records	Compare actual versus budgeted income and expenses

Perhaps you'll have little responsibility for financial matters other than approving expenditures and submitting receipts for reimbursements. However, many coaches are responsible not only for all of the expenses to be incurred, but also for raising the money to be spent.

Preseason

Here are some questions for you to consider regarding your financial responsibilities:

▶ Are you responsible for securing any or all team funds?

▶ If so, how will you acquire them? (See Sources of Funding for Sport Teams below.)

▶ Will you develop and maintain the team budget?

▶ Do you have a team budget that you control, or must you request approval of each expenditure?

▶ Do you understand the system for approving and making all expenditures?

▶ Who holds the money, and how do you get to it?

▶ What record keeping is required when you spend money?

▶ Who can spend it?

Sources of Funding for Sport Teams

▶ Funds from sponsoring organization
▶ Fund-raising events or projects
▶ Participant fees
▶ Booster donations
▶ Gate and concession receipts
▶ Parking fees
▶ Advertisement sales (ads in programs, on backs of tickets, and so on)
▶ Student activity fees
▶ Personal solicitation for donations

In-Season

Hopefully you are not burdened with raising money during the season, but you do have some ongoing financial responsibilities. Check that you are fulfilling your duties by answering these questions:

▶ Are you watching the budget and staying within it?

▶ Are you following the system for making expenditures?

▶ Are you keeping the records you or the organization will need?

Postseason

Now it's time to complete the "paperwork" by doing the following:

▶ Have you made certain that everyone who is owed money has been paid?

▶ Do you have all the records and receipts to account for all expenditures?

▶ Have you submitted a report to your sport administrator?

▶ Did you have enough money? What do you think you will need next season?

Coaching Yourself:
Managing Time

Do you find yourself doing any of the following things?

▶ *Relying on "mythical time."* If you sometimes tell yourself that you will have more time later and then put off completing the work to be done, you are relying on mythical time. When you do so, you squander the real time available to you for completing the work.

▶ *Underestimating the demands on your time.* We sometimes think we can do more than we actually can either because we are less efficient than we think we are or we have less free time than we recognize. Don't make the mistake of failing to expect the unexpected. In addition to your routine tasks you must also expect telephone calls, paperwork, conversations with athletes and assistants, and requests for information. Consider all of these part of your daily routine.

▶ *Task creeping.* If you fail to complete the current task before agreeing to take on another, you may find yourself creeping from one task to the next and getting further and further behind. This may cause you to rush through your work, making mistakes and sometimes costing others time, money, and opportunity. Don't be a task creeper.

▶ *Task hopping.* Task hopping is jumping from one task to another because of poor concentration, too many deadlines to meet, and little sense of priority. You may get a good idea, but lose it because you don't write it down and your mind is too full to remember it. Don't be a task hopper.

▶ *Ignoring reality.* Even the very best of coaches have limitations—on both time and energy. You may want to be involved in everything; when people request your services, you may feel flattered and see your involvement as an opportunity for personal advancement or to help others. By ignoring the reality of your own limitations, however, you may overextend yourself, which will adversely affect both you and others.

continued ☞

Coaching Yourself *(continued)*

Here are 15 things you can do to improve your time management:

1. Set aside time regularly to plan.

2. Plan by clearly defining your goals for the immediate future. Write down your weekly plans and review them at least once a day. Mark off those tasks that have been completed.

3. Set realistic goals. It's good to shoot high, but not so high that your goals become impossible to achieve. Be realistic, not only about the number of tasks you take on, but also about the time each task will require.

4. Determine what tasks must be done and how much time each will take. Give all other tasks a lower priority, working on them only when the "must do" tasks are completed.

5. Set limits. Do not take on more work unless you know that you will have spare time after completing your "must do" tasks.

6. Develop systems for completing routine work efficiently.

7. Control your time as much as possible. Create periods when you are inaccessible except for an emergency. Inform others that this is your time to complete work that will help you help them.

8. Develop concentration skills. Planning and efficient processing of routine work demand that you be able to concentrate.

9. Help yourself concentrate better by organizing a work area free of distractions. If possible, use this area only when you are working so that you associate it with work. Put other work out of sight so you are not tempted to task hop.

10. Record important details by writing them down.

11. Set and keep deadlines.

12. Delegate tasks to others when possible. Make certain they know what to do and when it is to be done. Monitor what you delegate so you are certain it will be completed on time.

13. Do not let other people waste your time. Learn how to close conversations in person and on the phone. In turn, don't waste other people's time.

14. Learn to make quick transitions between tasks.

15. Slow down and regroup when you feel overwhelmed. Reestablish your goals, develop your plans, and prioritize your work.

For additional information on time management see the To Learn More section.

Questions for Reflection

▶ How effective are you as a policy manager? Do you establish, enforce, and evaluate your policies? **(p. 416)**

▶ Do you have an organized information system? Coaching involves a lot of paperwork; an efficient system will keep you from drowning in forms! **(p. 417)**

▶ How effective are you at player recruitment, evaluation and selection, communication, and recognition? **(p. 420)**

▶ Do you have a player handbook ready to pass out at your first practice? **(p. 424)**

▶ Do you start the season with solid season and practice plans? How well do you implement them? **(p. 426)**

▶ What kind of events are you responsible for managing in addition to contests? Do you plan well for contests so you can concentrate on your coaching responsibilities on game day? **(p. 427)**

▶ Are you responsible for your facility and equipment and supplies? What routines do you have for ensuring that your responsibilities (and others') are met? **(p. 430)**

▶ To what degree are you responsible for the financial management of your team? **(p. 432)**

▶ How good are you at managing your time? What areas do you need to work on—organization? setting limits? being realistic about how long things take? minimizing distraction? **(p. 433)**

To Learn More

Bossidy, Larry, Ram Charan, and Charles Burck. 2002. *Execution: The discipline of getting things done.* New York: Crown.

Collins, Jim. 2001. *Good to great. Why some companies make the leap. . . and others don't.* New York: HarperCollins.

Grossman, Jack, and J. Robert Parkinson. 2001. *Becoming a successful manager: How to make a smooth transition from managing yourself to managing others.* New York: McGraw Hill.

Morgenstern, Julie. 2000. *Time management from the inside out: The foolproof system for taking control of your schedule and your life.* New York: Henry Holt.

19

Managing Relationships

Dear Coach:

I heard on the news today that you're in the hospital battling cancer. If courage can defeat this disease, I know you'll win the battle. You don't know me, but I know you and want to tell you how much you've influenced me.

When I was 10, we played your team in the YMCA Midget League. I remember the game because we won when the official made a mistake and gave our team the ball. Afterward you consoled your disappointed players and calmed their angry parents. Then I saw you congratulate our coach and thank both officials. I never forgot that! ☞

I watched you again when you became our high school basketball coach. I wanted to play for you, but I was a little short in stature and talent, so I watched you—every game all four years. I saw you win plenty, but what impressed me more was <u>how</u> you won. You always encouraged your players and treated them with respect. I never saw you stomping around on the sidelines like so many other coaches. I never saw you be disrespectful to officials or the opposing teams—even when you lost. I never forgot that!

Even though you don't know me, you've had a profound influence on my life. When I entered college, I knew that I wanted to be a coach—a coach just like you. May God speed your recovery.

Sincerely,

Coach Rita Walsh

Jackie Robinson said, "A life isn't significant except for its impact on other lives." In this chapter I hope to inspire you to be a coach of influence—positive influence—through skillful management of relationships. When you decided to become a coach, you certainly thought about the influence you would have on your athletes, but have you thought about the influence you may have on the many other people with whom you'll work?

You become a coach of positive influence only when you demonstrate that you care about others through meaningful relationships and when you act with integrity, which earns their trust. Through this trusting relationship you can help others "be the captain of their fate and master of their soul."

Coaching is about guiding other people to master skills and achieve more than perhaps they thought they could—and it's all done by managing relationships. Coaches seldom fail because they lack knowledge of technical and tactical skills in their sport. They fail more often because they lack skill in managing relationships with their sport administrators, the parents of their players, their assistant coaches, or the media.

☞ In this chapter you'll learn

▶ how to manage relationships by mastering four interpersonal skills that are vital to your coaching success; and

▶ how to work more effectively with your fellow coaches, administrators, medical personnel, officials, the parents of your players, and the media.

Through your skillful management of these interpersonal relationships you not only obtain the cooperation and respect of your support team and all who follow your team, but you also feel good about yourself as a person and as a coach.

Interpersonal Skills

Although we have to learn many interpersonal skills to be successful in working with others, four are especially important for coaches. Like the four points on a compass, as shown in figure 19.1, these interpersonal skills will point you in the right direction in developing and maintaining successful relationships.

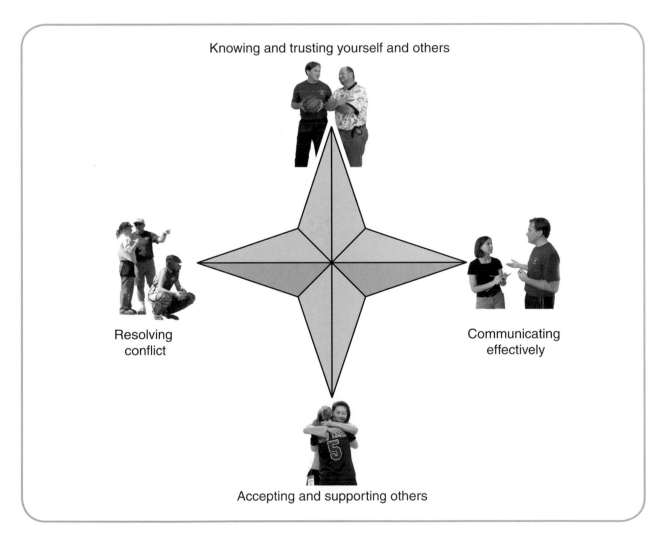

Knowing and trusting yourself and others

Resolving conflict

Communicating effectively

Accepting and supporting others

Figure 19.1   Four important interpersonal skills will point you, the coach, in the right direction.

Knowing and Trusting Yourself and Others

Duke University men's basketball coach Mike Krzyzewski said, "Almost everything in leadership comes back to relationships. The only way you can possibly lead people is to understand people. And the best way to understand them is to get to know them better" (Janssen and Dale 2002, p. 131). Relationships do indeed begin with you and those you work with getting to know each other. To know each other, you each must disclose yourself to the other person. We discussed this briefly in chapter 1.

You take a risk when you disclose yourself to another person—the person might not like you, or even worse, reject you. However, if you know who you are and like who you are (positive self-esteem), then you have confidence to take the risk of revealing yourself to others. When you appropriately let those you work with get to know you, they begin to trust you and in turn they'll let you get to know them. That's how a meaningful, successful relationship begins.

One quick way to damage trust is to show rejection, ridicule, or disrespect. If you make a joke or laugh at a person's self-disclosure or if you moralize or overevaluate the person's behavior, the person will quickly close up. You also can destroy trust if you are unwilling to reciprocate the self-disclosure of another person to you. If you're closed and the other person is open, then the other person will feel overexposed and vulnerable.

If people trust you, you can influence them. Trust is developed not only by appropriate self-disclosure, but also by being "real"—that is, honest, genuine, and authentic. Trust also is rooted in integrity, which means adhering to moral and ethical principles. If you intimidate officials, if you say one thing and do another, if you speak badly about others, you diminish your integrity. If you encourage others and help them achieve their goals, if you are caring, if you treat all those about you with respect, your integrity grows.

In chapter 4 I encouraged you to teach your athletes the moral values embodied in the Athletes Character Code. These values are to be respectful, responsible, caring, honest, fair, and a good citizen. When those moral values guide your relationships, integrity will be your reward. In those difficult moments in your coaching career—and there will be some—integrity will be your best friend.

Figure 19.2 shows the steps to becoming a coach of positive influence. Your climb begins by getting to know yourself, by taking a good look at who you arc and what you want to be. Next, you must like who you are (or become a person you can like). Then you must have the self-confidence to reveal yourself to others to develop meaningful relationships. Once you have developed a foundation of integrity, people will trust you, and through trusting relationships you'll become a positive coach of influence. This will give you a deep sense of personal satisfaction.

Figure 19.2 The steps to becoming a coach of positive influence.

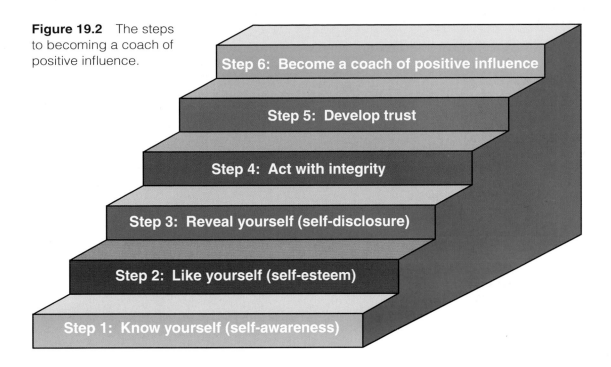

Step 6: Become a coach of positive influence

Step 5: Develop trust

Step 4: Act with integrity

Step 3: Reveal yourself (self-disclosure)

Step 2: Like yourself (self-esteem)

Step 1: Know yourself (self-awareness)

Communicating Effectively

No one needs to tell you that communication is vital to successful relationships. Chapter 6 addressed the basics of effective communication with your athletes, but those principles certainly apply to communicating with others as well. In this section I want to reemphasize one aspect of communication—listening. It's a powerful communication skill for developing relationships and one you'll have to master if you hope to become a coach of positive influence. You won't influence others by dumping information on them; you have to learn how to listen to them.

Here are four good reasons to listen to others in building relationships:

▶ *Listening demonstrates respect.* When you pay attention to your team manager who is telling you about a detail you'd rather she handle, you send a message that you value her. Listening to what she has to say demonstrates respect.

▶ *Listening builds relationships.* Take the time to inquire about your assistant coaches, athletes, and the parents of your athletes, and then listen to them when they respond so that you get to know them. In so doing, you have an opportunity to be a coach of positive influence.

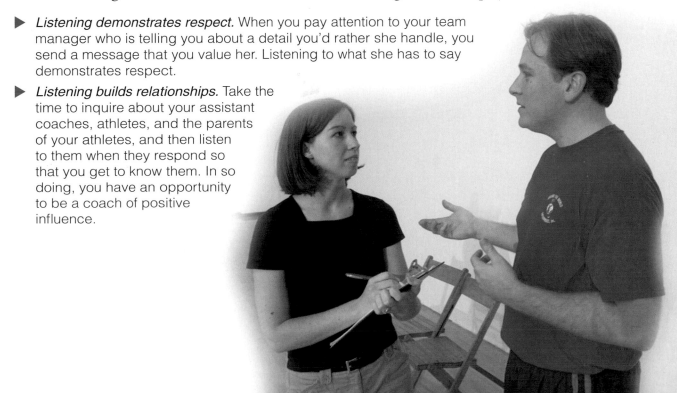

▶ *Listening increases knowledge.* It's OK not to have all the answers and to learn from other people. By listening you can learn much about your sport, your players, and your support team. Pat Summitt, the renowned University of Tennessee women's basketball coach, said, "You have to listen to develop effective, meaningful relationships with people. . . . Listening has allowed me to be a better coach" (Janssen and Dale 2002, p. 175).

▶ *Listening builds loyalty.* People stop talking to people who have stopped listening to them. When that happens, trust and loyalty can break down. Practice good listening skills and people will be drawn to you and will be loyal to you.

Remember this: Coaches without influence monopolize the talking. Coaches with influence monopolize the listening.

Accepting and Supporting Others

To build relationships, you must be not only *open with* others, but also *open to* them. If you want others to accept and support you, you must accept and support them. Acceptance of others does not mean approval of their every action. You may disapprove of certain behaviors, but still accept and care about the person. As a T-shirt I once saw touted: "I may not be perfect, but parts of me are very good!"

You must communicate acceptance of others for relationships to grow. People will feel "psychologically safe" with you if they know you accept them. You communicate this acceptance by being a good listener and expressing that you really understand them. You must also express that you like and care about them. You also can show that you accept others by being available when they need help, asking them to help you, and spending time with them.

Coaching, remember, is a helping profession. You must see the worth in people and care about them deeply if you want to be a coach of influence. Remember this: No one cares how much you know until they know how much you care.

In addition, the people around you need to feel nurtured. Just as people need food, water, and shelter to sustain life, they also need emotional nourishment in the form of encouragement, respect, a sense of security, and recognition. When you provide such sustenance to those with whom you work, you're nurturing them.

As a coach of influence, nurturing others through *encouragement* is your carrot that replaces the stick. Provide encouragement to those with whom you work and they'll walk on hot coals for you. Remember this:

Flatter me, and I may not believe you.
   Criticize me, and I may not like you.
Ignore me, and I may not forgive you.
   Encourage me, and I will not forget you.

William Ward (Maxwell and Dornan 1997)

Resolving Conflict

Your assistant coach disagrees with the way you're conducting practice. A parent confronts you angrily for not starting her daughter. An official embarrasses you by openly censuring you for your repeated complaints. We all have interpersonal conflicts, and you'll certainly have your share as a coach. Conflict occurs when the actions or inactions of one person prevent, obstruct, or interfere with the actions of another person. When coaching, you're likely to have conflicts with your athletes, support staff, and others over what you and they want to accomplish, the ways in which you or they want to pursue the team goals, each of your personal needs and wants, and the expectations you hold of them and they hold of you.

Stop for a moment and think about some of the conflicts you've had and how you managed or mismanaged them. What conflicts do you have in your life now, and how are you managing them? One of the most useful interpersonal skills you can develop as a coach is resolving conflict constructively. Failure to do so leads to the destruction of relationships, and you can't be a coach of positive influence without meaningful relationships. Although conflicts are often seen as negative events, when skillfully managed, they can be of great value to you by clarifying problems, encouraging change, and leading to better solutions. In this section I will discuss the basics of conflict management, which I hope will encourage you to learn more about this topic.

Your Approach to Conflicts

Because conflicts are typically highly charged emotional situations, all too often we let our emotions rule our actions before thinking about the consequences of those actions. When hurtful words are angrily expressed without thinking of the consequences, relationships can be damaged beyond repair. Thus, the most important step to managing conflict is controlling your emotions and recognizing that conflict is a normal and inevitable part of relationships. By approaching conflicts rationally and skillfully, you increase the likelihood of being a coach of positive influence.

How you respond to a conflict with another person depends on how you perceive the situation, which is determined by two major factors:

▶ The importance of achieving your personal goals

▶ The importance of keeping a good relationship with the other person

David Johnson (1981) described five styles of managing conflict based on these two concerns, as shown in figure 19.3.

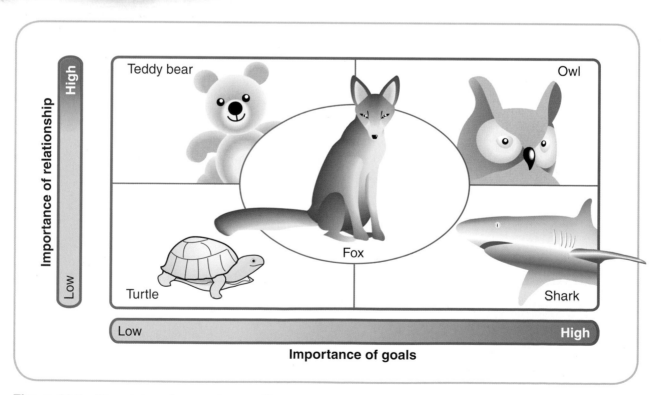

Figure 19.3 Five styles of managing conflict.

Because the relationship is of little importance and their goals are also of low importance, **turtles** withdraw from conflicts and avoid any type of confrontation. Often turtles see resolving the conflict as hopeless, and they feel helpless in changing the situation.

Because they value their own goals highly and give low priority to retaining relationships, **sharks** respond to conflict by attacking, overpowering, and intimidating others, forcing them to accept their solution to the conflict. Sharks consider conflicts contests in which one person wins and the other loses, and they want to win.

To **teddy bears** the relationship is of utmost importance, and thus they're willing to give up their own goals. They have a high need to be accepted and liked and avoid conflict because they believe conflicts can't be addressed without damaging relationships.

Foxes are moderately concerned with achieving their own goals and maintaining a good relationship, and consequently they seek compromise. They're willing to give up part of their goals if the other person will too; in that way both sides gain something.

Owls value their own goals as well as the relationship with the other person. Consequently their solution is to confront the other person to seek a solution that achieves both their own goals and the goals of the other person. This improves the relationship.

Each of the preceding approaches to conflict has its place, although the owl and fox are the two most effective strategies. To be effective at conflict management, however, you need to be skilled at all of the approaches, except for that of the shark. Here are some guidelines for when to use each strategy:

When the goal is unimportant and so is the relationship, be a turtle and withdraw. For example, you're leaving the playing field and a fan from the opposing team taunts you about losing the game; withdraw by walking away.

Although you may sometimes want to attack like a shark when the goal is highly important but the relationship is not, I can't think of an appropriate situation in which to do so in your role as a coach. Responding like a shark almost always provides a poor model to your athletes and others who work with you.

When your goal is of low importance and the relationship is of high importance, responding as a teddy bear is appropriate. For example, your spouse wants to play a round of golf, but you would rather watch a game on TV. Be a teddy bear and play golf. This will maintain the relationship.

When the goal and the relationship are moderately important to you and you and the person with whom you're in conflict both can't get what you want, compromise. For example, you meet with your athletic director in the hope of procuring funds and approval to attend three tournaments, but the athletic director says you can attend only one. Negotiate and see if you can compromise by going to two.

When both the goal and the relationship are highly important to you, you will want to cooperatively confront the person with whom you're having a conflict. We'll look at confrontation next.

Confrontation

Confrontation is an attempt to engage in a discussion with a person with whom you're having a conflict to see if you can solve the problem between you. Confrontation begins by you expressing your view of the conflict and your feeling about it and inviting the other person to do the same. Confrontation should always take place in private, away from athletes, parents, and bystanders. Through discussion you hope to clarify, explain, and resolve the issues with an agreement that satisfies both of you.

Confrontation is appropriate when a person you care about is keeping you from achieving goals that are important to you. You may be concerned that confronting the person will damage your relationship. You may also dislike confrontations in general. Confrontation, however, is sometimes the only way to address the situation. For example, as I discussed in chapter 17, when an athlete or member of your support staff has a substance abuse problem, your moral obligation is to confront, even if initially the person resents your involvement. Confrontation also can build a healthier relationship by alleviating the tension between you.

Once you've decided to confront a person, follow these steps:

1. *Reach agreement on what the conflict is about.* You can't begin to solve the problem if you're not clear about the issue. This can be very challenging because our emotions tend to distort our perception of the situation. We get angry or resentful or believe we're innocent victims representing truth and justice and are being attacked unfairly by an evil enemy. We tend to see things in black and white—we're right; they're wrong. In seeking agreement about the conflict, describe each other's actions without labeling or insulting each other. Describe the situation as a mutual problem to be solved, not a win–lose struggle.

2. *Communicate your cooperative intentions.* Let the other person know that you care about the relationship and that you want to resolve the conflict constructively. Be very careful not to exploit the other person's vulnerability because doing so will likely result in a breakdown in communication. Conflicts never get resolved when communication breaks down.

3. *Take the other person's perspective about the problem.* Use your empathy skills, your ability to put yourself in the other person's shoes, to understand how that person sees the conflict. Here's a place to use good listening skills.

4. *Motivate the other person to resolve the conflict.* You may want to resolve the conflict, but if the other person doesn't want to, you'll go nowhere. Look at the situation from a "cost–gain" perspective by asking these questions: (a) What does the other person gain or lose by continuing the conflict? (b) How can you motivate the other person by changing the cost or gain? For example, if you're having a serious disagreement with an assistant coach who prefers a command style of coaching, you could explain the benefits of your cooperative style for both the athletes and coaches, and the value of a consistent coaching style by all the coaching staff.

5. *Reach agreement.* Through discussion, understanding, and negotiation, you can reach an agreement that satisfies both of you. Be sure that both of you are clear about how you'll act differently in the future and how you'll restore cooperation if one person slips and acts inappropriately. Also, be sure to agree on how you both will communicate in the future to prevent future conflicts.

How to Respond to a Confrontation

In your leadership role as a coach, you are more likely to initiate confrontations than to be confronted. However, when you are confronted, follow these guidelines to ensure a constructive resolution of the conflict:

▶ Be sure that you understand the other person's position. Listen closely and ask questions for clarification, but don't interrupt.

▶ Seek to understand how the other person feels. Don't become defensive as the other person explains his or her emotional response to the conflict.

▶ Paraphrase back to the person his or her position and feelings as you understand them.

▶ Then describe your position and feelings, seeking to obtain agreement in defining the problem.

You've learned how the development of these skills can help you be a coach of positive influence—a coach with integrity and credibility who leads others to be more than they perhaps thought they could be. These skills, like motor skills, however, are not acquired merely by reading about them. You have to practice them, analyze your mistakes, and try to do them better next time. The good news is that as a coach you get the opportunity to practice every day.

Special Relationships

Now that you're wise beyond your years about managing relationships, let's consider your relationships with that inner circle of people who are so important in your life as a coach (figure 19.4). We'll look at the special nature of your relationship with each of these people and offer guidelines for building and maintaining these important relationships.

Figure 19.4 Inner circle of important relationships for coaches.

Fellow Coaches

You may be the head coach with several assistants, or you may be one of several assistants working with a head coach. We'll consider this relationship from both perspectives, and we'll briefly consider your relationship with coaches of other teams.

Relationship With Your Assistant Coaches

With most sport teams the head coach can't do it all alone. You'll benefit from having assistants, but you need to delegate responsibilities appropriately and develop and maintain effective relationships. Many people begin coaching as assistants, working as apprentices to learn the many roles of a head coach. The relationships you establish with your assistants will have a great impact not only on how well they help your team, but also on how well they learn the coaching profession. Consider the guidelines to the right in selecting your coaching assistants:

Once you've selected your assistants, you can manage your relationship with them in the following ways:

WANTED: An assistant coach who has a cooperative-style coaching philosophy or who will accept such a philosophy. Dictators, tyrants, and drill sergeants need not apply. The assistant should complement the head coach by having strengths where the head coach has weaknesses. (Call for details.) The assistant must be a good follower, but know how to lead when called upon. The successful candidate should enjoy working with young people, be respectful of others, and be supportive of the head coach. The assistant should have the courage to offer alternative viewpoints, but not be disagreeable in nature. Send resume to . . .

▶ Create a meaningful role for your assistants, giving them each responsibilities for some aspect of the program. Some coaches use assistants to do the tasks they find boring or undesirable, such as fetching things. It's OK for assistant coaches to do some boring tasks as long as they also get the opportunity to learn all aspects of coaching.

▶ Assign your assistants to positions for which they are qualified and in which they have interest, to the extent possible. Specify their responsibilities clearly.

▶ Help prepare your assistants for their duties. Teach them how to communicate with your players, your methods of instruction, and the specific tasks to be done in practices and contests.

▶ Be sure to give your assistant coaches time to communicate with you.

▶ Involve your assistants in as much decision making as possible. Their views may be helpful, and they'll learn from, and be motivated by, participating in the process.

▶ Provide your assistants with formal and informal evaluations throughout the season.

▶ Don't let situations arise in which players attempt to play you and your assistants against each other.

▶ Recognize your assistants' contributions to the team publicly and privately during and after the season.

▶ Just as your players should enjoy being members of the team, your assistants should too. Try to make the experience fun for them.

Relationship With Your Head Coach

As an assistant you're a part-time leader, especially with your players, and a part-time follower, primarily when working with your head coach. To be a good assistant, you have to have the capacity to be directed and guided by your head coach—that is, you need to be a good follower. You'll be appreciated as an assistant by demonstrating that you're someone your head coach can count on and that you will step up to take charge when called on. However, you don't have to be blindly obedient. Instead you should be a critical thinker and offer your suggestions respectfully to the coach.

As an assistant coach, you will likely have excellent relationships with the head coach, other assistant coaches, and the players if you do the following:

▶ Show initiative by knowing what to do without being told to do it.

▶ Keep the head coach informed.

▶ Think and act independently when it is appropriate to do so.

▶ Align your coaching behaviors with the head coach's philosophy and the team goals.

▶ Be another set of eyes to observe the team, offer opinions, and suggest alternative perspectives.

▶ Have the courage to disagree respectfully, and in private, with the head coach and other assistants when their actions are inconsistent with the team goals.

▶ Continually develop your knowledge of technical and tactical skills.

Relationship With Coaches of Other Teams

When I first began coaching, I saw the opposing team as the enemy, and therefore the opposing team's coach was not someone I wanted to fraternize with. However, the wrestling coach from the other high school in town knew I was a rookie and provided gentle counsel throughout my first season, which was immensely helpful. I'm glad he was more mature about the relationship with fellow coaches than I was.

Look on your fellow coaches as colleagues with whom you share the profession of coaching. At minimum they deserve your professional respect and preferably your friendship. You may be that rookie coach who needs a helping hand or the coach who can lend a helping hand. Before and after contests make an effort to meet your fellow coaches and seek to exchange information about coaching issues.

Many sports have local, state, and national coaches associations. I urge you to join your fellow coaches by becoming a member and active participant in these coaching associations. They will give you another opportunity to learn more, share what you've learned, and improve the coaching profession.

Administrators

You may be fortunate to have an athletic director or administrator to help you with many of the management functions described in chapter 18. If so, you will want to cultivate a cooperative relationship with that person. Here are a few important guidelines for nurturing it:

▶ Be certain that you understand what is expected of you and what procedures you are to follow for various management functions.

▶ Stay organized; submit your requests for items controlled by the administrator in sufficient time for processing.

- Keep your administrator informed of the team's activities through formal and informal communications, and invite your administrator to attend practices and contests.
- Keep requested records and stay within your budget.
- Know when to offer help without being asked to do so.
- Give credit to your administrator during and after the season for contributions to the team's achievements.

If an administrator is not fulfilling his or her responsibilities and thus is creating problems for your team, address the issue directly but politely. Don't start grumbling to others about the problem and allow your views to be communicated through others. Avoid going over the administrator's head unless the situation is very poor and you have first tried to solve any problems directly. Try to be the type of coach you would want to supervise if you were the athletic director.

Medical Personnel

If you coach a contact or collision sport, you'll definitely want to establish a working relationship with medical personnel. Your organization may have an arrangement with one or more team physicians, but if not, you should seek out a physician who has had training in sports medicine to serve as your team doctor. Medical doctors aren't likely to attend practices or contests regularly, but they should be available to your team on a priority basis when you have need for them.

Athletic trainers—trained specialists who provide preventive care for your athletes, respond to emergencies in practices and contests, and carry out rehabilitation programs under the direction of the team physician—can be helpful in many sports. Athletic trainers should be certified by the National Athletic Trainers Association, and they may recruit and train student athletic trainers to assist them.

Ideally, athletic trainers should be available at all practices and contests. However, your team may not be able to afford this support. A lower-cost alternative is to contract with a sports medicine clinic that provides the services of an athletic trainer and other specialists on an as needed basis.

Regardless of the availability of medical personnel to your team, as a coach you should always be qualified to respond to emergencies by being

certified in cardiopulmonary resuscitation and sport first aid (see the appendix to read about the ASEP Sport First Aid course). Moreover, as we'll discuss in chapter 20, you should have a written plan for responding to emergencies that you and all support personnel know well.

If you will have a physician and athletic trainer working with your team, here are some guidelines to keeping relationships with them productive:

▶ You, your sport administrator, and the medical personnel supporting your team need to know exactly what the responsibilities of the medical personnel are. Do they respond first to all injuries? Do they decide if a previously injured player can return to play?

▶ Do not interfere or try to influence the medical decisions of physicians or athletic trainers when they are functioning within their realms of responsibility. If something clearly seems contradictory to your common sense, first discuss it with the physician or athletic trainer. If you're still concerned after that, seek another medical opinion.

▶ Ask medical personnel not to interfere with nonmedical issues that are your responsibility to avoid situations in which they improperly offer counseling or attempt to take action that interferes with your management functions. But realize that your medical personnel can be a valuable source of information about team problems.

▶ Physicians and athletic trainers need to be appreciated, rewarded, and motivated. Give them attention, recognition, and respect, and you will find them eager to help your team achieve its goals.

Officials

Officiating sport contests is a very difficult job, and when coaches, players, and spectators abuse officials, the job is even harder. With increasing frequency we read of officials being not only verbally attacked but also physically assaulted. Is it any surprise then to learn that there is a severe shortage of qualified officials? Why subject oneself to all types of abuse for what often is minimum pay?

On the other hand, keeping your cool as a coach can be tough when you and your team have worked hard to play well and then a bad call deprives you of a well-deserved win. When you see an opposing coach's intimidation tactics with officials appear to be working, you may be tempted to employ the same tactics. And it's almost impossible to restrain yourself when an official not only makes repeatedly poor calls or fails to get in proper position, but then has a belligerent attitude when politely questioned about it.

Controlling your emotions when officials err is part of the challenge of coaching. Think about the consequences of yelling disparaging remarks, intimidating officials, or constantly chiding them. What do you get—a better-officiated game? No, not likely. Instead, you probably get these results:

▶ Your complaints become distractions, causing officials to lose some of their concentration on the game.

▶ With some officials you're more likely to get unfavorable calls.

▶ You damage the relationship between you and the official. Not only does this hurt your relationship, but it also could affect later contests because you may meet the official at another contest.

▶ You possibly incite spectators to become hostile toward the official.

▶ You model undesirable behavior to your players and support staff, damaging your own integrity.

Think for a moment about what you want from officials. You want them to apply and interpret the rules fairly and to ensure the safety of the participants. You recognize that officiating is not an exact science; interpreting and judging the actions of many players performing complex skills are immensely challenging tasks subject to considerable error. So you recognize that officials will make mistakes—and you also recognize that you will make mistakes about judging their mistakes!

Of course you don't want to see a contest officiated poorly, because athletes are denied the opportunity to make a fair comparison of their skills. Thus, if you are responsible for selecting officials, choose the very best you can find. Then help officials do their job by following these guidelines in working with them:

▶ Be prepared for the officials' arrival before the contest. You or someone you designate should greet them, show them their dressing facilities if they need them, and familiarize them with the facility.

▶ Treat the officials just as you would want to be treated, and require the same from your staff and players.

▶ Avoid constantly harassing officials from the sidelines. It seldom helps your cause, it distracts officials from performing their duties, and it diminishes your integrity.

▶ If you question a rule interpretation, express your concern to the official at the appropriate time and in an appropriate way. Many sports specify when coaches can talk with officials and what issues they are permitted to question.

▶ Avoid intimidation tactics. They set a very poor example for players, staff, and spectators. If you engage in this behavior, you will have a difficult time keeping your staff and players from doing the same.

▶ Help officials in every way possible to enforce the rules that protect the well-being of all players.

▶ Thank officials for their work after the contest. Even if you believe that the officials contributed to your team losing, maintain a respectful relationship.

▶ If officials perform poorly, do not employ them again, or write a report on their deficiencies to the person responsible for their hiring.

Parents

Many coaches find that the most challenging relationship to manage is their relationship with the parents of their athletes. Many parents can tell wonderful stories of effective and encouraging coaches, and unfortunately, others can tell horror stories of coaches mistreating and abusing their sons and daughters under the guise of sport. Some parents are completely apathetic to their offspring's participation in sport, and perhaps apathetic to most everything else their children do. Other parents are overly involved and become overbearing, both with the coach and with their child.

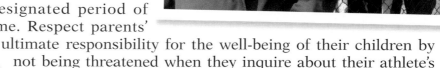

You need to foster appropriate involvement by giving parents clear guidelines about their roles and your expectations of them. In turn you need to remember that parents are ultimately responsible for their children and only desire the best for them. They are loaning you their daughter or son for a certain activity and a designated period of time. Respect parents' ultimate responsibility for the well-being of their children by not being threatened when they inquire about their athlete's participation.

Parents, in turn, need to respect your position. They should not interfere with your coaching unless there is reasonable cause for them to suspect that their son or daughter is being exposed to unnecessary physical or psychological risk or is being treated unfairly.

Your relationship with your athletes' parents is almost as important as the relationships you have with the athletes themselves. With a little effort you can have parents working with you and appreciating your efforts. The key is informing them about your program and listening to their concerns. I have found that many of the traditional problems between par-

ents and coaches can be avoided when coaches hold a preseason parent orientation program, and then maintain open lines of communication throughout the season. You will find an orientation program to be a wise investment in short-circuiting the parent–coach conflicts you often hear about.

Parent Orientation Program

The purpose of the preseason orientation is to do the following:

▶ Help parents understand the objectives of your team

▶ Allow parents to become acquainted with you and your assistants and to learn your coaching philosophy

▶ Inform parents about the nature of the sport and its potential risks

▶ Explain to parents the team rules or policies and procedures

▶ Let parents know what is expected of the athletes and of them

▶ Let parents express their own concerns

▶ Establish clear lines of communication between you and the parents

▶ Obtain help from parents in conducting the season's activities

Planning the Program

When should the meeting be held?

Schedule the meeting before the team begins practicing if you've selected your team, and if not, hold the meeting as soon after you've selected your team as possible. Choose a time when most parents can attend, and invite them individually by phone or personal letter. Consider making the meeting mandatory because of all the important information you will be covering.

How long should the meeting be?

You should be able to accomplish the stated objectives in under two hours.

Should the players attend the meeting?

Coaches have mixed opinions about this. Some think that the presence of players inhibits the communication between parents and coach, whereas others believe that it promotes communication among parents, coach, and athletes. Your coaching philosophy should help you make this decision. Personally I like to have the players attend.

Where should the meeting be held?

Select an accessible location. Be sure the room is suitable for your purposes, is well lighted, and has enough space and comfortable seating.

How should the meeting be conducted?

First, be well prepared and organized. I recommend that you distribute to players and their parents a copy of the player handbook discussed in chapter 18 and make reference to it throughout the meeting. Consider following the parent orientation program agenda shown on pages 456 to 457.

Parent Orientation Program Agenda

Introductions (10 minutes)

Introduce yourself and any assistant coaches. Give a little background about yourself: why you're coaching, your experience in the sport, what you do for a living. Let parents know what qualifies you to coach and why they should trust you in taking responsibility for their sons or daughters. Have your assistant coaches describe their responsibilities to help parents get to know their roles and feel comfortable with them.

Coaching philosophy (10 minutes)

Present a brief review of your coaching philosophy and refer parents to that section of the player handbook. You might want to reread part I of this book to prepare. Be sure to discuss at least the following points:

▶ The benefits their athletes are likely to derive from participation in the sport

▶ The methods you use to teach skills (you might describe a typical practice)

▶ The emphasis you give to winning; having fun; and helping athletes develop physically, psychologically, and socially

Demonstration (10-20 minutes)

Parents may not know much yet about your sport. To help them understand and appreciate it, give a demonstration and explanation of the skills, scoring, and rules. Use the entire team or select a few players to assist you in the demonstration. Pitch the demonstration at a level that is appropriate for the knowledge of your parents. If you cannot arrange a demonstration, perhaps you can locate a good film or video. The demonstration is an opportune time to discuss the equipment for your sport. Emphasize safety when discussing equipment and the rules, and don't forget to mention the role of the referee in ensuring athletes' safety.

Potential risks (10 minutes)

Be sure parents know the potential risks of participating in your sport. No one likes to hear about injuries, but it is your duty to inform parents of the inherent risks. They must make informed decisions about their children's participation. Be sure to be specific about the dangers of your sport. Keep your discussion upbeat by telling parents what precautions you take to minimize the risk of injury (see chapter 20).

Specifics of your program (15 minutes)

Now you are ready to describe the specific program you will be conducting. Following are some things parents will want to know. You may think of others.

▶ How much time will their sons or daughters be with you?

▶ How often and when does the team practice?

▶ How long is the season?

▶ How many contests will there be?

▶ How do you decide who plays and who doesn't?

▶ How frequently does the team travel, and who pays the expenses?

▶ What equipment does each athlete need to purchase?

▶ Where is equipment available, and how much does it cost?

▶ What insurance requirements are there, if any?

▶ How do parents communicate with you or your assistants?

▶ Are medical examinations necessary for the players to compete?

▶ Who decides when an athlete is ready to play after an injury?

▶ Are there special instructions for pregame meals?

▶ What can parents do at home to facilitate the athlete's physical development or learning of sport skills?

Player policies (15 minutes)

Refer parents to the player handbook and review your team policies. Invite questions from both players and parents.

Parent policies (15 minutes)

You may want to provide parents with a set of policies regarding what you expect of them. Here are some examples:

▶ Be supportive of your child's participation on the team, but don't pressure your child.

▶ Keep winning in perspective, and help your child do the same.

▶ Help your child set realistic performance goals.

▶ Help your child meet his or her responsibilities to the team and the coach.

▶ Inform the coach of any medical or physical ailments that your child may have that may affect performance or health.

Provide parents with guidelines for their behavior during practices and contests. See the miniposter for an example.

Question-and-answer session (15-18 minutes)

Throughout the program invite parents to ask questions. If sufficient time remains at the end of the program, invite parents to ask any other questions they may have.

Closing comments (2 minutes)

Thank the parents and players for attending and ask for their cooperation and commitment during the forthcoming season.

Parent Guidelines

➤ Remain in the spectator area.

➤ Let the coach be the coach.

➤ Provide only supportive comments to coaches, officials, and players of both teams. Avoid any derogatory comments.

➤ Do not coach your son or daughter during the contest.

➤ Do not drink alcohol at practices or contests or come having drunk too much.

➤ Cheer for your team.

➤ Show interest, enthusiasm, and support for your child.

➤ Be in control of your emotions.

➤ Help when asked by coaches or officials.

During the Season

After the preseason meeting continue to communicate with parents as needed. Here are a few suggestions for communicating with parents throughout the season:

▶ Keep parents informed and involve them constructively. Parents can fill many of the support roles outlined earlier.

▶ Don't allow athletes to play you and their parents against each other. You can usually avoid this problem by communicating directly with parents.

▶ Inform parents directly and immediately if a serious problem arises involving their child (injury, theft, drugs, ineligibility, or other disciplinary action).

▶ Not all parents will care about their son or daughter's participation, nor will they all respond as you would hope, but you still have a duty to inform them and request their help.

After the Season

At the end of the season, invite each parent to evaluate you and the program. Ask them to point out things that went well and to suggest what might be improved. See form 19.1 for a sample evaluation tool. Give copies to all parents and ask them to return them to you. Their feedback could help you become a better coach!

The Media

Your team may have little or no interest in media coverage except perhaps for some special event, achievement, or human-interest story. On the other hand, the community may have considerable interest in your team and its performance. In some communities a club team or high school team may be the source of considerable community pride and involvement. Thus you'll need to decide how much media attention you want, and how much media attention will be demanded of you as a coach of your team.

Coaches sometimes have a love–hate relationship with the media. As you can imagine, coaches typically like media attention when they're winning and all is going well with the team, and shun it when losing or having team problems. If your community seeks to know about your team through the media, then you need to prepare yourself, your assistants, and your players for successful interactions with media personnel.

How the media portrays you may substantially influence your career. It's been said that your community will judge you as a coach according to how your team performs in contests, and it will judge you as a person according to how you perform in the media. Media coverage may influence your career advancement, salary, ability to attract players, and gate receipts. Media coverage can also be very valuable in helping your players obtain scholarships and opportunities for advancement.

If media coverage goes with your coaching position, prepare yourself and your team for successful relationships with media

Postseason Parent Evaluation Form

A. Evaluate the degree to which you believe your son or daughter achieved the following (check one):

	Very much	Some-what	Not at all
My child had fun.			
My child learned the fundamentals of the sport.			

B. Evaluate the degree to which you believe your child changed on the following characteristics (check one):

	Improved	No change	Declined	Don't know
Physical fitness				
Learning to cooperate				
Self-confidence				
Desire to continue to play this sport				
Development of self-reliance				
Learning specific skills of this sport				
Leadership skills				
Sportsmanship				
Development of initiative				
Learning to compete				

continued

C. Evaluate how the coach did on the following items (check one):

	Excellent	Good	So-so	Weak	Poor	Don't know
Treated your child fairly						
Kept winning in perspective						
Took safety precautions						
Organized practice and contests						
Communicated with you						
Was effective in teaching skills						
Encouraged your child						
Recognized your child as a unique individual						
Held your child's respect						

D. Please give any additional comments in the space below and on the back, including any constructive criticism or praise you want to offer.

From *Successful Coaching, Third Edition,* by Rainer Martens, 2004, Champaign, IL: Human Kinetics.

personnel. You and your sport administrator may need to develop guidelines for the media regarding appropriate contact with players to avoid exploitation and invasion of privacy. You may also want to develop guidelines for the media with regard to contacting you, your assistants, and your sport administrator. Here are some additional guidelines to help you have successful relations with the media:

▶ If appropriate, provide the media with player information (name, height, weight, position, and so on) and a forecast of the team's prospects before the season.

▶ Invite the media to a preseason "picture day."

▶ If access to your contests is controlled, arrange passes for the media, and try to ensure adequate space and comfort for the media at contests.

▶ Let the media know when and where you can be reached before and after contests.

▶ Encourage players to give interviews at times that are convenient for both them and the media.

▶ Assign someone familiar with the spellings and pronunciations of players' names to help writers and broadcasters.

▶ Suggest appropriate human-interest stories concerning various team members.

▶ Arrange for copies of official game statistics to be delivered promptly to the press after the contest.

Coaching Yourself:
Controlling Your Anger

The very nature of sport—the potential for injustice and for physical and mental injury—increases the likelihood of coaches experiencing anger. Anger is a completely normal emotion that we all experience, but we have a choice about how we respond to it. We can be out of control and respond destructively, or we can be in control and respond constructively.

Coaches are most often angered when they perceive injustice to themselves or their team. Because officials are the judge and jury of sport, anger is often directed their way. Anger also arises when coaches perceive that there was intent to injure their players or themselves physically or mentally by demonstrating disrespect through insults and humiliation tactics. Coaches also experience anger when their autonomy and personal space are invaded or their self-worth and integrity are threatened.

When you experience anger, you can respond in one of the following three ways:

- ▶ Spontaneously and destructively
- ▶ Purposefully and destructively
- ▶ Purposefully and constructively

Spontaneous and destructive anger often takes the form of yelling, swearing, pushing and hitting, or more serious violence. Of course nothing constructive comes from expressing such rage. It destroys your credibility, it damages relationships, and of course it's a poor model of behavior for the athletes and others who observe such behavior.

Another way to respond to anger is to be in control of yourself, but to choose to engage in destructive behavior. With what may best be termed hostility, you may choose to make condescending remarks or use sarcasm, "put downs," and hurtful humor to retaliate. This form of anger focuses on revenge by hurting those who angered you.

Of course the optimal choice is to respond to your anger in a purposeful and constructive way. Consider these points:

- ▶ Anger is a common and appropriate emotion in some situations. How you respond to this emotion is under your control. You can choose to respond constructively or destructively.

- ▶ Learn what triggers your anger. Avoid those situations if that's a reasonable choice, or prepare yourself mentally to respond more constructively to these triggers.

- ▶ Change the way you think. You may think that you should always be treated fairly, maybe even a little more fairly than others, and that it's awful and terrible if you or your team is treated unfairly. Change that thinking by recognizing that destructive anger achieves nothing positive! Use logic to defeat your angry emotions. Remind yourself that the world is not always fair; you do not always get your way. Accept frustration and disappointment; don't let them turn to anger.

- ▶ Problem solve. Feeling angry is appropriate and healthy under certain circumstances. Rather than respond destructively, identify ways you can solve the problem constructively.

If anger is a serious problem for you, perhaps damaging your relationships with family and friends or holding you back in your career, seek professional help. To read more on anger, see the To Learn More section.

Questions for Reflection

▶ Do you feel comfortable disclosing yourself to others? How do you respond when others disclose themselves to you? **(p. 440)**

▶ Are you a good listener? Listening demonstrates respect, builds relationships, increases knowledge, and builds loyalty. **(p. 441)**

▶ How can you communicate acceptance and support to the people with whom you interact as a coach? **(p. 442)**

▶ In conflict situations do you usually respond like a turtle, a shark, a teddy bear, a fox, or an owl? Does your style tend to build relationships or damage them? **(p. 444)**

▶ How can you improve your relationships with assistant coaches (or your head coach if you are an assistant), coaches of other teams, administrators, medical personnel, officials, athletes' parents, and the media? **(p. 448)**

▶ How do you act when angry? Is your reaction generally purposeful and constructive? If not, what can you do to respond differently? **(p. 462)**

References

Janssen, Jeff, and Greg Dale. 2002. *The seven secrets of successful coaches.* Tucson, AZ: Winning the Mental Game.

Johnson, David W. 1981. *Reaching out.* 2nd ed. Englewood Cliffs, NJ: Prentice Hall.

Maxwell, John C., and Jim Dornan. 1997. *Becoming a person of influence.* Nashville, TN: Thomas Nelson.

To Learn More

Carter, Les, and Frank Minirth. 1993. *The anger workbook.* Nashville, TN: Thomas Nelson.

Toropov, Brandon. 1997. *The art and skill of dealing with people.* Paramus, NJ: Prentice Hall.

20

Managing Risk

Chris Thompson, a football player for West Seattle (Washington) High School, was paralyzed in a football game when he lowered his head and tackled an opponent, severing his spinal cord. The coach and school district were sued on the grounds that the coach should have warned Chris about the dangers of tackling with his head down. The court ruled in favor of Chris, who was awarded $6.3 million. This famous, if not infamous, case shocked the sport world and, more than any other event, led to the recognition that coaches have a duty to warn their players of the risks in their sport.

The last thing I want to do is frighten you away from coaching, but in today's litigious society you need to know your legal duties as a coach, not only to avoid a lawsuit such as the one just mentioned, but more important, to reduce the risk of injury to your athletes and others.

☞ **In this chapter you'll learn about**

▶ our legal system and the definition of negligence,

▶ what risk management means for coaches,

▶ immunity laws, and

▶ your nine legal duties as a coach.

Although there certainly is a negative side to the increased litigation in sports, it has had the positive effect of making sports safer. Your legal duties as a coach, as now prescribed by numerous court rulings, encourage responsible and professional conduct to protect your athletes and others. When you take appropriate actions to meet these legal duties, you are *managing risk*.

As every coach knows, the best defense is a good offense. So don't focus on protecting yourself from lawsuits. Rather, begin your risk management program with the Athletes First, Winning Second perspective. You want to manage risk because you want to do what is best for your athletes. Focus on the positive side of helping your athletes play safe, and you will minimize the risk of litigation.

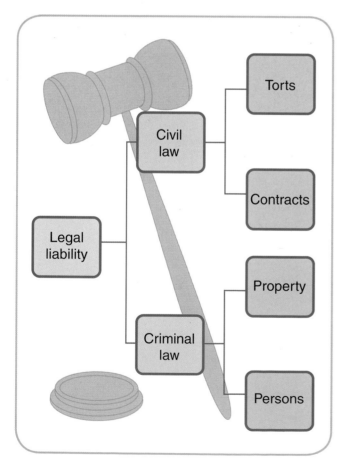

Figure 20.1 The American legal system.

The Legal System

Legal liability refers to the responsibilities and duties between persons that are enforceable by the courts. As you can see in figure 20.1, legal wrongs may be either civil or criminal. Under civil law, legal wrongs are classified as either torts or contract liabilities. In this chapter we do not consider criminal or contract law, but focus on tort law, which is applicable to most litigations involving coaches.

Negligence

Tort law is concerned with determining if a person has failed to conform to a legal duty. As a coach you have certain legal duties to fulfill. If you fail to do so, and this failure results in injury, you can be sued under tort law. The legal term for failing to fulfill your legal duty is *negligence*.

When coaching, you are negligent if you fail to exercise the skill and knowledge normally possessed by fellow coaches in working with those to whom you have a legal duty. Negligence may occur because of an inappropriate act or a failure to act.

Determining Negligence

In our legal system, anyone can sue another person for negligence. If you are sued for negligence and the case goes to trial, the court will determine whether you have been negligent by making a judgment on the following four key questions:

▶ Did you indeed have a legal duty to the injured party in this situation?

▶ Did you fail to fulfill this duty?

▶ Was there injury to the party to whom you owed the duty?

▶ Did your failure to fulfill the duty cause the injury?

All four questions must be answered yes for you to be found negligent.

A frequent defense in sport negligence cases is that an injury occurred as the result of the inherent risk in that sport and not a failure on the coach's part to fulfill a legal duty. For example, you have properly instructed a young girl in diving, the board is in excellent condition, and the pool is sufficiently deep. As the girl executes a one-and-one-half inward dive, she strikes her head on the board, sustaining a serious injury. If no other factors are involved, her injury is the result of a risk inherent in diving, not of negligence on your part.

A second common defense is that the injured party, often an athlete, may have contributed to the injury, such as by failing to follow instructions. It may be that you failed to fully meet your legal duty and that the athlete also contributed to the cause of the injury. This is known as *contributory negligence*. In many states if an athlete contributed to the negligence in any way, you may not be found negligent. Recently, though, more states have adopted *comparative negligence* laws, in which the negligence of each party involved is compared on a percentage basis. Most commonly, a player who contributed to the negligence by 50 percent or more cannot recover any damages.

Risk Management Process

The objective of risk management is to produce the safest environment possible for your athletes and others and to avoid litigation. Follow these four steps to managing risk in your sport.

STEP 1: Identify the Risks

Determine the likely risks you face when coaching your team by carefully reviewing the nine legal duties discussed in this chapter. You need to consider your players and others for whom you have responsibility, the activity, environment, equipment, methods of instruction, and supervision in identifying risks. As you review these legal duties, make note of those you think are the greatest risks in your situation.

Example: In a contact sport such as wrestling, you recognize that infectious skin diseases such as impetigo are a risk.

STEP 2: Evaluate the Risks

Assign a probability to the likelihood that each risk may lead to an injury and the likely severity of that injury. Begin by determining whether an injury is likely to occur often, infrequently, or seldom. Next, decide whether the severity of the injury and its financial impact are likely to be high, medium, or low, with high representing a severe injury with great financial impact and low representing a slight injury with little financial impact.

Example: You decide that the likelihood of an infectious skin disease occurring is high, and that its severity and financial impact are likely to be low.

STEP 3: Select an Approach to Manage the Risk

Your preferred course of action is to *eliminate the risk* by removing the hazard or by fulfilling your duties competently. When you cannot eliminate the risk, however, use table 20.1 to determine your approach to the identified risk based on how frequently you determined the injury is likely to occur and how severe the injury and its financial impact would be. Find the column that represents your response to the likely frequency of occurrence. Then find the row that represents your response to the likely severity of injury or impact. The box in which the row and column intersect contains a recommended course of action for this risk. The meaning of each of these courses of action is explained in step 4.

Example: Your first approach would be to do all that you can to prevent the occurrence of infectious skin diseases by educating your wrestlers about the problem and following good sanitation practices. Then, based on your assessment that the frequency of occurrence is often and the severity is low, the recommended course of action is that you *accept* this risk.

Table 20.1—Determining Your Approach to the Identified Risk

Severity of injury or financial impact	Frequency of occurrence		
	Often	**Infrequently**	**Seldom**
High	Avoid or transfer	Transfer	Transfer
Medium	Transfer	Transfer or accept	Transfer or accept
Low	Accept	Accept	Accept

STEP 4: Implement the Approach

Your first course of action will always be to eliminate or minimize the risk by acting reasonably and prudently. Thereafter, you have three options to consider in managing the identified risk:

▶ You can *avoid the risk* by not engaging in the activity. You decide the risk is too high to teach an advanced routine on the uneven parallel bars or an advanced dive on the 10-meter tower.

▶ You can *accept the risk.* If you judge the risk to be minor, you may decide that you can live with it. Stated differently, you may determine that the benefits of proceeding with the risk at hand outweigh the potential costs of avoiding it.

▶ You can *transfer the risk* in several ways: For example, (a) rather than driving your own car when transporting athletes, you can use the school's vehicle or public transportation; (b) you can transfer the financial risk by being insured for legal liability costs (see page 496 for more information about insurance); or (c) under certain circumstances you can transfer the inherent risks through participation agreements (see page 495).Remember, you cannot transfer your legal duties, but you can transfer some or all of the risk.

Example: You accept the risk of infectious skin diseases and make certain that the team is covered by health insurance.

Immunity

A 10-year-old New Jersey boy who had played second base during the regular season was transferred to the outfield in preparation for an all-star game. During practice in the outfield the boy misjudged a ball, which hit him in the eye and caused permanent damage. The parents sued the coaches for $750,000, charging them with negligence for placing the boy in a position he was not trained to play.

The coaches were able to document that the boy had played outfield the previous season. Nevertheless, the insurance company decided to settle out of court for $25,000. The immediate consequence was skyrocketing insurance rates and coaches quitting in anger. Eventually the New Jersey legislature passed the first law providing immunity to volunteer coaches against frivolous and ordinary negligence lawsuits.

More than a dozen states passed similar legislation, followed in 1997 by the U.S. Congress passing the Volunteer Protection Act. This Good Samaritan law provides volunteer coaches of nonprofit organizations with immunity against frivolous lawsuits. Volunteers are people who receive less that $500 compensation, excluding reimbursement for expenses. The federal law does not protect volunteer coaches against gross negligence. The courts must decide whether a lawsuit is frivolous and if it involves either ordinary or gross negligence.

Although the intent of such legislation is positive, these immunity laws actually provide little protection. In fact, in a few situations the perception of protection has led sport administrators to de-emphasize the education of their coaches, an unintended adverse response to these laws.

If Athletes First, Winning Second is your philosophy, then you will want to do all you can to protect your athletes. That requires you to become the best-trained coach possible. Do not rely on these immunity laws for protection, but instead rely on yourself to provide a safe environment through competent coaching.

Coaches' Legal Duties

Over the past 20 years, through thousands of lawsuits, the courts have defined and continue to define your legal duties as a coach. These duties may vary from state to state and may change as sport litigation continues unabatedly. This section describes the most well-established duties (figure 20.2) and at least some of the actions that you can take to fulfill your legal duties as a coach. Actually, much of this book advises you directly or indirectly on how to fulfill your legal responsibilities. The case studies that introduce each of the duties are based on actual court cases.

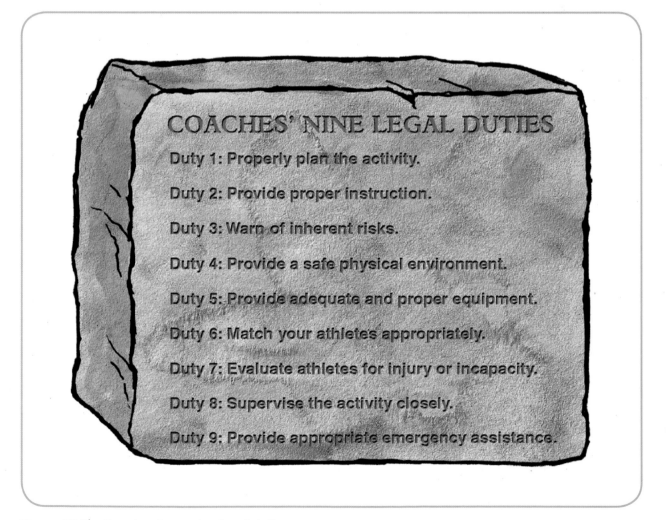

COACHES' NINE LEGAL DUTIES

Duty 1: Properly plan the activity.

Duty 2: Provide proper instruction.

Duty 3: Warn of inherent risks.

Duty 4: Provide a safe physical environment.

Duty 5: Provide adequate and proper equipment.

Duty 6: Match your athletes appropriately.

Duty 7: Evaluate athletes for injury or incapacity.

Duty 8: Supervise the activity closely.

Duty 9: Provide appropriate emergency assistance.

Figure 20.2 Coaches have nine legal duties.

DUTY 1: Properly Plan the Activity

In the second week of practice, first-year wrestling coach John Sterling wanted to impress his team with his knowledge of the sport. He showed them an advanced takedown technique called "souple," in which the wrestler lifts the opponent and then falls back on his neck and shoulder with the weight of the opponent on top of him. Manuel Garcia, a 15-year-old in his first year of wrestling, attempted the takedown and broke his neck, which left him paralyzed. The coach and school district were sued and ruled negligent because Coach Sterling failed to prepare Manuel for this advanced skill with proper strength training and lead-up skills.

Understanding Your Duty

The courts have repeatedly ruled that coaches have a duty to properly plan the activities for the athletes participating under their supervision. You will go a long way toward fulfilling this duty if you do what is described in chapter 12, Planning for Teaching.

Among your essential duties is to teach the skills of the sport in the correct progression. Avoid teaching advanced skills too quickly just because a few of your better athletes are ready or because you are getting bored. Practicing advanced skills can be very dangerous, and you can be found negligent, as the wrestling coach was, if you don't follow a reasonable progression. "A reasonable progression" will be judged relative to the progression used by other prudent coaches and the readiness of the individual athletes.

To fulfill your planning duty, you must consider each athlete's developmental level and current physical condition. You will not fulfill your duty to properly plan activities if you prescribe the same plan for all of your athletes. Thus, at least at the beginning of the season, evaluate your athletes' readiness with the fitness tests described in chapters 14 and 15. Not only is this a good coaching practice for planning practices, but it will also provide a written record validating your effort to plan your activities properly.

Fulfilling Your Duty

1. Develop a season plan using progressions that are appropriate for your athletes.
2. Test players to determine their physical capacity and skill level for your sport.
3. Develop written practice plans that adhere to the recommendations in chapter 12.
4. Adapt your plans to the individual needs of your athletes.
5. Don't deviate from your plans without good cause.
6. Keep all records of your planning and testing.

DUTY 2: Provide Proper Instruction

Spear tackling, a form of tackling in football in which the tackler's head is "speared" into the ball carrier's chest, was the accepted way to tackle in the 1960s. Because many spinal injuries resulted from this technique, however, and several studies demonstrated how vulnerable the spine is in this tackle, the technique was no longer recommended, especially for high school players. Unfortunately, high school coach Mike Douglas did not know that spear tackling was contraindicated. He had learned tackling that way, and so he taught it to his players. Using the technique resulted in quadriplegia for his middle linebacker and a $2.8 million court ruling against Mike and his school.

Understanding Your Duty

You have a duty to teach technical and tactical skills correctly and thoroughly so athletes are not injured and their actions do not injure others. In general, the law requires you to teach athletes in accordance with accepted procedures of the sport, allowing for individual variations as long as those variations are not radical or dangerous. For example, you can use a number of approaches to teach feet-first sliding in baseball, but if you teach head-first sliding and the athlete is injured, you have a good chance of being found negligent. Although many advanced baseball players slide head first, the technique is not accepted as the correct way to slide.

If you are the head coach, your instructional duty cannot be delegated. If you ask assistant coaches or more skilled athletes to teach skills, you must supervise their instruction because you are responsible for ensuring that it is correct.

Fulfilling Your Duty

1. Keep abreast of current instructional standards for your sport and use them.
2. Teach techniques, tactics, and rules in accordance with customary methods of your sport and the developmental level of your athletes.
3. Make your instructions clear, complete, and consistent. Provide adequate feedback on how your athletes are progressing.
4. If you are a head coach, you must supervise any instruction that you delegate to others.

DUTY 3: Warn of Inherent Risks

Bill Edgar, a 16-year-old, was awarded $1.8 million after sustaining permanent paralysis playing baseball. He attempted to score by diving headlong into the catcher. The coach, one of several defendants in the lawsuit, was found negligent for failing to warn Bill that this action could result in serious injury.

Understanding Your Duty

You are responsible for providing instructions regarding the safety of the sport. For example, you are expected to teach your athletes how to react to potentially dangerous situations. When a 10-year-old boy was injured in soccer because he collided with another player, as they both were going for a loose ball, the court ruled that the coach was negligent because he had failed to teach what should be done in this foreseeable and potentially dangerous situation.

Although you cannot protect athletes from all risks in the sport, athletes must know, understand, and appreciate the risks inherent in the sport to be able to assume them. Just how much understanding is required is not clear, but one warning may not be sufficient. Your warnings should be thorough, clear, and repeated.

Accepted ways of warning athletes of inherent risks in the sport include the following:

▶ Posting signs describing risks and how to perform the sport skills properly

▶ Meeting with the team to explain the risks, followed by repeated warnings in practices and contests

▶ Including descriptions of risks in player handbooks and parent orientation programs

▶ Using participation agreements, which are signed by parents and athletes, to explain the risk in specific terms (see page 474, form 20.1, for an example)

▶ Showing films or videotapes that illustrate the risks

Fulfilling Your Duty

1. Warn your athletes of the inherent risks of the sport so they know, understand, and appreciate them.

2. Use written notices, releases, videos, and repeated warnings to make certain your athletes understand the risks and are mindful of them.

Inherent Risks and Participation Agreement for Soccer

Soccer is an exciting sport that often involves forceful contact with the ground or another player. The sport is also frequently played during hot, humid seasons. Because of these conditions inherent to the sport, participating in soccer exposes an athlete to many risks of injury. Those injuries include, but are not limited to, death; paralysis due to serious neck and back injuries; brain damage; damage to internal organs; serious injuries to the bones, ligaments, joints, and tendons; and general deterioration of health. Such injuries can result not only in temporary loss of function, but also in serious impairment of future physical, psychological, and social abilities, including the ability to earn a living.

In an effort to make the sport of soccer as safe as it can be, the coaching staff will instruct players concerning the rules of soccer and the correct mechanics of all skills. It is vital that athletes follow the coach's skill instructions, training rules, and team policies to decrease the possibility of serious injury. Team rules and policies are listed in the team handbook each athlete receives at the preseason meeting.

We have read the information above concerning the risks of playing soccer. We understand and assume all risks associated with trying out, practicing, or playing soccer. We further agree to hold _____ [School District] and its employees, representatives, coaches, volunteers, and agents harmless in any and all liability actions, claims, or additional legal action in connection with participation in any activities related to participation on the _____ [High School] soccer team.

In signing this form, we assume the inherent risks of soccer and waive future legal action by our heirs, estate, executor, administrator, assignees, family members, and ourselves.

Note: The athlete and both parents or legal guardians (if living) must sign this form before any athlete may participate in interscholastic sport practices or games. If one parent or guardian is deceased, please indicate so on the appropriate line.

Date: _____

Signature of athlete: _____

Signature of mother (or legal guardian): _____

Signature of father (or legal guardian): _____

DUTY 4: Provide a Safe Physical Environment

After a short but heavy rain the barren softball infield was too muddy to use for practice, so Coach Ellen Archer moved the team to a large grass field. Kelly Smith stepped in a hole, breaking her leg in three places. The resulting litigation found Coach Archer negligent for not properly inspecting the playing facility.

Understanding Your Duty

Playing sports holds an inherent risk in any physical environment, but as a coach you are responsible for regularly and thoroughly inspecting the facility. How regularly depends on the activity. A good rule of thumb: The greater the risk is, the more frequent your inspections should be. If you want to be a good risk manager, I recommend that you develop a facilities inspection checklist for your sport by adapting the one on pages 476 to 478, form 20.2, to your sport.

You also have a duty to notice hazards and to do what you can to reduce their risks. When you cannot eliminate a hazard, such as a protruding rock on a playing field or a wall too close to the end line of a basketball court, you are responsible for trying to reduce the hazard and for warning your players about it. You might place a bright cloth over the rock or pad the wall, and warn players to avoid them. Again, you are expected to do what a prudent coach would do in the same situation.

When you encounter a facility that does not conform to the standards set by the governing body of your sport, you have a duty to notify the facility manager that the facility is unsafe and to recommend corrective action. If you and the facility manager are unfamiliar with these standards, you should contact the governing body of your sport.

Remember too that the physical environment can change when you are practicing or competing, whether you are inside or out. Rain-slick playing surfaces, high winds, and lightning can make outdoor environments unsafe quickly. Although changes are less likely indoors, facilities can still become hazardous quickly if there is a loss of lighting, heat, or moisture control. You must continuously monitor a changing environment to determine whether it is safe for your athletes and to take appropriate action if it isn't.

Fulfilling Your Duty

1. Note and remedy hazardous conditions through regular inspections of the playing facility and the warm-up, training, and dressing areas.

2. Develop a facilities inspection checklist for the facilities and equipment used in your sport. Use it regularly, and keep these checklists on file.

3. Change any dangerous conditions that you can; reduce the hazard if you cannot remove it. Warn your players of the hazard and notify the facility manager through written recommendations about correcting the hazard.

4. Give precise rules for using the facility. Post the rules, remind the players of them, and enforce them consistently.

5. Monitor the changing environment and make prudent judgments about continued participation if it becomes hazardous.

Facilities Inspection Checklist

Name of inspector: _____ Date of inspection: _____

Name and location of facility: _____

_____

Note: This form is an incomplete checklist provided as an example. Use it to develop a checklist specific to your facilities.

Facility Condition

Circle Y (yes) if the facility is in good condition or N (no) if something needs to be done to make it acceptable. In the space provided, note what needs to be done.

Gymnasium

Y N Floor (water spots, buckling, loose sections)

Y N Walls (vandalism free)

Y N Lights (all functioning)

Y N Windows (secure)

Y N Roof (adverse impact of weather)

Y N Stairs (well lighted)

Y N Bleachers (support structure sound)

Y N Exits (lights working)

Y N Basketball rims (level, securely attached)

Y N Basketball backboards (no cracks, clean)

Y N Mats (clean, properly stored, no defects)

Y N Uprights or projections

Y N Wall plugs (covered)

Y N Light switches (all functioning)

Y N Heating or cooling system (temperature control)

Y N Ducts, radiators, and pipes

Y N Thermostats

Y N Fire alarms (regularly checked)

Y N Directions posted for evacuating the gym in case of fire

Y N Fire extinguishers (regularly checked)

Other (list):_____

_____

Locker rooms

Y N Floor

Y N Walls

Y N Lights

Y N Windows

Y N Roof

Y N Showers

Y N Drains

Y N Benches

Y N Lockers

Y N Exits

Y N Water fountains

Y N Toilets

Y N Athletic trainer's room

Other (list):_____

_____

Form 20.2 *(continued)*

Field or outside playing area

Y N   Stands   Y N   Sprinklers
Y N   Pitching mound   Y N   Garbage
Y N   Dugouts   Y N   Security fences
Y N   Track and fences   Y N   Water fountain
Y N   Sidelines   Y N   Storage sheds

Other (list): _____

_____

Pool

Y N   Equipment in good repair   Y N   Chemicals safely stored
Y N   Sanitary   Y N   Regulations and safety rules
Y N   Slipperiness on decks and   posted
        diving board controlled

Lighting—adequate visibility

Y N   No glare   Y N   Light switches properly
Y N   Penetrates to bottom of pool   grounded
Y N   Exit light in good repair   Y N   Has emergency generator to
Y N   Halls and locker rooms meet   back up regular power source
        code requirements

Exits—accessible and secure

Y N   Adequate size, number   Y N   No obstacles or debris
Y N   Self-closing doors   Y N   Office and storage rooms
Y N   Self-locking doors   locked
Y N   Striker plates secure

Ring buoys

Y N   20-inch diameter   Y N   50-foot rope length

Guard chairs

Y N   Unobstructed view   Y N   Tall enough to see bottom of
                                            pool

Safety line at break point in the pool grade (deep end)

Y N   Bright color floats   Y N   3/4-inch rope

First aid kit

Y N   Inventoried and replenished regularly

Stretcher, two blankets, and spine board

Y N   Inventoried and in good repair

continued ☞

Track

Y N Throwing circles

Y N Fences

Y N Water fountain

Surface

Y N Free of debris

Y N Free of holes and bumps

Other (list):_____

_____

Recommendations/observations: _____

_____

_____

_____

_____

_____

_____

_____

_____

_____

_____

_____

_____

_____

_____

_____

_____

_____

_____

_____

_____

_____

_____

DUTY 5: Provide Adequate and Proper Equipment

Robert Bloom thought he was making a good buy when he purchased new plastic face masks for his hockey team. The masks were mounted in the helmets by the school maintenance man, although no instructions were provided on how to do so. Four weeks into the season Brad Kosnick was hit in the mask by a high stick, which shattered the mask and sent a plastic splinter into his left eye. Brad lost the sight in that eye, and in the court trial the mask manufacturer, the coach, and the school were found negligent.

Understanding Your Duty

Your duty here is generally the same as for duty 3. You have a duty not only to provide adequate and proper equipment, but also to explain its correct use and any unique characteristics. For example, a football helmet is intended to protect the player, but used incorrectly it can be dangerous to both the player and those he plays with. Similarly, gymnastics apparatuses are designed to be as safe as possible for specific events, but used incorrectly they can be highly dangerous.

Just as with facilities, you must inspect equipment regularly. If it is worn or broken, you must remove it from use or have it properly repaired. Use the large equipment inspection checklist (form 20.3) and personal equipment inspection checklist (form 20.4) to routinely inspect the team's equipment.

When purchasing equipment, you should buy the best you can afford. Also be sure that it meets the standards of the National Operating Committee on Standards for Athletic Equipment (www.nocsae.org) or of the national governing body for your sport. Always purchase equipment with the age and skill level of your athletes in mind. When equipment is furnished by the player or by the school, you have less legal responsibility for its meeting these standards or being safe.

Much of the responsibility for equipment safety falls on the manufacturers, partly because of the "deep pockets" approach to litigation.

Nevertheless, you have a duty to see that equipment fits properly and is used according to the manufacturer's specifications.

You also are responsible for seeing that equipment is properly stored. Leaving equipment, such as weights or springboards, in unlocked and unattended areas invites injury and litigation.

Fulfilling Your Duty

1. Buy the best equipment you can afford, considering the age and skill of your athletes.

2. Teach your athletes how to fit, use, and inspect their equipment. Encourage them to return any equipment that does not fit or appears defective.

3. Inspect equipment regularly; the more stress placed on the equipment, the more frequently you should examine it.

4. If players bring their own equipment, you still have a responsibility to inspect it and ensure that it complies with safety standards.

5. Allow only qualified people to install, fit, adjust, and repair equipment. You may want to insist that a manufacturer's representative fit all equipment (e.g., helmets, pads, and mouth guards).

6. Warn players of potentially hazardous equipment, and give verbal and written instructions on using it.

7. Be aware of changes in equipment by keeping current on accepted standards.

Large Equipment Inspection Checklist

Date of inspection: _____

Equipment inspected: _____

Current condition: _____

Inspector: _____

	Satisfactory	Unsatisfactory	Comments
Clean	_____	_____	_____
Free of rust	_____	_____	_____
Free of splinters or sharp edges	_____	_____	_____
All parts (original factory parts) in place	_____	_____	_____
All parts (from manufacturer's repair facility) in place	_____	_____	_____
All parts in working order	_____	_____	_____
All repairs done by authorized personnel	_____	_____	_____
Nuts and bolts tightened appropriately	_____	_____	_____
Placed correctly for use	_____	_____	_____
Secured properly for use	_____	_____	_____
Padding installed according to specifications	_____	_____	_____

Received by: _____ Date: _____

Repair work scheduled: _____

Date repairs completed: _____

Signature of supervisor: _____

Follow-up inspection date: _____

From *Successful Coaching, Third Edition*, by Rainer Martens, 2004, Champaign, IL: Human Kinetics.

Personal Equipment Inspection Checklist

Date of inspection: _____

Equipment inspected: _____

Condition of equipment when issued: _____ New _____ Reconditioned

Condition of equipment now: _____

Inspector: _____

	Satisfactory	Unsatisfactory	Comments
Clean	_____	_____	_____
Free of rust, splinters, and sharp edges	_____	_____	_____
Fits appropriately	_____	_____	_____
Padding in place	_____	_____	_____
All integral parts in place	_____	_____	_____
All integral parts operational	_____	_____	_____
No modification from factory specifications	_____	_____	_____
All repairs done by authorized personnel	_____	_____	_____

Received by: _____

Date: _____

Repair work scheduled: _____

Date repairs completed: _____

Signature of supervisor: _____

Follow-up inspection date: _____

From *Successful Coaching, Third Edition*, by Rainer Martens, 2004, Champaign, IL: Human Kinetics.

DUTY 6: Match Your Athletes Appropriately

Randy Brooks was a 115-pound (52-kilogram) football player who irritated Coach Jack Bennis with his continual misbehavior and boasting of unfounded ability. After an hour of Randy's provocations one day, Coach Bennis organized a one-on-one tackling drill and matched Randy with Tom McNab, a 205-pound (93-kilogram) tackle and the strongest player on the team. In the drill Randy suffered a serious concussion and was hospitalized. The court found Coach Bennis negligent for his imprudent judgment in matching the players.

Understanding Your Duty

This duty is especially pertinent to contact and collision sports, but it is also relevant in sports in which balls are thrown or hit to other players. Although matching athletes by age is common in sports, as we discussed in chapter 5, doing so may not necessarily ensure that they are well matched in size and experience. Two boys with a chronological age of 14 can differ by 5 or 6 years in biological age (physical maturity). One boy might weigh 75 pounds (34 kilograms) and have the biological age of an 11-year-old, and the other might weigh 240 pounds (109 kilograms) and have a biological age of 17. Matching these two players in a contact sport is obviously dangerous, and the courts have found coaches like Coach Brooks who do so to be negligent.

Your duty is to see that your players are not placed in situations in which they are at such a disadvantage that their risk of injury is increased. You should consider the following factors when matching athletes:

- Age
- Size
- Physical maturity
- Technical skill
- Experience
- Conditioning level
- Sex, especially on mixed teams
- Athletes returning after recovering from an injury
- Athletes with disabilities

Fulfilling Your Duty

1. Match players according to size, maturity, skill, and experience as well as age so that they are not placed in situations in which the risk of injury is increased.
2. Enforce eligibility rules; they often are intended to provide equitable competition.
3. Modify the drill or practice structure when mismatches in ability cannot easily be corrected.
4. Be especially alert to mismatches between the sexes, when athletes are recovering from injury, and among athletes with disabilities.

DUTY 7: Evaluate Athletes for Injury or Incapacity

Andy Jacobs was knocked unconscious for about 30 seconds when he was slammed to the mat by his opponent in a high school wrestling match. After 15 minutes Andy insisted that he was all right and demanded to continue the match. His coach reluctantly agreed. Andy died 20 minutes after the match from a cerebral hemorrhage. The two physicians who testified at the trial stated unequivocally that the coach should not have permitted Andy to return to the mat. The jury found the coach negligent.

Understanding Your Duty

You have three important responsibilities to fulfill this duty:

▶ You must ensure that an athlete's health is satisfactory for participation in your sport at the beginning of the season.

▶ You must determine whether an illness or injury during practice or competition is sufficiently threatening that participation should be stopped.

▶ You must ensure that an injured athlete is ready to return to play.

These responsibilities are not yours solely, but are shared with parents, athletic trainers, and physicians. In fact, good risk managers transfer as much of these responsibilities as possible to the team physician or athletic trainer. Because such a transfer of responsibility is often not possible, however, you should learn more about the preparticipation physical examination, coaching athletes with disabilities, and making prudent decisions about injured athletes.

Preparticipation physical evaluation.

Various medical associations recommend that athletes have preparticipation physical examinations every two or three years. Every athlete may not need a preseason physical for your sport, but all athletes should provide evidence of having passed a preparticipation medical examination within the past two or three years.

The primary objectives of preparticipation physical examinations are to identify conditions that may be life threatening or disabling to players and that may predispose them to injury, and to meet legal and insurance requirements. A good examination should include the following:

▶ *A completed health history.* Some states and organizations require that specific forms be completed. Five medical associations have developed a standard medical history form for athletes that I recommend if your organization does not have a form (American Academy of Family Physicians et al. 1996).

▶ *A physical examination.* Physical examinations for sport participation should measure weight, height, visual acuity, blood pressure, and heart rate. Thereafter, the extent of the examination may depend on the sport, but for any sport involving strenuous activity I recommend that the preparticipation physical examination guidelines of the five medical associations noted previously be followed.

If any health conditions are identified in the medical history or preparticipation examination, then the physician, in consultation with the athlete and the athlete's parents, must determine whether the athlete can safely participate. Then, the physician, parents, athlete, you, and possibly your sport administrator should agree on the conditions and limitations of the athlete's participation.

Coaching athletes with disabilities.

When considering whether an athlete is physically capable of participating on your team, keep in mind the implications of the Americans With Disabilities Act (ADA). The act's intent is to provide people with disabilities with the same opportunities for involvement as those afforded to people without disabilities, which is a good thing.

What do you do if an athlete who is blind, deaf, or confined to a wheelchair or has a chronic illness or psychological disorder wants to play on your team? I recommend that you follow the guidelines of the National Collegiate Athletic Association (NCAA) unless your organization has more specific guidelines.

The NCAA recognizes the right of impaired people to an equal opportunity to participate in high-quality sport or recreational programs. These people should be eligible for intercollegiate programs if they qualify for a team without any lowering of standards for achievement, attendance, or completion of the required tasks, and if their participation does not put others or themselves at significant risk of substantial harm (National Collegiate Athletic Association 2000).

Before you decide to exclude any athlete from participating on your team on the basis of a disability, be sure to discuss the issue with your sport director or chief administrator to consider the implications of the ADA.

Injured athletes.

When athletes are injured during practice or competition, you must judge the risk of returning them to play. When a physician or athletic trainer is present, you can transfer that responsibility to that person. If you do not hire the services of a physician or athletic trainer, the best thing you can do is take a sport first aid course to learn how to respond to a variety of sport injuries. (See the appendix for a description of the American Sport Education Program Sport First Aid course.)

Fulfilling Your Duty

1. In cooperation with your medical support team, require evidence that all athletes have received preparticipation physical examinations in the past two or three years.

2. Keep a medical history of every athlete on file.

3. Recommend that your medical support team follow the American Academy of Pediatrics (AAP) guidelines in determining whether and under what conditions persons with special conditions can participate.

4. Follow the NCAA guidelines in seeking to accommodate people with impairments who want to participate on your team.

5. Use extraordinary judgment in identifying athletes who are injured or so ill that they should not participate.

6. Get medical and parental approval before permitting seriously ill or injured athletes to return to participation.

DUTY 8: Supervise the Activity Closely

High school basketball coach Sue Emmerling was in a practice session working on speed drills when a student assistant called her to the office for an important telephone call. The team continued to practice but became reckless, and the drill degenerated into horseplay. Two players collided; one broke her jaw and knocked out several teeth. Coach Emmerling was sued and found negligent for failing to fulfill her duty to supervise properly.

Understanding Your Duty

Your duty to supervise will require general supervision at times and more specific supervision at other times. *General supervision* is being in the area of activity so that you can see and hear what is happening. General supervision is required of all preparation areas, such as locker rooms and playing facilities before and after practice. You are expected to be

▶ immediately accessible to the activity and able to oversee the entire program systematically;

▶ alert to conditions that may be dangerous to players and to take action to protect them; and

▶ able to react immediately and appropriately to emergencies.

Specific supervision is direct supervision at the immediate location of an activity; it is more action oriented than general supervision. You should provide specific supervision when you teach new skills and continue it until your athletes understand the requirements of the activity, the risks involved, and their own ability to perform in light of these risks. Specific supervision is also advised when you notice athletes breaking rules or a change in the condition of your athletes.

As a general rule, the more dangerous the activity is, the more specific the supervision should be. This suggests that more specific supervision is required with younger and less experienced athletes.

As part of your supervision duty, you are expected to foresee potentially dangerous situations and to be positioned to help prevent them from occurring. This requires that you know your sport well, especially the rules that are intended to provide for the safety of the athletes.

Failure to supervise adequately is among the most common sources of lawsuits in sport. You cannot take this legal duty lightly. Supervision is a form of management; it's not only being there, it's actively directing and controlling the activity when appropriate. In a lawsuit, the court will consider the activity, the type of supervision provided, and the location and competency of the coach in determining negligence. Remember that the degree of supervision is expected to be proportional to the risk of injury that is known or can be reasonably expected.

Fulfilling Your Duty

1. Always provide general supervision for all facilities and playing areas your team uses.
2. Provide specific supervision when teaching new skills and when the risk of injury increases.

3. Know your sport so well that you can anticipate potentially dangerous situations and be positioned to prevent them from occurring.

4. Use posters, notices, and signs to support but not replace your supervision.

5. Do not condone reckless or overly aggressive behavior that threatens the safety of any athlete.

DUTY 9: Provide Appropriate Emergency Assistance

Field hockey player Jill Donovan passed out during practice on a hot, sultry day. Coach Ellis failed to recognize the common symptoms of heatstroke, and so rather than seeking immediate medical assistance, she instructed Jill to sit under a shade tree while practice continued. Jill slipped into shock and another team member urged Coach Ellis to get help, but the plea fell on deaf ears. The next morning Jill died. Coach Ellis was found negligent in the lawsuit that followed for failing to provide appropriate emergency assistance.

Understanding Your Duty

You have a duty to provide or secure appropriate medical assistance for injured athletes you coach. If medical assistance is not immediately available, you have a duty to provide appropriate first aid. Every coach should complete a sport first aid course such as the one offered by ASEP (see the appendix).

To meet your duty to provide emergency assistance, you should first obtain consent to provide emergency assistance from the athlete's legal guardian if the athlete is not of majority age. Form 20.5 on page 488 is a sample of such a form. Next you should develop a written emergency plan that you keep readily available. On page 489, form 20.6, I've provided a sample of such a plan. It describes what is to be done immediately, who contacts emergency medical help and how, how to transport an injured athlete, who contacts parents and school officials, and how to complete an injury report. Know this plan and follow it when an emergency occurs.

After an injury, you should complete an injury report form, a sample of which you'll find on page 491, form 20.7. This form should be completed after any serious injury, meaning any injury that causes the athlete to miss at least one practice.

Whenever possible, transfer the risk associated with emergencies to more qualified people. Have a team physician on site whenever possible, and employ an athletic trainer if you possibly can. When an injury occurs, provide only the first aid you are qualified to perform and then immediately obtain medical assistance. Do no more and no less.

Fulfilling Your Duty

1. Obtain a consent form for each athlete at the beginning of the season.
2. Protect the injured athlete from further harm.
3. Provide appropriate first aid.
4. Attempt to maintain or restore life using CPR when required.
5. Comfort and reassure the athlete.
6. Activate your emergency plan, transferring the treatment responsibility to trained medical personnel.
7. Complete your injury report form as soon after the injury occurrence as possible.

Form 20.5

Informed Consent Form

I hereby give my permission for _____ to participate in _____ during the athletic season beginning in _____. Further, I authorize the school to provide emergency treatment of any injury or illness my child may experience if qualified medical personnel consider treatment necessary and perform the treatment. This authorization is granted only if I cannot be reached and a reasonable effort has been made to do so.

Date _____ Parent or guardian _____

Address _____ Home phone (   ) _____

Cell phone (   ) _____ Beeper number (   ) _____

Family physician _____ Phone (   ) _____

Medical conditions (e.g., allergies or chronic illnesses) _____

_____

Other person to contact in case of emergency _____

Relationship with person _____ Phone (   ) _____

My child and I are aware that participating in _____ is a potentially hazardous activity. We assume all risks associated with participation in this sport, including, but not limited to, falls, contact with other participants, the effects of the weather, traffic, and other reasonable risk conditions associated with the sport. All such risks to my child are known and appreciated by my child and me.

We understand this informed consent form and agree to its conditions.

Child's signature _____ Date _____

Parent's or guardian's signature _____ Date _____

From *Successful Coaching, Third Edition*, by Rainer Martens, 2004, Champaign, IL: Human Kinetics.

Emergency Plan for Field Hockey

Immediate actions:

1. Head coach Joan Ellis will stay with the athlete and keep her calm. She will also keep other nonmedical personnel away from the area.

2. No one will move the injured athlete until the possibility of serious injury (especially head, neck, or back injury) has been ruled out. If Joan Ellis decides that it is safe to move the athlete, she will be moved only after all injuries have been stabilized. Procedures covered in first aid training will be used.

3. Joan Ellis will provide first aid until medical assistance arrives.

4. Assistant coach Anne Phillips will summon the school nurse or contact the emergency medical system (EMS) immediately.

If the EMS is activated:

1. The EMS phone number is 555-1234. A cell phone will be accessible at all times.

2. Anne Phillips will give the following information to the EMS dispatcher:

   a. Her name, her position, and the school name

   b. The athlete's name, age, and suspected injury

   c. The address of the field and directions for access

   d. Any additional information requested

   Important: Anne Phillips will not hang up until the EMS dispatcher has hung up.

3. Anne Phillips will then go to the school entrance to direct medical personnel to the field.

4. Student manager Carol Fields will pull the athlete's emergency card, which includes phone numbers for parents and important medical history information. She will also note the names of adult witnesses to the injury for the injury report form.

5. Joan Ellis will contact the parents as soon as the medical personnel have examined the athlete and prepared her for transport to a medical facility. The athlete will be transported to the medical facility only in an EMS vehicle. School or personal vehicles will not be used.

6. Joan Ellis will then inform the athletic director of the activation of the emergency plan.

In any injury situation:

1. Joan Ellis will complete the injury report. Names of adult witnesses were previously taken by Carol Fields. This information should be included on the report.

2. Joan Ellis will file copies of the injury report form with the athletic director, principal, and school nurse. She will keep one copy on file with the team records and another as a personal record.

3. Joan Ellis will follow up with medical personnel to determine any role she will need to play in the recovery and rehabilitation process.

Important phone numbers:

EMS dispatcher: 555-1234   School nurse: Ext. 1621
Fire department: 555-5678   Principal: 555-1357
Police department: 555-0987   Athletic director: 555-2468

Form 20.7

Injury Report Form

Date of report: _____

1. Name: _____

2. Home address: _____

3. Organization: _____ 4. Sex: M ❑ F ❑ 5. Age: ____ 6. Sport: ____

7. Time accident occurred: _____ Date: _____

8. Place of accident: _____

9. Nature of injury (check):

Abrasion	❑	Concussion	❑	Puncture	❑
Amputation	❑	Cut	❑	Scalds	❑
Asphyxiation	❑	Dislocation	❑	Scratches	❑
Bite	❑	Fracture	❑	Shock (elec.)	❑
Bruise	❑	Laceration	❑	Sprain	❑
Burn	❑	Poisoning	❑	Other (specify)	❑

Part of body injured (check):

Abdomen	❑	Eye	❑	Leg	❑
Ankle	❑	Face	❑	Mouth	❑
Arm	❑	Finger	❑	Nose	❑
Back	❑	Foot	❑	Scalp	❑
Chest	❑	Hand	❑	Tooth	❑
Ear	❑	Head	❑	Wrist	❑
Elbow	❑	Knee	❑	Other	❑

What object or substance was the source of injury? _____

_____

How did the source of injury come into contact with the athlete? _____

_____

10. Protective equipment worn? No ❑ Yes ❑ Type of equipment: _____

_____

11. Degree of injury: Death ❑ Permanent impairment ❑ Temporary disability ❑ Nondisabling ❑

continued ☞

12. Coach in charge when accident occurred (name): _____

    Present at scene of accident: No ☐ Yes ☐

13. Immediate action taken:

    First aid steps taken? No ☐ Yes ☐ By (name): _____

    Sent to physician? No ☐ Yes ☐ By (name): _____

    How transported? _____

    Physician's name: _____

    Sent to hospital No ☐ Yes ☐ By (name): _____

    How transported? _____

    Hospital name: _____

    Was parent or other individual notified? No ☐ Yes ☐ When? _____

    How? _____

    Name of individual notified: _____

    By whom? (enter name) _____

    Restricted activity time: _____

14. Corrective actions taken or recommended to prevent future incidents: _____

    _____

    _____

    _____

Witnesses:

1. Name: _____ Address: _____

2. Name: _____ Address: _____

Remarks: _____

_____

_____

_____

Signed: (Coach) _____

        (Sport administrator) _____

From *Successful Coaching, Third Edition*, by Rainer Martens, 2004, Champaign, IL: Human Kinetics.

Other Duties

You have reviewed the nine major duties required of coaches to help manage the risk of injury to your athletes and the risk of legal liability to yourself. Several additional duties also warrant your consideration.

Keep Adequate Records

You can reduce your risk of losing a lawsuit by keeping the following records regarding your nine legal duties:

- ▶ Preseason and periodic player evaluations
- ▶ Season and practice plans
- ▶ Season schedule
- ▶ Health history forms
- ▶ Emergency information cards
- ▶ Medical clearances based on preparticipation physical examinations
- ▶ Completed facility and equipment checklists
- ▶ Emergency plan
- ▶ Informed consent forms
- ▶ Eligibility records
- ▶ Injury reports

Provide Safe Transportation

The best way to transport your athletes in terms of liability is by public carrier. You thus transfer the responsibility to them, and often they offer the safest and most convenient way to travel. The next best option is to use a vehicle owned by the school or agency for which you coach. Be certain that whoever drives the vehicle has the proper license if a special classification is required.

The least preferred choice is to drive your automobile. If you transport athletes in your car, be certain that you are properly licensed and insured and that the vehicle is in good repair. Some insurance policies invalidate the personal liability section of a policy if the driver is compensated for transporting others. If your school or sponsoring agency asks you to drive your car, find out whether any insurance coverage is provided. Never allow athletes to transport other athletes to competitions.

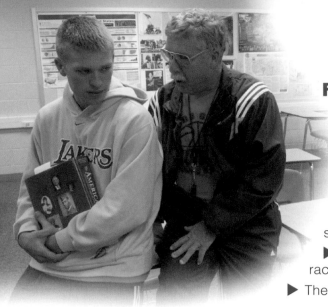

Follow Due Process

You are expected to protect the constitutional rights of your athletes, including the following:

▶ The right to fair treatment and not to be subject to arbitrary or capricious rules

▶ The right to free expression (meaning that you cannot impose unreasonable requirements regarding dress or hair styles, for example)

▶ The right not to be discriminated against because of race, sex, or religion

▶ The right to confidentiality regarding medical information

These rights complement and affirm the Bill of Rights for Young Athletes, which was presented on page 23.

When you see the need to discipline athletes by imposing significant punishments on them such as suspending them from practices or games or dismissing them from the team, you will want to be cognizant of athletes' rights to due process. Many state associations and other sport organizations have imposed specific requirements for the procedure you must follow to meet athletes' rights to due process. Check with your sport administrator for any specific requirements. These procedures commonly consist of the following three steps:

1. Provide athletes with notice of charges or violations and the penalty to be imposed.
2. Allow athletes to present their side of the situation.
3. Provide a written record of findings.

In minor cases, these requirements can be met by telling athletes what rule they have violated and what penalty will be imposed, and by then pausing to allow them to respond. For major violations, you may need to provide a written notice of the violation and the penalty, conduct a formal hearing, and follow up with a written record of findings from that hearing. One of the most frequent problems coaches encounter is reacting too quickly without giving athletes an opportunity to respond until a penalty has been imposed. You can avoid most problems with due process by making sure you have given athletes a chance to present their side of the situation.

Pursue Proper Training

By now you should realize that as a coach you have a legal responsibility to be properly trained to fulfill your duties. Without appropriate training, the risk of injury for athletes and lawsuits for you and your sponsoring agency increases greatly. The courts are telling us that it is no longer acceptable to place an unqualified person into the position of coach to supervise athletes.

If you are a head coach, you also are responsible, along with your sponsoring agency, for ensuring that your assistants are qualified. If you use untrained assistants, you must provide close and direct supervision until they demonstrate competency.

As coaching becomes a more formally recognized profession, mandatory training and certification are rapidly approaching reality. Although certification is no guarantee of competency, it is a big step in the right direction. Certification does not guarantee protection from lawsuits, but it will help you defend yourself against them.

Waivers and Participation Agreements

As lawsuits have increased in sport, many sponsoring agencies have turned to using waivers of responsibility to absolve or indemnify themselves (hold themselves harmless). The waiver or release is a contract signed by participants or their parents that seeks to transfer responsibility from the sponsoring agency to the participant. Waivers have limited legal value for several reasons:

▶ Minors cannot enter into contracts, and parents cannot waive minors' rights to sue.

▶ The courts reject contracts to waive negligence.

▶ It is frequently considered a violation of public policy to require a release prior to participation in a sport.

Although waivers may have some psychological value in discouraging people who have signed them from suing, don't put confidence in waivers as part of your risk management plan. Instead, consider using participation agreements, which are not contracts, but signed documents stating that your athletes

▶ understand the dangers inherent in the sport;

▶ appreciate the consequences of the risks involved, including the possibility of injury and death;

▶ know the rules and procedures of the sport and the importance of following them; and,

▶ knowing all this, request to participate in the sport.

Participation agreements must be stated explicitly, they must list the rules to be followed, and they must spell out clearly the possible dangers. Participation agreements cannot prevent lawsuits or absolve you from negligence, but they clearly establish that you fulfilled your duty to warn. Remember, athletes cannot

assume risk for something about which they are ignorant; participation agreements spell out the inherent risks in your sport. Form 20.1 on page 474 is an example of such an agreement.

Insurance

In our litigious society, insurance is essential in managing risk. You simply should not coach without liability insurance, and sponsoring agencies should not permit anyone to coach without it.

Simply knowing that you have insurance is not sufficient. You need to know the specific coverage. Before your next season, find out from your sponsoring agency or school whether it has liability coverage for you and what this coverage is. Get answers to the following questions:

- What events are covered?
- What property is covered?
- What activities are covered?
- What locations are covered?
- What losses are covered?
- What amount of loss will the insurer pay?
- What time period is covered?
- What special conditions are excluded?
- What steps must be taken following a loss?
- What is the coverage for transportation when using an agency vehicle? Your own vehicle?

If the sponsoring agency does not have liability coverage or you consider it inadequate, buy your own liability insurance. You have at least three options for doing so.

- You can add this coverage to your homeowner's policy for a relatively small sum.
- If you belong to a professional organization (such as the National Recreation and Park Association, a national governing body for your sport, or a national or state coaching association), it may offer personal liability insurance at low rates.
- You can purchase a separate personal liability policy.

A policy should provide a minimum of $1 million in coverage as well as pay for the costs associated with the investigation and defense of lawsuits. Review policies carefully because they differ widely in coverage for the premiums charged.

Some insurance policies are only secondary policies, meaning that they provide coverage only after any other existing policy pays. Although some of these policies are useful supplements, others have so many exclusions that your actual coverage is very limited.

Questions for Reflection

▶ Do you generally have a positive attitude about managing the risk inherent in your sport in order to protect your athletes? If so, you are doing much to avoid litigation. **(p. 466)**

▶ What are the definitions of *legal liability* and *negligence?* **(p. 466)**

▶ What are the four conditions that must be met to prove negligence? **(p. 467)**

▶ What are the four steps to managing risk in sport? **(p. 468)**

▶ To what degree are you protected by the immunity laws in your state? **(p. 469)**

▶ What are the nine principal legal duties of a coach? **(p. 470)**

▶ What are some other ways to reduce your risk of liability? **(p. 491)**

▶ Why are participation agreements considered superior to waivers? **(p. 493)**

▶ How much liability insurance should you carry as a coach? Are you adequately covered? **(p. 494)**

References

American Academy of Family Physicians, American Academy of Pediatrics, American Medical Society for Sports Medicine, American Orthopaedic Society for Sports Medicine, American Osteopathic Academy of Sports Medicine. 1996. *Preparticipation physical evaluation.* 2nd ed. New York: McGraw-Hill.

National Collegiate Athletic Association. 2000. Guideline 3a. Participation by the impaired student-athlete. Indianapolis: National Collegiate Athletic Association.

Van der Smissen, Betty. 1990. *Legal liability and risk management for public and private entities.* Vol. 2, Cincinnati, OH: Anderson.

To Learn More

American Academy of Pediatrics. 2001. Medical conditions affecting sports participation (RE0046). *Pediatrics,* 107 (5): 1205-1209. Accessible on the Internet at www.aap.org/policy/re0046.html.

Appendix

ASEP COACHES EDUCATION PROGRAMS

The question no longer is whether coaches should be trained, but *how* coaches should be trained. The American Sport Education Program (ASEP) has been offering the solution to this question since 1981 through the development and implementation of coaching education courses and resources. ASEP has educated more than one million coaches, officials, sport administrators, and parents over the past 20 years.

ASEP Professional Education Program

The ASEP Professional Education Program is composed of three levels—Bronze, Silver, and Gold. The Bronze Level offers coaches of athletes age 14 and older a three-course credentialing program geared toward educating the entire coach. Bronze Level courses include *Coaching Principles, Sport First Aid,* and *Coaching [Sport] Technical and Tactical Skills.* To receive the Bronze Level credential, coaches must complete these courses and also be certified in CPR. The Bronze Level is especially appropriate for coaches at the high school, college, Olympic, and serious club sport levels. In fact, 35 state high school associations, 200 colleges and universities, and 13 national governing bodies currently use, require, or recommend the Bronze Level in whole or in part to meet coaching education requirements for their organizations.

Coaching Principles provides essential education for the serious coach. *Successful Coaching, Third Edition,* is the text for the course, and through this course, coaches are challenged to define who they are as coaches (their coaching philosophy, objectives, and style); enhance communication and motivational skills; become more effective teachers and trainers; and improve team, relationship, risk, and self-management skills. *Coaching Principles* is a study of the fundamentals of being a successful coach—before even stepping on the playing field.

Sport First Aid, with the course text of the same title, provides clear and up-to-date information on preventing, evaluating, and responding to more than 110 athletic injuries and illnesses. Potentially life-saving actions covered in this course are developing a sport first aid game plan, conducting a primary survey and providing life support, moving injured athletes, and step-by-step protocols for injuries and illnesses.

Coaching [Sport] Technical and Tactical Skills Courses (all available exclusively online)
Coaching Baseball Technical and Tactical Skills
Coaching Basketball Technical and Tactical Skills
Coaching Football Technical and Tactical Skills
Coaching Soccer Technical and Tactical Skills
Coaching Wrestling Technical and Tactical Skills
Coaching Cheerleading Technical and Tactical Skills
Coaching Ice Hockey Technical and Tactical Skills
Coaching Softball Technical and Tactical Skills
Coaching Swimming Technical and Tactical Skills
Coaching Track & Field Technical and Tactical Skills
Coaching Volleyball Technical and Tactical Skills
Coaching Field Hockey Technical and Tactical Skills
Coaching Golf Technical and Tactical Skills
Coaching Gymnastics Technical and Tactical Skills
Coaching Lacrosse Technical and Tactical Skills
Coaching Tennis Technical and Tactical Skills

Watch the ASEP Web site at www.ASEP.com for updates on course release dates.

Coaching [Sport] Technical and Tactical Skills is a sport-specific, Xs and Os course providing coaches with technical and tactical skills, as well as two options for how to teach them: the traditional approach and the games approach. Sports and release dates for these courses are given in the table above.

Coaching Principles and *Sport First Aid* are offered as classroom courses, taught by certified instructors, and alternatively as online courses. The *Coaching Principles* classroom course consists of a seven-hour clinic followed by self-study of the course's text and a test. The self-study and test require three to five hours to complete. The *Sport First Aid* classroom course follows the same format, with the exception that it's a four-hour clinic.

Coaches may also complete the *Coaching Principles* and *Sport First Aid* courses via the Internet—on a schedule that's right for them. After registering, each coach receives a copy of the book *Successful Coaching, Third Edition,* or *Sport First Aid, Fourth Edition,* and a course CD-ROM containing video clips. In this interactive environment, coaches read sections of the book, view video, and participate in virtual exercises that simulate classroom learning and put the coach in practice and game-day situations. These online courses provide a convenient way for coaches to learn at their own pace and save time attending in-person classroom clinics.

For coaches who have completed the Bronze Level and would like to continue their professional development, ASEP Silver Level courses are the next step. The Silver Level curriculum consists of advanced courses on sport-specific techniques and tactics, sport physiology, sport psychology, mechanics of sport, and teaching sport skills.

ASEP Gold Level courses continue the education of coaches in the sport sciences and provide advanced knowledge of conditioning and instructional methods specific to each sport, plus advanced courses in sport nutrition, risk management, and social issues in coaching.

Watch the ASEP Web site, www.ASEP.com, for timelines on Silver and Gold Level course release dates.

ASEP Silver Level Courses
Coaching [Sport]: Advanced Skills
Coaching [Sport]: Advanced Strategies
Sport Biomechanics for Coaches
Sport Physiology for Coaches
Sport Psychology for Coaches
Sport Skill Instruction for Coaches

ASEP Gold Level Courses
Coaching [Sport]: Advanced Practice Plans
Coaching [Sport]: Advanced Conditioning
Sport Nutrition for Coaches
Risk Management for Coaches
Social Issues in Coaching

ASEP Volunteer Education Program

For the volunteer coach, the ASEP Volunteer Education Program provides beginning and intermediate education for coaches of athletes 13 years of age and younger, plus courses and resources for parents, officials, and sport administrators working with this age group. Ideal for park and recreation departments, national youth sport organizations, YMCAs, Boys and Girls Clubs, junior high schools, military and religious sport teams, and nonaffiliated local sport clubs, *Coaching Youth [Sport]* courses are available as online courses or through classroom instruction for baseball, basketball, football, soccer, softball, tennis, volleyball, and wrestling.

ASEP Philosophy

Built on the philosophy of Athletes First, Winning Second, ASEP is committed to improving amateur sport by providing coaches with the education to put that philosophy to work. For additional information on ASEP professional and volunteer education programs, visit www.ASEP.com or call 800-747-5698.

INDEX

Note: Page numbers followed by an italicized f or t refer to the figure or table on that page, respectively.

ABOUT THE AUTHOR

Sport has always been a vital part of Rainer Martens' life. He has coached at the youth, high school, and collegiate levels and has studied sport as a research scientist. The founder and president of Human Kinetics, he also started the American Sport Education Program, the largest coaching education program in the United States. An internationally recognized sport psychologist, Martens is the author of more than 80 scholarly articles and 15 books, including *Successful Coaching*, the best-selling coaching book ever published, and *Directing Youth Sport Programs*. He has also been a featured speaker at more than 100 conferences around the world and has conducted more than 150 workshops and clinics for coaches and athletes at all levels.

After receiving his PhD in physical education from the University of Illinois at Urbana-Champaign in 1968, Martens was a member of its faculty for 16 years. A past president of the American Academy of Kinesiology and Physical Education, he has been recognized for his contribution to sport by the National Recreation and Park Association and by his induction into the National Association of Sport and Physical Education Hall of Fame. He has received Distinguished Alumni awards from Emporia State University in Kansas (where he earned a bachelor's degree), the University of Montana (where he earned a master's degree), the University of Illinois, and Hutchinson High School.

Martens continues to enjoy sport today, especially senior softball. As a member of the world champion 60+ Florida Legends, Martens has been named to six all-world teams.

IT STARTS WITH THE COACH

Much is expected of today's high school coach. On any given day, you may play the role of mentor, motivator, mediator, medic, psychologist, strategist, or trainer. Each requiring a separate set of skills and tactics that together make you a "coach."

The **Bronze Level** credential—offered through the ASEP Professional Coaches Education Program—is designed with all of these roles in mind. It includes courses on coaching principles, sport first aid, and sport-specific techniques and tactics, and requires CPR certification. The Bronze Level prepares you for all aspects of coaching and is a recognized and respected credential for all who earn it.

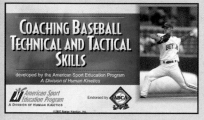
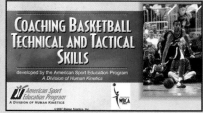
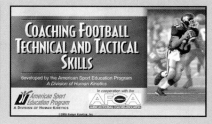

To enroll in any of these courses, visit the ASEP Web site at **www.ASEP.com** or contact your state association.

To learn more about how you can adopt the program for your state association or organization, contact Jerry Reeder, ASEP Sales Consultant, at **800-747-5698, ext. 2325** or e-mail **JerryR@hkusa.com**.

Developed, delivered, and supported by the American Sport Education Program, a 25-year leader in the sport education field, the ASEP Professional Coaches Education Program fulfills the coaching education requirements of nearly 40 state high school associations.

A DIVISION OF HUMAN KINETICS

WWW.ASEP.COM